The
Middle School
Program

The Middle School Program

John H. Hansen
University of Oregon

Arthur C. Hearn
University of Oregon

Rand McNally & Company
Chicago

RAND McNALLY EDUCATION SERIES
B. OTHANEL SMITH, *Advisory Editor*

To SAL and MARION
in return
for the hours they didn't see us

Preface

The official foreign policy of the United States of America for the past seventy years has been a gradual enlargement of the "open door policy" initiated during the last decade of the previous century. It is with the conviction that American education needs an open door policy that the authors wrote this book. For too long, teachers in the junior high and in the middle schools, in particular, (as in most schools at all levels) have operated behind closed doors with the attitude that what happens in *their* classroom is so relative, pertinent, and important that they need not be concerned with what happens in the classroom of the other staff members. This attitude is unfortunate wherever it appears in American education. In particular, it is criminal when it happens in a school setting that purports to be designed solely to meet the needs of the early adolescent.

The primary purpose of this book, then, is to present a survey of current thoughts about what should be happening in each of the various subject matter divisions of the middle school program. The reader will note that two of the five sections of this book are devoted to this purpose. Because of this emphasis, the material was written so that it could be read by teachers. If the reader wants up-to-date information on the architectural designs of the middle schools, a thorough analysis of administrative trends or problems, an in-depth discussion of theories of learning that particularly appertain to the early adolescent, or a sociological or historical discussion of the place of the middle school during the 1970s, the authors respectively submit that, though these topics are touched briefly, other books are now on the market that will provide these better than this one will.

The secondary purpose of the book is in response to an unfortunate repetition of 1900–1915 events which concern the authors. At that time, in reaction to supposed evils of the existing 8-4 administrative organization, an institution—a middle school which popularly became known as a junior high school—was formed without an educational philosophy for a base. In the mid-1960s, in reaction to supposed evils of the existing 6-3-3 administrative organization, an institution—a middle school which was called a middle or intermediate school—was formed for the same expedient reasons (building problems, desegregation, rapid population expansion, etc.) used fifty years earlier. It is the authors' contention that the generic term "middle school" needs to be accepted as "an education program designed to meet the needs of early adolescents" and that school design, curricular offerings, grade groupings, and staffing are local problems that demand local decisions. The authors are adamant that a middle school program for grade seven, for example, should be very similar even though in one instance it might be in a 6-7-8 school, in another in a 7-8 school, in another in a 5-6-7-8 school, and yet another in a 7-8-9 school. The existence of grade 9 in the fourth instance does not rule out the possibility that this is a middle school.

The authors are deeply indebted to colleagues and students who, for the past five years, have contributed ideas and materials which eventually found a place in the manuscript. Since it would be impossible to include all, we must apologize in advance to those who felt they deserved special mention but were not mentioned. We are especially grateful for the work of Alvin W. Howard, University of New Mexico, whose recently published text, *Teaching in Middle Schools*, is an excellent discussion of methods that pertain to the middle school classroom. His forthcoming book of readings with George Stoumbis will be an excellent complement to this text.

A number of individuals are worthy of note for special tasks. We must also express our sincere appreciation to the patient Joyce Anderson who authored the chapter on Instructional Materials Centers and to Patricia Jackson, formerly of Nova Schools, who authored the chapter on Learning Activity Packages. Similarly, we would like to thank William Moore, a Carlsbad, California principal, for the case study (Chapter 16) he wrote, and Donald Darling, Consultant on Secondary Guidance for the state of Florida, for his help with Chapter 15. As is true with all books, preparing the manuscript is often more arduous than writing the material. We must thank Sally Hansen, Chester Dugger, Judith Margulies, and Laurie Barnard for their excellent assistance.

Finally, we are grateful to a number of publishers and authors, without whose permission to use their copyrighted material the manuscript would be incomplete.

J. H. H.
A. C. H.

Eugene, Oregon
June, 1970

xi

Tables

Section One

The People
and the Place

Overview

For over fifty years we have had an intermediate school to cope with
the education of early adolescents, but the question has never been completely settled: What grades should be included in this school? What is
the best school for the child in this age group? While the most common
combination is grades 7-8-9, there is nothing absolute about this pattern nor, for that matter, much documented research on any organizational plan. More recent dissatisfaction with and critical scrutiny of
the junior high school has encouraged expansion, innovation, and experimentation in what might now be called a "middle school." Such
schools usually contain grades 6-7-8, and 5-3-4 organization, or four
grades in the middle school, 5-6-7-8, a 4-4-4 plan.

A generic definition of the term "middle" or "intermediate school"
designates a school which is between elementary and high school; is
housed in separate buildings (preferably designed for this purpose);
includes some of the grades five through nine; makes use of a variety of
instructional innovations; is highly flexible; and is neither elementary
nor secondary in basic characteristics, but strives to make use of the
best features of each. The junior high school is one form of the middle
school. Lest we make the same errors which were made a half century
ago when the junior high school was formed, the authors have tried to
delineate in this section the largely expedient reasons behind the
formation of the junior high school. This information, along with a
discussion of the adolescent and the teacher, will serve as excellent
background data for the discussion of definition and function.

The section, as a whole, is designed to provide an understanding of
the institution, now and in the past, for the student and his teacher.
The reader should thus be prepared with a foundation upon which the
data contained in the remainder of the book can be placed in appropriate perspective.

3

Chapter 1

The Institution:
Its History,
Function and
Definition

The history of the first middle school, the junior high school, indicates that it was conceived not as a movement to introduce something new into American education but as an expedient endeavor to ease several supposed deficiencies. Because it was thought that the cause of these deficiencies was inherent in the 8-4 organizational pattern, this pattern was questioned. This questioning intensified and multiplied during the last decade of the previous century and the first decade of this century. In the forefront of the criticism were such noted educators as William T. Harris, Charles W. Eliot, and G. Stanley Hall.

William T. Harris criticized the eight-year elementary school because of the absence therein of any provision for individual differences, use of ability grouping and developmental teaching, i. e., teaching without repetition. As is common among the three educators mentioned, Harris did not call for a specific new organizational design. He merely made educators aware of the weaknesses of the existing system and the imperative need for change.[1]

---

[1] Frank Parker, "Fifty Years of the Junior High School," *National Association of Secondary School Principals Bulletin* (February 1962) : 46:435–445, p. 435.

G. Stanley Hall, because of his scientific study of the child, provided protagonists with physical, emotional, and social evidence of these respective differences among the children.[2]

Charles W. Eliot, in his annual report in 1885–1886, in his speech to the National Education Association in 1888, in his speech to the New England Association of Colleges and Preparatory Schools in 1891, and in his work for the Committee of Ten, continually pointed out what he felt to be the inadequacies of the existing system in Elementary Education.[3] Eliot found the years at the end of the elementary experience to be wasted years (some Massachusetts communities at this time had a nine-year elementary school). He lamented this in his speeches and endeavored to correct it through the Committee of Ten recommendations suggesting a six-year elementary school and the introduction of secondary subjects into grades seven and eight. His arguments were continued in the Committee on the Economy of Time but, as was true with others mentioned, he never advocated outright an institution similar to the present junior high schools. Eliot's purposes throughout his efforts for economy of time and improvement of the 8-4 system were directed at enriching the secondary school and strengthening the base for college preparation.[4] The fact that his arguments coincided with those of the junior high school advocates added prestige to their contentions.

Dissatisfaction with the 8-4 system mounted in the first decade of this century as John Dewey added his prestige to the cause with pronouncements such as the one resulting from the 1901 Conference of the University of Chicago, which stated that the elementary school was too long—especially so when the secondary school needed at least six years to do an adequate job of developing cultural appreciation needed for civic competence.[5]

Both the educators dissatisfied with the 8-4 system and those proposing the secondary pattern for grades seven, eight, and nine (either 6-6 or 6-3-3) continually discussed the ills and weaknesses they saw in the old system as it existed at the turn of the century. Sometimes these discussions were as hypothetical and argumentative as the pro-8-4 justifications they were decrying. A good example of such a discussion is that found in T. H. Briggs when he discussed the following weaknesses of the 8-4 system:[6]

1. The 8-4 system is not justified by psychology, comparative education, historical development, or its results.

[2] *Ibid.*, p. 436.

[3] Editorial, *"Educational Review"* (November 1891) : 2:384–386, p. 384.

[4] *Ibid.*, p. 384.

[5] John Dewey, "Discussion: Shortening the Years of Elementary School," *School Review* (January 1903) : 11:17–20, pp. 18–20.

[6] T. H. Briggs, *The Junior High School* (Boston: Houghton Mifflin Company, 1920), pp. 4–20.

2. Isolated and small grammar and high schools are very impractical and uneconomical.
3. Due to the 73 percent dropout rate in the ninth grade, building and equipping high schools for these students is very costly.
4. Elementary schools do not and cannot prepare students for life and higher education as well as the junior high school can.
5. Male teacher influence while possible in a junior high school is hard to obtain in an elementary school.
6. A program or an organizational technique is needed to bridge the gap between the elementary and secondary years.
7. The seventh and eighth grade organized in 8-4 system makes provision for individual differences, educational guidance, and vocational guidance difficult.

With arguments such as these, educators began looking to the junior high school as a panacea which would solve all their educational problems at once.[7]

The junior high school is said to be a uniquely American organization, but precedents can be found for it in the upper division of the lower class *Bürgerschuler* and the intermediate stage of the upper class *Realschule* in Germany and in France in the Higher Primary School and the first cycle of the *lycée*. These European schools were designed for twelve-to-fifteen-year-old students, and featured diversification of instruction, introduction of foreign languages, prevocational training, and, in some cases, terminal education.[8]

Simultaneously with the arguments against the 8-4 mode of organization, prototypes of the junior high school were springing up in the East, the Midwest, and the Far West. Despite all the arguments being voiced against the old system, few voices proposed a positive philosophy for the establishment of the junior high school. Historians today, as well as critics of the institution, are quick to point out that expedience was often the reason for its inception. D. W. Lentz' statement is representative of these remarks:

It is apparent that . . . it (the junior high school) was established, not because of any strong and proved educational values, but as an expedient, usually to solve a housing problem; in many cases because it was the thing to do in educational circles. . . .[9]

Even Frank Bunker, the Superintendent in Berkeley, given credit by many for establishing the first "real" junior high school, stated that the institution was established:

[7] Joseph Abelson, "A Study of the Junior High School Project," *Education* (September 1916) : 37:1–19, p. 13.
[8] D. W. Lentz, "History and Development of the Junior High School," *Teachers College Record* (May 1956) : 57:522–30, p. 523.
[9] Ibid.

in order to lessen the congestion in the High School and in hopes that the tendency will be to hold the children in school at least a year longer. . . .[10]

The argument as to where the first junior high school was established resembles the Fitch-Fulton, chicken-egg, and Shakespeare-Bacon controversies and depending on your semantics, your assumptions, and your prejudices, arguments can be stated for Richmond, Indiana, New York City, Columbus, Ohio, and Berkeley, California. Will French states that historians are simply unable to determine when and where the first junior high school was organized.[11] Briggs states that active development of the junior high school can be dated from the reorganization planned in Berkeley in 1909.[12] Since Bunker used the term "Introductory High Schools," educators in Columbus, Ohio, claim their schools were the first junior high schools because they inaugurated the term in actual practice.[13]

In 1905–1907, the New York City school system converted PS #24, 62, and 159 into intermediate schools along the lines advocated by a Brooklyn teacher, Charles Hartwell.[14] It was not until 1914–1916, however, that the ninth grade was added along with commercial and prevocational subjects.

Berkeley, California opened its first "Introductory High School" January 1, 1910, but the story of the development of the junior high school in that city goes back to a 1904 Committee report which came out of a joint group made up of representatives of the California High School Teachers Association, the California Teachers Association, and the University of California at Berkeley. This committee dealt with secondary school reform and recommended a 6-6 organization with a seventh and eighth grade of high school character.[15] As cited earlier, due to a seat shortage in the high schools and room in the elementary schools, Bunker, in the fall of 1909, advocated formation of Introductory High Schools. McKinley Elementary School under Principal Biedenbach opened its doors as an introductory high school on the first day of this century's second decade. Bennett relates some of the early difficulties:

> . . . So great were the difficulties (K-6 in the same building, 7-8 allowed in other schools if the parents objected), so new the plan, and

---

[10] Frank Bunker, "The Better Articulation of the Parts of the Public School System," *Education Review* (March 1914) : 47:249–268, p. 251.

[11] Will French, *American Secondary Education* (New York: Odyssey Press, 1957), p. 18.

[12] Briggs, *op. cit.*, p. 32.

[13] M. M. Smith, L. L. Stanley, and C. L. Hughes, *Junior High School Education* (New York: McGraw-Hill Book Company, Inc., 1942) p. 21.

[14] Charles Hartwell, "Economy in Education," *Education Review*, September, 1905, pp. 162–63.

[15] Parker, *op. cit.*, p. 437.

so fundamental the change it became necessary to appeal to the people for ratification of the scheme . . .[16]

Bunker immediately organized so efficient a public information campaign that he convinced not only the citizens of Berkeley but also those of Los Angeles and educators from coast to coast.[17]

Detroit is representative of the effect of Bunker's publicity. From 1911–1919, the city experimented with the junior high school, became convinced, and in 1919, shifted over entirely to the 6-3-3 design. Elementary buildings were used, foreign languages and commercial subjects were introduced, exploration experiences in Home Economics and Industrial Arts were provided, and, it was believed, the students were given an organization adapted to their physical, social, and mental development. Twenty-two schools were planned and twenty-one were built before the depression.[18]

In general, the early junior high schools were a reaction against the presumed failures of the 8-4 plan; they were measures of expediency; and they were formed prior to the development of a positive philosophy but, in a large measure, they attempted to serve the needs, interests, and abilities of the early adolescent as well as a contemporary knowledge of these aspects would allow. For the most part, however, the early junior high schools were simply a downward extension of the senior high schools with no particular means for facilitating elementary-secondary transition, with few unique operational devices, and with no depth in the exploratory courses offered for the terminal student.[19] In the words of G. N. Fraser:

Junior high schools were set up for one purpose—economy of time; they were spread because of another—to remedy the housing problem; and some years later developed a philosophy totally unrelated to either.[20]

Research by Briggs during the last half of the second decade concerning the reasons various communities gave for starting a junior high school program provides an excellent summary of the philosophy behind the early years of the institution. Briggs surveyed 266 junior high schools across the nation and tabulated the results as they appear in Table I following.[21]

[16] Bennett, op. cit., p. 47.

[17] Bunker, op. cit., p. 253.

[18] H. L. Harrington, "Detroit Expands its Junior High School Policy," National Association of Secondary School Principals Bulletin (February 1962) : 46:34–38, p. 34.

[19] C. F. Toepfer, "Historical Development of Curriculum Patterns of Junior High School Organizations in America," National Association of Secondary School Principals Bulletin (February 1962) : 46:181–183, p. 182.

[20] French, op. cit., p. 234.

[21] Briggs, op. cit., p. 34.

Table I. Early Justification for Junior High Schools

Reason For Initiation	Number of Communities
To provide better educational opportunities	60
To relieve pupil congestion	36
To utilize old facilities	26
To improve instruction in grades seven, eight, and nine	21
To increase retention of students	18
To provide earlier differentiation	15
To bridge the gap	15
To introduce prevocational work	11
Miscellaneous reasons*	64

* No reason listed as common to more than three school systems.

The literature between 1910 and 1925 was voluminous concerning all aspects of the junior high school program: the *Junior High School Clearing House,* a magazine sponsored by Briggs, Judd, Cox, and others, being the central spokesman after 1920. Included in this literature were many attempts to give the school some positive purposes rather than to allow it to remain characterized as a negative reaction against the 8-4 plan. For example, the first four issues of the *Clearing House* contained nine articles which tried to answer some form of the question, "What is a Junior High School?" The positive arguments which resulted were aimed at curing most, if not all, of the problems of public education.[22]

Regardless of which of the early discussions of the function and purpose of the junior high school one reads, he finds that the conclusions reached are usually stated as broad generalizations. Many of them are hypothetical since the fields of guidance and adolescent psychology were as new and as unproven as the institution itself. Often one gets the impression that the activities and curricula of grades seven, eight, and nine, if not in an 8-4 administrative design, can do all things equally well for all students. Most of the arguments are presented in such a way as to seem based on the assumption that the first six years of the elementary school and the last three years of the high school are, by comparison, without fault. One also gets the obviously erroneous impression that all a school system needs to do is to create the ideal program for grades seven, eight, and nine (junior high school, 6-6, or

[22] Abelson, *op. cit.,* p. 13.

whatever), incorporate it with the existing K-6 and 10-12 program, and all educational ills will be solved. In general, educational theorists tried to apply all desirable attributes in an effort to give a positive philosophy to these schools which often had resulted out of mere expediency.

Just what was the early junior high school like? To answer this, let us examine three schools that appear to be representative of the programs offered—one each in New York City, Detroit, and St. Louis.

PS #62 in New York was a Manhattan school converted into an intermediate school in 1905. It operated with just the seventh and eighth grades until 1916 when the ninth was added. Its aims, as stated by the city Board of Education, were to sift and grade students according to their personal aims and aptitudes, to direct and equip those who would pursue higher education (both high school and college) for courses and institutions, and to prepare those terminal students enrolled for vocational schools, the commercial world, or the trades.[23] Upon matriculation each student had to choose between several tracks—two academic, an industrial or vocational one, and three commercial sequences. The academic tracks were identical in content, the only difference being that one could be completed by the more able students in two years rather than three. The subjects offered included Language Arts (English and foreign, spelling, penmanship), Social Studies, Science, and Mathematics. The other tracks considered the same subjects but differed in emphasis and the nature of the required exploratory courses (Home Economics, Industrial Arts, Music, and Art). The industrial track was a terminal program aimed at instilling within each pupil the basic facility for civic responsibility and, at the same time, preparing him to take a place in the vocational climate of the city. The commercial sequence offered three programs—one for the student capable of normal progress who expected to go to high school prior to his entrance into the vocational world, one for the student capable of rapid advancement who could complete the normal three-year course in two years, and the third for the terminal student who chose to prepare himself for immediate entrance into commercial life. The commercial program contained a heavy concentration of typing, bookkeeping, and general business courses. The industrial track was designed to give the students facility in the use of his hands and a basic vocabulary from which he could build his life in the trades. In addition to the classroom activities, the school offered thirty-nine extracurricular activities, ranging from girls' and boys' athletic teams to Science clubs, fine arts clubs, and mechanical or electrical workshops. Through school personnel, emotional, dental, medical, and nutritional aid was given to those students in such need.[24]

[23] R. L. Lyman, and P. W. L. Cox, eds., *Junior High School Practices* (Chicago: Laidlaw Brothers, 1925), p. 27.
[24] *Ibid.*, pp. 27–38.

The Detroit schools, as they were systematized in 1919, were three-year schools organized for both the continuing and the terminal student. Although no track differentiation was set up, almost an identical program with that of PS #62, described above, was available to the student. Each school was organized into six departments and all students were required to take courses in each department in each year. Although names differ slightly, these departments are the same as those now present in most modern junior high schools. Physical Education was required for all three years; it included calisthenics, team games, swimming, and intramural sports. Social Studies consisted of Civics, World History and United States History. The Department of Exact Science offered arithmetic in grades seven and eight, and Algebra and General Science in grade nine. English, French, and Latin made up the courses offered in the Language Arts department. Election by the students was allowed in the departments of Vocational Arts and Fine Arts. Courses offered in the Vocational department included a General Shop with work in wood, metal, printing, auto mechanics, and electrical and mechanical drawing. Typing, Business, and Bookkeeping, along with the normal range of Domestic Science subjects were also included. The Fine Arts program differed from that of today with classroom instruction in the dramatic arts for those so inclined. Each school was designed to hold 1800 students in classes of thirty-five.[25]

The Ben Blewett Junior High School in St. Louis, Missouri was established in 1917 with two fundamental purposes in mind: to provide for individual differences to reproduce life situations as Dewey had suggested in his book the year before. More time was spent by this school system than by the New York or Detroit system devising procedural instructions for the principal and the teachers. The principal of each school was to be the intellectual leader of his teachers, working to lead each along the way to freedom and ease of instruction. The students were to be grouped according to ability in all academic subjects with all objectives of instruction subordinated to the first aim—developing good citizenship. Each student was to be promoted on the basis of his performance in the grade. The school day was divided into six periods with each teacher responsible for four periods of recitation and one period of advisory activities. The seventh grade was identical for each of the students regardless of his educational or vocational plans. In the eighth grade the students were divided into Academic, Commercial, and Technical tracks according to their desires and abilities. The ninth grade merely reproduced those tracks which previously existed in the senior high schools except for a liberalization of the election policy.[26]

The above accounts of representative schools in the early years of the junior high school show the effect of the aforementioned verbalized

[25] Harrington, *op. cit.*, p. 35.
[26] Lyman, and Cox, *op. cit.*, pp. 61–76.

theories upon the institution in actual practice. By the end of the first period of development, about 1928, the institution had found its way into the large cities and the small towns. In the concluding paragraph of their introduction, Lyman and Cox said that the junior high school was definitely no longer an experiment.[27] Part of the reason for the general acceptance of the schools by the middle of the twenties was the emphasis, publicity, and investigation provided by the National Education Association. The organization's conventions served as a platform for the discussion of the pros and cons of the 6-3-3, the 6-6, and the 8-4, and other designs. After 1911, the NEA took a positive stand for school reorganization. In a 1914 commission report the eight-year elementary school was labeled "obsolete."

Professor Johnston opened his 1916 NEA convention address with the statement, "The Junior High School movement is sweeping the country."[28] Reports were published indicating progress and investigation going on in connection with the school such as Table II reproduced in Briggs.[29] With information as this provided by a reputable organization, the junior high school movement indeed swept the country. Only ten states, among them Wisconsin, had no junior high school by 1917. Indiana and Minnesota had more than any other state—twenty-four each—with North Dakota with twenty and Pennsylvania following with sixteen.

The advent of a new administrative design with its fresh curricular innovations did not, however, seem to demand thorough changes in the method of educating the teachers to be used in the institution. Although several discussions in magazines and books point out the educational world's obligation to provide adequately prepared teachers, only two of the early advocates included in their publications an extended discussion of teacher qualifications or teacher preparation. Briggs stated that the success of the new movement was dependent upon the use of teachers prepared for the task.[30] Bennett probably went beyond all others when he said:

> . . . A whole curriculum, devoted exclusively and pointedly to preparation for junior high school teaching only, would seem to be the next logical step . . . in the near future we may look for this curriculum . . .[31]

Bennett's dream of a separate collegiate curriculum came true in a Wisconsin State Normal School in the thirties, but the program was dropped because of lack of funds and scarcity of student population.

Collegiate activities provided for prospective junior high school

---

[27] *Ibid.*, p. 13.
[28] Bennett, *op. cit.*, p. 50.
[29] Briggs, *op. cit.*, p. 32.
[30] *Ibid.*, p. 210.
[31] Bennett, *op. cit.*, p. 56.

Table II.   Junior High Schools Formed Each Year—1905–1917

YEAR	NUMBER	YEAR	NUMBER
PRE-1900	2	1911	9
1905	1	1912	21
1906	—	1913	27
1907	3	1914	44
1908	3	1915	76
1909	3	1916	68
1910	11	1917	60

Range in Student Population—23 to 2,465 pupils
75% of the schools have less than 496
Median School—248

teachers were usually limited to one or two courses in either Junior High School Curriculum or Adolescent Growth or Development. Some of the first of such courses were initiated at the University of Southern California and at Bridgewater State Normal School in Massachusetts in 1918. By 1925 seventy Normal Schools, Teachers Colleges, Schools of Education, etc. offered a course in some phase of junior high school education. However, not one offered more than one course and no course provided more than three semester credits for the work involved.[32]

Growth is a peculiar phenomenon, whether it appears in the animal world, the botanical world, or the social world. In the embryonic, pre-natal, or formative stages of growth, the organism goes through a cycle of advancement with little regard or worry about its surroundings. Following this, there comes a period of adjustment where the organism modifies itself or is modified by external forces so as to fit into its environment. Such was the story of the junior high school during the years between 1927 and 1947. Few innovations took place during this period of adjustment when the more radical claims of the school were toned down and the more doubtful of the skeptics were presented with evidence that, despite its defects, the institution had valuable contributions to make to American public education.

As far as teacher preparation was concerned, the writers merely looked to the future as Bennett had done earlier—a future which would provide some unique form of teacher preparation for junior high school teachers. Some writers[33] continued to say nothing about this problem

[32] Ibid., p. 55.
[33] L. V. Koos, F. T. Spaulding, and O. I. Frederick, Reorganization of Secondary Education (United States Office of Education Bulletin #17, 1932, Monograph #2, National Survey of Education, 1933).

while others[34] stated something had to be done, and in one case, accurately predicted a situation found today.

> .... It is not at all unlikely that the professional education of junior high school teachers will begin at the graduate level . . . the fifth year being a full year of internship (sic) . . . the intern will serve as a teaching assistant and will receive one-half the minimum salary . . . .

Negative comments concerning the junior high schools between 1927 and 1947 should not be interpreted as meaning that no new schools were formed during this period. The numbers steadily increased from 2,268 in 1925 to 10,322 junior high schools in 1947. The character, curriculum, administrative procedures, and philosophical justification of these 1927–1947 schools were, however, merely borrowed from schools and publications in the score of years prior to this period. Little money was available during the depression to finance investigations and studies, and when the nation's economy recovered in the early 1940s a war was being fought which demanded the resources and talents of those who might otherwise be interested in such improvement. Few new buildings were built in the 1930s because of the lack of money, and in the 1940s building material had been commandeered for the war effort.

By 1930, twenty-five publications had appeared on different aspects of the junior high school. Twenty percent of the secondary students were enrolled in reorganized schools and interest was just beyond its peak. As the years of the depression went by, the schools continued to be formed but the zeal of their advocates steadily waned. Only two books seem to have been published between 1930 and 1947 on the junior high school, and both were McGraw-Hill publications. Magazine articles and research papers on the graduate level declined almost to the point of nonexistence. Quotes such as "the junior high school is a failure" and "it will gradually pass from the picture as a separate school" were not uncommon in speeches and periodicals.[35]

Pringle, author of one of the two publications the authors found on the junior high school during this period, summarizes the state of the institution in the following manner. Generally, faith in the worth, possibilities, effectiveness, and future of the junior high school had been realized and accepted. The initial period of experimentation had passed and it was then the job of the educators to substantiate the fact that their subject matter and activities were suited to the interests and capabilities of the students. The institution had finally realized its unique identity; therefore, effort had to be made to develop its own positive philosophy based on educational objectives clearly recognized

---

[34] Smith, et al., op. cit., p. 450.

[35] John H. Lounsbury, "What Has Happened to the Junior High School?" *Educational Leadership* (March 1956) : 13:368–73, p. 369.

as within the domain of the school. Special education programs on both the pre-service and in-service level had to be provided for those teachers involved with the school, for it had to contain teachers of content material as well as teachers of children.

> In a word, the junior high school must standardize its activities, its teacher preparation, its administrative organization, and its philosophy if it is going to make its maximum contribution to education in the America of 1940.[36]

Taking Detroit, Michigan as an example of what happened during this period we find the following situation. No new schools were built, although some older buildings were converted to junior high schools. This shift in the use of the older buildings coupled with the failure to provide facilities peculiar to the junior high school caused the average class size during the years 1912–1930 to increase from thirty-five to forty-three. For the same reason, as well as for lack of funds, special services and extracurricular activities had to be stopped or greatly curtailed in comparison with the preceding years. The only positive action during this period was a reaffirmation of the 1919 stand by the Board of Education, in effect, saying, "We still believe as we did but we see no way of continuing to implement that policy at the present time."[37]

Following the war, the abilities and interests of the nation once again turned toward peaceful ends. Included in this emphasis was a revival of concern for the junior high school. In 1945, the National Association of Secondary School Principals devoted an entire issue of their bulletin (as it has since—in 1952, 1958, and 1962) to the philosophy, practices, and policies of the junior high school. As the money was being poured into the elementary program to meet the urgent need caused by the coming of the "war babies," investigations were being started to examine the junior high school.

Probably the most complete investigation was conducted by William T. Gruhn and Harl R. Douglass and published in book form in 1947. This study delved into primary source materials as well as the publications of the twenties in an effort to ascertain the origin, purposes, and progress of the junior high school. Definitions and statements of function were rewritten in light of the changes which had taken place in American society. The greatest value of the work has been found in the delineation of need changes provided by the authors who are presently publishing their second revision of the book. Not only were the weaknesses of the institution cited but constructive criticism was offered to correct these ills. In general, the book is a comprehensive presentation of the functions of the junior high school, its instructional program,

---

[36] R. W. Pringle, *The Junior High School* (New York: McGraw-Hill Book Company, Inc., 1937), pp. 27–30.

[37] Harrington, *op. cit.*, pp. 37–38.

guidance, extracurricular activities, organization, and evaluation, and improvement.

The "new" functions of the junior high school that Gruhn and Douglass discussed were merely modernizations of the older ones. The purposes of exploration, guidance, and bridging the gap were just as pronounced in their list as they were in any lists of the 1910s or 1920s.[38] The arguments for retention and economy of time, negated by external forces, have been replaced with efforts toward moral and social effectiveness. The function of differentiation was simply a recognition of the continuing importance of providing for individual differences among the students.

The revival of interest initiated by Gruhn and Douglass has not as yet reached an end. Both in theory and practice, educators have intensified their efforts within the last fifteen years to produce an institution built on solid philosophical grounds which could provide the best possible education for the early adolescent youth of America. Gruhn and Douglass prophetically cited this desire for the best educational program possible as the most important reason for continued growth in the junior high school.[39] In addition to the publications by Gruhn and Douglass, Koos, and Noar, in the last fifteen years several agencies and organizations have stimulated interest and growth. The United States Office of Education has held several national conventions dealing with the subject and has published numerous circulars, bulletins, and bibliographies. The Southern States Work Conference inaugurated and supported a three-year study of adolescent educational needs in the mid-1950s. New York State and the California Administrators financed and conducted studies, produced films, and published reports directly related to current practices in junior high schools. Publications of the Association for Supervision and Curriculum Development and the National Association of Secondary School Principals have reproduced and circulated questions, studies, reports, and other information of pertinent value to junior high school educators.[40]

In recent publications, Gruhn,[41] French,[42] and Juilfs[43] provide a fairly comprehensive list of the problems facing the junior high school at the present time. Unfortunately, for the pride of American educa-

[38] W. T. Gruhn, and H. Douglass, *The Modern Junior High School* (New York: Ronald Press Company, 1947), pp. 59–60.

[39] Gruhn, and Douglass, *op. cit.*, pp. 39–41.

[40] Lounsbury, *op. cit.*, pp. 369–71.

[41] W. T. Gruhn, "Major Issues in Junior High School Education," *National Association of Secondary School Principals Bulletin* (September 1961): 45:18–24.

[42] French, *op. cit.*, pp 233–35.

[43] Erwin Juilfs, "History of the Junior High School in Oregon," *National Association of Secondary School Principals Bulletin* (February 1962): 46:338–40.

worthwhile and worth striving for in a community, family, school, and all-agency effort. However, it was said to be a digression from purpose and out of reach for the individual junior high.

Consider what the (junior) high schools promised. They proposed to develop healthy individuals of sound moral character who were guaranteed not only to be competent in their jobs and wise in their use of leisure, but worthy parents and good citizens to boot. Indeed, some assurance was offered that in the process the pupil might enjoy popularity among his peers, a tranquil adolescence, and protection from a sense of failure and frustration.[46]

A junior high must have a program of its own especially geared to the preadolescent and early adolescent. With the ninth grade gone and with it the Carnegie Unit limitations and the other credit and subject restrictions, a 5-8 middle school is able to produce a better, different, sounder program aimed at satisfying the curricular and educational needs of its age groups first.

What of the exploratory aspect of the junior high program? There has been increasing emphasis on the academics which, in many cases, limits this exploratory characteristic. Again, with the ninth grade out, opportunities to provide exploratory experiences multiply—such experiences include newer educational methods and techniques such as flexible scheduling, independent study, special interest centers, team teaching, ungraded classes, and new course content.

Functions of the Middle School

In an attempt to define the functions of the junior high and middle schools a number of statements have been made, most of which find it necessary to discuss purposes and characteristics as part of the functions of this organizational pattern. Many such statements promise such a variety of benefits as to lead one to believe that the adoption of the middle school concept will solve most, if not all, of the educational ills with which a district may suffer. Other statements of functions are either of so general and amorphous a nature that it is difficult to know precisely what is meant, or can apply equally to schools and children of all grade levels and, therefore, are not valid reasons for establishing any particular kind of school organization.

For example, we are told that the junior high school will develop physical and mental fitness, so should any well-run school, whether 8-4, 6-3-3, 5-3-4, or 6-6. Neither is it reasonable to assume as a function peculiar to the middle school the development of appreciation of moral and ethical principles, as frequently claimed.

[46] Mauritz Johnson, Jr., "The Dynamic Junior High School," *National Association of Secondary School Principals Bulletin* (March 1964) : 48:119–28, p. 122.

If the middle school has any real and valid reason for existence, it must be based upon the ability to do something for children of this age group that cannot be done as well by other organizational patterns or cannot be done at all. At its inception, the junior high school was expected to reduce the number of dropouts, push the academic disciplines downward, increase departmentalized instruction, provide an economy of time in total years of instruction, and permit some pre-vocational and vocational training.

As time passed, it became apparent that a middle school could and did provide a kind of atmosphere, guidance, and instruction for the adolescent which had been slighted previously. To the extent that the adolescent is a unique person, the middle school can provide something for him—attention to his particular needs not usually found in either the high school or the elementary school. A statement of functions, taking cognizance of the needs of the adolescent, will, of necessity, include comments relating to the purposes and characteristics of this middle school.

Providing a Program for the Early Adolescent

Children enter a critical stage of their development at this age. Their interests are widened. They become increasingly ready for opportunities for independent functioning and responsible self-management. This is not to say that early teenagers should be given carte blanche. They need the security of wise supervision and direction. It is necessary to provide a sound guidance program, one which directs without rigidity and guides with a nice balance between authoritarianism and laissez-faire. Where the elementary school does not have the personnel nor the time to devote to this and the high school is concerned with pre-college, vocational training, and graduation, the middle school can and should have the trained personnel, the time, and the interest to work with its students.

Establishing a block of time, where the students are with the same teacher two or three periods as in the lowest grade of the school, and allowing departmentalized instruction by subject matter specialists, for the balance of the day, will permit the middle school to make an even transition from elementary school to high school. Transition, of itself, should never be the sole function of the middle school.

Exploration

In addition to the broad and general education desirable and necessary for children, the middle school should provide a wide program of elective subjects and activities. At no grade level in this intermediate school should the curriculum be completely required and restrictive. A good school should establish a program of supplemental courses geared to the interests and abilities of its students. Such a list of offerings includes, as a matter of course, industrial arts and homemaking (for boys and girls) ; at least one foreign language; music, both vocal and instrumental; arts and crafts. A better program should include such courses as journalism, dramatics, speech, and typing. Students should be given an opportunity to choose at least one or two electives at the lowest grade level of the school; and the oldest group, whether grade eight, nine, or ten, should have at least two or three electives each semester. Permitting a wide range of elective courses and experiences fulfills a very real function of the middle school, that of exploration.

Activities

A well-planned and properly organized program of school activities, aimed at meeting the needs of early adolescents, is difficult to accomplish in the regular curriculum. Children of this age have a real desire to participate, to belong, to do things which may be related to but are not directly labelled, school work. Children who have been unable to achieve to the degree that their classmates have and who seek opportunities not found in the regular curriculum may find interests in the school activity program which can engage their attention and reflect their overall attitude and effort. It is possible to teach democratic processes and still provide a large field of electives and develop widespread participation, effort, learning, and enjoyment. Special interest clubs, service groups, student government, and social organizations all have their role. The problem here is a common one for middle schools: too often school activities become little more than a slightly diluted high school activity program. Again, the middle school is in a position to offer experiences to its students which are beyond those available in the elementary school, and, with care and judgment, can satisfy the needs of its own age group.

Special Facilities

If the middle school is to do things for early adolescents that other grade patterns do poorly or not at all, it is essential that facilities for these purposes be provided. Characteristics and needs of young adolescents are best met in schools that have facilities designed expressly for them. Unfortunately, it was frequently the case that the junior high school was established because of problems a district was having with enrollment, finances, buildings, or consolidation. In these instances, the junior high school was handicapped because it closely resembled the school organization, elementary or high school, from which it inherited its building. The same situation continues today.

A satisfactory middle school program needs more than classrooms; it should have facilities for art, music, science, industrial arts, homemaking, and physical education. It is desirable to have an auditorium or cafetorium—some sort of central meeting place—as well as adequate grounds and playfields. It is possible to have excellent teaching with the teacher on one end of the log and the student on the other end. Of course, it is considerably easier to teach children in buildings and equipment designed for specific instructional purposes.

Since the early adolescent is unique, providing him with the best learning experiences requires a school intended and designed for this purpose—an organization which in itself is unique. Education must include the development of basic skills—reading, writing, arithmetic, thinking, and reasoning. A good middle school has more than this to offer. Since individual differences are aggravated in children in the early adolescent stage, they need a program designed specifically for them, as well as personnel trained to work with them. Such a program must provide necessary guidance and counselling, permit early differentiation in elective subjects and activities, and ensure the segregation of these children from both the elementary and high school students. The middle school is more than buildings and facilities; it is an idea, a concept, a belief that such a school can best educate children who need that kind of attention, teaching, and learning which this program best provides.

Proposals and Innovations

Few will advocate the abolition of a separate school for adolescents and a return to the 8-4 system. Seventh and eighth grade children need the facilities and resources for intellectual development which can be more readily provided by secondary or middle schools. There is a growing trend for a reorganization of the school system with the hope of solving several problems. Various proposals and arguments are being pursued. It has been suggested that grades seven and eight be eliminated and that the schools adopt a six-year elementary and four-year secondary pattern similar to some European schools on the basis that seventh and eighth grades are largely review, watered down, and time-wasting.[47]

Another proposal is that the schools be organized 5-3-3-3 with the last two years of high school part of a junior college. Students would be introduced to lab experiences in science, industrial arts, home economics, fine arts, modern foreign language, physical education and advanced mathematics at an earlier age. This program, to meet the needs of children in today's world, requires more specialized classes, rooms, labs, shops, and equipment than elementary schools have.[48]

A somewhat different plan is to have children begin the first grade at age five; departmentalize grades five and six and begin foreign languages, algebra, geometry, astronomy, biology, chemistry, and physics at this level; a middle school of grades seven to ten; and a high school

[47] Charles H. Schutter, "Should We Abolish the 7th and 8th Grades?" *School Executive* (May 1955), p. 53.

[48] Lawrence Vredevoe, "Let's Reorganize our School System," *National Association of Secondary School Principals Bulletin* (May 1958): 42:40–44, p. 40.

with three different tracks—a two year program for terminal education, four years for a community college, and four years with only three
years in the middle school for those going to a liberal arts college.[49]
The author goes on to say:[50]

> While the aims of American education have changed drastically
> since 1900 there has been little basic change in the organization of
> public education during this period. The most significant changes
> have been found in the establishment of the junior high school and
> the public community college. . . .

Another suggestion is that the American school system be reorganized on a more flexible basis: an ungraded primary for slow children ages 5-9 and fast children ages 5-7, the equivalent of grades K-2;
an elementary or middle school for slow children ages 9-14 and fast
children ages 7-12, equivalent to grades 3-6; and a high school including grades 7-10.[51] Many educators are examining middle schools, both
4-4-4 and 5-3-4, in the hope of finding solutions to problems of segregation, finances, and administration. There is considerable activity in
school reorganization, and those most often incorporated are 4-4-4 and
5-3-4. Such reorganization places considerable emphasis upon the nature of the new unit, a middle school separate from that usually designated as a junior high school, neither elementary nor secondary.

This recent development is based on the premise that ninth graders
are more physically and socially mature compared with seventh graders,
and that academically and mentally they are capable of higher achievement and more advanced work. Omitting the ninth grade relieves some
of the pressure toward preoccupation with college entrance units, interscholastic sports, and marching bands. In addition, it eliminates restrictions upon seventh and eighth grade curricula caused by scheduling
courses for the ninth grade.

> Possibilities for varied programs in the seventh and eighth grades
> are hedged in scheduling by the need to establish the pattern for the
> ninth grade and the lower grades are fitted around this as can best
> be done. . . . We conclude by gearing and twisting the seventh grade
> and eighth grade programs to fit the ninth grade requirements.[52]

Claimed advantages of this type of middle school are:
   1. Permits some departmentalizing and instruction by specialists
      in the lower grades of the middle school and at the same time

[49] R. Baird Shuman, "Reorganization in Public Education," *Peabody Journal of Education* (May 1963), p. 239.

[50] *Ibid.*, pp. 239–240.

[51] Paul Woodring, *A Fourth of a Nation* (New York: McGraw-Hill Book
   Company, Inc., 1957), p. 153.

[52] Alvin W. Howard, "Which Years in the Junior High?" *Clearing House*
   (March 1959), p. 406.

reduces somewhat the fragmentation into which some junior highs have wandered.

2. Allows a more logical grouping in terms of social maturity and sophistication.
3. Encourages the elimination of activities and attitudes which are too mature.
4. Permits enrichment of the sixth grade program as well as the fifth if it is included in the middle school by introduction of areas as foreign language, science, art, shop, homemaking, music, and physical education.
5. Provides far better facilities for use with sixth grades—library, shops, homemaking and art rooms, language labs, science labs, gymnasium, locker, and shower rooms.
6. Encourages creativity in developing new techniques in both administration and teaching. This in turn contributes to high teacher morale.
7. Creates more opportunities for staff utilization, flexible scheduling with modules, independent study, and team teaching.
8. Permits a school to work into ungraded classes—by subject, if desirable.
9. Allows other forms of ability grouping, if wished.
10. This unit, the middle or intermediate school, now has a status of its own—not a "junior" classification.
11. Provides a better guidance program for fifth and sixth graders and improved discipline because there is a lessened conflict of interest.

The elimination of the ninth grade does not eliminate certain disadvantages:

1. Girls in the middle school still mature more rapidly than the boys.
2. If the school works toward ungrading, more time is required of the teachers to devise new techniques, select materials, and evaluate the program.
3. It is hard to drop the habit of rigid scheduling and even harder to work out a flexible schedule, particularly if it involves grouping and an ungraded school.
4. If each child is given individual attention within an ungraded situation, grading and reporting become an aggravated problem.
5. While students apparently mature at an earlier age and are often capable of doing more than they are accustomed, it is easy to overload them.
6. Sometimes these middle schools, as the junior high school, are handicapped by inherited building facilities which are unsuited to the program.

The Ideal Middle School
(With or Without Grades Five, Six, or Nine)

Advocates are pretty clear as to what the middle school should be. What is most sought for in middle schools is a curriculum which is truly aimed at engrossing the attention of the junior high school pupil and one which attempts to satisfy the needs of the wide range of individual differences found in this age group—children approximately ten to fourteen years old.

The middle school must emphasize individualized instruction. To help in this, various aids—consideration for independent study, individual projects, opportunities to use a variety of learning resources—should be available. Grade six (and grade five, if included) will have not less than a three-hour block with the same teacher. Grades seven and eight will have two-hour blocks with the same teacher. Grade nine should be departmentalized. There must be a time and place for independent study and every effort must be made to create an intellectual climate in which learning is exciting and worth doing.

It is usually recommended that progress groupings be used in the academic areas and opportunities provided for accelerated, individualized programs for those students who are capable and interested; for instance, algebra in grade eight or in a lower grade. Foreign language, open to all who wish it, should be available beginning at the lowest grade of the middle school. Industrial arts, homemaking, art, music, arts and crafts, and typing will be offered at each grade level, varying from grade to grade and school to school. Electives will be open at least in a limited way at all grade levels. A real strength of the junior high school has been the exploratory program. Moving children into the middle school earlier will permit increased opportunity for a sound program to be developed.

Common learnings include those of the language arts: reading, writing, spelling, speaking, literature; mathematics, on an ability-grouped basis; science; certain of the fine arts; health and physical education.

Use will be made of team teaching, differentiated staffing, learning activity packages and an instructional materials center.

A team of three to five teachers (one or two especially competent in language arts and social studies, one or two in science and mathematics, and one in fine arts and/or languages) could be organized and assigned to each group of seventy-five to 150 pupils, either on a single grade or multi-grade basis. These teachers would be responsible for about two-thirds of the instruction of these pupils.[53]

Students will be grouped heterogeneously for non-academic classes. Building facilities will include team teaching or large group instruction

[53] William Alexander, "The Junior High School: A Changing View," *National Association of Secondary School Principals Bulletin* (March 1964), p. 23.

areas, small group instruction areas, and space for independent study. Care must be taken to avoid forcing all students to take the same subjects for the same length of time. Varying interests and abilities preclude the lockstep design. Extended day opportunities may be used to provide part or additional programs in certain areas. There must be increased use of technological aids to instruction.

To provide the most opportunities for each child and still avoid advanced socialization, there should be a basic club program, simplified student government, and restrictions (but not necessarily elimination) of cheer leaders, school yearbook, marching band, and interschool athletics. Sports for all boys and girls can be provided by a strong intramural program with teams made up on an age, weight, and height basis.

A Look at Some Middle Schools

Schools planned and built specifically to be middle schools can, of course, come much closer to having the necessary facilities. In one of these, a southern school, which includes grades five through eight, school personnel believe that a 4-4-4 plan with a strong middle unit is far superior to junior high; it is a "school for growing up."

Grade five is almost completely self-contained; grade six has team teaching; grades seven and eight are departmentalized. There is no marching band, no interschool sports activity. There is a large materials resource center to expose children to arts and crafts, science, shop, and homemaking. There is a big library with facilities for independent study. Use is made of specialized teachers, facilities, and equipment.

A Michigan school district which has adopted the 4-4-4 plan built its building three-sided with three classrooms to a side; it has openness, freedom, and spaciousness. There is a raised "mall" down the center of the wing between the classrooms which may be used for large group instruction since the classrooms are open on the side facing it. The mall is a common work area, multipurpose, and is used for homemaking, arts and crafts, and industrial arts. Quiet spaces for individual study carrels are available. The children eat in a "dining room," not a cafeteria, which has booths, round tables, and chairs. There is a library, a gymnasium, and a social center. Teachers for grades five and six plan together for team teaching, although fifth and sixth grades are essentially self-contained. Grades seven and eight are blocked for language arts and social studies. They are departmentalized for foreign language, mathematics, science, arts and crafts, homemaking, industrial arts, music, physical education, and health. Special classrooms, designed for teaching these areas, are used for most departmentalized subjects. There is a large well-equipped instructional materials center. Students are grouped on a "performance level" basis by means of scores achieved in a reading test.

A New York State school district planned and built a 6-7-8 school designed for 1,000 students. The course of study includes a unified arts program composed of industrial arts, art, music, and theater. The school is organized around teaching teams. There are no rigid grade levels or labels.

Another New York State district has built two 7-8-9 schools. Designed to hold 1,000 students each, they are organized on the house plan. There are three subdivisions or houses in the school, each containing fourteen classrooms. Three hundred and forty pupils from all three grades are assigned a house and remain there for three years. Teachers are carefully selected and matched for suitable balance within and between houses. Art, general music, science, mathematics, English and related subjects, and social studies are taught within each house. There is a large visual aid room in each house for projection, informal dramatics, and house meetings. Shared areas include general administration, library, auditorium, specialized music, gyms, dining rooms, shops, and homemaking rooms. There are four classes in each grade in each house with remedial classes and a gift program. The lowest grade ignores the bells; they are self-contained except for physical education, art, music, shop, and homemaking. Science teachers are available to teachers as consultants. Classes for the other grades are forty-two minutes long, activity classes have double periods. Classes are organized in heterogeneous groupings for English, social studies, art, music, physical education, and French, and in homogeneous groupings for science, reading, and mathematics. All three houses participate jointly in orchestra, band, chorus, student council, special interest clubs, and intramural sports.

An Illinois school district has spent considerable time in planning and constructing a new middle school. Even more time has been expended in selection of staff, development of curriculum, and determining methods and materials. The school is completely carpeted throughout, has no interior doors, has movable partitions but no interior roof supports, air conditioning, and a ceiling lighting system. The school includes grades six, seven, and eight, and was specifically designed to replace the traditional junior high school. Heavy emphasis is placed upon team teaching in the belief that through this method each student can be placed in the proper class for each subject. There are about 100 children in each of three learning groups in the three grades. Classes are divided into fourteen modules of thirty minutes each and the lengths of periods are based on the activities of the subject and its long range importance to the students. Language arts are given eight modules a week. Local personnel regard their school as a transitional school with a curriculum for specific groups of people at specific learning stages. The literal center of the school is a 7,000 square foot learning center. All pupils spend some time in the center every week and, since it is in the center of the building, all must pass through it to get to the dining area, the gym, or the arts and crafts wing. The center was planned without barriers and walls to provide a sense of freedom. In the center there are also audiovisual equipment areas, a listening center, a meditation area, individual study sections, and a project center. There is also a center for theatrical and special projects, as well as a planetarium which is integrated with the school's overall science program.

Proponents of the newer forms of the middle school are confident that the pattern that they are developing is educationally and logically sound. It satisfies those who favor a four year high school, agrees with advocates of a separate middle school, and is in accord with those who want pupils introduced at an earlier age to more specialized instruction.

The oft-mentioned explosion of knowledge and the expansion of the elementary curriculum gives more responsibility than ever to the elementary teachers who cannot be expected to be trained for the requisite competence needed in so many subject areas.

The question has been seriously raised as to whether or not the middle school should continue to include the ninth grade. It may be of more value to begin the middle school with the fifth or sixth grade, returning the ninth grade to the senior high school. This would help those students who are in the college preparatory program and remove the Carnegie Unit from the junior high schools.

If an individual approach were possible, it might be best to enter junior high school at different ages and remain varying lengths of time. In the past the greatest concentration of pupils who reached pubertal status was in grades 7-8-9. However, we now find that children in many communities reach pubescence before seventh grade. In these situations the beginning phase of adolescence may occur primarily in grades 6, 7, and 8. If so, this would lend support to a 5-3-4 division.[54]

However, applying a new label, changing grade levels, or reorganizing in the hope that this alone will produce the desired educational transitions is not enough. Ultimately all depends upon the efforts and attitudes of the teachers and administration involved.

These factors, coupled with the belief that early adolescents are ready for an educational program materially different and more extensive than that generally available in the elementary school, lend strength to the proposals of those who would revise the organizational pattern to permit operation for the non-junior high middle school. Still,

The decision as to form of organization will have to be made on practical grounds and on the basis of social and administrative viability. Any pattern is satisfactory that gives identity to youths during early adolescence, includes at least three grades for stability, and brackets those grades in which significant numbers reach pubescence.[55]

[54] Alfred Skogsberg, and Mauritz Johnson, Jr., "The Magic Numbers of 7-8-9," *NEA Journal* (March 1963), p. 51.

[55] *Ibid.*, p. 51.

Summary

The junior high, an educational development of the early 1900s, appears to have acquired its most prevalent type of grade organization. 7-8-9, more by accident than by design. In the past few years an increasing criticism of and dissatisfaction with the junior high has brought about a number of reorganizations of the grade patterns of the American schools. These reorganizations involve a variety of different grade arrangements, the most common changes being to 5-3-4, with grades 6-7-8 in the middle school, or 4-4-4, with a middle school of 5-6-7-8. Many districts have adopted the middle school concept and have planned and built schools specifically for these grades and have revised and adapted their curricula accordingly. Some form of large scale reorganization appears possible, perhaps even probable, with accompanying curricular innovations and revisions.

School organization is far from being static; reorganization has involved such a variety of patterns as to bewilder any investigation. Suggestions, experiments, and new patterns are constantly being tried. From this welter of diversity, the middle schools of 4-4-4 or 5-3-4 appear to be gaining considerable acceptance.

Chapter 1 Bibliography

Abelson, Joseph. "A Study of the Junior High School Project," *Education* (September 1916): 37:1–19.

Alexander, William M. "The Junior High School: A Changing View," *National Association of Secondary School Principals Bulletin* (March 1964).

Bennett, G. V. *The Junior High School*. Baltimore: Houghton Mifflin Company, 1920.

Bunker, Frank. "The Better Articulation of the Parts of the Public School System," *Educational Review* (March 1914): 47:249–268.

Grambs, Jean D., and others. "The Junior High School We Need," *ASCD Bulletin* (1961).

Harrington, H. L. "Detroit Expands Its Junior High School Policy," *National Association of Secondary School Principals Bulletin* (February 1962): 46:34–38.

Hartwell, Charles. "Economy in Education," *Education Review*, September, 1905.

Howard, Alvin W. "Which Years in Junior High School?" *Clearing House* (March 1959).

_____. "The Middle School in Oregon and Washington, 1965–1966." Unpublished doctoral dissertation, University of Oregon, 1966.

Juilfs, Erwin. "History of Junior High Schools in Oregon," *National Association of Secondary School Principals Bulletin* (February 1962): 46:338–340.

Lentz, D. W. "History and Development of the Junior High School," *Teachers College Record* (May 1956): 57:522–530.

Lounsbury, John H. "What Has Happened to the Junior High School?" *Educational Leadership* (March 1956): 13:368–373.

Lyman, R. L., and Cox, P. W. L., eds. *Junior High School Practices.* Chicago: Laidlaw Brothers, 1925.

Parker, Frank. "Fifty Years of the Junior High School," *National Association of Secondary School Principals Bulletin* (February 1962): 46:435–445.

Pringle, R. W. *The Junior High School.* New York: McGraw-Hill Book Company, Inc., 1937.

Schutter, Charles H. "Should We Abolish the 7th and 8th Grades?" *School Executive* (May 1955).

Shuman, R. Baird. "Reorganization in Public Education," *Peabody Journal of Education* (May 1963).

The Adolescent

Introduction

To the human organism few aspects of development are so dramatically evident as the physical change which takes place during the junior high school years. This change is an involved process in which a great variety of events are taking place simultaneously. To compound this phenomenon further, an adolescent has few companions who are concurrently experiencing the same things he is experiencing. Subject to some modifications, each individual experiences adolescent growth at a rate and quantity unique to him.

Who are these adolescents? How do they learn? What should teachers know about them? Writers agree that these questions must be answered if middle school teachers are to be successful in their work. A perusal of the writings of these scholars indicates the belief that present middle school teachers lack answers.

This chapter does not represent a study in depth but is intended as a summary of salient points of the study of adolescents which have implications for the school program and school teacher. Readers should pursue this subject by perusal of the writings of adolescent psychologists, not curriculum professors.

Before discussing the many aspects of adolescent change, it would be expedient to define our terms. Adolescence refers to that period of time during which the growing individual makes the transition from childhood to adulthood. This period begins and ends at different points for everyone, as there is no precise span of years. Because of this, adolescence is viewed as beginning roughly when children show signs of puberty and continuing until both sexual and physical maturation has been achieved. General agreement—using averages—puts this period between the ages of twelve and twenty.[1] Some children enter this period in grade five or six while others do not enter it until grade ten—the range, however, is age nine-seventeen for girls and eleven-nineteen for boys.[2] Most adolescents experience the majority of their changes between the ages of 11.8 and 14.6—approximately the ages of grades seven, eight, and nine.

Physical Factors

The adolescent spurt of physical growth is most visible to onlookers through observations of changes in height and weight. Both height and weight changes are accelerated during two periods of rapid growth. All children, regardless of sex, experience a period of rapid growth during the first two years of their life. Girls experience a second period of accelerated growth between the years of nine and twelve. The second period of rapid physical change for boys appears between the ages of eleven and fourteen.[3] For both sexes, this second period of rapid physical growth is followed by a period of diminished velocity until, after a period of years, mature height and weight are achieved. Caution must be used in regard to all averages or central tendencies which refer to growth; for more than any other "average" terms, they seldom refer to a specific growth pattern.[4]

During adolescence, height increases 25 percent while body weight doubles. Leg height at age fourteen makes up 48 percent of the total where it formerly made up only 33 percent.[5] Also, during adolescence, other parts of the body—hips, arms, trunk, head—assume their adult proportions.

The changes which take place completely within the growing organism do not hold the social and personal importance and interest that

[1] A. T. Jersild, *Psychology of Adolescence* (New York: The Macmillan Company, 1957), p. 4.

[2] R. G. Kuhlen, *Psychology of Adolescent Development* (New York: Harper and Row, Publishers, 1952), p. 40.

[3] M. E. Breckenridge, and E. L. Vincent, *Child Development* (Philadelphia: W. B. Saunders Company, 1949), p. 242.

[4] J. M. Seidman, *The Adolescent Years* (New York: Dryden Press, 1963), p. 125.

[5] J. M. Stephens, *Educational Psychology* (New York: Holt, Rinehart and Winston, Inc., 1962), p. 136.

external changes do, but they are much more complicated. Throughout life, the processes of growth and development are guided and controlled by the secretions of several of the endocrine glands. The "growth" hormone, gonadotrophin, a product of the pituitary gland, controls the rate of growth during the adolescent years. When secretions of this growth hormone increase, growth is accelerated. Conversely, when these secretions are reduced or shut off, growth slows or stops.

Ossification, a process which begins during the embryonic stage, is completed during adolescence. For the most part, adolescence is occupied with growth of existing bones. Some new bones do appear, however, the most interesting of which is the sesamoid bone which appears in the hands of children at about the same time as the onset of puberty, though unfortunately for the teacher this fact is not externally observable. Several authors indicate the importance of knowledge concerning ossification and skeletal development because it can give the teacher help in interpreting scholastic success, mental development, and social adjustment. These physical phenomena parallel sexual maturation and give observers the best external evidence of it. The most conclusive evidence which indicates the above is a study of Cleveland youngsters during the depression.[6]

Muscular growth has reached mature weight and development by age twelve, so the period of adolescence is the time for shaping, molding, and strengthening these muscles for later adult use. During this adjustment of the muscles to their uses there are numerous periods of sluggishness and ineptness when fatigue comes quickly. Lack of muscular coordinations, poor posture, awkwardness, and feeling of discomfort often occur in middle school students. Because of these phenomena the students stumble into furniture, feel overly conscious of their hands or feet, or slouch at the desk in an unsightly manner. Although such activity cannot be condoned or encouraged, the teacher must have sufficient background in the physical development of his youngsters to accept some of this as normal and unavoidable. Physical educators must plan activities geared to the retention of old skills and the development of new ones rather than activities that put great stress on coordinated muscular movement.

All authors, however, are not in agreement concerning coordination or motor ability. Motor ability matures at different rates, reaches its maximum at different ages, shows no partiality to sex, and fails to reach its peak in any form during the adolescent years. Most of the few studies that have been made are often negated in importance because of the lack of correlation which exists between simple functions, as tested in many motor ability studies, and manipulative skill, as used by the adult on his job.

If graphed, coordination would show a slowing down during the adolescent growth spurt but would not show the reversal or "dip" that

[6] Breckenridge, *op. cit.*, p. 268–70.

most people attribute to adolescence. In one study, the pubescent boy was actually found to be better coordinated than the post-pubescent one.[7] The awkwardness which society often points to is usually a function of social uneasiness rather than lack of physical coordination.

Physical endurance increases continually for boys until it reaches its peak between seventeen and twenty. Physical endurance for girls increases until age thirteen when it regresses so much that by age eighteen they are no better in their performance than are children between the ages of six and eight.[8] Physical endurance, coordination, and motor ability certainly have direct implications for Physical Education and Home Economics (social graces). From our knowledge concerning endurance, fatigue, and attention span, the teacher can gather data which will give him some help in conducting his class. Since endurance is short for some and ample for others, some activities must be planned to allow for a change of focus for those who find it difficult to dwell for long periods on one subject or activity. This idea can be interpreted to indicate that profitable use can be made of more than one method of teaching, especially in grade seven, in presenting a single lesson. This change of pace should be designed to catch the eye or interest of those who might have lost the train of thought. We could conclude from this same idea that nine-week units on some large concepts present an unscalable mountain of information to the students whose interests are constantly changing. In planning units, provision also must be made for a wide variety of options in the required projects, activities, and reports. Such provision will allow the students, despite their multiplicity of interests, to find something of interest to them. Again, because of the multiplicity of interests and the inability to dwell on one subject for a long time it is often prudent for the teacher to allow some supervised study time to clear up puzzling questions which in unsupervised situations could prevent effective work from being done. Supervised study should be available at all grade levels but it seems especially appropriate for the adolescent student.

The most controversial argument growing out of the discussion of physical changes concerns competitive athletic events. A thorough discussion of this debate is included in a later chapter. While some authors decry[9] the injury inflicted on all aspects of our youth's growth cycles, others point to desirable mental, emotional, and physical advantages. Although sheer weight of numbers of advocates certainly does not make an activity correct, research such as the study reported in the *National Association of Secondary School Principals Bulletin* of February, 1958, indicates that an overwhelming majority of junior high schools (85 per-

[7] T. W. Todd, *Physical Developments from Eight to Fifteen Years* (New York: Progressive Education Association, 1936), pp. 67–72.

[8] Kuhlen, *op. cit.*, p. 50.

[9] Breckenridge, *op. cit.*, p. 286.

cent) have competitive athletics.[10] What effects the loss of school time, study time, and the intense competition between academic and athletic interests have on the scholastic success of the students should be the topic of consideration for future studies.

Mental Factors

> Mental growth is now recognized as a pattern of cycles. Childhood cycles have been more clearly indicated than adolescent cycles. . . . It is consistent with the accumulating evidence about other aspects of growth to suppose that there is an adolescent cycle of mental growth. . . . The most striking feature of this pattern is what appears to be a plateau during the early adolescent years.[11]

The most significant word in the foregoing is "suppose," because it typifies the whole attitude concerning discussions of mental development which takes place during the junior high school years. Numerous studies by many authorities cite conflicting data concerning this growth factor.

Early studies speak of a steady and constant development of mental ability but more recent data seem to indicate that this development is steady up to age twelve, is interrupted briefly, and then goes through a growth spurt in the post-pubescent period.[12] Adolescents experience continual mental growth, although the rate of growth sometimes slows markedly. Dull, bright, and average students all seem to grow at the same rate and for the same length of time during this adolescent slowdown. The study from which the title quoted above was taken indicates that during early adolescence a plateau of mental development is experienced when very little physical growth takes place. This is based on a study of over 1,000 youngsters and was found to be true in 75 percent of the males and 60 percent of the females.[13] As was mentioned earlier, knowledge of one's students, both from reading materials and from personal contact, will enable the teacher to vary his scholastic demands to meet the various needs of the students.

Based on this information and data similar to the above, some writers demand that middle school educators reevaluate their programs and increase the minimum achievement levels in all ninth grade courses, particularly mathematics and science; in fact, an increase in minimum

[10] Ellsworth Tompkins, and D. M. Roe, "Interscholastic Athletics in the Junior High School," *National Association of Secondary School Principals Bulletin* (February 1958), p. 7.

[11] Ellsworth Tompkins, and D. M. Roe, *A Design for Early Secondary Education* (Albany, N. Y.: The State Department of Education, 1954), p. 10.

[12] H. E. James, and H. C. Conrad, *Mental Development in Adolescents* (Chicago: University of Chicago Press, 1944), pp. 154–155.

[13] Design, *op. cit.*, p. 11.

achievement levels for mathematics and science is also recommended for the eighth grade.[14] It should be noted that this argument, which definitely emphasizes science and mathematics, was written shortly after the Russians launched their Sputniks.

Of all the differences and variances between individuals which are being discussed here, one of the most important from an instructional point of view is the difference found in reading ability. Reading ability must be of special concern to all educators for without it their task would be insurmountable. Understanding the normal variations in the development of reading skills is paramount in meeting the needs of the adolescent, for although a class is composed entirely of students with eighth grade reading ability, individual capacity may still vary as much as ten to twelve months in the reading level. In an actual eighth grade class one is likely to find students with primary grade reading ability alongside those with college reading ability. On the average, boys will differ as much as ten school years while girls will differ seven years. The sex difference could easily be as much a function of peer pressure as it is an indication of actual physical differences in situations where the group-conscious boys try to emulate a leader who finds school, particularly reading, outside his popular interests.

For the teacher, these facts concerning reading ability indicate caution when common readings are assigned. They certainly would indicate that one of the teacher's first tasks is to determine the range of ability in reading among his students. Textbooks must be advanced enough to provide for the needs of the rapid reader, yet elementary enough for the slow reader. Classes sectioned for ability in reading, the use of multiple textbooks, or individual learning packages might resolve this dilemma in reading. Social Living teachers who make extensive use of book reviews to supplement their classroom activities must be prepared to demand very difficult and advanced material (in terms of the grade level) from the rapid reader and, at the same time, accept material containing below-grade-level reading from the slow reader.

The junior high school student is able to transfer much of the curiosity and concern for himself, his future, and the world around him to the printed page, and often the problem is one of channeling this interest rather than having to work to arouse it. Characteristics of the mental development of junior high school students provide several implications for instruction in all classes. It seems that the wide variety of individual differences found in a class calls for units of instruction that seek to meet the needs of the student in a number of ways so as to provide activities for the slow, the average, and the advanced students.

---

[14] M. A. Shirts, "Ninth Grade—Curriculum Misfits," *National Association of Secondary School Principals Bulletin* (November 1957): 41-232, p. 137.

Social and Emotional Development

Early maturation can present a series of emotional stresses which offset many of the apparent advantages. Earlier maturing girls, for instance, are big, physically conspicuous, too advanced for age-mates among boys, too young for the social activity they crave, and generally out of contact with their age-sex mates. Since the terms "early" and "late" are relative, it could be advantageous for a child to mature early—especially if this will increase his peer group acceptance. In such cases, it will be the late maturer who finds himself left out and alone. Early or late maturation seldom results in permanent aftereffects, even though it often seems to be a major crisis at the time. Early or late maturation leaves harmful effects only when the child is the sole member of his peer group who is either late or early. The boy who matures early will be bigger, stronger, more handsome, and should enjoy more prestige than his late maturing friend during the period of time prior to maturation.

Studies of the psychological impact of sexual maturation are best documented and most conclusive when they speak specifically of the impact of menstruation. Because it is difficult to pinpoint a time to conduct a related study among boys and because studies of behavioral activities of adolescents often involve much more than just sexual maturation, studies concerning the emotional effects of menstruation come closer than any others to approximating the psychological impact of sexual maturation. As one might expect, girls differ greatly in their emotional response to menarche.[15] Of 153 apparently normal women, 42 percent reported no emotional response, 18 percent had a positive response of pride and excitement, 32 percent were moderately disturbed or angry, and 7 percent were definitely disturbed, shocked, or frightened. A girl's response to menstruation seems to be affected by her attitude toward herself as a female, her general outlook on life, her knowledge of what is happening, her self-confidence, and her natural tendency toward anxiety. The school and its teachers should do their part to help the girls achieve "normal" attitudes, outlooks, knowledge, and confidence, thereby lessening the possible negative emotional effects of this physical phenomenon.

The adolescent's physical abilities have an important bearing on his approach to life, his self-concept, and the role he plays in his relation to others. There is a more pronounced gain in physical strength during the adolescent growth spurt than there is in size. Four-fifths of an adult's strength, as compared with one-third of his height, is acquired during this spurt.[16] A spurt in the development of strength bears close relation-

---

[15] C. Landis, A. T. Landis, and M. M. Bolles, *Sex in Development* (New York: Paul B. Hoeber, 1940), pp. 282–83.

[16] H. E. Jones, *Motor Performance and Growth* (Berkeley: University of California Press, 1949), pp. 42–44.

ship to pubescence and is a good index of sexual changes. Boys always have the edge in body strength, but this edge widens to more than its adult proportions during adolescence.

Again, as above, an adequate knowledge of the changing adolescent will greatly aid the teacher when he plans activities and works with students. The seventh graders are more interested in group rather than individual activities and successes, so role-playing, discussion, and group enterprises should be more successful than individual reports, projects, or assignments. This characteristic reverses itself during the eighth grade and then reverses again in the ninth grade. Especially in social studies, where emphasis is often put on cooperation and group dynamics, knowledge of these facts is important.[17]

Peer acceptance is a major factor in the life of the middle school student. In everything he thinks and does, the student tries to conform to the norms of his peers. This fact would seem to indicate that a teacher must be cognizant of pupil needs and desires when planning a unit, conducting a lesson, or working individually with his students. Also, when a teacher is attempting to motivate his class, it would seem prudent to concentrate on the class leaders, for the others will often follow. Peer acceptance also indicates the need for an extracurricular program of clubs and activities whose membership is open to all those wishing to join.

Because of the confusing nature of the student's environment, his physical development, his unstable peer relationship, and his uncertain future, the student needs something or someone to whom he can attach. If this student's daily schedule is one involving seven subjects, each with a different teacher in a separate room, he may receive little security from it. One of the arguments given for "core" and "common learning" programs is that students are provided with a central classroom and a teacher or pair of teachers in whom they can place their trust. Advocates of block scheduling in English and social studies, and, to a lesser degree, in mathematics and science, are quick to point out that the stabilizing aspect of the "core" also is found in any scheduling device where students are with a teacher for more than one hour in a school day. Guidance personnel, although decrying the fact that untrained people are doing the work, express interest in all arrangements involving dual periods because they give the teachers an opportunity to know students better and, therefore, present ready-made situations where counsel and advice may be given.

Undoubtedly, the greatest emotional change during the adolescent period is the transference of interest and satisfaction in relationships with members of one's own sex to those of the opposite sex. Because this change does not take place at one time or at one age, special problems are created for the social aspects of the middle schools. The heels and

[17] M. H. Ahrens, *Junior High School Program* (Atlanta: Southern Association of Colleges and Secondary Schools, July, 1960), p. 11.

hose of the ninth grade girl and her accompanying interests seem somewhat ludicrous when viewed alongside the pigtailed sixth grader. Realizing again that the average means little in light of the wide variations,
it is possible to say that the average girl matures sexually at the age of
13.5 and the corresponding boy at fifteen. The insinuation is that his
transference of interest shortly follows this maturation. Table III below
illustrates this.[18]

Table III.   When Boys and Girls Mature Sexually

AGE	CHILDHOOD	PUBERTY	MATURATION
9½	FFFFFFFFFF MMMMMMMMMM		
11½	FFFFFFF MMMMMMMMM	FFF M	
13½	F MMMMMM	FFFFF MMMM	FFFF
15½	 M	F MMM	FFFFFFFFF MMMMMM

M represents 10 percent of all boys at the given age.
F represents 10 percent of all girls at the given age.

The range of puberty among girls is from age ten to seventeen and in
boys from age twelve to nineteen. Table III documents the fact that the
school is obligated to provide activities designed to meet the needs of
individuals who have the ideals and interests of children, of teenagers,
and, in some cases, of adults.

Gertrude Noar, in her work on the junior high school, stated that the
responsibility of the school in its instruction and co-curricular program
was to meet four needs which related to children's emotions. They are as
follows:

1. The need for security and affection which creates feelings of being
   wanted and a sense of belongingness.
2. The need for recognition and reward.
3. The need for achievement and success.
4. The need for fun and adventure: new experiences—both educational and recreational.[19]

The change and development which takes place during the junior high
school years in the social and emotional areas of the student's life can

[18] A. V. Keliher, *Life and Growth* (New York: Appleton-Century-Crofts,
1968), p. 159.
[19] Gertrude Noar, *The Junior High School—Today and Tomorrow* (Englewood Cliffs, N.J.: Prentice-Hall, Inc., 1961), p. 32.

best be summarized in Table IV following, which compares the person who enters grade seven with the one who leaves grade nine almost three years later.

Table IV. Social and Emotional Development of Adolescents[20]

Aspects of Personality Grade 7–Age 12	Aspects of Personality Grade 9–Age 14.75
Variety and instability of interests	Narrowing and deepening of interests
Talkative, noisy, daring; a great deal of activity	More dignified, controlled masculine-feminine behavior
Seeking peer status with a high regard for peer standards	Mimicry of adult cultural patterns
Desire for identification with the herd	Identification with a more select group
Family status relatively unimportant in influencing peer relations	Family socioeconomic status an increasingly important factor in peer relations
Informal social activities	Formal social activities
Dating present but rare	Steady dating not unusual
Emphasis on building relations with peers	Increasing concern with preparation for life
Friendships quite temporary	Lengthening friendships
Many friends	Selective friendships
Willingness to accept activities providing opportunities for social relations	Initiative in setting up own social relations and function
Little insight in behavior	Increasing insight
Acceptance of reasonable rules important	Making own code and standards with definite goals
Ambivalence in accepting adult authority	Growing independence from adults; dependence on self

Implications for Education

In summarizing the foregoing, it is possible to list several areas of instruction—both in the classroom and outside—where the teacher can improve his teaching through the knowledge of children and their unique stage of development.

[20] A condensation of material which originally appeared in A. Gesell, F. L. Ilg, and L. B. Ames, *Youth, the Years from 10 to 16* (New York: Harper and Row, Publishers, 1956), pp. 101–138, 214–249.

Each child is an individual developing at his own rate and experiencing growth in his own unique order. Therefore, his interests could be quite varied from those of his peers. Provision in instruction must be made for this.

In spite of the change necessitated in some teacher education programs, it would be more profitable in terms of the total development of the child to sacrifice the scheduling flexibility and content mastery available with complete departmentalization in order to provide the need for security present in most early adolescents. Most youngsters enter the middle school after spending four to six years with one teacher in a self-contained classroom except, possibly, for art, music, and physical education. In grade seven, the student usually begins to experience changes in his body which leave him unsure of himself. In some schools, he experiences the phenomenon of having seven classes with seven teachers in seven different rooms. When these two situations exist, insecurity is a major possibility.

If we know that one age group enjoys itself and functions best when involved in group activities and another age group is at its poorest in such a situation, should we not capitalize on this information by providing group activities for those grade groups seventh and ninth that can best use them, while offering individual activities to the sixth and eighth graders who would profit most from those projects?

If the need for peer group acceptance, excellence and security is coupled with doubts about those who do not "make the team" as well as for those who do, would it not be prudent to concentrate on a well-developed intramural program in lieu of an adult-accepted interscholastic athletic schedule?

When the "average" class has a reading level differential of from seven to ten years, might it not be beneficial for the teacher to provide textbooks and individual activities of varying difficulty which would challenge the excellent student and instruct the poorest one?

Because an internally overworked body suffers from fatigue, lack of endurance, and short attention span, would it not be best for teachers to provide a variety of activities in order to combat this?

If the curiosity of adolescents toward their new bodily functions turns outward and they develop a curiosity about their neighbors and their environment, should we not be able to recognize it and use it for constructive purposes rather than to ignore it and invite discipline problems? When anyone becomes curious about something, he asks questions, he investigates, and he inquires. Intellectual curiosity operates in the same way. Teachers should organize their courses to provide for the continual asking of why, and how.

A Look at Some Early Adolescents

Following are several vignettes depicting memorable adolescents from the authors' past. They are provided to illustrate some of the difficulties caused by the differences in adolescents and to stimulate discussion and investigation.

1. Jim and Mike

Like many teachers, I feel that I "understand" the conscientious, eager student; he is my "type." In my dreams, I visualize classes in which he is the only type. Unfortunately, he is not the only type; with him in that sea of faces are all grades of intelligence and conscientiousness. This is difficult to forget when one faces the actual class, but difficult to remember when one plans a lesson or designs a test. This study will look at two extreme groups who are consistently near failure and who are consistently "less understood." The groups are those that apparently would like to do better but for some reason cannot, represented by Jim, and those who at least appear not to care, represented by Mike.

In both cases, low intelligence can be ruled out as the primary cause of failure. Both have scored slightly above 100 on IQ tests. Mike's Iowa Test Cumulative score is close to the class average; Jim's is lower but still above other class members. Both demonstrate intelligence in occasional class participation.

Personality conflict with the teacher and an emotionalized attitude toward one subject can also be discarded safely as both are presently failing in other classes.

Therefore, other possible causes of failure must be considered. Among these we might include:
1. Lack of training in study procedures.
2. Emotional upsets due to out-of-school situations.
3. Lack of any motivation to grasp subject matter.
4. Extreme nervousness in an evaluative situation.

Observation of Jim, the student who does care, has led to the conclusion that lack of study habits and nervousness in the face of evaluation are his key problems. He is obviously somewhat motivated in this class, since he at times makes valuable oral contributions and at times attends this class while skipping others. No abnormal emotional problems have been noted by myself or by his counselor, although he is the child of a broken home.

Jim's motivation and classroom participation do not influence him to turn in written work or to succeed in a testing situation. A test day last week was typical. Students were given dittoed sheets of the information needed; these were discussed and carefully reviewed in class on the day of the test. Jim joined in the discussion with intelligent comments which, however, showed that he had been unable to gain very much from studying the written materials. While taking the test, he was unable to answer any test items from the written material and few from class discussion, including the material which he himself had discussed in class the same day.

In a conference the following day, Jim's comments confirmed my opinions that,

1. he finds it possible to recall and to reason in a discussion but not in a test.
2. he finds concentrating upon and assimilating written material impossible but feels that he can learn readily from class discussion.
3. he can answer questions directed to the class but not those directed exclusively to himself.

Jim has had failing and near-failing grades throughout his secondary school experience. For Mike, however, his failing grades started with his move to Madison from a small Iowa town at the beginning of junior high school. He had demonstrated study ability previously and has continued to do so in scattered bursts of enthusiasm; he reacts equally well to testing situations and to casual questioning. Thus, the causes of Jim's troubles can be ruled out. Mike can study. It is necessary to probe elsewhere to see why Mike does not study and why he appears not to care.

The fact that failure began soon after his transfer is undoubtedly significant; the change from a small school to a large, strange one has evidently influenced his attitude towards scholastic achievement. This is evidenced in a constant attempt to win approval from his peer group throught frequent wisecracks and other attention-demanding devices. When not seeking attention from the rest of the class, he admits he is daydreaming about one of a variety of other interests.

Other students work, transfer, and have outside interests, but their insecurities and preoccupations do not prevent success in school. In conference, Mike asserts that his parents have no true interest in him, that his father always disagrees with him, and that he would like to quit school but he cannot get permission. Further study is admittedly necessary but it would appear that Mike's family situation has served as a catalyst to intensify his problems.

2. Milton

Milton, an underachiever, is dirty and smelly. His father is poor; their financial position is due to poor money management and heavy drinking. His father has been able to maintain a steady job in the community for the past decade despite his problems. Milton has an older brother who was an accomplished athlete and an older sister who apparently does not have the best reputation. There are younger children in the family, so Milton is a "middle" child.

Socially, Milton is not well-accepted. He is belligerent and often disrespectful, although at times he is considerate and polite. In the hall, Milton is usually loud spoken and harsh. For a period of time, he attempted to join "the group" of boys who are known as delinquents. In order to qualify for consideration for this "elite" group, he had to display his physical prowess and his disregard for school. Milton did his best to meet these requirements but he was not accepted.

Earlier in the year, he was involved in a car stealing episode. Somehow, the authorities did not inform his family and Milton did not tell them for some time. During the period between the incident and Milton's confession to his father, Milton developed an extremely negative attitude. He was truant several days and was asked to leave several classes due to discipline problems. Although he was finally persuaded to inform his parents, he did not lose his negative attitude.

In order for Milton to keep working, or to work at all, he requires an extreme amount of attention which frequently he cannot receive. On seeing that he must wait his turn, he will throw down his books and pencil and pursue less desirable means to achieve attention. The tragedy involved in this action is that he alienates himself from the class as a whole. Like all people his age, he needs to be needed and liked. Unfortunately, he attempts to fulfill his needs the wrong way. In his desire to be accepted, Milton tends only to make himself less liked.

3. Nell

Nell is a slight, attractive, dark-haired fifteen-year-old girl. She lives with her real mother, a housewife, and her stepfather, a mill worker. She has four brothers and two sisters, all younger. Her hobbies include sewing and cooking. She studies about two hours each evening, her favorite subject being science. Nell likes to have many friends, but has few good friends. She seems to be an average student without serious problems.

Her peers describe Nell as quiet and shy. Most believe that she is average to well-liked. The girls say that she likes to cook, sew, and date. She especially likes to double date and go to dances. She dislikes large groups and parties unless there is dancing. Her peers say she is a hard worker and usually does whatever is asked of her. Her teachers describe her as plastic, i.e., agreeable to anything suggested, a "yes man."

At times, she sits and gazes or stares at nothing for long periods of time—daydreaming. She looks at her books, or the blackboard, and does not appear to see them.

The counselor's and doctor's reports indicate that Nell has a long history of chronic illness, dating back to grade school. She had rheumatic fever and still carries some of its effects in her poor physical condition. Nell's mother has been under psychiatric care for a number of years and her doctor believes some of her problems are "rubbing off" on Nell. She seems to be over-sheltered by her mother who, at the same time, is pushing her into dating relationships and encouraging her to "go steady."

Nell's problems at home, combined with a below-average ability (thirteenth percentile on the CTMM), give her almost no academic encouragement. She daydreams in class, seems be be "away from reality," lacks drive, enthusiasm, and common sense.

4. Dave, Steve, and George

Dave is a fifteen-year-old ninth grade student. He has above average intelligence (125 I.Q.) and is correspondingly enrolled in above average sections in his junior high school. Dave is the oldest of three boys, all of whom are in attendance at the same school. Dave is quite proficient in sports activities, able in the classroom, and a social leader among his peers.

Dave is engaged in keen scholastic competition with his peers and, although he has just missed twice, he is striving to "make" the honor roll this year. Dave is courteous in class and, at times, uses his size and prestige to force some rebellious peers to be orderly in class.

Steve, the youngest of the three boys, is a slightly built thirteen-year-old carbon copy of his brother, David. He is active in junior high school athletics and very well liked by his teachers and his peers. He does not quite have the potential of his oldest brother but he continually works up to his capacity. The presence of two older brothers in the same school has undoubtedly helped Steve become a leader among his peers.

George is a fourteen-year-old eighth grade student. George's problem is that he is average—in intelligence, in athletics, in social leadership, etc. His "averageness" is a problem because he is continually compared to David. Since the last grading period, George's grades have fallen from their customary "C" level to a low "D." When George was approached about his problems, he was arrogant and uncooperative; his haughty attitude made the entire effort worthless. A conference with guidance personnel and his parents was equally fruitless—his parents could not see why he should not follow in Dave's footsteps.

Chapter 2 Bibliography

Breckenridge, M. E., and Vincent, E. L., *Child Development*. Philadelphia: W. B. Saunders, 1949.

————. *Design for Early Secondary Education*. Albany: The University of the State of New York Bulletin, State Education Department, 1954.

Eash, M. J. "Grouping: What have we learned," *Educational Leadership* (April 1961): 18:429–435.

Ferguson, William. "A Report on a Junior High School Program for the Gifted," *National Association of Secondary School Principals Bulletin,* (November 1960): 40:79–87.

Gesell, A., Ilg, F. L., and Ames, L. B. *Youth, the Years from 10–16*. New York: Harper Brothers, 1956.

James, H. E., and Conrad, H. S. *Mental Development in Adolescence.* Chicago: NSSE Yearbook, University of Chicago Press, 1944.

Jersild, A. T. *Psychology of Adolescence.* New York: The Macmillan Company, 1957.

Jones, H. E. *Motor Performance and Growth.* Berkeley: University of California Press, 1949.

Keliher, A. V. *Life and Growth.* New York: Appleton-Century-Crofts, 1968.

Kuhlen, R. G. *Psychology of Adolescent Development.* New York: Harper Brothers, 1952.

Landis, C., Landis, A. T., and Bolles, M. M. *Sex in Development.* New York: Paul B. Hoeber, 1940.

Seidman, J. M. *The Adolescent.* New York: Dryden Press, 1963.

Shirts, M. A. "Ninth Grade—Curriculum Misfits," *National Association of Secondary School Principals Bulletin* (November 1958) : 41:232.

Todd, T. W. *Physical Development from 8 to 15 Years.* New York: Progressive Education Association, 1936.

Tompkins, E., and Roe, D. M. "Interscholastic Athletics in the Junior High Schools," *National Association of Secondary School Principals Bulletin* (February 1958) : 42:3–16.

Wilhelms, F. T., and Westby-Gibson, D. "Group Research Offers Leads," *Educational Leadership* (April 1961) : 18:410–414.

Chapter 3

The Teacher

Having then gifts differing according to the
grace that is given to us, whether prophecy,
let us prophesy according to the proportion of
faith; or ministry, let us wait in our ministering;
or he that teacheth, on teaching. . . .
Romans XII - 6

Newspaper cartoons offer much food for thought about the American scene. The reader may recall one of the *Sideglances* series drawn by the cartoonist Galbraith, where a young stalwart remarks to a parent upon presenting his report card, "Yes, they are low marks, Dad. But why shouldn't I seem stupid to my teacher? She's a college graduate!"

If being a college graduate only were the making of a teacher, America would not be faced with one of its greatest problems—how can enough *good* teachers be graduated from its Colleges of Education and be retained in the public schools?

Characteristics of a Middle School Teacher

Prior to any discussion of the training necessary for teachers, it is imperative that we first define our terms. It is not the intent of the authors to confuse the issue by trying to define a "good" teacher—that value judgment must be made on the basis of specific criteria. Too often teacher-educators have so ladened their criteria with value judgments that their objective implementation is impossible.

Basically, a middle school teacher is a hybrid whose preparation contains more subject matter content than his fellows in the lower grades and more knowledge of and empathy for children than his fellows in the senior high school. This preparation, which will be amplified below, should have been directed toward the fulfilling of seven roles the teacher plays:

1. as a professional
2. as a manager of learning
3. as an interactor
4. as a counselor
5. as a mediator
6. as an organization man
7. as a liaison

The Teacher as a Professional

A professional is an individual whose years of training and accumulated skills (whether earned, learned, or inherited) enable him to make instantaneous, autonomous decisions concerning his duties. In addition, he has acquired an attitudinal base which provides him with esprit de corps, ethical mores, a penchant for recruitment, and a zest for continual improvement.

The concept of a teacher as a decision-maker is often verbalized but seldom discernible in the classroom. To be sure, disciplinary, managerial, and planning decisions are made—the former two often in class but the latter usually out of class. Once learning activities start, unfortunately most decision-making functions cease. A true professional teacher must be able to define and describe the active learning sequence as a series of events which happened because the role of the student consciously *decided* such events were the best possible means to a given end.

When a student gets "out of hand," a teacher must be able to choose from a large repertoire the one means which is most appropriate for the situation. When a student responds with a creative idea, a teacher must choose from an entirely different but equally large repertoire of responses that one which best suits the student, the idea and the lesson. The automaton teacher who has a limited number of stereotyped means of dealing with problems, interacting, presenting material, or organizing activities will not produce the same quality of results as the teacher who consciously structures his mode of operation.

Similarly, a teacher with a professional attitude will feel some responsibility for knowing his students, studying their environment, inducting new members into the profession—directly by involvement in pre-service functions or indirectly by "selling" his students on the profession—and helping new colleagues adjust to specific school requirements and continual self-improvement.

Self-improvement is considerably more than taking "x" number of hours of in-service credits—it is an attitude of introspection that continually operates while the teacher functions; it is listening to oneself on audio or video recordings; it is asking colleagues as well as superiors for constant observation and critiques. If a teacher is to change his behavior in the classroom he must do it himself on the basis of information about such behavior that is acceptable to him. What better way to gather such data than for an individual to do it himself? In-service and summer courses are treatments administered after needs are identified.

Actually, a professional teacher is intimately and personally involved with not only his own problems in the classroom but with the problems of his school and the profession as a whole. The natural corollary to this involvement is professional contacts through organizations formed for specific purposes.

The Teacher as a Manager of Learning

In order to teach a concept you must first know it well, but simply knowing a concept "well" does not insure the ability to teach it. This can be attested to by anyone who has survived the multitudinous survey classes at the modern multi-versity. Such instructors know their material well but many are unable to teach it to others. At any level instructors must be able to take concepts known to themselves and effectively order, manage, plan or direct a series of learning experiences which will result in the transference of the concept from themselves to their students. It is significant and should be especially noted by the pre-service teachers among the readers that the teacher is a manager of learning, not a giver of information. The concepts we learn are those we assimilate and accommodate from within—concepts which must be acquired by *many* means of which an effective lecture is *only one*. This discussion would not be necessary if we were writing in Gaelic. In that language there is no infinitive similar to our "to teach." If one wanted to talk about "teaching" he would have to use "to learn." Such a change in emphasis is sorely needed in professional education.

The term "management" is used because its definition connotes several situations analogous to the teaching-learning act. It connotes something less than final authority for the prescribed actions—just as the manager of the Atlanta Braves is responsible to the owners so the classroom teacher is responsible to district administrators, parents, and society as a whole. It connotes an image of a benevolent dictator who has determined the overall direction and limits for activities but provides for considerable latitude and freedom within such limits so that a climate encouraging civic (i.e., student) participation is maintained. It connotes the picture of a factory manager identifying peer leaders who can provide him (as foreman) with necessary assistance in implementing the goals and quotas of his particular firm. Finally, it also connotes the idea represented by a Park and Recreation District manager, one of whose responsibilities is the maintenance of a multitude of activities and approaches to satisfy the needs of all the participants.

As can be readily subsumed from the above analogies, the teacher as a manager of learning activities in a middle school classroom must do so (1) within the context of societal, parental, district, and ethical prerogatives; (2) in firm but fair control of such activities but with considerable provision for pupil involvement at all stages—planning, introducing, implementing, and evaluating; (3) by identifying those able students who have earned the respect of their peers and using them for both managerial and instructional purposes; (4) with intensively planned functions which provide variety in approach, content, materials, evaluation, and analysis without impairing their quality; and (5) without sacrificing the continual attention which must be focused on the student—his needs, problems, successes, interests and plans.

The Teacher as an Interactor

The most ineffectual way for one person to teach another person a concept is to have the latter simply read it or hear it. However, teachers must be adept at interacting—both verbally and non-verbally —with their students as individuals and as members of a group. This is an aspect of the teaching act which educators largely ignored until the last decade. The works of John Withall, Ned Flanders, Edward Amidon, Robert Spaulding, Del Shallock, and John Hansen have produced new insights into the analysis of teaching.

Basically, teachers talk! Often they talk without paying any attention to the effect such verbiage is having on their audience. To be sure they measure the cognitive (as opposed to the affective) effects via tests, quizzes and reports, but what about the affective domain? Why is it that teachers seldom deal with students' feelings in a verbal manner? Are we creating the neurotics of modern society by setting an example which inhibits talking about feelings? Why is it that teachers repeat student answers as a reinforcement technique to such an extreme that students learn they do not have to listen to each other because they know that the teacher will repeat it? Why is it that teachers often respond to one student by asking another to add to, detract from, or discuss the first student's comments without at least accepting the fact that the first student made a contribution? Why is it that teachers do not make more effective use of silence? We ask for responses requiring thought on the part of the students and become impatient after a few seconds of silence. If we expect thought, then let us provide time for it. Such questions could be continued indefinitely but the point would be the same—teachers must become aware of their verbal interaction. They must be so aware that they can choose the most appropriate verbal or non-verbal response to a given classroom stimulus.

In the cognitive domain, teachers must have further training— either internal or external—in the use of questions both on their part and on their students' part. An adept questioner is a highly skilled individual whose classroom performance differs markedly from other teachers or students. Examine these questioning problems:

1. Mrs. Hilary asks a question, gets no response, rewords the question, pauses and rewords it again before a student answers. In all likelihood the content asked for in the first version was the content which fits into her lesson plan. Also, the student probably answered the third version which typically had little relation to the first. Such is the source of many unexplained classroom diversions.

2. Mr. Hunter firmly believes that students must be afforded an opportunity to ask questions about the topics at hand. Accordingly, as a first year teacher, he allotted ten minutes every day for this activity in plans he made during the in-service workshop prior to the opening of the school year. He abandoned this idea after two weeks because the students either did not ask questions or they merely asked for facts they had missed while taking notes. Mr. Hunter did so because he failed to realize that just as students need to be taught study skills so they need to be taught questioning techniques. Richard Suchman's work in Inquiry Training was designed specifically with this in mind—not as a method of teaching but as a means to teach students how to ask questions about the unknowns.

3. Mrs. Roma asks, "What were the causes of World War I and which cause had the most influence on America's entry into that conflict?" In so doing she has effectively eliminated from responding all those who cannot answer both parts as well as asking students who can respond to both aspects to use two different mental processes (as defined by Sanders, Guilford, and Gallagher) in determining one answer. If a teacher wants two separate and unique answers, he would be far more successful asking two separate and unique questions.

While emphasizing verbal interaction we must not ignore the non-verbal side. The intonation, facial expressions, gestures, and mobility of a teacher in a classroom do much to communicate meaning and feeling to his audience. The most effective means of analyzing this phenomenon is the videotape recording. There is something quite revealing, impersonal, and, at times, traumatic about seeing oneself on a screen in front of a classroom.

The Teacher as a Counselor

It is unavoidable that every teacher is called upon to perform counseling and guidance functions during the day-to-day implementation of classroom activities. The early adolescent passes through myriad minute crises that to him seem to be insurmountable. All adults with whom he comes in contact—teachers, parents, neighbors, professional counselors, and others—at times play this role. This is not to deny or in any way detract from the very real need for full-time professional guidance counselors on a school staff. It is a role that at once complements and supplements the professional's responsibilities.

The teacher needs to have at his disposal techniques usable in classroom and in informal settings to help him fulfill this role. He also needs to be thoroughly acquainted with the limitations of his abilities and his obligation to both society and the student to seek professional help as soon as such assistance is necessary. No middle school should be without such professional assistance on a full-time in-school basis.

To be effective in this role, a teacher must (1) have the time and inclination to hear what a student says and what he thinks his problem is, (2) be able to function in an indirect verbal manner in order to achieve the objective of a student talking about his problem, (3) be thoroughly grounded in the knowledge of the physical, psychological, mental, and social characteristics of his students, and (4) have the ability to convey sincerity and empathy to the point that the student can feel he is accepted as an individual. In addition, the teacher must personally have the characteristics that would make it possible to earn the student's confidence—confidence must be a matter of selective criteria at pre-service institutions if it is to be fully realized.

The Teacher as a Mediator

As Christ Jesus to the Christian is a mediator between God and man so must the teacher be a mediator between the student's cultural heritage and himself, between the past and the present, between the daily events and the adolescent's perception, and between racial, ethnic and socioeconomic differences within a community, school, and classroom. It is not the role of the teacher merely to transmit culture, to interpret our heritage, or to propagandize the students. It is rather his responsibility to see that culture is transmitted, interpreted, and realistically evaluated. The religious analogy also brings to mind that when Christ fills the mediation role he does so from an omniscient position. Unfortunately, the teacher must fill this role from a position which is far from omniscience.

As a mediator, the teacher must function from a firm understanding of the needs, problems, strengths, and weaknesses of the early adolescent. The receptiveness of one group of adolescents for concepts of a cultural nature will differ markedly from that of other groups within the same community. The teacher must, of course, have a thorough knowledge of the nation's cultural heritage—broad enough to be able to channel questions from several disciplines yet specific enough to deal with problems in a few given areas. An effective mediator must have an attitude toward the task which demands consideration of all points of view as well as respect for and faith in humanity. Such an attitude undoubtedly will also result in a belief in the value and workableness of democratic processes—a concept basic to the western world.

While functioning as a mediator, it is imperative that the teacher help each child to discover and examine all the facts and, in addition, to help the child arrive at his own conclusion. Using totalitarian methods to implement democratic processes is the height of inconsistency.

Throughout the task of cultural transmission one of the major difficulties a teacher experiences is the problem of how to handle his own opinions, biases, and beliefs. It is unrealistic to assume that any but the rare few would be able to conceal their opinions—if such concealment were advantageous. The degree of revelation of a teacher's bias is the actual point of contention. Any revelation would be dependent upon community readiness, student maturation level, theoretical bases for the opinion, and personal objectives. Bias is neither a negative nor a positive phenomenon. It is one or the other depending upon the reciprocal biases of the hearers. Further, it is the contention of the authors that an objective analysis of our cultural heritage will result in patriotic fervor, faith in democracy, and respect for humanity much more effectively than if these "positive biases" were allowed to become propaganda.

The Teacher as an "Organization Man"

Students attend formal educational programs in our society for at least ten consecutive years and, for a few, as many as twenty-two years. In addition, during six to eight years of this schooling the student typically works with four to seven teachers per day. In all, a student beginning kindergarten this fall might expect to come in contact with up to 200 teachers in his scholastic endeavors. Furthermore, the five to eight schools he is likely to attend will each have administrative, guidance, secretarial, medical, and other personnel who will play roles in his development. Why is it, then, that a specific teacher continually conceives his function in isolation from the total situation? The educative process is the prerogative of a massive, complex social institution—teachers and students mere cogs in its operation. No teacher presently in the profession would deny this; he sees many reminders each year.

Within the organization, in spite of its bureaucratic tendencies, are many provisions which insure that a student will have a multitude of supportive data and personnel at his disposal. By the time a student reaches adolescence at least a dozen school personnel have worked with him. In addition, the student's own behavior patterns (intellectual, as well as societal) are sources of data. After adolescence, he will probably work with another dozen educators each year. In addition, throughout his childhood, non-school community sources (church, recreation districts, employers, family, etc.) will have had social contact with him. A teacher who does not use as many of these sources of data as are available to him is remiss in his duties. Please note that sources of data are stressed rather than sources of conclusions or interpretations. A teacher must be cautious when accepting another teacher's conclusion about a student, especially so when supportive data are so readily available. If a teacher is a professional, he should be able to gather information from several sources, to interpret the data, to form those judgments as new data are gathered in his own classroom.

Another aspect of the role of the teacher as a member of an organization is his responsibility to the organization, its goals, and its means. The teacher who sees no need to communicate with the non-school public, who votes against school budget elections, who is unwilling to carry a share of the student activity program, or who views school hall, assembly, and playground disorders as administrative problems not to be "messed with" does not fully understand the "give and take" necessary for effective education of our children.

The teacher can get immeasurable assistance from personnel files and records available to him for problems with students. In return, however, he must see that he has a responsibility to contribute to others as well as to the total school program.

The Teacher as a Liaison

A teacher's liaison with the community can be a successful relationship with support for the school program or it can result in alienation of the community from the school program. To insure the former type of relationship, teacher training institutions must orient teacher candidates to their responsibilities to the total community. Administrators recognize that liaison between the community and the school is both oral and written. Administrative screening of written reports of beginning teachers is necessary to insure good relations. The fact that teachers are highly quotable out of context needs to be emphasized. Teachers should guard against misunderstanding of class procedure or of the semantics of the classroom situation. Teachers become interpreters of the school in their participation in community life. This is a responsibility that must be recognized and exercised.

The closest liaison with the community can be through the school program in civic and classroom learning activities. The school can rally the support of the community through close liaison in matters of learning through the use of community resources and awareness of student government responsibilities. Teachers who are long-time residents of the community can help new teachers and students in their relations with the community.

Furthermore, a teacher often struggles through technical information which can be done effectively by community personnel who are often quite willing to play the role of community experts. Consistent use of community resource personnel produces positive public relations toward the total school program which in turn can result in direct benefits to the children. Along the same line, a teacher often relies on films, models, and slides to convey information (as discrimination in housing, for example) that can be inadequate when a visit by the class to an area, a factory, or a business could say it more effectively.

The liaison aspect of a teacher's role then is two-fold: the responsibility to carry to the community information relative to school operation and the responsibility to use the community as a resource center when such use meets the objectives of the classroom instructional program.

Middle School Teacher Education

Special programs focusing on junior high school teacher education have operated since the beginning of the junior high school movement. The first issues of the *Junior High School Clearing House* in the early 1920s carried listings of institutions that offered courses for the junior high school and programs for prospective teachers. Bridgewater State Normal School, Bridgewater, Massachusetts, and Stevens Point State College, now the Wisconsin State University at Stevens Point were among the early institutions which offered such programs.

Unfortunately, another common factor in the preparation of junior high school teachers has been that most programs as the ones in the two institutions just named were eventually cancelled because the institutions were unable to fill the program with sufficient students to make it economical. Although the next sections will deal with programs deemed adequate to prepare teachers for the middle school, the reader must remember that regardless of the quality the program will be useless unless public schools, institutions of higher education, and society in general can convince individuals to prepare to teach at this level.

There is no doubt that teacher education institutions place more emphasis on the training of elementary and high school teachers than they do on the training of middle school teachers. Undoubtedly, one of the reasons for this is the continuing inability of the middle school to identify a national model to which teacher educators can aim their program. Furthermore, only twenty states have certification programs for junior high school or middle school teaching. In spite of this, in some of those twenty states, it is still possible to teach in the middle school without such certificate. Students often "hedge their bets" by preparing for either elementary certification or senior high school certification knowing that if they have difficulty finding jobs or become interested in other matters they can always teach in the middle school. In teacher education as in other aspects of the public school program the middle school does not want what is LEFT from the other programs; it simply wants what is RIGHT for it.

In the past decade more than a dozen fairly sophisticated studies have been conducted on the question of how teachers should be prepared for the junior high school. These studies, most of which were conducted as doctoral dissertations by individuals currently prominent in junior high school education in their individual states, have shown that there is considerable agreement across the country as to what ingredients make up the junior high school teacher education program. How much of each, and in what order, does not have the same universal agreement, however.

Ralph Ackerman[1] in a study completed in 1960 analyzed the programs of thirty-six NCATE approved institutions which provided a special curriculum for the preparation of junior high school teachers. He conducted this analysis by using a list of the component parts for teacher education programs developed from a consensus of 209 educators across the country. Ackerman concluded that most of the special junior high school teacher education programs were simply modifications of the curricula for either elementary or general secondary teachers. If the junior high school is in reality a unique educational institution and if the needs of the early adolescent are in fact unique, it appears completely untenable to say that teachers trained for either the elementary or the secondary school, with or without minor adjustments in requirements, are equally prepared to teach the early adolescent. Ackerman further stated that the educators were almost unanimous in their demand for a thorough knowledge of the junior high school child on the part of prospective teachers.

John Conway in a study which was instrumental in setting up the certification requirements for junior high school teaching in the State of Oregon summarized the issue in the following manner:[2]

[1] Ralph E. Ackerman, "A Critical Analysis of Program For Junior High School Teachers in Teacher Education Institutions of the United States." Unpublished doctoral dissertation, University of Connecticut, 1960.

[2] John S. Conway, "A Study to Determine Criteria for State Standards for Junior High Schools of the State of Oregon." Unpublished doctoral dissertation, University of Oregon, 1963.

The question of the best type of preparation for junior high school teachers has been one that has received an increasing amount of attention in the literature of the past few years. Probably in no other single aspect concerning the school has there been such a lack of agreement. The only consensus appears to be of dissatisfaction with existing practices whatever they may be.

As a result of the work of Van Til at George Peabody College for Teachers several significant studies of the junior high school have been produced there in addition to the excellent text that he coauthored with two of his students, Gordon Vars and John Lounsbury.[3] One of the most interesting of these studies was the one conducted by Elizabeth Lambeth Dalton which attempted to measure the effectiveness of junior high school teachers and to analyze the differences that existed in the preparation of programs of teachers having significant differences in effectiveness.[4]

The sixty-eight teachers in each of Dalton's samples were compared with respect to (1) general scholastic achievement, (2) liberal arts education, (3) professional education, (4) levels and extent of teaching experiences, (5) teaching assignments, (6) degrees and certification, and (7) experiences with children and youth other than in school situations. An analysis of the comparison of the pre-service preparation program of two groups which differ significantly in effectiveness as teachers indicated that those in the high group had better undergraduate records academically (e.g., GPA) and more hours in methods, guidance, and psychology courses. Other than in these areas, the preservice preparation program of the two groups had no significant differences. This would only add to the controversy that Conway suggests—that we cannot agree, but we know that we disagree.

Leland W. Dean conducted a study similar to the previous three at Michigan State University in the mid-1950s.[5] His study attempted to analyze the differences in the reactions to pre-service programs expressed by teachers at the time teaching at the upper elementary level, the senior high school level, or the junior high school level. The study found significant differences in the areas of specialized subject matter, guidance and counseling, special education, reading methods, and core curriculum. The teachers who had actual teaching experience in the junior high school indicated that these areas needed consideration in a

[3] William Van Til, Gordon Vars, and John Lounsbury, *Modern Education for the Junior High School Years* (New York: The Bobbs-Merrill Company, Inc., 1967).

[4] Elizabeth L. Dalton, "Preparation Programs for Junior High School Teachers." Unpublished doctoral dissertation, George Peabody College for Teachers, 1962.

[5] Leland W. Dean, "A Preparation Program for Junior High School Teachers." Unpublished doctoral dissertation, Michigan State University, 1956.

specific curriculum for prospective junior high school teachers. They further indicated that the specific curriculum needed to be permeated with the child-centered approach commonly associated with elementary teacher preparation.

Drayton Marsh in a study of in-service teacher education for junior high school teachers completed in 1960 concluded that junior high school teachers in their own opinion have not been adequately trained to teach children in this separately organized educational unit.[6] It is interesting to note that the other conclusions which Marsh reached in his study of the needs of in-service programs coincided with those that Dean found as necessary for pre-service programs. Since the same groups were asked similar questions, the obvious conclusion which can be drawn is that in-service teachers feel they should have more information on adolescents and the techniques of working with adolescents than they received either prior to their initial teaching experience or since their initial teaching experience. It is entirely unrealistic to assume that prospective teachers are adequately prepared for teaching when they complete their four-year program at an institution of higher learning. Means must be implemented in every state to provide for a continuing program of preparation throughout a teacher's career and not simply prior to that career.

H. Glenn Maynard working at Colorado State University made a study of the preparation of junior high school teachers in 1960.[7] Maynard gathered his data from 140 junior high school principals in forty-nine states. He found that the program of preparation developed from a composite of the component parts deemed desirable by his respondents who were identified with the two prevailing preparation programs in wide use, i.e., elementary teacher education programs and senior high school teacher education programs. The composite of their desirable components, however, was markedly similar to junior high school teacher preparation programs being followed at that time in institutions of higher education. As with the other investigators mentioned above, he found considerable agreement as to the courses that were necessary in a basic junior high school teacher education program.

Several other studies, including some conducted by the authors, could be cited but they would merely repeat the general conclusions indicated above. What can be derived from current literature are the parts necessary in a program to prepare junior high school teachers. What educators must do is to combine these experiences in such a way

[6] Drayton E. Marsh, "In-service Teacher Education in Oregon Junior High Schools." Unpublished doctoral dissertation, University of Oregon, 1960.

[7] H. Glenn Maynard, "A Study of the Professional Preparation of Junior High School Teachers." Unpublished doctoral dissertation, Colorado State University, 1960.

that they will attract students or to devise other means of attracting students so that the critical need for teachers prepared to teach in a middle school can be met.

Pre-Service Teacher Education

The authors would like to suggest the following teacher education program for middle school teachers as an indication of what they feel would be the most advantageous combination of the component parts that are held in wide agreement. No apology is offered for the fact that the program of preparation bears little resemblance to that suggested in the past by a noted chemist or a famous naval officer. The basic philosophy underlying the program of preparation is one represented by a continuous program of preparation characterized by a gradual induction into the profession. Just as no one ever is able to acquire the ultimate in subject matter comprehension, teaching skill, or knowledge of the student so also no one is ever able by legislative fiat or institutional approval to suddenly perform in the classroom when previously he was unable to do so. Plotted schematically, the line of preparation for middle school teachers should be an ever-ascending one starting somewhere above zero and rising at various levels throughout the individual's career.

There are three categories of pre-service teacher preparation—general education, subject matter specialization, and professional education. The combination of experiences in these three areas must produce at the end of four academic years an individual ready to embark on a career in teaching. The authors firmly believe that a five-year program of preparation, including a paid teaching internship, is a necessary aspect of teacher training at all levels.

General Education

The first phase of the teacher education program endeavors to provide a general cultural background while satisfying specific graduation requirements demanded by the teaching institution. This phase of the program should account for between 40 and 50 percent of the time the student spends in college. Courses in the arts, humanities, social sciences, sciences, and physical education must make up the balance of his time at school.

It is unfortunate that the general education courses are usually found in the lower division of work a student completes on campus (especially so when his work is carried on in shallow survey courses in classes of several hundred students). Although the nature and style of such courses are firmly entrenched on most college and university campuses, several studies have indicated that a majority of the work undertaken in these courses is repetitious of conscientious high school programs. The ideal pre-service program would be so constructed that a good proportion of the general education requirements could be met through small groups and seminar class situations. We now have college students who have experienced their entire secondary education program in classes taught through the inductive method.

As these students become involved in the current revolution on campus it seems highly probable that a change in the nature of university courses and graduation requirements will be necessary. The disadvantage in the way current general education requirements are met is compounded by the fact that a good proportion of the courses are designed with no utilitarian value to the prospective teacher. It is suggested that something other than emphasis on research as found in the sciences will be of value to a far greater number of students than is presently being reached. For instance, on the University of Oregon campus, 500 chemistry students enrolled in freshman chemistry classes. Four years later one percent of these students will graduate with a degree in chemistry. Yet, unashamedly, the chemistry professors designed their courses at both the freshman and the sophomore levels towards that one percent.

The ideal general education requirements for prospective teachers would include work in history, philosophy, sociology (including group dynamics), laboratory science, composition (including linguistics), literature, mathematics, foreign language, and, if at all possible, art and music. In addition, prospective teachers should have had some experience with non-school community services at some time during their four years in college. The obvious advantages of continued contact with community service organizations and with youngsters and adults in a non-school, non-threatening relationship are highly desirable. This would be similar to the 100-hour requirement that some teacher training institutions have. Unfortunately, such a requirement usually involves the student counting minutes and hours rather than participating in worthwhile experiences. As more and more students interrupt their collegiate training for junior years abroad, civil rights activity, VISTA or Peace Corps experiences, and local social welfare activities, realization of this requirement will become easier.

Subject Matter Preparation

A third of the work that a prospective junior high school teacher completes in the normal four year undergraduate teacher preparation program should be in the area of specialized preparation in subject matter. Because of the nature of the instructional programs found in most of the junior high schools, the program is similar to the subject matter preparation required for high school teachers.

In the early 1960s, teams of teachers throughout the state of Oregon (each team representing a different discipline) met with college and university personnel and individuals from the State Department of Education, and after reviewing available related literature, produced the following specific subject matter requirements as the minimum accepted for prospective junior high school teachers:

Art

Thirty-six quarter hours in art, with preparation in each of the following areas: drawing and painting, sculpture, art history, crafts, and basic design. Twenty-seven of the thirty-six quarter hours in studio work; six quarter hours of the twenty-seven in basic design.

Business Education

Forty-two quarter hours in business education, to include:
a. A minimum of nine quarter hours from one or more of the following areas: economics, business law, and business fundamentals.
b. Thirty-three quarter hours in business education courses taught in high schools, to include any three of the following: typing, shorthand, bookkeeping, and office practice.
c. Teachers who teach typing only may substitute evidence of proficiency in typing in lieu of college credit and will not be required to meet the business education norm.

Foreign Language

Forty-five quarter hours in any one language or the equivalent, to include preparation in the following fields:
a. Language (composition and conversation)
b. Literature

Health Education

Forty-two quarter hours in health education, to include:
School health service
Human anatomy
Human physiology
Nutrition
Safety and first aid
Personal health
Community health and communication
Family living
Communicable and noncommunicable diseases

Health and Physical Education

Forty-five quarter hours in health and physical education, to include preparation in each of the following areas:

a. Twenty-four quarter hours in professional health and physical education to include each of the following:
Human anatomy
Human physiology
Health services
Principles of physical education
Organization and administration of health
and physical education
b. Twelve quarter hours in physical education laboratory, to include:
Fundamentals of body movement and mechanics
Rhythms
Gymnastics
Sports (individual, dual, and team)
Aquatics
Games, relays, stunts, and self-testing activities
c. Nine quarter hours in health education, to include:
Nutrition
Safety and first aid
Personal health
Community health and sanitation
Family living
Communicable and noncommunicable diseases

Home Economics

Thirty-six quarter hours in home economics, to include preparation in the following areas:
Child development
Clothing
Family relationships
Foods and nutrition
Housing and home furnishings
Home management

Industrial Arts

Forty-five quarter hours, to include preparation in the following:
Drawing related to industrial arts
Woodwork
Metalwork
and any two from the following areas:
Electricity and electronics
Graphic arts
Photography
Auto mechanics
Shop crafts in leather, plastic, and lapidary

Journalism

Eighteen quarter hours, to include advanced news writing, advanced copy editing, and makeup or production of high school publications

Library

Eighteen hours in library science, to include preparation in the following areas:
Cataloguing and classification
Reference
Selection
Library administration

Mathematics

Thirty-six quarter hours of mathematics at the college level, to include preparation in algebra, geometry, trigonometry, calculus, and contemporary mathematics

Music

Forty-two quarter hours in music, to include preparation from each of the following areas:
Theory, composition, and keyboard harmony
Music literature and music history
Conducting
Analysis (form)
Applied music

Physical Education

Thirty-five quarter hours, to include:
a. Twenty-one quarter hours in physical education with preparation in each of the following areas:
Human anatomy
Human physiology
Principles of physical education
Physical education curriculum
Organization and administration of physical education programs
b. Fourteen quarter hours in physical education laboratory with preparation in each of the following areas:
Games, relays, stunts, and self-testing activities
Rhythms
Gymnastics
Fundamentals of body movement and mechanics
Sports (individual, dual, and team)
Aquatics

Science

a. Biology

Thirty-six quarter hours in biological sciences, to include preparation in general biology, anatomy, physiology, developmental biology, genetics, evolution, and ecology.

b. Chemistry

Thirty-six hours in chemistry, to include preparation in general chemistry, analytical chemistry, and organic chemistry.

NOTE: Teachers who have completed preparation in physics will also qualify as teachers of physics when this is a minor assignment.

c. Physics

Thirty-six quarter hours of physics, to include preparation in the following areas: general physics, advanced physics, and modern physics.

NOTE: Teachers who have completed a preparation in physics and who have twelve quarter hours in chemistry will also qualify as teachers of chemistry when this is a minor assignment.

d. General Science

Thirty-six quarter hours in college science, to include preparation in biology, general chemistry, general physics, and earth science.

Speech and Drama

Thirty quarter hours including oral interpretation and the fundamentals of acting and advanced preparation in fundamentals of speech, speech arts.

These teams further recommended that before final recognition as a prepared teacher, individuals either meet two of the above groups of requirements or complete an additional twenty-four specified hours in one of them. This additional work was to be done subsequent to the first teaching job to complement whatever teaching assignment the teacher experienced during the initial teaching year. This provision was made to accommodate both the teacher in the small school who was forced to teach in two subject fields and the teacher in a large school who was able to work in his field of specialization.

The reader will note that preparation in language arts-social studies is not included in the listing above. The preparation of language arts-social studies teachers in the middle school is an issue currently being debated throughout the country. The studies quoted in later sections dealing with language arts-social studies indicate that in approximately half of the junior high schools in the country, language arts and social studies are combined in some form of block of time courses. Every state has block of time courses of one form or another ranging from 3.5 percent of the schools in the state of Indiana to close to 80 percent of the schools in the state of Oregon. Professional educators involved in the teacher education process are faced with a dilemma in regard to how they prepare teachers for a block of time language arts-social science course. Fifty percent of the beginning teachers who will find themselves teaching either language arts or social studies, but not both, after completing a language arts-social studies combined program of preparation will certainly be desirous of further preparation in their specific field. If educators decide to train either language arts or social science teachers without paying attention to the combination of the two, 50 percent of the students will find themselves lacking both in subject matter preparation and in the techniques of correlations so vital to a block of time program. It would appear that the prudent course would be to train language arts-social science teachers in a way that would prepare them for work in block of time courses and, in addition, to provide sufficient work in either one of the areas so that they could comfortably function if they were assigned to teach that area alone. Admittedly, it would be a compromise, but it would provide fewer disadvantages and handicaps for the beginning teacher than either of the other alternatives. Language arts-social science teachers and educators have suggested the following teacher education program for prospective language arts-social science teachers:

In Four Years

A. Thirty quarter hours of preparation in literature, writing, and language to include:
   1. Composition
   2. American literature
   3. World literature
   4. English literature
   5. Development of the English Language
   6. Speech
B. Thirty-three quarter hours of preparation in social studies to include:
   1. Nine quarter hours in each of American history, European or world history, and geography.
   2. Six quarter hours in a behavioral science.

In Five Years

Twelve additional quarter hours each in social science and English.

Professional Education

Prospective teachers need to be gradually inducted into every part of their program of teacher education particularly in the professional education aspect of that program. Throughout the four years in college and including the fifth year of the five-year teacher education programs, students must be given opportunities to work with students both in and out of the classrooms to augment the on-going campus program. In addition, the students need thorough grounding in what has been mis-named foundation courses in education—in the methods and techniques of teaching and in the ability to analyze teaching. Zealous teacher educators must guard against making the program of preparation for middle school teachers more stringent than the program set for elementary or senior high school teachers. If the middle school program of preparation takes an additional number of hours and demands an additional one or two terms, it is highly unlikely that students, indecisive as they are at the time, will choose a longer, more complex program. Parenthetically, please note, nothing is said about the comparative strengths of the program.

Professional Education Course Work

Professional education courses are continually the butt of campus humor because the typical education student looks for tricks of the trade, gimmicks, and other survival techniques for his initial teaching experience. The professor of education on the other hand knows that these gimmicks and tricks of the trade are insufficient as preparation and so he deals in broader concepts and deeper ideas with a more theoretical base. Both teacher educators and prospective teachers must be able to function at and deal with both levels—a theoretical base giving structure to the gimmicks and tricks of the trade as presented. An ideal program of professional education for the prospective middle school teacher should involve no formal course work during the first five quarters the student is on campus.

During the sixth quarter on campus, the student will be enrolled in a five-hour course in human development and learning. The course would be a team-taught course with responsibility shared by individuals from the Psychology Department and the School of Education. The course would focus on the adolescent, with some attention paid to the years before adolescence and subsequent to the middle school years. In addition there will be a survey of significant learning theories, their application in the classroom, and techniques of measurement and evaluation. At the same time students enroll in this course, they would concurrently enroll in a half-day observation experience, a half-day simulation experience, and a related two-hour seminar which might be called Introduction to Classroom Procedures.

The work in the three aspects of this additional experience would be coordinated to such an extent that a number of assignments would be given from both classes for the observation period. The syllabus of Introduction to Classroom Procedures would be divided between the discussion of specific classroom techniques about which the students gathered data prior to a specific seminar and an analysis of teacher verbal behavior. The authors have found Interaction Analysis as developed by Ned Flanders, Verbal Interaction Categories as developed by Edward Amidon, and Content Analysis developed by John Hansen as successful vehicles for the analysis of verbal behavior.

As a result of the analysis of verbal behavior, students were forced to limit the verbal behavior they use in assigned group discussions such as one wherein students are forced to lead a six-minute micro-lesson during which they are prohibited from asking questions, giving information, giving directions, or criticizing other students. The attempt is not to teach students one method of operating in the classroom but to force them to focus on how they can control their verbal behavior and to see the results. In other role-playing situations students might be told to respond to male members of the class in a negative fashion and to female members of the class in a positive fashion, or they might be told to respond to specific individuals in specific ways such as ignoring them, using their ideas, questioning them, praising them, or criticizing their right to speak. Following such discussion the class would have a wealth of data to use for an analysis of how people react to a teacher's verbal behavior.

During their junior year on campus, prospective junior high school teachers would take course work in the Principles of Guidance and Counseling, Diagnosis and Remediation, Teaching of Reading in their content field, and Special Methods. Concurrent field experiences will be required for the Diagnosis and Remediation and the Special Methods courses. The field experience associated with the Diagnosis and Remediation would involve working in a remediation clinic with educationally handicapped students from the public schools under the supervision of experts in the field. Field experiences associated with the Special Methods course may be a fabricated experience using video tapes and other electronic devices such as the simulation techniques developed by Bert Kersh at the Teaching Research Division of the Oregon State System of Higher Education. The objectives of this field experience, whether live or simulated, would be to provide opportunities to experiment with techniques of presentation and organization discussed in the methods course.

During the senior year, students will enroll in a course entitled, The Junior High School, which would function as a seminar concurrently with their student teaching experience.

Professional Education Field Experiences

Just as it is extremely difficult to master the use of a complicated machine tool by reading about its use, so it is extremely difficult to acquire the skills necessary for teaching through the same method. Teacher education programs must be heavily saturated with field experiences.

This is not to say that teaching is merely a skill that could be taught to any individual, given enough patience and a long enough period of time; there are many aspects of teaching that are more analogous to artistry than they are to skill. Emphasis on field experiences is derived from the fact that the more skilled we are at the specific aspects of teaching, the better artists we will be. If it were possible for someone to become highly skilled in all aspects of the teaching act, there would still need to be something more before we would have the master teacher. This difficulty, however, should not deter us from providing as many field experiences as are physically possible during the pre-service teacher preparation program.

There are five organized field experiences that should be a part of the professional education of a prospective junior high school teacher— "September" experience, human development field experience, remediation and diagnostic experience, methods experience, and student teaching. The internship possibilities will be discussed in the following section.

"September Experience" is a name given by several institutions to the observation experience that is given college students during the interim period between the opening of public schools and the opening of colleges and universities each fall. Public schools typically start the school year during the last week in August or the day following Labor Day. Typically, the universities start their fall term during the last week in September or the first week of October. The two to four weeks that intervene encompass a period that is extremely vital to a successful teacher and, at the same time, one which colleges and universities cannot effectively reproduce. Required "September Experience" has been found to be one of the most efficient ways of getting prospective teachers to start the gradual change in attitude from that of a student to that of a teacher. Usually the students are assigned to an individual or a department for two, three, or four weeks simply as "shadows."

The field experience associated with the combination of Human Development and Learning-Introduction to Classroom Procedures is designed to give the students a window through which they can watch both students and teachers function in an on-going classroom setting. With the advances in simulation and video tape, this experience can be duplicated in campus studios. Wherever possible, it would seem most advantageous to allow the students to spend their time in actual classroom settings. Observation assignments should be structured in such a way that students will be forced to gather data about their experiences rather than opinions or value judgments. The data could then be used for the analysis of teaching in a more realistic fashion than were value judgments used. An objective that might be realized from this would be the introduction of the students to ways and means of gathering objective data about teaching.

Student teaching experience required of all students is preferable during the fall or winter quarter of a school year. Student teaching experience should be a minimum of half a day and when possible, a full day assignment where the students are given an opportunity to practice in a classroom and at the same time to see all the various demands that are made upon a teacher. Organization on a semester basis provides ease in scheduling the student teaching experience. College administrators can set up a block semester in which the students can teach full time for ten weeks and spend the remaining six to eight weeks on campus taking courses every day. Quarter system colleges and universities do not have this privilege and so can have difficulties at times.

Student teachers should be expected to follow whatever assignment the cooperating teachers have. They should be expected to fulfill supervisory duties, chaperone activities, attend faculty meetings, PTA, and other school responsibilities as well as function as teachers in a classroom where their field of specialization is being taught.

Supervision for the student teaching experience must be provided both in a school setting through a *trained* cooperating teacher and in a university either through a university staff member assigned to supervision or clinical professors employed jointly by both the university and the school district. It is difficult to conceive of a student teaching experience as "graded" activity. However, care should be taken in determining just who passes and who fails.

Fifth Year Teacher Preparation

General education, subject matter specialization, and professional education course work should be continued over a fifth year period of preparation. It may be completed contiguously with the four years of preparation or, more desirably, it could be completed after a year or two of an initial teaching experience.

General education requirements would be reserved for those areas that are identified as neglected after a careful analysis of the four-year preparation program. Teachers are a mobile group—general education which may be desirable for teaching in one area may not fit the need in another region. Legislative requirements may have a role here; e.g., all social studies teachers in the state of Wisconsin must have had a course about dairy cooperatives.

Fifth year requirements in the field of specialization are devoted to deficiencies identified in particular teaching jobs—teachers may find themselves teaching in an area of their field that was given only minor emphasis in their four-year preparation program. It is during the fifth year that the full requirements of the norms listed above will be fully met.

It is in the area of field experiences that the authors feel the strongest about the fifth-year teacher preparation program. *Every* teacher should serve as an intern just as every doctor and dentist fulfills a period of internship. The period of internship should be a joint responsibility of colleges and school districts supported financially by local and state Departments of Education. This experience would be a school year in length, at reduced pay, spent under the tutelage of master teachers who would aid and support every first year teacher regardless of the quality of his four year preparation program. If teachers are to learn to teach they must teach and they must do so under the expert guidance of individuals trained in the ability to change a teacher's behavior. The work of the Northwest Regional Education Laboratory particularly deals with the selection of individuals who would work as master teachers with the interns. An excellent teacher may not be an excellent master teacher. The key to the successful operation of an internship program is the training and skill of the master teachers. A careful analysis of the characteristics of successful master teachers has resulted in the following list of "preferred capabilities":

A. Orient the intern to the school and community in which he will teach.

B. Help clarify policies and procedures of the school district and building for the intern.

C. Acquaint the intern with the instructional program, the availability of materials and supplies and special resource personnel.
   1. Secure all guides and manuals that are to be used by the intern.
   2. Explore IMC and other catalogs of materials and supplies.
   3. Arrange to use the services of district consultants.

D. Help the intern to develop skill in the analysis of teaching.
   1. Plan for individual observations on a regular basis to gather data by means of one or more of the following:
      a. Verbatim
      b. At Task
      c. Teacher Flow Chart
      d. Verbal Analysis
      e. Other Suitable Instruments
   2. Give intern opportunities to analyze data:
      a. Encourage and help interns to analyze written data
      b. Encourage interns to gather data on themselves by means of the following:
         (1) Tape Recorder
            (a) Intern records class session and analysis
            (b) Supervision group or supervisor records and analyzes these cooperatively with intern
         (2) Video Tape
            (a) Televise class session

      (b) Intern and class observe

      (c) Intern analyzes alone

      (d) Intern and team, or supervisor, analyze together

    (3) Follow-up observations or data-gathering with conferences

3. Arrange clinical supervision on a regular basis:
   a. Planning conference
   b. Observe to gather data
   c. Allow time for intern to read data
   d. Analyze data
   e. Hold a group conference, including intern, to discuss data gathered
   f. Post-analysis of conference
4. Provide time for intern to observe other teachers:
   a. Intern to gather data
   b. Intern to analyze data
   c. Intern conferences with teacher
5. Relieve intern to participate on clinical supervision teams.

E. Teach cooperatively in the classroom with the intern.
1. Follow predetermined plan for the lesson.
2. Confer with intern whenever possible during the lesson.
3. Confer following the lesson.

F. Serve as a consultant to the intern in planning and implementing the instructional program.
1. Make available a weekly individual conference time.
2. Help interns establish the habit of making written weekly lesson plans. These plans should include behavioral objectives and specific procedures.
3. Help the intern interpret courses of study and assist him in selecting and preparing teaching units for the year.

G. Organize a series of classroom demonstrations by competent teachers to illustrate teaching procedures.

H. Serve as a resource to the intern through sharing new ideas, suggesting professional reading, introducing the use of new supplies and equipment, etc.

I. Help the intern find a place in the faculty.

J. Confer regularly with the intern concerning the ever-recurring problems in the life of a new teacher.

K. Periodically release the intern from teaching his class for visitation with other teachers or to do other professional tasks.

L. Plan cooperatively with the University supervisor ways to help the intern increase his competence.

M. Continue professional development in supervision through reading, attending seminars for supervising teachers, taking classes in supervision, and/or discussing teaching competence and its improvement with professional colleagues.

N. Assume joint teaching responsibility with the intern in a team organization for certain phases of the instructional program.

Summary

The ideal program of preparation for prospective teachers would include approximately 40 percent general education, 35 percent specialized subject matter training, and 25 percent professional education. The first is designed to provide a broad background of knowledge, the second to provide depth in one area, and the third to correlate the other two with practical means of using them in classroom teaching-learning situations. The latter two can be summarized in this way:

Junior High School Teacher Preparation

A. Within Four Years
  a. Thirty quarter hours of secondary teacher preparation to include experiences in:
    1. Educational psychology
    2. Child psychology
    3. Adolescent psychology
    4. Teaching of reading
    5. Methods of teaching including special emphasis in a subject taught in junior high school
    6. The junior high school, its role in education and its curriculum
    7. Junior high supervised teaching
  b. One norm in a subject field taught in junior high school, or a four-year norm in Language Arts-Social Studies
B. Within Five Years
  a. Forty-five quarter hours in teacher preparation taken to include experiences in:
    1. Educational psychology
    2. Child psychology
    3. Adolescent psychology
    4. Teaching of reading
    5. Methods of teaching including special emphasis in a subject taught in junior high school
    6. The junior high school, its role in education and its curriculum
    7. Guidance and counseling
    8. Philosophy and/or history of education
    9. Diagnostic and remedial techniques in the basic skills
    10. Junior high supervised teaching
  b. Two norms taught in junior high school or a fifth year norm in Language Arts-Social Studies

Chapter 3 Bibliography

Ackerman, Ralph E. "A Critical Analysis of Program For Junior High School Teachers in Teacher Education Institutions of the United States." Unpublished doctoral dissertation, University of Connecticut, 1960.

Association for Student Teaching. *Internships in Teacher Education*. Washington: National Education Association, 1968.

Conway, John S. "A Study to Determine Criteria for State Standards for Junior High Schools of the State of Oregon." Unpublished doctoral dissertation, University of Oregon, 1963.

Dalton, Elizabeth L. "Preparation Programs for Junior High School Teachers." Unpublished doctoral dissertation, George Peabody College for Teachers, 1962.

Dean, Leland W. "A Preparation Program for Junior High School Teachers." Unpublished doctoral dissertation, Michigan State University, 1956.

Gray, Jenny. *The Teacher's Survival Guide*. Palo Alto, Calif.: Fearon Publishers, 1967.

Harris, Ben, and Bessent, Wailand. *Inservice Education: A Guide to Better Practice*. Englewood Cliffs, N. J.: Prentice-Hall, Inc., 1969.

Howard, Alvin W. *Teaching in Middle Schools*. Scranton, Pa.: International Textbook Company, 1968.

Kindred, Leslie W., and Associates. *The Intermediate Schools*. Englewood Cliffs, N. J.: Prentice-Hall, Inc., 1968.

Marsh, Drayton E. "In-service Teacher Education in Oregon Junior High Schools." Unpublished doctoral dissertation, University of Oregon, 1960.

Massey, Harold W., and Vineyard, Edwin E. *The Profession of Teaching*. New York: Odyssey Press, Inc., 1961.

Maynard, H. Glenn. "A Study of the Professional Preparation of Junior High School Teachers." Unpublished doctoral dissertation, Colorado State University, 1960.

Popper, Samuel H. *The American Middle School*. Waltham, Mass.: Blaisdell Publishing Company, 1967.

Wiles, Kimball. *Supervision for Better Schools*, 3rd ed. Englewood Cliffs, N. J.: Prentice-Hall, Inc., 1967.

Section Two

The Rationale
of the Program

Overview

Educators are often accused, and justly so, of talking in a language all their own—pedaguese, if you will. Although this general situation is little different from that found among engineers, architects, medical doctors, and others, it appears that not only do educators speak in their own idiom, but that this idiom, in itself, differs among educators at different times and in different places. Not only would one find variance between laymen and professionals concerning concepts such as curriculum, core, and ability grouping, but one would also find considerable differences among professionals themselves. Particularly in the area of classroom organization, professional educators are susceptible to the malady known as pedaguese. It seems prudent, therefore, prior to a discussion of the various instructional areas, to comment upon the various means of classroom organization, instructional process, and curriculum considerations. Thus this section is designed to share with the reader the various rationales and definitions held by the authors.

Chapter VI in this section is regarded by the authors as one of the unique contributions of the book. Learning Activity Packages, LAPs, which originated at the Nova Schools in Florida, are, in the authors' minds, the most useful recently developed technique to aid teachers in their effort to individualize instruction. Not programmed learning but a variety of carefully thought out avenues to achieve specific behavioral objectives, LAPs are useful in helping the teacher to stop dealing with a group, which by definition learns nothing as a group, and to start dealing with individual learners.

Chapter 4

Some Thoughts
Concerning Curriculum

*... I dipt into the future, as far as
human eye could see
Saw the vision of the world, and all
the wonder that would be; ...
Yet I doubt not thro' the ages and
increasing purpose runs,
And the thoughts of men are widen'd
with the* process *of the suns.*
Locksley Hall
Alfred Lord Tennyson

In ancient Rome thousands of citizens would journey to the "Colosseum" in their "curride" to see several "curricula." In time, a word that once meant "a race" or "running" has come to stand for the planned program of instruction provided by a school for its students. The authors use "Curriculum" to mean more than a specific course of study—indeed, even more than all the courses of study in a school. A school's curriculum includes the instructional program, the student activities, the pupil-personnel services, and everything else planned by the school to be vehicles for meeting the objectives set by or for the children.[1]

Of course, the major vehicle for fulfilling the school objectives is the instructional program—that part of the curriculum which includes the formal classroom and intellectual pursuits usually associated with "school." The authors intend to discuss general instructional considerations in this chapter and follow it with several others each devoted to one subject or a group of subjects included in the junior high school instructional program.

Change and the Curriculum

Change in the rhythm of change is one of the most important and far-reaching aspects of the contemporary world. Few people would disagree with the contention that in the next few decades changes in our lives will be so rapid and numerous that we shall have to develop a new attitude towards change, and that we shall have to learn to live with this quickening of pace. Even more important, we shall have to learn to control and direct the changes that go on about us.

No matter what our view of this quickening pace, progress or revolution, it bears investigation, for it influences our lives today and will to an even greater extent tomorrow. But why the revolution, the change of pace? An early indication of today's revolution is contained in Ralph Waldo Emerson's address to Phi Beta Kappa at Harvard in 1837.

> We do not meet for games of strength or skill, for the recitation of histories, tragedies, and odes, like the ancient Greeks; for parliaments of love and poesy, like the Troubadours; nor for the advancement of science, like our contemporaries in the British and European capitals. Thus far, our holiday has been simply a friendly sign of the survival of the love of letters amongst a people too busy to give to letters any more. As such it is precious as the sign of an indestructible instinct. Perhaps the time is already come when it ought to be, and will be, something else: when the sluggard intellect of this continent will look from under its iron lids and fill the postponed expectation of the world with something better than the exertions of the mechanical skill. Our day of dependence, our long apprenticeship to the learning of other lands, draws to a close. The millions that around us are rushing into life, cannot always be fed on the mere remains of foreign harvests. . . .

[1] See Chapter XXI in E. A. Krug, *The Secondary School Curriculum* (New York: Harper and Brothers, 1960), for a more thorough discussion of the "everything else."

A second cause for the revolution in curriculum today is the re-search that has and is taking place in the various disciplines. It takes only limited insight to realize the vast amount of information that has been added in the last few years to the sum of man's knowledge. Man has more than doubled his total knowledge in the last twenty years. That is, the knowledge gained since Genesis until 1951 was equalled between 1951 and 1971. Old curricula must be changed to accommodate this new knowledge, and the large amount of new knowledge requires vast changes.

A third factor causing a need for change in today's curriculum is the continuation of the industrial revolution now called automation. To live fully in today's world, one must be able to cope with today's machines. New machines require new skills to displace old ones. This ever-changing picture requires on-going change in the schools if the schools are to help prepare students to live in today's and tomorrow's environment. An excellent example of this process is shown by today's learning of logarithms. Logarithms were introduced centuries ago, and have been widely taught as an important tool. Logarithms, how-ever, are no longer important for calculations; small calculations being performed on desk calculators, and large calculations on computers. The question could be asked, Shall we stop teaching logarithms? Not at all, but the emphasis should be not on logarithms as a tool for cal-culations but as a study of the properties of the logarithm function.

A fourth cause of the contemporary revolution in curriculum is the need for a greater degree of knowledge for the individual in his particu-lar discipline. The geographer of today must have a more comprehensive knowledge of his field. If the knowledge required to be proficient in a field is double what it was fifty years ago, then today's "expert" is re-quired to go to school twice as long or the curriculum and teaching must be much more efficient than it was fifty years ago. Who can afford to finish college and receive the BS or BA degree at thirty-five years of age?

The fifth change agent is the effect of our culture on the curriculum. Curricula both reflect and lead cultural changes in a society. Our culture has gone through a series of almost explosive changes in the last fifty years. We have changed from a small rural society to a large urban one, from a politically small ex-colony to the most powerful country in the world. School curricula have to undergo almost radical change just to reflect this cultural change. Yet they need to prepare students to live in tomorrow's world, the adult world for today's students.

The basic change agents of today's curriculum, then, are the im-pact of the new knowledge created by research, the continuing indus-trial revolution, the need of specialization and expertness, and the cultural rural-urban transformation. If these are accepted, what do they demand of today's curriculum created for today's child?

Contemporary curricula must develop the intellectual abilities of all children to the highest degree possible. This must be true for the culturally deprived, the gifted, and the large and often forgotten middle group. Of these three areas, the former has been most neglected in the past. The American culture must produce its own "brain trust" if it is to survive in tomorrow's world or must develop every child to his fullest ability while giving equal educational opportunity to all.

Contemporary curricula must incorporate the new knowledge exposed by contemporary research. Who would knowingly teach a child a falsehood or half-truth? Yesterday's common sense is often tomorrow's blatant ignorance. But who can know all of man's present knowledge? We must pick and choose carefully that knowledge which is basic for the student to know and understand. And the emphasis on this basic knowledge must give the student the skills and understanding required for the adult world in which he will compete.

Today's curriculum must change to reinforce and further the skills and attitudes of the child in the culture in which he will live. Johnny must learn and accept laws and attitudes so that he can be a productive person and citizen. The school's responsibility is to help the student to function effectively as a member of society while at the same time help him preserve his integrity as an individual.

A visit to a middle school today will quickly convince one that the conscientious teacher and administrator are struggling, with a high degree of success, to meet these needs. Change is apparent everywhere. Tucker Junior High School (a composite, fictitious school) is involved with new math, new biology, new geography, and new English. It is experimenting with a pilot science program in the ninth grade. The social studies curriculum is being revised in an effort to make it meet the aforementioned needs. The physical education program had just gone through a reemphasis period. Change indeed; the focus is on change. "Let us find a better way and do it!" seems to be the motto.

The change does not end with the curriculum but extends into all other aspects of the school. The educational literature relates efforts to create better means, designs, and organization patterns. School architects build all sorts of innovations to meet educators' needs. Better time-use patterns or schedules are coming into use. The list is as diverse as creativity will allow.

Along with the new curriculum come new teaching techniques and organization patterns. The training and retraining of teachers is at the largest scale of production in educational history. Never have the universities produced so many new teachers, and never have so many teachers gone back to school to get new knowledge and to learn better ways of using that knowledge.

The principal of Tucker Junior High could state that it is not difficult to get many of his teachers to change. Several of his staff have initiated improved materials and techniques themselves. Others needed only to be shown a better way of teaching and they wanted to try it. The principal could feel that change is positively accepted if the teacher views it as better than what he is doing now. Unstated, but implied, was that most teachers are looking for a better way.

What is common in the large majority of these curriculum changes? Analysis indicates the following eight points as threads of concern in modern curriculum designs.

1. Knowledge to be taught came from experts in the disciplines.
2. Technique for teaching came from classroom teachers.
3. The marriage of items one and two was tried out and revised in actual classrooms until it was satisfactory to all concerned.
4. Each curriculum has attempted to allow for differences in individual needs and abilities by one or more of the following devices:
   a. Tracking of some sort
   b. Ungraded rooms
   c. Multi-level texts and materials
   d. Exercises in one text that progressively become more difficult.
5. Teach the student skills that allow him to go on teaching himself without a teacher.
6. Place emphasis on inductive learning rather than on a deductive learning process.
7. Concern exists for not only knowledge, but understanding and attitudes developed in the child.
8. Lessons that develop the thinking skills and means of dealing with raw data for the students.

We must remember that curriculum is change and not an end nor an experience nor a recipe; that the time for change is now.

Strategies for Teaching

For the past several years public education has been besieged by the "new" material, "new" courses, "new" methods, "new" curricula, and "new" schools alluded to above. An individual does not have to be a very serious student of education to realize that little of what is presently being proposed is actually new. Nor is there a great deal of difference between the several approaches to the same problem. Team teaching and staff utilization, two of the older "new" ideas in education, were actually part of the scene during the sixteenth century when it was known as the Lancasterian method of teaching. An educator would be far more accurate in calling the new ideas "currently espoused ideas" since trends and fads in education seem to be cyclic in nature. Such things as the kernel sentence, an integral part of the new approach in English, was suggested at one time by John Locke in *Some Thoughts Concerning Education*. Despite the fact that we can criticize the use of the word "new," we should not detract from the important contributions that both process and curricular studies of the past decade have made to the on-going program in the public schools. Research study after research study currently being discussed in the literature indicates that the students in the schools are better off because of the change in approach in the public schools of the day.

The common elements of the "new" curricula (above), particularly items 5-8, indicate that it would be prudent to preface the discussion of the instructional program with some attention to teaching approaches.

Educators talk! Not only do they talk, but they write. Since often promotion and tenure are based on what is written, premium is placed on new and original ideas. Since new and original ideas are few and far between and since expedience dictates that one needs to write whether or not he has a new and original idea, writers in the field of education in an attempt to appear new and original take an accepted concept and simply give it a new and original name. This phenomenon which we will find recurring several times in the following chapters operates particularly in the field of inductive teaching. The authors have chosen to call the common elements of the new approaches "inductive teaching"—simply because it is the least original of the various new terms and is most likely to convey similar ideas to the readers. Several other terms could have been chosen and they, in the authors' minds, mean the same thing—inquiry, discovery, productive thinking, problem solving, and divergent thinking, among others.

Advocates of inductive thinking, regardless of what they call their approach, would all agree that thinking is a process, a skill, an ability that can be taught and learned. While they differ slightly in the structure of this skill and greatly in the semantics they use to discuss the skill, for the most part they start from a common foundation. This foundation is the division of the thinking skill into several different strata which are possible of definition and observation and can provide the teacher with a means of structuring a lesson so that specific thinking skills are necessary. The works of three researchers will be discussed as illustrative of this foundation.

Taxonomy of Educational Objectives
—Cognitive Domain

During the early 1950s Benjamin S. Bloom and a team of professional educators published some ideas concerning the process of teaching.[2] They did this not from the standpoint of talking about specific acts of thinking or acts of teaching but rather by dividing up what is "knowable" and what it means to know something at several levels. They

[2] Benjamin S. Bloom, *Taxonomy of Educational Objectives, The Classification of Educational Goals, Cognitive and Affective Domain* (New York: David McKay Co., Inc., 1961).

looked at two areas of the teaching act: (1) the cognitive domain—that which deals with knowing something, and (2) the affective domain—that which deals with feeling something. A summary of their work in the cognitive domain is pertinent here.

According to Bloom there are six steps in the process of knowing something—knowledge, understanding, application, analysis, synthesis, and evaluation. These six steps, listed in ascending order of importance, form a stepladder, the rungs of which an individual must climb or be able to leap over before he can arrive at the next step. The stepladder analogy is weaker at the upper levels than it is at the lower levels of this thinking process.

1. KNOWLEDGE. Bloom's first step in the hierarchy of thinking skills is the ability to know something which he calls Knowledge. This ability to "Know" is defined as the immediate recall aspect of thinking. Upon hearing a definition, a student is able to give the definition a correct label—simple matching, dates and figures, mathematical formulas but not the working or derivation thereof, etc. This first step in the thinking process is the vocabulary "sine qua non."

2. UNDERSTANDING. Understanding is the ability to add perception to immediate recall. This involves being able to recognize a definition instead of being able to give one. It is an ability which forces a student to be able to recognize relationships between simple facts.

3. APPLICATION. Assuming that we know an arithmetical formula and we understand the relationship between the specific parts, then and only then, are we able to apply that formula to a known or unknown situation. As another example, if one knows what a piston is and understands how it works, then he has the ability to apply this knowledge and so construct a simple piston operation. The application aspect of the thinking process is simply the ability to put the knowledge and understanding of information to work.

4. ANALYSIS. This aspect of the thinking act connotes the ability to examine the unknown situation and from a repertoire of knowledge, understanding and application (as defined above) to be able to solve the problem. It may be deriving an equation or locating a malfunction in an engine. It may be finding generalizations in a social problem or breaking down a chemical compound.

5. SYNTHESIS. As the dictionary definition of the word would indicate, this stratum in the teaching process is the reverse of the previous one. Rather than taking a given situation and solving it for an unknown component or breaking it down into its many components, a student is able to take the components and put them together in some permutation or combination. It could be a simple matter of putting an engine back together or reconstruct-

ing a situation; or it might be a situation such as knowing
_____ would happen if _____.

6. EVALUATION. The most difficult aspect of the thinking process
is the combination of the previous five. All are necessary in order
to evaluate a situation. More than the ability to analyze, more
than the ability to synthesize is the ability to attach value judgments to that which is analyzed or synthesized. It is more difficult to break something down into its component parts and construct a priority for these various parts than it is simply to do
the breaking down.

As is also the case for the two summaries listed below, the authors
suggest the reader spend time in further consideration of these topics
in the original sources as footnoted. Beyond the basic foundation presented here, these three researchers diverge into several interesting
viewpoints which would be pertinent at both the pre-service and in-
service level.

Gallagher's Productive Thinking Strategies

At approximately the same time that Bloom and his colleagues were
working on the task that they undertook, J. P. Guilford was looking at
thinking from another aspect.[3] What he did was to take all the known
variables in the thinking act and apply statistical factor analysis
treatment to these variables to determine relationships, correlations,
and importance. The result of the factor analysis was to divide intellectual processes into three categories. Guilford laid the groundwork for
the following studies which were carried out under the leadership of
James Gallagher at the University of Illinois.[4]

Gallagher selected that portion of the structure of the intellect that
dealt with the operational phase and using the component parts developed a strategy which teachers could use to conduct lessons demanding
thinking at various levels. Guilford's structure divided the intellectual
operation into five parts: memory, cognition (description), evaluative
thinking, convergent thinking (explorative), and divergent thinking
(expansion). Rather than the stepladder analogy that Bloom saw, Guilford indicated there were two strata of processes: at one level, the cog-
nitive-memory aspects, and at the other level, the remaining three. It
was further indicated that the three at the higher level are more or less
equal. While research was needed to differentiate between them, it was
the conjecture of the original study that divergent thinking was the most
difficult.

[3] J. P. Guilford, *Nature of Human Intelligence* (New York: McGraw-Hill
Book Company, Inc., 1967).

[4] James A. Gallagher, *The Gifted Child in the Elementary School* (Washington, D. C.: National Education Association, 1959).

1. MEMORY. The memory operation can best be described with a literal definition of the word memory or factual recall—the simple act of knowing something by rote and the act where the only operation involved is one of recognition. One can easily see the similarity between memory as defined by Guilford and knowledge as defined by Bloom.

2. COGNITION. The cognition operation is one of combining, relating, and explaining known facts. The describing or defining process involves more than simple recognition and recall. This is an operation that demands some evidence of understanding, some evidence of knowledge in something other than the vacuum which is acceptable for the previous step. Again it is very easy to see the similarity between this operation and the levels of thinking in Bloom's *Taxonomy* which he described as understanding and application. To be sure, cognition as defined by Guilford is more than understanding as defined by Bloom but there is a distinct similarity between the two.

3. EVALUATIVE THINKING. Evaluative thinking does not quite have the position of preeminence in Guilford's (structure as modified by Gallagher) that it does in Bloom's work. The definition is, however, the same: the ability to compare and contrast and give priorities or the ability to simply give priority judgments to a given situation.

4. CONVERGENT THINKING. Convergent thinking is the operation which describes the ability to take several specific bits of data and relate them or combine them in some form and arrive at a generalization. (If this operation were to be drawn schematically it would look like an arrowhead.) From a body of knowledge an individual selects several points, combines them, narrows them, until a generalization is reached. A similarity can be seen between this operation and that which Bloom calls a synthesis.

4. DIVERGENT THINKING. Divergent thinking is the ability of an individual, given a generalization, to break it down into its many component parts. For example, a student could, after being given a situation, discuss the causes or effects of that situation. (This operation appears to be the reverse of the convergent operation and schematically could be drawn as an arrowhead but would be placed in the reverse position from that of the arrowhead that would describe convergent thinking. The action here stems from the point rather than leading to the point.) This operation is given the preeminent position because it demands the abilities to apply all that is known from other situations in projecting what could be.

Gallagher attempted to modify these ideas by redefining them as ways to ask questions. By asking a convergent question, a teacher could force a student to think using this process. *Similarly,* by asking a memory question the teacher would know what mental processes the students would have to use in order to answer it. As so often happens, the original five operations were not workable when Gallagher and his team began to work on specific strategies for teaching. These original five operations were redefined by Gallagher in the following way: Cognition and Memory were combined into a single operation and called Description. The single operation carries the definition which would include that given to Memory and that given to Cognition. The Evaluative operation was subdivided into two parts: one, dealing with an evaluative operation against an unknown criterion; the other with a judgment made according to exposed criteria. There seemed to be a difference in the research conducted by Gallagher between the ability to evaluate something against a given checklist and the ability to evaluate something when no checklist was available. Convergent and Divergent remained the same although they were retitled Explanation and Expansion, respectively. By dividing content that was dealt with into three parts— data level, concept level, and generalization level—Gallagher further suggested that the resulting grid could be used not only as a means of insuring various kinds of thought level exercises on the part of the student but also as a means of planning lessons with this specifically in mind. Gallagher offers an intriguing possibility for the use of inductive teaching and readers are encouraged to pursue his works.

Taba's Higher Level Thinking Strategies[5]

Taking a different tack from those of the previous two researchers— basing her work to a considerable extent on that of Piaget[6]—Hilda Taba arrived at a stratification of the thinking process which is to a surprising degree similar to that of Bloom and Gallagher. When Professor Taba and her research team divided up the process of thinking they saw three distinct thinking tasks that a student became involved in as he went through the process from being initiated to the topic to the ability to apply principles that he could derive from that topic. The three cognitive tasks as they are known in Hilda Taba's work relate to the three levels of thinking skills—each level involving several different operations.

COGNITIVE TASK I. Cognitive Task I is the group of actions containing the initial steps or the lowest level of thinking. This cognitive task is further subdivided into three separate and distinct processes: (1) The ability to enumerate or list known facts. The process of recall

---

[5] Hilda Taba, *Curriculum Development: Theory and Practice* (New York: Harcourt, Brace, and World, 1962).

[6] Jean Piaget, *Origins of Intelligence in Children* (New York: W. W. Norton & Co., Inc., 1963).

of specific facts known about a given problem. (2) The ability to group these enumerated facts into some meaningful categories. Meaningful is defined individually so what may be a meaningful category to one group or individual may not be a meaningful category to another. The example is given of a first grade social studies lesson which is dealing with community agencies. Following a visit to a supermarket the students have enumerated the various things that they saw. The students then proceed to group these into meaningful categories. Johnny decided that peaches and ice cream should be grouped together. When queried by the teacher as to this grouping of fruit and a dairy product Johnny informed the teacher that peaches and ice cream went very well together. They had had that combination for dessert the night before. (3) The ability to take an enumerated list of facts that are grouped into meaningful categories and attach names to the various categories. Quite often this name is more than a name and is actually a concept. A stepladder analogy that Bloom referred to would pertain here in that each subdivision is dependent upon the one beneath it and each cognitive task becomes increasingly difficult as you go up.

COGNITIVE TASK II. Cognitive Task II involves several operations that can generally be grouped under the title, "Generalizing" or "Inferencing." The operations involved are such that ultimately they lead the students to forming generalizations or making inferences about the data. Something is happening to the data that had been dealt with in Cognitive Task I. At the simplest level it may merely be relating, explaining, defining, comparing, or contrasting. This would proceed to combinations of explained or compared facts into a generalization or a combination of generalizations into what we might call inferences. Most of the time spent in the public school classroom is in either Cognitive Task I or Task II.

COGNITIVE TASK III. Cognitive Task III is the most difficult of thinking tasks and is one that rarely occurs in the public school classroom unless specifically planned, according to Taba. This is the process of applying principles, generalizations, and inferences derived in Cognitive Task II to unknown situations and the analysis of the resultant data.

Again if comparisons were to be made one could see a striking similarity between Bloom's first three categories, and Gallagher-Guilford's first two categories, and Taba's Cognitive Task I. One could also see a similarity between Evaluation and Synthesis of Bloom, Evaluative and Convergent of the Gallagher-Guilford model, and Cognitive Task II of the Hilda Taba model. Similarly, Bloom's analysis, Gallagher-Guilford's divergent thinking, and Taba's Cognitive Task III are related to each other.

These three models form the foundation in the authors' viewpoint of inductive thinking as it is used in most of the "new" instructional programs current today. Names are changed, the order is changed, the alleged results differ but basically whether it is "new" English, "new" social studies, or the alphabetical soup of the "new" science, the inductive approach found therein is similar.

Content Analysis

Because teachers can often verbalize about inductive teaching but seldom know precisely what they are doing in this regard, an instrument has been developed which affords teachers and supervisors the opportunity to observe themselves through electronic means or to observe one another and determine at what level of thinking a class is operating during any given lesson. This instrument combines the techniques suggested by Ned Flanders,[7] James Gallagher, and Hilda Taba into one instrument that is useful for a cursory examination of the thinking levels taking place in an individual classroom. It is designed not as a research instrument but as a supervisory tool to provide limited feedback as to the quality of inductive thinking which is taking place during any given lesson. The instruments developed by the three individuals mentioned are much more useful for research purposes into this question than is the limited Content Analysis. Considerable success has been found, however, in using Content Analysis as a means of providing a teacher with immediate feed back about the quality of interaction that takes place in an inductive lesson. Content Analysis is a thirteen-part category system which divides classroom verbal behavior as suggested in Table V. A trained observer who is thoroughly familiar with the thirteen categories sits in a classroom and records data every three seconds differentiating according to columns and categories as shown in the data below.

After recording data in the above manner for the duration of a lesson (Table VI), the material is then summarized as indicated in Table VII for use by the teacher in evaluating the levels of interaction found therein.

An examination of Tables V, VI, and VII gives the teacher information for use in analyzing her performance.

Information from Table VII:

1. The teacher talked 43.5% of the time. Most of this was spent "seeking."
2. The students talked 56% of the time, virtually all of it providing answers.
3. 57.6% of the time was spent in what Hilda Taba calls Cognitive Task I.
   a. 49.6% seeking or giving information.

[7] Ned A. Flanders, Project Director, *Helping Teachers Change Their Behavior*, Rev. ed. (Ann Arbor: The University of Michigan School of Education, 1965).

Table V.   Content Analysis

1. Seeks Information	Specific information is sought with no demand for any action other than presentation.
2. Gives Information	Specific facts are given—most one word answers, dates, unexplained data, lists, etc.
3. Seeks Labels and Groups	Naming, classifying, categorizing and grouping of information is sought.
4. Gives Labels and Groups	Specific facts are classified, categorized, or grouped.
5. Seeks Interrelationships	Requests for responses which explain or organize data already known.
6. Gives Interrelationships	Explanations or organization of information already presented.
7. Seeks Inferences and Generalizations	Asks for comparison, contrasts, consequences, etc. which demand inclusion of information not already stated.
8. Gives Inferences and Generalizations	Provides (specifically or through implications) comparisons, contrasts, consequences, principles, generalizations, etc.
9. Seeks Predictions and Hypothesis	Requests to apply known information to situations in order to predict events, outcomes, etc.
10. Gives Predictions and Hypothesis	Use of information and deduction to predict unknown facts, events, actions, etc.
11. Procedural Remarks	Those statements which are made in class which are intended as agreement, disapproval, management, reiteration, feeling, encouragement, etc.
12. Focus	Those statements which are made to keep students working towards the proposed objectives.
13. Nonverbal	All classroom activity which is nonverbal or does not contribute to the lesson (confusion or out-of-focus remarks).

Table VI.   Content Analysis Data Sheet

	1	2	3	4	5	6	7	8	9	10	11	12	13	14	15	16	17	18
S			2				6	6		2			11					
T	1	1		5	5	5			1		8	8		11	12	12	12	12
S	8	8			8	8	11		11					8		2	2	
T			2	7				11		2	2	7	7		1			1
S		2	2	2		8	8				8	8	8	8				
T	7				2			11	11	11					5	5	5	5
S	2	2	2	2	2	2	2	2	8	8	8	8		2	2	2		
T													1				7	7
S	2		2		1	2	8	8	8	8	8	8		8	8	8	2	2
T		7		4									11					
S	8	8	8					2	2		8		2		2		8	
T				12	12	12	3			1		1		1		1		1
S	2	8	8		2	2			2			2		2		2	2	2
T				1			1	1		1	5		7		1			
S						8		8	8	8	8		2			8		6
T	12	12	12	7	1		1					1		1	1		1	
S		2		6		4	4	4				4	4		4	4	4	
T	1		1		3				3	3	3	3			1			
S	2	6		2		2		2		2	2		6	2				2
T			1		1		11		1			11			1	1	1	
S	2	1	2	2	13	2		2	2							2		2
T						1			12	12	12	12	1			1		1
S							2	2	3	2	2	2	2	2			4	
T	12	12	12	12	12	1									1	1		1

Table VII.   Content Analysis Data Summary

							TEACHER TALK—43.5%						
Category	1	2	3	4	5	6	7	8	9	10	11	12	13
Tallies	39	4	6	—	9	—	7	—	—	—	8	17	—
% of Total	19.2	1.9	3.0	—	4.8	—	3.5	—	—	—	4.8	8.3	—
			24.1				8.3					4.8	8.3

Total TG—1.9%   Total TS—29.5%

							STUDENT TALK—56%						
Category	1	2	3	4	5	6	7	8	9	10	11	12	13
Tallies	1	62	—	10	8	8	3	34	—	—	3	—	1
% of Total	.5	28	—	5	—	4	—	17	—	—	1.5	—	.5
			33.5			21				1.5			.5

Total SS—.5%   Total SG—54.5%

Teacher Category   Student Response

1   Category   T   2   4   6   8
     Tallies   32   24   2   1   5

Student Category   Teacher Response

2   Category   T   1   2   5   7   11   12
     Tallies   26   17   1   1   3   3   1

Student Category   Teacher Response

8   Category   T   1   6   11   12
     Tallies   11   7   1   2   1

4. 29.3% of the time was spent in what Hilda Taba calls Cognitive Task II.
   a. TS—8.3%   SG—21%
5. No time was spent on predicting or hypothesizing.
6. The teacher spent 8.3% of time establishing or reestablishing focus.
7. Students responded thirty-two times following teacher category 1.
   a. Twenty-four times by giving information
   b. Two times by giving labels and groups
   c. One time by giving interrelationships
   d. Five times by giving inferences and generalizations

8. The teacher talked twenty-six times following student category 2.
   a. Seventeen times by seeking more information
   b. One time by seeking information
   c. One time by seeking interrelationships
   d. Three times by seeking inferences
   e. Three times by making procedural remarks
   f. One time *he* focused discussion
9. The teacher talked eleven times following student category 8.
   a. Seven times he sought information
   b. One time he sought interrelationships
   c. Two times he repeated
   d. One time he refocused
10. Only one teacher category 3 was not followed by student category 4.
11. Only one teacher category 5 was not followed by student category 6.
12. Three of four teacher category 7s were followed with student category 2.

The behavioral dimension in the process of education is crucial for education is modification of behavior. In the inductive approach, inquiry as a sophisticated and disciplined mode of thought in fashioning knowledge and in solving problems is perceived as the central component. The role of the student, then, is that of a seeker of truth and reality about phenomena in the social domain, and the mode of inquiry guiding thought is grounded in the logic inherent in the discipline. Since each of the disciplines has its own unique mode and logic, there are many ways of knowing. Students must learn that a particular problem defined in a particular way prescribes a mode of solution. For example, the problem of overpopulation in India may generate many questions. The question: "What is the effect of overpopulation on the distribution of the food produced?" invokes the mode of inquiry of the discipline of economics. "How does crowdedness affect the behavior of the hungry?" This question invokes the mode of inquiry of the discipline of sociology. "For how long has India confronted the problem of overpopulation, and what has been its effect on the people of India?" This question invokes the mode of inquiry of the discipline of history. "What is the nature of the land on which Indian peoples live and how do they utilize this land?" This question invokes the discipline of geography. The nature of the question prescribes the mode of intellectual operation.

If teachers and students are to know how well they are moving and the direction in which they are moving, instruments must be devised. Social studies tests loaded with questions on names, dates, and isolated facts of history purporting to measure students' knowledge of and ability to do history; tests replete with queries on location of cities, rivers, meridians, and longitudes purporting to measure students' knowledge of and ability to do geography not only are invalid but also have debilitating influences on teaching as well as student inquiry. Test-makers must become adept in devising valid, reliable instruments. Worthy of note are attempts to utilize Bloom's *Taxonomy of Educational Objectives* (discussed above) as a model for the making of tests compatible with the multiple dimensions of the process of thinking. If it is true that the nature of tests given determines to a large extent students' learning behavior, then it is imperative that teachers become expert in designing appropriate measuring instruments.

Chapter 4 Bibliography

Amidon, Edmund J. "Group Supervision: A Technique for Improving Teaching Behavior," *National Elementary Principals* (April 1966) : 45.

Commission on the Reorganization of Secondary Education. *Cardinal Principles of Secondary Education.* Washington, D. C.: U. S. Office of Education Bulletin, No. 35, 1918.

Conant, James B. *The Education of the American Teacher.* New York: McGraw-Hill Book Company, Inc., 1963.

Downey, L. W. *Secondary Phase of Education.* Waltham, Mass.: Blaisdell Publishing Company, 1965.

Educational Policies Commission. *The Purpose of Education in American Democracy.* Washington, D. C.: National Education Association, 1938.

Fenton, Edwin. *Teaching The New Social Studies in Secondary Schools, an Inductive Approach.* New York: Harper & Row, Publishers, 1966.

Flanders, Ned A., Project Director. *Helping Teachers Change Their Behavior.* Rev. ed. Ann Arbor: The University of Michigan School of Education, 1965.

Gallagher, James A. *The Gifted Child in the Elementary School.* Washington, D. C.: National Education Association, 1959.

Guilford, J. P. *Nature of Human Intelligence.* New York: McGraw-Hill Book Company, Inc., 1967.

Hansen, John H., and Anderson, Robert. *Interaction Analysis: Manual for Workshops.* Portland, Ore.: Northwest Education Research Laboratory, 1970.

Krug, E. A. *Secondary School Curriculum.* New York: Harper & Row, Publishers, 1960.

Pace, Clinton, Director. *White House Conference on Education Report.* Washington, D. C.: 1955.

Piaget, Jean. *Origins of Intelligence in Children.* New York: W. W. Norton & Co., Inc., 1963.

Schwab, Joseph J., and Branwein, Paul. *Teaching of Science.* Minneapolis: University of Minnesota Press, 1962.

Taba, Hilda. *Curriculum Development: Theory and Practice.* New York: Harcourt, Brace, and World, 1962.

Thelen, H. A. *Classroom Grouping for Teachability.* New York: John Wiley & Sons, Inc., 1967.

Organization for Instruction

Middle schools organized in a traditional mode which encompass grades five and six usually operate those grades on a self-contained basis. By *self-contained* we mean a method of classroom organization wherein one teacher is responsible for one group of children for most, if not all, of the school day. Many such schools have adopted a highly desirable modification of the self-contained organization which provides for instruction in art, music, physical education, industrial arts, and home economics by specialists in the field. Also, team teaching and cooperative planning activities as augmentations of self-contained classes have further provided assistance for the beleaguered teacher who must operate with competence in several subject matter areas. While the emotional and personal advantages of prolonged contact between a teacher and the children of eleven and twelve years far outweigh the advantages of fully departmentalized instruction at this level, nothing can hide the fact that the teachers at this level must be close to being intellectual supermen if they are to do their job well.

Grades seven and eight in middle schools organized along traditional lines will be departmentalized in some but not all subjects while grade nine is likely to be departmentalized in all subjects. Indeed, one of the current issues in junior high school education is the degree to which departmentalization should be used below grade nine. Supporters of departmentalization, correlation, fusion, block-of-time, and core organization, are currently vying with one another for space in administrative periodicals.

Those who support departmentalization believe that this will provide the time necessary and desirable for specific disciplines; it is usually the case that the disciplines thus encouraged are not narrowly defined but are fused, as American History, not Colonial History, History of the West, or History of the Civil War. Although there has been, through the years, considerable criticism of the subject matter organization, recent developments, such as the writings of a noted chemist and the aroused interest of the academicians, have strengthened the position of the departmentalized approach.

When subject matter lines are maintained but materials from other subjects are brought in as seems necessary or desirable, we are dealing with correlated subjects. *Correlation* is a conscious effort to integrate materials, concepts, and learnings so that relationships between various subjects may be more readily seen. A common example of correlation may be found where students who are studying the westward movement in social studies are, in language arts, reading literature which concerns that period. A more complex example involves an examination of the social and economic conditions existing at the time which contributed to the westward movement. Those aspects of other disciplines which may relate or fit logically are introduced by the teacher as they become of value. Teachers still feel quite secure in teaching subject matter but they are, in fact, teaching correlated subjects and do not have to be so narrowly specialized. Effective correlation requires teachers who are flexible, adaptable, and who are quick to take advantage of student interest. Good correlation is not an unplanned nor accidental event.

Carried a little further, correlation becomes *fusion,* in its simplest form. Under this organizational plan the content of several, or conceivably all, of the social studies subjects are consolidated into what is sometimes called the "broad fields" approach. Such a course, usually labeled "Social Studies," is generally composed of elements from several behavioral disciplines and often includes geography, history, and civics. A change in name is no guarantee of a change in content, method, nor approach, and many of these courses are the same old subjects with different nomenclature. A course such as Problems in Democracy, however, is apt to be a fused course which takes what it needs from history, sociology, civics, and economics. Fused courses require major reorganization of content, method, materials, and approach, and, because there is much diversity in the treatment of fused courses, there are likely to be more obvious cases of extremes which, too often, emphasize poor planning. In many instances fusion has joined subjects from completely different areas, such as language arts and social studies (both of these already correlated or fused) in a course which may be titled, "Living in Our Community," or "Problems of Today's World," or "Finding My Place Today." There have been examples of excellent planning, organizing, presenting, and teaching of units and courses of this nature but, unfortunately, there have also been examples of poorly prepared units presented by teachers who were unsure of themselves or students who were not interested, motivated, or reached. Too, academicians and university scholars are apt to be highly critical of the breakdown of subject matter lines and feel that it is difficult to accomplish a synthesis in one subject alone, to say nothing of attempting to fuse and relate six to twelve other disciplines.

A method of organization which has enjoyed increasing use and popularity on the junior high school levels is *block-time*. A block-time class is a class which the same teacher meets for two or more periods daily and which may or may not break down subject matter lines. When this plan includes two or more subject areas within the block, it is essential that teachers be equally qualified in two or more subjects as well as being thoroughly competent and enthusiastic. The block-time program permits a teacher to know his pupils better and, presumably, affords the pupils somewhat more security. The block-time increases advantages for more effective teaching because the longer period of time makes possible better utilization of audiovisual materials, field trips, and related activities. Wright's study[1] indicated that the most common combination of subject areas was English (or language arts) and social studies—72 percent of the block-time classes reporting this pairing. Some schools reported a science-mathematics block (14 percent of those replying), while a few schools operated two blocks, one for English-Social Studies, and one for Science-Mathematics.

In Howard's study of Oregon and Washington middle schools, block-time classes were reported in 72 percent of junior high school seventh grades, 40 percent of junior high school eighth grades, and only 8 percent of the ninth grades. Again the most common combination was language arts and social studies, inclusion of mathematics and science in a block-time program has virtually disappeared for middle schools.

A number of other studies have been made of block-time scheduling, most of them before 1960. These studies indicated that block-time was found to be relatively common in the seventh grade.

A great deal of discussion, pro and con, and a considerable amount of heat has been generated by the organizational pattern known as *core*. Indeed, there are those who say that the outstanding characteristic of core is lack of organization. In a genuine core program there are no commitments to any subject or content areas. Student selected topics are

[1] Grace S. Wright, *Block Time Classes and the Core Program in the Junior High School* (Washington, D. C.: U. S. Office of Education Bulletin #6, 1958), p. 21.

frequently utilized for the course content, and subject matter from any area is brought in as it may be used to assist in solving the problems selected. Sometimes referred to as the common learnings approach, a true core depends upon teacher-pupil planning around broad problem areas, purportedly satisfying individual, group, and societal needs important to the development and education of all students. It is claimed that there is increased motivation for learning in core because the students are working on real, self-selected problems. Unfortunately, there is little evidence either for or against this statement. It is also asserted that individual differences are better met by a core program since it emphasizes small group and individual work. Thus, the gifted child and the slow child will both be stimulated to a greater extent. Properly organized, a functioning core class, it is said, makes full use of problem solving and critical thinking, working around problems of real significance, meaning, and concern for the students. Such may be the case; again, there is little evidence either to support or deny this statement. One of the main obstacles to successful core programs is the lack of properly trained, thoroughly qualified, and willing teachers to teach core. It has been remarked that this is the main problem in any organizational plan, and there is considerable truth in such a comment. A good teacher who has a solid knowledge of the subjects taught, who is an autonomous decision maker in classroom activities, and who understands, likes, and has the respect of adolescents, is almost certainly going to be successful in any type of organizational plan. With the imagination and creativity necessary for top level teaching, plus the sensitivity requisite for working with children, such a teacher should prove successful in each of the plans discussed.

Critics of core point to statements such as that of a noted chemist in which he supports a block-time without breaking down subject matter lines but does not endorse core. At the same time the proponents of core teaching say quite firmly that there is an increased interest in and widespread acceptance of core, and, as evidence, they mention the amount of attention given to core in educational writings.

In all honesty it must be said that the potential of core has never been fully reached. In equal honesty it must be pointed out that the most complete survey made of core in the junior high schools, Grace Wright's,[2] indicated that of the schools which used some form of block-time organization, a relatively small number of schools, 12 percent, had a program which could be considered core, and there is little evidence to indicate any increase in application of core since 1958. If anything, there has been at least a tendency to turn toward more individualization or departmentalization. It should be mentioned, too, that while a proliferation of writing concerning a practice may indicate interest and even concern, it certainly is not proof that such a practice is

[2] *Ibid.*, p. 21.

approved nor even becoming more common. There has been an indicated increase in uSe of block-time in junior high and it is likely that much which is reported as core is, in reality, a block of time—two or more subjects, probably within subject matter lines within two or more periods, with the same teacher. The oft-mentioned explosion of knowledge makes it increasingly difficult for one teacher to be thoroughly trained in a variety of subjects.

Innovations in Organization for Instruction

In recent years the middle schools have been subjected to ever increasing pressures, both from the society it serves and from the larger educational institution of which it is a part. Bases for these pressures have included increased school enrollments, shortage of competent teachers, rapidly expanding knowledge, greater numbers of students going on to universities, changing national vocational and residential patterns, a fierce competition between nations, and the adoption of the view that schools are an institution to be used to facilitate social change. As might be expected, numerous changes have been proposed in the organization, curricular content, and methodology of the middle school.

Team Teaching

Kenneth D. Jenkins has given the following definition: Classically, team teaching has come to be regarded as a means by which a group of teachers coordinate their particular abilities for the purpose of improved instruction, the rationale being that one teacher cannot be an authority on all knowledge for all students.[3]

Carl Olson would further add that team teaching must include cooperative planning, mutual evaluation, flexible scheduling, and grouping.[4] But Trump and Miller[5] would not call any method team teaching unless it included large and small group instruction and some provision for individual independent study. If team teaching were to mean bringing two or more classrooms of students together so that a teacher could teach a lesson once instead of having to teach it several times, it would mean nothing more than a matter of convenience for the teacher. Even though this arrangement has merit in that it would save teacher time and energy, little extra value would be derived by the student. Criticism has long been directed toward the teacher who tends only to "talk at" students. Reinforcement through small group discussion is necessary to

[3] Kenneth D. Jenkins, "Teaming and Teaching," *Clearing House* (October 1967) : 42:80–82, p. 80.

[4] Carl O. Olson, Jr., "Teaching Team in the Elementary School," *Education* (April 1968) : 88:345–349, p. 345.

[5] J. Lloyd Trump, and Delmas Miller, *Secondary School Curriculum Improvement* (Boston: Allyn and Bacon, Inc., 1968) p. 318.

allow students to share each other's views and questions. Students must also be provided with the opportunity to explore their own individual interests and strengths as well.

Small group discussion and individual study are not new concepts since teachers in conventional classrooms have used these methods for a long time. Team teaching merely affords these teachers a more convenient and effective way of employing these methods.

Team teaching should be a cooperative effort by two or more teachers in which together they plan, instruct, and evaluate the work of their students so that maximum learning takes place. What is important in the schools is not so much what the teachers do, but what the students do. For this reason, any definition of team teaching must be in terms of how it influences or enhances learning.

It is essential that teachers embarking on a team teaching program of instruction must first define for themselves what team teaching is in terms of their particular situation.

Much has been written in current periodicals and books concerning the problems that have arisen in past team teaching experiences. It is well for all those contemplating the use of this method of organization to study such problems carefully so that these problems may more easily be solved, or so that some or all of the undesirable factors may either be avoided or eliminated.

Inadequate teacher selection has probably given rise to most of the problems arising out of team teaching. Some teachers simply are not prone to change. Teachers who have been teaching in a self-contained classroom for a number of years and who have been relatively sheltered from newer trends and philosophies, could not be placed into a team teaching assignment without a considerable amount of difficulty. Generally, these people are too self-conscious about other professionals observing them to do an adequate job. Many teachers cannot work in a give-and-take situation. In team teaching it is necessary to be able to receive professional criticism and evaluation from others.

Teachers with little or no teaching experience, or teachers who do not perform well in front of large groups, do not feel adequate in a team. This then puts a greater burden on the other team members. Other teachers do not perform well in small groups. They either control the discussion or fail to understand group dynamics.

The inability or failure of teams to clearly determine both long and short range objectives causes the teams to wander aimlessly through units of work. Guiding principles are sometimes overlooked in the desire to get at the job. Teams that do not plan and evaluate their progress daily soon lose their enthusiasm because what they do seems to lack direction. Students also become disinterested and difficult to manage.

In cases where teachers are forced to do their planning after school hours, teachers soon tire of the heavier than normal teaching load. The first thing the teachers tend to give up are the planning sessions. Teachers must have some school time to plan so that team teaching can be effective.

Inadequate space and building facilities have handicapped some teams in what otherwise might have been a successful teaching experience. Since team teaching implies the cooperation of two or more teachers with large numbers of children, ordinary classrooms are not sufficient for large group instruction. Use of auditorium, gymnasium, cafeteria, or library space has not always been successful. Provision for large and small group instruction and individual study is essential.

It has been noted in quite a number of instances that staff relationships suffer because some staff members are involved in team teaching while others remain in traditional classrooms. Teachers not selected for team teaching duty are often envious of those who have. Because many team teaching practices have been established on an experimental basis in a particular school, extra equipment and facilities have been provided for that area. Then again, team teaching experiments are often visited by other teachers and school officials and in so doing, give added popularity and recognition to members of the team.

It is not uncommon for teaching teams, because of added responsibility and teaching load, to see less and less of teachers in the other areas of the school. What results is a staff within a staff. In some instances, members of the team talk too much at staff meetings. Because they develop habits of speaking freely at their own planning meetings, they tend to overpower other teachers with their ideas and suggestions. Moreover, because they may be enthused about their team teaching involvement, they want to share their experiences with other teachers.

Lack of continued support from the principal or other administrators has sometimes been the cause of team teaching efforts to fail. A priority of other concerns or a gradual disenchantment with the process have caused decay in support. Inadequate communication with the local community often results in the failure of the parents to see the value of team teaching. Pressure groups may form to persuade the principal, the superintendent, or the school to discontinue the operation or to have their children transferred to a traditional classroom.

Administrators have often found that rather than cutting instructional costs, as they had at first anticipated, team teaching increases the cost. The demand for teaching assistants, secretaries, and additional equipment and supplies has been responsible for much of the increased cost. As teaching teams become more fully aware of their potential, they see more productive ways of spending their time. Consequently, the need for nonprofessional assistance increases. They also see ways of improving instruction with the help of mechanical aids.

In some instances, teaching teams have been so successful that in their enthusiasm they have tended to overwork the students. Teams have sometimes devoted too much time to large group instruction and information giving and have deprived the students of time to digest the information through small group work and individual study.

A good team must plan carefully, taking advantage of the best each teacher has to offer. Each team member contributes the best of his or her resource material and techniques. Improved quality of instruction often is the result of cooperative planning. The team shares its understanding and the needs of each student. What might go by undetected by one teacher might be observed by another. Included here might be personal problems or a particular weakness or strength either in an academic or social area. Having other professionals observing their teaching along with more intensive preparation on their part tends to make the teaching act much more vital and alive. The value to the student is obvious.

With larger numbers of students gathered together for large group instruction, the teacher is spared the tiring task of having to present the same materials a number of times as would be the case in a traditional classroom. Time saved can be spent in other constructive professional activities. All students have the advantage of listening to a fresh presentation rather than perhaps the last of a number of identical presentations a teacher is required to give in a traditional setting. Students also benefit by having the most capable member of the team present the lesson. Students in a self-contained or traditional classroom with a poor teacher have only to look forward to poor instruction in that particular subject for the entire year. A weak teacher in a team situation can learn by observing other members teaching and benefit from their ideas and suggestions.

In a self-contained classroom, the teacher tends to teach to the average achieving student. While much can be done for the exceptional students at either end of the scale, limited class time does not always permit the teacher to give as much individual attention as it would be possible in a team situation.

In most schools where there are more than one classroom of students in each grade, students are generally grouped homogeneously. While this may make for ease of instruction, it does not allow for the heterogeneous interaction of students that is necessary for the wholesome development of the child. A student in a low ability room is often stigmatized while those in high ability rooms often develop a superior attitude toward others. It is possible in a large group for a student to be a member of a remedial reading group, and still be with the other students for many activities.

The possibility for social interaction is also increased in a large team approach. Each individual has an opportunity to identify himself with a greater number of students with like interests. At the same time each individual can benefit from a greater exposure to more students of other interests, races, religions, and beliefs. An understanding and appreciation of all people is an important need of all youth. This interaction can occur in informal activities or it can be planned by teachers in setting up small groups.

Students, particularly middle school students, often identify themselves with certain members of a staff more than with others. In a team situation, they have more opportunity to seek out that teacher and enjoy that association for more time each day. This being the case, more effective guidance can be done right in the classroom as the teachers are able to better identify the needs and problems of these students. Cooperative assessment of the group needs and problems leads to more effective group guidance as well.

A team teaching setting can provide an excellent training ground for new teachers. A new teacher can reach maximum performance more quickly by receiving commendation for strengths and constructive criticism for weaknesses. The new teacher can also contribute to the team effort by suggesting recent ideas received as a result of more recent training.

Teachers working in an interdisciplinary team have an excellent opportunity to more clearly gain an overview of the total educational program. They are forced to recognize the aims, objectives and problems of other disciplines as well as their own. Teachers in traditional settings are often accused of possessing a limited point of view.

Implications for the Design and Construction of Team Teaching Areas

It is difficult to carry on team teaching programs without suitable building space and facilities. Team teaching, of course, implies grouping together of larger numbers of students in one room. It also implies providing space in which students can get together in small groups for discussion. As in any school, students must have facility for carrying on individual study.

Existing buildings must make some modifications to their structures or use large spaces intended for some other purpose. Many schools have removed nonsupporting walls from between two traditional classrooms to provide for the larger space. Some use this large room for all the activities and some use them in addition to homerooms. Large instructional rooms have been built onto existing units. Homerooms remain as the base of activities for the classes. Many schools have made use of lunchrooms, gymnasiums, auditoriums, and rotundas for large group instruction. For obvious reasons, this handicaps a teaching team.

Schools designed and constructed especially for team teaching have a decided advantage. Such designs can be commonly found in editions of *Nation's Schools*. One design calls for a large flat or tiered room which is used exclusively for large group instruction. Classes of students are scheduled into these areas for the lecture, film, or speaker. Individual and small group work are scheduled in some other room or facility of the school. This type of space can be used extremely well by either the single-discipline team and by the team using the block-of-time approach. Since a room of this type is scheduled with classes for most of the day, audiovisual equipment remains in the room permanently. If the area is used exclusively by one team, or discipline, the instructional materials for that team are stored in it as well.

An increasing number of school designs feature the open pod facility in which students remain for almost all of their academic subjects. Students in these areas generally move to other facilities in the school for instruction in the fine arts, physical education, industrial arts, and home economics. This arrangement is extremely advantageous to the interdisciplinary team approach. Some of the rationale behind the open pod concept is that a school can provide more actual classroom space without making the total building area larger simply by removing interior walls and corridors. This point can probably be brought out more strongly in terms of the number of square feet of floor space per student. A cluster of four traditional classrooms, each containing 900 square feet of floor space, would give each of the thirty students thirty square feet of floor space. The total floor space of the four classrooms would be 3,600 square feet. By removing the interior walls and including the corridor, the total unobstructed floor space would be 4,800 square feet. This would provide forty square feet of floor space for each of the 120 students assigned to that cluster.

The use of acoustic tile and carpeted floors reduces most of the noise that one would expect from so many students working within one enclosure. Also, trapezoidal tables are extremely functional in the large team areas. They can be easily arranged for small group discussions as well as for large group instruction. Some schools have the students store their books in trays or wall compartments along the outside wall so that the desks or tables remain light for easy handling.

Some schools provide retractable walls to divide the large area into smaller units whenever it would seem necessary. The extremely high cost of these walls have encouraged many schools to provide only portable chalkboard dividers for smaller groups. Movable book and supply shelves can also serve as dividers.

Flexible Scheduling

In traditional schedules each instructional period is the same length of time, usually forty-five minutes, and each class meets daily. Flexible scheduling, popularly, refers to any deviation from this format. It may be as simple as combining two periods into one larger block of time or as complex as the plan recommended by J. Lloyd Trump.[6]

6 J. Lloyd Trump, and Dorsey Baynham, *Guide to Better Schools* (Chicago: Rand McNally and Co., 1961).

The objectives of flexible scheduling are fourfold.[7]

1. To allow for the different time demands of different subjects. An obvious example of this is the laboratory type class such as industrial arts or home economics. It might be desirable, when students are doing laboratory work, to meet less days during the week but for longer periods of time.

2. To permit different kinds of time arrangements to better meet the needs of students with different learning problems. As an example, very able math students may be able to master certain mathematical skills with relatively little supervised drill. However, the student who finds math difficult may need longer periods of drill, with a teacher available for assistance.

3. To provide for different time demands for different activities in the same subject area. In a general science class, one teacher who is particularly knowledgeable in electricity might present a lecture-demonstration to a large group of three classes in thirty minutes. This might be followed by a one hour laboratory session in three groups of thirty students each.

4. To provide a block of time for students in one classroom to aid in the transition from the self-contained classroom concept of the elementary school to the six period day of the high school.

Many schools have adopted something comparable to Trump's proposed modular schedule. Whittier Junior High School in Livonia, Michigan, has maintained a two-hour block in English-Social Studies every day but operates the rest of its schedule on fifteen-minute modules. Classes meet for differing amounts of time on different days or, in some cases, do not meet every day.[8]

At Nichols Junior High School in Evanston, Illinois, the schedule is based on thirty-minute modules. The homeroom and activity period concept has been maintained. Art and Science meet for the same total time but do so in three periods per week.[9] The schedule at Euclid Junior High School, Euclid, Ohio, based on a twenty-two-minute module allots the available time according to the needs of different subjects. In their case, the seventh grade core has five modules, English three modules, and Art and Foreign Language one module each. These classes meet every day.[10]

[7] Donald Manlove, and David Beggs, *Flexible Scheduling* (Bloomington: Indiana University Press, 1965), pp. 23–25.

[8] Bruce M. Hudson, "An Experiment in Flexible Scheduling," *Michigan Education Journal* (November 1964): 42:12–13.

[9] Thomas Sinks, "Data Processing in the Schools," *Clearing House* (October 1964): 39:118–120.

[10] Robert Bush, and Dwight Allen, "Flexible Scheduling," *National Association of Secondary School Principals Bulletin* (May 1963): 47:73–98, p. 96.

Some other schools that operate modular schedules are Meadow-brook Junior High School, Newton, Massachusetts; Shawnee Junior High School, Lima, Ohio; University Junior High School, Bloomington, Indiana; Stanforth Junior High School, Elmont, New York; and Grover Cleveland Junior High School, Caldwell, New Jersey.

One of the more extreme examples of flexible scheduling operates at Brookhurst Junior High School in Anaheim, California. In attempting to develop a more adequate instructional framework, Brookhurst inaugurated the Daily Demand Schedule in 1962. Prior to 1962, a full year was spent in research. Parents of all eighth grade students were contacted and goals of the program were explained. School Board acceptance was obtained and a three-week summer workshop was approved. Committees of teachers under the guidance of Gardner Swenson,[11] began devising forms and techniques necessary for scheduling. The following basic assumptions served as guidelines:

1. All subjects do not require the same amount of time or method of instruction.
2. All students do not have equal abilities nor do they learn at the same rate.
3. The teacher is best qualified to determine the students' academic needs, the method of instruction, and the time required.

From these assumptions the Daily Demand Schedule at Brookhurst evolved.

Independent Study

Winslow Hatch and Ann Bennet define independent study as:

> . . . independent work or reading, sometimes on one's own, sometimes in small groups, but with such work taking place in the absence of the teacher and in lieu of regularly scheduled class meetings.[12]

Among the frequently mentioned objectives of independent study programs are:

1. To develop creativity, adaptability, responsibility, and habits of inquiry in students.
2. To permit different rates of progress.
3. To enable students to pursue elective interests on their own.
4. To encourage and facilitate development of good study habits.
5. To permit program adaptation to individual student needs.

---

[11] For more information on this idea see: Gardner Swenson, and Donald Keys, *Providing for Flexibility in Scheduling and Instruction* (Englewood Cliffs, N. J.: Prentice-Hall, Inc., 1966).

[12] Winslow Hatch, and Ann Bennet, *Independent Study* (Washington, D. C.: U. S. Office of Education, 1960), p. 3.

6. To permit program adaptation in individual student problem-solving skills.[13]

Jacques Barzun in his book, *Teacher in America,* stated:
The whole aim of good teaching is to turn the young learner, by nature a little copycat, into an independent self-propelling creature, who cannot merely study but learn—that is, work as his own boss to the limits of his powers. This is to turn pupils into students, and it can be done on any rung of the ladder of learning.[14]

In a few cases independent study time is built into each student's schedule, as at Brookhurst. However, there appear to be few schools having independent study programs involving a high percentage of their students. Broome Junior High School in Rockville, Maryland,[15] and University Junior High School in Bloomington, Indiana,[16] according to the literature, appear to have a large portion of their student bodies with regularly scheduled independent study time.

A more common arrangement is to involve just a few of the more able students and release them from some regular class time. Skokie Junior High School in Winnetka, Illinois, has provided a learning laboratory. Students are released from regular classes for varying amounts of time to work on predetermined projects of their choice in the learning lab. A staff member is employed to operate the lab and assist students in their independent efforts.[17]

Pimlico Junior High School in Baltimore releases a few highly select students to pursue independent studies. Students must be at least two years above grade level on standardized achievement tests and in the superior range on intelligence tests. Most of the work done is through library research although some science lab work is also done.[18]

Independent study is often coupled with team teaching efforts. In addition to satisfying some of the previously mentioned objectives, this makes it possible for the teachers to work with smaller groups of students. For example, a team of two teachers and sixty students may have thirty students doing independent study while two discussion groups of fifteen each are being conducted by the two teachers.

---

[13] William Rogge, "Independent Study is Self-Directed Learning," *Independent Study* (Bloomington: Indiana University Press, 1965), p. 19.

[14] Jacques Barzun, *Teacher in America,* (Boston: Little, Brown and Company, 1945), p. 21.

[15] Carl Michael, in Manlove and Beggs, *op. cit.,* p. 58.

[16] Manlove, and Beggs, *op. cit.,* p. 58.

[17] S. P. Marland, Jr., "Winnetka's Learning Laboratory," *Educational Leadership* (April 1963) : 20:459.

[18] E. L. Goldsmith, "Independent Study in the Junior High School," *Education Digest* (February 1965) : 30:40–42.

Chapter 5 Bibliography

Barzun, Jacques, *Teacher in America*. Boston: Little, Brown and Company, 1945.

Beggs, David W. III, *Team Teaching*. Indianapolis: Unified College Press, 1964.

————, and Buffie, Edward G. *Independent Study*. Bloomington: Indiana University Press, 1965.

Brubaker, Charles William, and Leggett, Stanton. "How to Create Territory for Learning in the Secondary Schools," *Nation's Schools* (March 1968): 81:67–98.

Bush, R. N., and Dwight, Allen. "Flexible Scheduling," *National Association of Secondary School Principals Bulletin* (May 1963): 47:73–98.

Goldsmith, E. L. "Independent Study in the Junior High School," *Education Digest* (February 1965): 30:40–42.

Hatch, Winslow, and Bennet, Ann. *Independent Study*. Washington, D. C.: U. S. Office of Education, 1960.

Hoffman, E. B. "Brookhurst Plan—Flexible Scheduling," *NEA Journal* (September 1965): 54:50–52.

Hudson, Bruce M. "An Experiment in Flexible Scheduling," *Michigan Education Journal* (November 1964): 42:12–13.

Jenkins, Kenneth. "Teaming and Teaching," *The Clearing House* (October 1967): 42:83–86.

Manlove, Donald C., and Beggs, David W. III, *Flexible Scheduling*. Bloomington: Indiana University Press, 1965.

Marland, S. P., Jr. "Winnetka's Learning Laboratory," *Education Leadership* (April 1963): 20:459.

Olson, Carl D., Jr. "Teaching Team in the Elementary School," *Education* (April 1968): 88:345–349.

Sinks, Thomas A. "Data Processing in the Schools," *Clearing House* (October 1964): 39:118–120.

Swenson, Gardner, and Keys, Donald. *Providing for Flexibility in Scheduling and Instruction*. Englewood Cliffs, N. J.: Prentice-Hall, Inc., 1966.

Trump, J. Lloyd, and Baynham, Doris. *Guide to Better Schools*. Chicago: Rand McNally and Company, 1961).

————, and Miller, Delmas. *Secondary School Curriculum Improvement*. Boston: Allyn and Bacon, Inc., 1968.

Wright, Grace S. *Block-Time Classes and the Core Program in the Junior High School*. Washington, D. C.: U. S. Office of Education Bulletin #6, 1958.

Learning Activity Packages

The advent of the middle school has encouraged innovative thinking by those administrators and curriculum planners involved with it. Restructuring implies concomitant changes and the purposes of the restructuring dictate what those changes should be, or at least, parameters within which the changes should occur.

If we can assume that any change in education is designed to facilitate more effective learning, then individualized instruction must be one focus of the middle school. Research has shown that students achieve better when their curriculum is individualized, and the dedicated teacher has long felt pangs of conscience over what research shows and what he is physically incapable of doing. The already overburdened teacher, who does much of his work after school hours, is equipped neither emotionally nor academically to individualize materials for an overload of students. The complexity of the task is so overwhelming that few will attempt it. Yet there is a way—which, while time-consuming at the outset, provides the teacher with opportunities to know more students better, individualize their instruction, encourage the development of responsibility for learning in the student, and develop a more positive self-concept in the student. In addition, students become more aware of the intrinsic rewards of learning, while teachers develop more creativity and a direction of purpose they have rarely had before.

This approach to individualizing called variously "Learning Activity Package," "LAP," or just "package," was developed at the Nova Schools in Fort Lauderdale, Florida, as an offshoot of the UNIPAC idea disseminated by the Kettering Foundation. Schools across the country have been offering in-service training to their teachers in the development and use of packages because of the sound learning theory which underlies them. The LAP is designed without the sophistication of the computer, but offers a similar range of components and can be used anywhere from the one-room school to the college. It is written within the school or district by the teachers, for use with their own students as those students' needs have been diagnosed.

The Learning Activity Package has seven basic components: (1) the pretest, (2) the rationale, (3) the behavioral objectives, (4) activities, (5) self-evaluation, (6) the post-test, and (7) in-depth opportunities. It is generally designed to cover one month's work for an average student. It functions best in the non-graded school where students are self-paced. This creates a wide variety of places in which any one group of students might be working. It would not be unusual for a class of thirty-two to be in twenty different LAPs if they are allowed to work as they choose.

While the middle school is a period where flexibility should be the keynote of structure, even an experience curriculum should be planned with regard to what experiences are to be included, which should come before others, and how much the student should know before he can effectively use it as a tool. Whatever the point of view of the curriculum planner, articulation is a necessary component of the curriculum.

The LAP is based on the scope and sequence of the curriculum. If, for example, thirty-six experiences (or concepts) are enumerated for the middle school in a particular subject area, then thirty-six LAPs would be written, one for each experience.

There may be sub-concepts or intermediate steps desirable in developing each concept or experience; the LAP might then be divided into sections, one for each sub-concept or step. Teachers may prefer to have students work through one of the sections, before giving them the next section in the LAP, feeling that "a month's work" might overwhelm some students. It is a mark of the flexibility of the LAP that this is possible, while still allowing those students who prefer the overview to have the entire package at once. If the LAP is broken into sections, each section would be devoted to a sub-concept with its behavioral objective, activities to attain that objective and self-evaluation and post-testing to see that the objective is met. The pretest would determine which sections the student needed. In-depth work would be offered at the conclusion of the LAP.

The scope and sequence should be developed as a cooperative effort of the teachers at the grade level as well as the curriculum planner, if the school has one. It is possible that the scope and sequence has been developed by the school district already. However, if such a program exists, teachers should be given an opportunity to examine it carefully and decide if it is relevant for the students in their school. The district-developed program of instruction is often perceived as irrelevant by teachers, and their participation in the development of one of their own produces an enthusiasm for it. Research shows that enthusiasm—believing in what one is doing—is a prerequisite for successful teaching.

In preparing their scope and sequence, teachers may work with their teams, in subject areas, in grade achievement or at whatever level they are assigned. Opportunity to meet together to exchange ideas should be provided to prevent undesirable repetition. Certain concepts or skills may need to be reintroduced, but it probably is not necessary for the students to have a LAP each year on a subject like library research skills.

There will be *approximately* nine skills or concepts (perhaps as few as five or as many as eighteen) per year in each subject area. While generally, they would be sequential, it would be quite possible to combine two subject areas where concepts overlap or the concepts of one could be used to practice skills in the other as in social studies and language arts for example.

To summarize, the platform on which LAPs are based should be relevant for the students and engender enthusiasm in the teachers.

The Rationale

The rationale of the Learning Activity Package is the first contact the student has with the package. It is, in a sense, his introduction to it. However, its purpose is far more encompassing than that of the usual introduction. The rationale tells the student why the package has a place in his learning. It is the justification for occupying the student's time and energy with this particular concept or skill. Justifying the inclusion of a concept or skill in the curriculum gives cause for a great amount of soul-searching on the part of the LAP writer and/or curriculum planner. The inability of the writers to find a good reason for a particular experience might well bring about a long-needed streamlining of course content in almost every area. It is difficult to sound credible to the student when the only reason a writer can think of for content is that "we've always done it." Even little children—perhaps most likely, little children—can see through that.

If the LAP is concerned with a concept which is part of a scope and sequence, the rationale should tell the student how this package fits into the scope and sequence. It might say, "Your last package was about the United States growing in size; this package is about the United States growing in population; and your next package will be about the growth of industry in the United States."

If the package is based on a skill, such as using the card catalogue in the media center, the rationale would explain to the student why he might find it necessary to possess such a skill.

The rationale is written simply and concisely. It might be analogous to a one-minute television commercial "selling" the package to the student. It serves a two-fold purpose—it shows the relevance of the package and is motivational.

Behavioral Objectives

Behavioral objectives, instructional objectives or goals are currently being much discussed in educational circles. The nebulous goals with which many teachers begin the year, or worse, the goal of finishing the prescribed textbook by the end of the year, are unacceptable to the innovator. Yet, setting individual goals in each subject area for each student appears an impossible task.

Several educators have contributed to partially solving this problem. Benjamin Bloom,[1] David Krathwohl,[2] and their associates have developed taxonomies in the cognitive and affective domain. These taxonomies offer a hierarchical scale from which a curriculum writer of behavioral objectives (and LAPs) may select in order to offer challenges to the individual learning styles of students. In writing behavioral objectives for a LAP, at least three levels of difficulty should be included. For example, Bloom's lowest level is knowledge, and all students could be expected to experience success in attaining behavioral objectives on this level. Application is a higher level of *behavior* and many students might be able to achieve such objectives successfully. There are students who can successfully achieve objectives written at Bloom's highest levels, and they should not be denied the opportunity to do so. Behavioral objectives calling for synthesis and evaluation can be written for these students. In this way, students are challenged to the extent of their ability, through their choice of the objective they will work toward attaining. A student who consistently chooses to operate on a knowledge level, when all indications are that he might be successful on higher levels, may be afraid of failure or in need of improving his study skills. Diagnosis of the problem is facilitated by the continuing interpersonal relationship between student and teacher provided for in the Learning Activity Package.

Behavioral objectives serve a two-fold purpose. They let the student know exactly what is expected of him when he has successfully completed the learning experience. They also serve as guide lines for the

[1] Benjamin S. Bloom, ed., *Taxonomy of Educational Objectives, Handbook I: Cognitive Domain* (New York: David McKay Company, Inc., 1956).
[2] David R. Krathwohl, Benjamin S. Bloom, and Bertram B. Masia, *Taxonomy of Educational Objectives, Handbook II: Affective Domain* (New York: David McKay Company, Inc., 1964).

LAP writer. Every activity and all evaluations are based on the objectives.

Robert Mager, in his book *Preparing Instructional Objectives,* has suggested three elements of objectives: performance, conditions, and extent. Each objective, based on the concept (or sub-concept, if the LAP is to be broken down into sections) or skill which is the subject of the LAP, should contain each of the elements.

The task of the LAP writer is to examine the concept or skill, decide exactly how a student is to be able to perform if he has mastered the concept.

The student may paint a picture which demonstrates his internalization of the concept—or he may role play, make a speech, or build something. Matching two columns of words, one column containing ten words, the other containing fourteen is another example of performance. Writing answers to questions is a performance, but the student should be told ahead of time how many and what kind of questions they will be.

The second element of the behavioral objective is condition. The student is told what conditions will be prevalent while he is performing. If he is to have an open book test, he is told that this condition will prevail. If he is to perform from memory, that is the prevailing condition. Using a board, hammer and nails, if he is to build something, or using a tape recorder and self-developed notes not to exceed one page, are conditions.

The conditions might be called the "given." Many objective writers begin "Given—(conditions)—, you will be able to—(perform)—."

Extent is the third element of the behavioral objective. To what extent must the student be able to perform in order to meet the objective? If he is to be given a grade, what will be acceptable as passing?

"Given ten problems of addition of two-place numbers, you will be able to add at least seven correctly." In this example, "Given ten problems of addition of two-place numbers—" is the condition, "You will be able to add—" is the performance, and "—at least seven correctly" is the extent.

It is apparent that developing behavioral objectives for affective behaviors is a challenge to the writer because of the subjectivity involved. Every writer's (or teacher's) idea of what constitutes "an interest in good books" might differ both in depth and content. One possibility is the bringing together of a team of teachers of the subject area in question and asking them to enumerate those behaviors in students which make them think, "He's interested in good books!" Consensus on certain behaviors, while highly subjective, is better than no specific objective at all. From the objective can evolve activities which will lead the student to attain the objective.[3]

[3] *Ibid.*

Testing

The package-writer has also developed guidelines for testing once the objectives have been established. The testing will be whatever the behavioral objectives have stated it will be.

Each LAP contains a pretest and a post-test, and where desirable, opportunities for self-evaluation by the student.

The pretest is given to the student at the beginning of the package to determine whether or not he needs to go through that particular package. In an area such as foreign language or higher mathematics the pretest may be omitted; however, its purpose is to assure that students work only on those things they cannot already do, and it is always better to use a pretest if there is even the remotest possibility of the student having an understanding of the concept. Placement-type tests are useful in determining which LAP the student is to work through; however, they are usually too general in nature to replace the pretest.

The self-evaluations are designed to allow the student to see how well he is doing, and rechannel himself, or ask for help in rechanneling if he feels it is necessary. The self-evaluation answers are included in the package, so that he can assess himself and make his own decisions about what to do next. If he decides he is ready, he then proceeds to the post-test. The teacher does not make these decisions for him unless he requests such counsel. He assumes the responsibility himself.

The post-test, like the pretest, is based on the behavioral objectives. If the objective stated that the student would be given ten multiple choice questions, then the post-test would, of course, contain ten multiple choice questions. Generally, the questions on the pretest and post-test would be different.

Wherever possible, students using LAPs are encouraged to do their own evaluating, including checking pre- and post-tests. With careful orientation and development of a trust relationship between student and teacher, the student is unafraid to face his deficiencies, and when he finds he has them, he knows what to do about them. He literally becomes responsible for his own learning, and experiences intrinsic rewards. His self-concept improves as his decision-making ability improves.

Activities

The activities, the heart of the package, lead the student through experiences which will help him attain the objective. They should offer a multi-media, multi-model approach to the student so that whatever may be his learning style, there are activities for him. Some students learn by reading, some by observation, some by writing, some by doing. The Learning Activity Package provides the opportunity for the student to learn in whatever way he learns best.

There are two kinds of activities—those required of all students and those from which the student chooses for himself. Even in the required activities, however, he has a choice, for while it may be desirable for everyone to have a common core of knowledge in this LAP, he may choose how he will get that core. Perhaps, upon examining ten books on a topic in the media center, the LAP writer finds six which contain the particular concept the LAP is about. He might then choose one on a very low reading level, one of about average reading level, and one which is more detailed or goes into the concept at greater depth. He would then list the three books in his required activity section, but give the student the option of which one to read. If a film, filmstrip, tape, or recording is available on the concept, they might also be an option on the required activity list. A multi-media approach is desirable. Care should be taken, however, that only those materials which actually contain the concept are listed. Titles of books and films are frequently misleading and only careful perusal by the LAP writer of everything available will assure that the student is getting the best use of his time by using only relevant materials.

Following the required activities are those from which the student may choose whatever he would like to do. These should offer something for every possible learning style. The choice for inclusion is almost endless; however, there should be a notation made that if a student wishes to develop an activity of his own, he is free to do so. He should write a short proposal or outline of what he would like to do and submit it for teacher approval before he begins. This is to insure the "intellectual honesty" and relevance of his proposed project to the concept being studied.

The following chart (Table VIII) may prove helpful to those wishing to develop LAPs of their own. It graphically illustrates numerous possibilities for activities.

Table VIII.   LAP Activities

READ	WRITE	LISTEN	MAKE	DO
(List not only books, but plays, poems, primary sources, newspapers, magazines...)	(Stories, dialogues, plays, diaries, newspaper articles...)	(Tapes—commercial student, and teacher prepared, records, dialogues...)	(Collages, diagrams, maps, charts, relief maps, tapes...)	(Investigations, role playing, academic games, problem solving...)

Multi-model activities should be included in the LAP as well as the multi-media activities previously described. Multi-mode implies a variety of environments available for the student's learning. Besides large group presentations such as films and lectures, opportunities should be offered for small group discussion and dialogue between student and teacher. One page in the activity section might say, "When you reach this page, sign up on the appropriate sheet on the bulletin board." When six students have signed up, the teacher will call them together for a discussion on "Are Immigration Laws Needed in the United States Today?"

The large group presentations are sharply curtailed in the LAPped curriculum. When students are allowed to proceed at their own pace, they spread out along the continuum, and there are few topics that are relevant to all students simultaneously. Lectures can be taped, and films can be reordered so that the lecture or film has relevance for the student when he hears or sees it.

The student-teacher dialogue is invaluable as a diagnostic tool, as a trust-builder, and as an opportunity for tutoring. At the end of each step in the concept, there should be a note to the student to see the teacher. A sign-up system works well for this. The teacher notes in the record book each time there is a student-teacher conference. This allows the teacher to keep a record of the student's progress in time as well as concept-formation.

Activities should enable the student to meet the behavioral objective. As mentioned before, Bloom's *Taxonomy* is helpful in writing activities for the package. If the objectives have been written on levels, then activities should be included which allow the student to operate on those levels. For example, if the objective states that the student will synthesize certain information, then he should be given opportunities to practice synthesization.

Some LAP writers include a section *after* the post-test containing in-depth opportunities. These are for students who like to "posthole" something that has aroused their interest, or develop an investigation into a related topic. In the in-depth section, the student may go off on a tangent—in fact, he is encouraged to do so. Not all students care to work in this way, so this is left entirely up to the student.

Use of LAPs

Some LAP writers have found it helpful to print each component of the LAP on different colors of paper. All tests are printed on green, for example; the rationale on blue; all behavioral objectives on yellow; activity pages on white. If the pages are color-keyed, then the student can refer back quite easily to the objectives or the activities whenever he needs to do so. Including pre- and post-tests in the LAP which is given to the student are a prerogative of the writer. Once the student begins to develop self-confidence, he can be trusted to use such information as it is best for him.

Color-keying adds to the attractiveness of the package as do cartoon illustrations and changes of type styles. Inclusion of maps and diagrams often aids clarity.

Writing the LAP at the lowest possible vocabulary level is recommended. The LAP is meant to be a road map to guide the student through activities to attain the objective. The language of the LAP should not be a challenge for the student; the activities are arranged to accomplish the task.

Students should receive orientation in the use of LAPs before they start working in them. A LAP on "How to Use a LAP" has been found to be successful. There is an adjustment period as students learn how to work on their own. Students who have been told what page to be on and what questions to answer need some time to learn to operate independently. Occasionally, students are found to be so dependent on the teacher that they cannot function otherwise. These may need to be grouped together to work in LAPs under teacher direction and then gradually weaned away.

When using Learning Activity Packages, students need no longer fear failure. LAPs encourage rechanneling through material, so that no one fails. Based on Jerome Bruner's statement ". . . the foundations of any subject may be taught to anybody at any age in some form."[4] If a student cannot meet the objective, he may have chosen to work on a level beyond his capacity. Student-teacher counseling may help him make a wiser selection next time.

Self-pacing by students implies responsibility on their part, and to say that the student may move as quickly or as slowly through the LAP as he chooses, also implies *within reason*. A large calendar with room for names within each date is helpful. If, on glancing through the record book, the teacher observes that a student has not had a conference with the teacher for a considerable length of time, the teacher schedules one. If at that time it seems necessary, the student is invited to put his name on the calendar under the date he thinks he will be finished with that section of the LAP. This makes a time-contract for the student to fulfill. Since he sets the date himself, he usually honors it.

Organization

Stations or learning centers are set up in the classroom or pod so that students may move from one to the other as needed. There may be an area designated as a listening center with tape recorder, record player, and language master,[5] earphones if possible, a multi-level textbook center, a painting-drawing-doing center, a center for simple science investigations, desks or chairs arranged for small group discussion, a space which can be partially shielded for individual viewings of films or filmstrips, and desks or tables set aside for independent study. Even

[4] Jerome S. Bruner, *The Process of Education* (New York: Vintage Books, 1960), p. 12.
[5] Language Master is trademarked by Bell and Howell.

the traditional classroom can accommodate such arrangements as shown in Table IX.

While the diagram shows seating for thirty-two students, probably those working at the painting and science centers would be standing. Flexible use of space in a traditional area is a point to be noted in the diagram; another is the number of tables and chairs being used instead of desks. The package concept encourages students to relate to each other in a free learning climate. They learn with and from each other as well as to operate independently.

Teacher Role

It becomes obvious that the role of the teacher in the LAP-oriented curriculum is a drastic change from the traditional "center of attention." The teacher becomes counselor, diagnostician, facilitator, and most important, friend. The teacher's day is spent counseling with students, usually one at a time, but occasionally two. In a traditional sixty-minute time period the teacher would confer with about ten students (the others working independently in their stations). Every three days or so the student talks on a one-to-one basis with the teacher. The personal relationship which develops from these short conferences establishes a rapport that the lecture never attains.

While the student signs up for the conferences at the end of each completed section, he may sign up for help any time he needs it. As soon as the conference in progress is completed, the teacher sees those who have asked for help. On days overbooked with conferences and help calls, students who have already attained the objective may be utilized to expedite matters. Such student activity should be noted in the record book, however, and no student should have to confer with another student in more than one of three conferences. One of the purposes of the conference is to know the student better and, therefore, be able to diagnose his problems more accurately. Too frequent use of students in the teacher role will impair this ability.

Summary

The Learning Activity Package, while designed to be self-instructional, is a device for more effective use of teacher and student time.

Each component of the package is an attempt to make the learning relevant to the learner.

1. The pretest determines whether the student needs to do the work in the package.
2. The rationale tells the student how this package fits into his learning and why he needs it.
3. The behavioral objectives let the student know exactly how he is to perform when he has completed the package, under what con-

Table IX.   LAP Classroom Arrangement

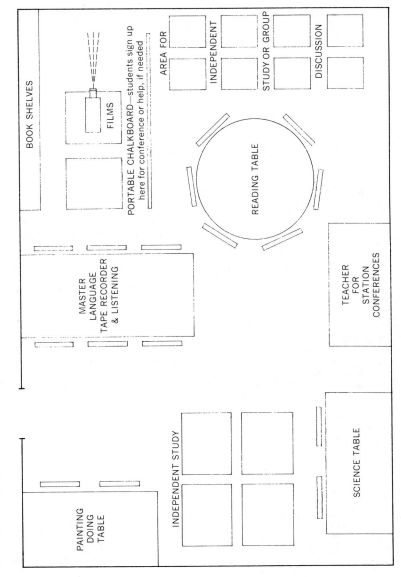

ditions he will perform and to what extent he must be able to perform in order to meet the objective.

4. The activities give the student a multi-media, multi-model approach to his learning so that every learning style will have an activity to accommodate it.

5. The self-evaluation allows the student to assess his learning and make adjustments himself. It enables him to make decisions, and to learn to live with decisions of his own making.

6. The post-test determines whether the student advances to the next section of LAP or is rechanneled by the teacher through the current one. No one who fails to meet the objective is considered a failure. He has not yet chosen those activities which enable him to learn. (Once again the words "within reason" are used. If the package is well written, and if the student's intelligence meets the minimum school standard, he will be able to meet the objective.) The LAP is designed to assure success. Success is the key to a positive self-concept.

7. The in-depth opportunity affords students who enjoy independent research the opportunity to continue in something they have found particularly meaningful. The teacher, by conferring with students, learns about them and their needs. His goal is for them to learn to work independently and to come to love learning.

Chapter 6 Bibliography

Bloom, Benjamin S., ed. *Taxonomy of Educational Objectives, Handbook I: Cognitive Domain.* New York: David McKay Co., Inc., 1956.

Bruner, Jerome S. *The Process of Education.* New York: Vintage Books, 1960.

Jones, Richard. "Learning Activity Packages: An Approach to Individualized Instruction," *Journal of Secondary Education* (April 1968) : 43:178–183.

Kapfer, Philip G. "An Instructional Management Strategy for Individualized Learning," *Phi Delta Kappan* (January 1968) : 49:260–263.

Krathwohl, David R., Bloom, Benjamin S., and Masia, Bertram B. *Taxonomy of Educational Objectives, Handbook II: Affective Domain.* New York: David McKay Co., Inc., 1964.

Mager, Robert F. *Preparing Instructional Objectives.* Palo Alto, Calif.: Fearon Publishers, Inc., 1962.

Talbert, Ray L. "A Learning Activity Package, What is It?" *Educational Screen and Audiovisual Guide* (January 1968) : 47:20–21.

Wolfe, Arthur B., and Smith, James E. "At Nova, Education Comes in Small Packages," *Nation's Schools* (June 1968) : 81:48–49.

Section Three

The Instructional Program, Part I

Overview

This section is not designed to be a prediction of what the instructional program of the 1980 middle school content areas will look like. Neither is it intended to provide a discussion of "how to teach" the various disciplines included here. Rather, it is simply a survey of what is being taught *now* in a typical middle school, the rationale behind it, and the questions that are being asked. To a very real extent, it is inaccurate since any description of a dynamic student and culturally oriented educational program, as the middle school should be, cannot describe "what is," only "what was." But this is the ideal; one needs only to compare the social studies program in our schools in 1920 and 1971 to know that there is much that is static (even stagnant), unfortunate as it may be, about our educational system.

The rationale underlying both this section and the next is that before you can realistically revise, change, create, or develop a "better" program you must understand the existing program thoroughly. Thus, the authors have described the existing content of the instructional areas in the hope that it will better prepare teachers to be the dynamic, autonomous, innovative individuals early adolescents need and deserve as their teachers.

Chapter 7
The English Language Arts

The modern English language arts curriculum, a composite of four broad areas, reading, writing, speaking, and listening, occupies a favored position in the schools. Most school districts and states require courses in English longer, and to a greater extent, than any other academic subject. Virtually all students are enrolled in language arts of one form or another through grades ten or eleven in the United States.

Frequently described as consisting only of literature, language, and composition, the English language arts actually include a wide range of subjects formerly taught as individual offerings. The academy, successor to the Latin Grammar School and precursor of the American public high school, offered an almost bewildering selection of subjects in the area of English language arts, such as:

Spelling	Writing	Penmanship
Composition	Declamation	Literature
Word Analysis	Word Study	Forensics
English Grammar	Debate	Elocution
Rhetoric	Punctuation	Semantics
Reading	Drama	Literary History

Slow to change, the English language arts have been in greater ferment in the past few years than in generations previous. Some innovations and suggestions have found ready acceptance while there has been community and academic resistance to others. Research has frequently been confusing or disappointing and too often there is no clearly defined path indicated. Indeed, it has been cynically observed that the proper attitude toward research will provide evidence for nearly any point of view.

Spelling

Accurate spelling is visible proof to many people of the amount and quality of education a person has had. Almost a status symbol, correct spelling may have a pronounced effect upon the individual's future, particularly when encountered in applications for a position or other openings of competitive selection.

English spelling lacks consistency in that a number of sounds may be represented by one letter, or a number of letters may represent the same sound. A classic example of this is the nonsense syllable, "ghoti," where "gh" represents the "f" sound in tough; "o" is the "i" sound in women; and "ti" is the "sh" sound of motion. "Ghoti" in this context spells "fish."

As a contrast, an examination of the Russian language, which has thirty-six symbols and thirty-four basic sounds, is about 90 percent efficient in its sound letter relationships, while English, which has 379 symbols for forty to forty-four basic sounds, is only about 20 percent efficient. Adding to the difficulties are the many sources and origins of the English language. It is no wonder that spelling becomes a frightening thing to so many people. The implications of this diversity in origin, sounds, and symbols for the teaching of spelling, as well as reading, are readily apparent.

Research in the teaching of spelling is not lacking although this is one area which has produced confusing and contradictory results. There is agreement, however, that better results are achieved with two or three short periods each week of fifteen to twenty minutes, rather than one weekly lesson. As much as the use of drill is decried, it appears that drill and memorization, combined with use, produces more growth in spelling.

Further, never underestimate the power of motivation. A factor in any kind of learning, motivation is of first importance in spelling. Literally, if a student decides that he really wants to become a better speller, he will very likely become a better speller.

To assist in developing student interest and the desire to improve one's spelling, one or more of the following may be useful:[1]

1. Help students to see that words are interesting; that they have personalities. It is often interesting to a class to discover the origin of words.

[1] J. N. Hook, *The Teaching of High School English*, 3rd ed. (New York: Ronald Press Company, 1965), pp. 353–354.

2. Demonstrate why spelling has become standardized. Have each student write a few sentences and spell each word phonetically; then exchange papers and attempt to read what others have written.
3. Show how much importance the community and employers place upon correct spelling.
4. Make correct spelling a challenge, a contest, even a game.
5. Praise improvement. This, of course, is useful in nearly every area of endeavor.

Time spent in studying spelling should be applied to words which the student uses. There is little value for the average student in learning to spell words which are seldom, if ever, encountered in his regular schooling.

The basic English vocabulary employs approximately 1,000 words while a list of about 2,500 words includes 95 percent of the average person's written vocabulary. These are the words which a student should be taught to spell. Since not all the words on these lists constitute problems, mastery of those which present difficulties, the spelling demons, should reduce spelling errors significantly. Lists of spelling demons may be compiled by students or classroom teachers; several such lists exist and are presently available.[2]

All students do not need the same amount of instruction and practice in spelling nor do all students have trouble with the same words. Ideally, each student would make up his own list of words which he needs to learn to spell; then he would study, learn, use, and write the words, and develop subsequent lists as he improves.[3]

A student is more likely to improve in spelling if these suggestions are followed:

1. Work on spelling two or three times weekly for fifteen to twenty minutes.
2. Motivate—help the students to see good reasons for learning to spell.
3. Make the words interesting.
4. Praise improvement.
5. Work toward student developed lists.
6. Be sure the student knows the correct pronunciation of the words.
7. Make use of phonetics where necessary and desirable.
8. Suggest and use several approaches to spelling problems.
9. Use words from "demon" lists as well as from class readings and discussions.

[2] "Spelling Report" available from National Council of Teachers of English.
[3] The work of R. Van Allen for Encyclopedia Britannica is particularly useful in this area.

10. Work for word visualization.
11. Develop spelling as a part of work in other subjects.
12. Keep spelling rules at a minimum.
13. Teach the words that are used.
14. Use spelling games for variety and interest.

Research and investigation in the teaching of spelling has, in many cases, produced contradictory results. Positive findings indicate that correct spelling requires drill and memorization, steady application, and that better results will be achieved with the individualized approach.

Reading

The Last Shall be First; and the First, Last

The early settlers in America instituted schools for the purpose of teaching their young to read. The development of the American school system has been rapid since that time, with stress applied to different skills at different times in history. The "Three R's" have become R, R, r: 'RITHMETIC, 'RITIN, and reading, for students who are enrolled in middle schools today.

Reading is still the fundamental skill which must be acquired by persons who desire to advance through the school system with any measure of academic success. Guy Bond and Miles Tinker make this point clearly in the introductory remarks of their text, *Reading Difficulties: Their Diagnosis and Correction:*[4]

> The ability to read well constitutes one of the most important skills a person can acquire. In fact, satisfactory adjustment to living in the complex modern world requires effective reading. Our world is a reading world. It is difficult to discover any activity, whether in school, in business, even in recreational pursuits and daily life, that does not require more or less reading in order to do it as well as it should be done.

These reading specialists estimate that 80 to 90 percent of all study activities in the typical high school require reading.

Further substantiation of the importance of reading is reflected in studies of the relationship of subject matter achievement to reading skill. Elden A. Bond states, "general reading comprehension is significantly related to achievement in each of the content areas except mathematics."[5]

[4] Guy L. Bond, and Miles A. Tinker, *Reading Difficulties: Their Diagnosis and Correction* (New York: Appleton-Century-Crofts, Inc., 1957), p. 53.
[5] Elden A. Bond, *Tenth Grade Abilities and Achievements* (New York: Bureau of Publications, Teachers College, Columbia University, 1940), p. 130.

James B. Conant, scientist and modern school critic, is unequivocal in his endorsement of the importance of reading: "I especially stress reading because pupils will not succeed in high school unless they can read at least at the sixth grade level. *The ability to read is imperative to success in secondary school.*"[6]

The importance of teaching reading in the middle school is present; however, instruction in reading in the school appears to be lacking in quality and quantity. The most noticeable deficiency is in the area of developmental reading—providing a program for students who, although progressing satisfactorily, could profit from additional help. Remedial reading, either within the framework of the regular class or in a special program, seems to be available to students who are reading two or more years below grade level.

Various estimates are given for the amount of reading retardation among middle school students. Preston states, "One-eighth of the seventh-grade pupils throughout the United States are functionally illiterate. This means that they read below the fifth grade level."[7] Statements such as this focus the attention of educators and of the American public on programs of remediation. When asked if his school has a reading program, almost every principal will give an affirmative answer and begin to explain his school's program for the student who is reading below grade level. Patient listening does not result in hearing many principals speak about their positive programs of developmental reading instruction designed to meet the needs of the average and above average student.

Research and Experimental Programs in Reading

Research studies of experimental programs in reading improvement make one thing clear: no matter what method is used in the experimental program, if the program is well organized gains in reading skill will result. These gains vary from three to fifteen months above the gains anticipated from normal development.

Eight weeks of lab instruction resulted in eight months' growth for Centinela Valley Union High School freshmen.[8] Summers reports "each of the intellectual ability level groups made significant gains from

[6] James B. Conant, *Recommendations for Education in the Junior High School Years* (Princeton, N. J.: Educational Testing Program, 1960), p. 21.

[7] Ralph C. Preston, "A Foreign Image of American Reading Instruction," *Reading Teacher* (December 1962): 16:158–162, p. 159.

[8] Edward G. Summers, "Evaluation of Reading Gains in a Secondary School Reading Laboratory," *Reading Teacher* (January 1964): 17:255–259, p. 256.

pretest to post-test scores after six weeks of instruction."[9] Both of these programs were laboratory experiences taking a block of time from the regular English class.

After conducting a modest program of fifty-five minutes a day three times a week for seventh graders, the following statement was made by Johnson and Howard: ". . . results seem to indicate that three hours a week of specific reading instruction is definitely worthwhile in the seventh grade."[10] Of interest in this study was the reported slight loss in reading skill of the very capable reader. This phenomenon was also reported by Bottomly in his study of the use of the Controlled Reader with eighth grade students in Spokane, Washington.[11]

The value of supervision in establishing systematic programs of developmental reading was reported by Sister Josephina.[12] The school principal met with teachers to assist them in the preparation of lesson plans. Supervisory conferences were held to work out improvements cooperatively. The result was an increase in reading skill which exceeded the expected rate.

Barry and Smith conducted experiments in 1951–52 and 1952–53 in an attempt to establish the value of different methods of teaching developmental reading. The 1951–52 experiment involved 473 ninth grade students. These students were divided into two equal groups. The series of fourteen State University of Iowa Reading Films was shown to the group; one group viewed one film per week, the other group saw two films per week. Students in both groups also read *Reader's Digest* timed articles and made graphs of their progress. The students in this experiment gained 8.5 months beyond expectations. In 1952–53 a larger experiment was conducted using 2,166 ninth graders in eight groups. Seven of the groups were instructed with varying combinations and quantities of the Iowa Reading Films and *Reader's Digest* articles. One group received only a pretest and a post-test. All eight groups gained from six to nine months beyond expectations. Students who ranked in the bottom one-quarter in reading ability gained the most from the instruction. No particular advantage was attributed to any of the eight methods and the researchers concluded:

> The experiments seem to imply that the critical factors in increasing reading ability of pupils are (1) the focusing of attention of the teacher on reading improvement of the pupils, and (2) the focusing of attention of each pupil on the possibility of his own self-improve-

---

[9] *Ibid.*, p. 258.

[10] Patricia Johnson, and Alvin W. Howard, "You Can Teach Reading," *Clearing House* (May 1960) : 34:545–546, p. 546.

[11] Forbes Bottomly, "An Experiment with the Controlled Reader," *Journal of Educational Research* (March 1951) : 54:265–269, p. 269.

[12] Sister C. S. J. Josephina, "The Role of Supervision in Improving Reading," *Elementary School Journal* (April 1965) : 65:375–380.

ment in reading. This may be accomplished through a systematic, planned procedure.[13]

All of the experiments summarized above may have profited from the Hawthorne effect. Nevertheless, the assertion that the reading level of middle school students can be raised markedly seems to be justified. What is necessary is a systematic program designed to result in higher reading levels for all youth.

Organization for Reading

The programs of reading which are being used in middle schools vary in quality from school to school and from district to district. One of the most obvious variations is the classification or naming system for the various parts of the reading program. The San Francisco Unified Schools name three kinds of reading which should take place in all classrooms: developmental, functional, and recreational.[14] Robert Karlin, in his book *Teaching Reading In High School,* defines the different phases of reading instruction as follows:[15]

Developmental reading is provided for students who can profit from additional help although they are progressing satisfactorily. Learning to read is a continuous process, the complexities of which are not completely resolved at any one stage of development.

Corrective reading is remedial-reading instruction given within the framework of the regular class.

Remedial reading instruction ordinarily is reserved for special teachers who work with the seriously handicapped.

Reading instruction as stated is noticeably weak in the developmental phase. This phase consists of three areas. Basic instruction in the fundamentals of learning to read is the first area. A great deal of attention is directed toward this area in the primary grades, but middle school teachers must realize that part of their time should be devoted to stressing this area. A second area of the developmental program consists of organized instruction in each content area. This instruction must be systematically conducted in all of the content areas in the middle school. Encouragement of personal and recreational reading is the third area of the program. Again, this is a responsibility of all classroom teachers in any school.

13 Robert F. Barry, and Paul E. Smith, "An Experiment in Ninth-Grade Reading Improvement," *Journal of Educational Psychology* (November 1964) : 45:407–414.

14 San Francisco Unified School District, *Reading Guide* (San Francisco: 1964).

15 Robert Karlin, *Teaching Reading in High School* (New York: Bobbs-Merrill Co., Inc., 1964), pp. 15–16.

Within the framework of the middle school, many systems of organization exist for teaching reading. One system assigns the primary responsibility for developmental reading to the English curriculum. Reading may be taught by the English teacher in her classroom as a regular part of the program or by a reading specialist for six to eight weeks in a reading laboratory. The laboratory method appears to be particularly suited to a situation where the English teacher lacks proficiency in teaching reading. The program thus serves as an in-service device while assisting students to develop their reading skill.

While the laboratory block-time method has proved successful and surely has much to recommend it, some disadvantages are present. Placing students in a special type of room for a special period of reading gives the impression that reading is an isolated skill. This method does not promote the attitude that reading is a continuous, sequential development process. Not only is the English teacher inclined to reduce the stress on reading during the remainder of the year, but also other subject matter teachers do not feel the need to teach reading during their class periods. A general atmosphere of satisfaction that reading instruction is being provided seems to prevail. A laboratory program with a concentration on developmental skills is an excellent *supplement* to the reading program. Under no circumstances should it be considered a *substitute* for reading taught by all teachers.

Another system of organization utilizes the skills of the reading specialist in a different way. In cooperation with the regular teacher, the specialist provides special help to students within the framework of the classroom situation. This may be done in small groups in a corner of the room, with individuals, or by periodically directing the attention of the entire class to a special aspect of reading improvement. The classroom teacher benefits from this program by receiving assistance in learning how to provide for individual differences and by learning teaching techniques for reading instruction. This system of organization requires a coordinated team approach. The advantage of using the special competencies of the reading specialist and the regular teacher is that reading is more likely to be seen as a year-long project for all teachers. The reading specialist's assistance should be utilized in the classrooms in all subject-matter areas. Scheduling problems may occasionally result but can be resolved with planning and coordination.

The developmental reading program may be organized around the services of a reading consultant. This system of organization places the responsibility for reading instruction in the hands of all classroom teachers. The consultant conducts demonstration lessons in class, small group and individual techniques, holds conferences with individual teachers, assists in the development of overall programs to assure continuous, systematic growth in reading skills, assists in the preparation of lesson plans; participates in parent-teacher conferences when a reading problem is present, and coordinates testing programs. Probably the most significant contribution of the reading consultant will be in the evaluation of the reading program. The involvement with each teacher provides many opportunities to stress the importance of reading in all subjects and to stimulate an interest in reading among the entire staff.

Whatever the system of organization may be, developmental reading instruction must be part of every classroom in every subject. Where concentrated effort, cooperatively planned, has been present, successful programs have resulted. A school principal who desires emphasis on reading in all classrooms must provide time and opportunities for teachers of different subject matter areas to meet and cooperatively plan a systematic program. Administrative support must then be given to providing in-service training and specialized assistance to put the program into operation. Particular attention should be devoted to programs of evaluation and maintenance. Many programs are conceived and put into operation, but die because of lack of support from the school administrator.

The duties of teachers in curriculum fields must include provision of optimum conditions for reading growth, promotion of growth in aspects of reading unique to the subject, and stimulation of interest in recreational reading. This means that every teacher should have training in the teaching of reading.

Problems of Reading in Content Areas

The following examples of the special kinds of problems of specific subjects are taken from seventh, eighth, and ninth grade texts. Textbooks in most subjects, other than English, are not graded in difficulty. If the books are graded in difficulty, the grading is based upon skill in the subject, not reading level. This is understandable because textbook writers are usually experts in their own field and do not possess special knowledge about reading difficulties.

Since students differ considerably in their ability to perform in different subjects, it is quite possible that students advanced in mathematics or science may be retarded in reading. If this is the case, errors in reading could result when the student encounters such similarities as *multiplication* and *multiplicative; radical, rational, radius, ratio;* and *commutative* and *cumulative*. A story problem based on the following advertisement appeared in a seventh grade arithmetic text: "Quarter Horse Auction Spurs Lively Bidding." A student reading at fourth grade level (and there are likely to be several in the classroom) may misread *Auction* as *Action* or may mispronounce *Lively* if he is sounding out the root word *live*. These may not be serious problems to the understanding of this particular story problem, but they cause discomfort to the youngster. The student who reads word by word may have difficulty understanding the following explanation: "To multiply a fraction by a fraction, we multiply the denominator to get the size of the new fractional unit and multiply the numerators to get the total number of equal parts." The following sentence from a science text requires reading and vocabulary skill in order to understand the scientific principle: "A concept of the molecule itself, in fact, demands the ability to conceive of something that is invisible and strangely intangible."

The above examples are not intended to be critical of textbook writers, but to illustrate the difficulties encountered by a student and his classroom teacher. Reading instruction must be part of every classroom.

Trends in Teaching Reading

Teaching methods and materials in the reading instructional program do not appear to be undergoing the revolution which is taking place in other subject matter fields. The use of teaching machines is not new in reading. Flash-meters (tachistoscopes), pacers, and films have been utilized for many years in remedial and developmental programs. After a careful review of the research on machines and reading, Karlin concluded:[16]

> In eleven of the twelve investigations which measured natural reading against machine reading, the groups that received training in the former either equaled or surpassed the machine group in rate of reading. From these data it can be said that outcomes in speed of reading similar to those achieved through the use of special instruments may be expected from suitable reading instruction which does not include these same instruments . . . it is reasonable to suggest from what information is presently available that perhaps the monies which might be spent for the purchase of reading machines be used for other purposes.

Perhaps great strides have been made since Karlin's 1958 study; if so, these advances were not reported in the current literature.

Likewise, programmed instruction has yet to be evaluated accurately to establish its value in teaching reading. After the standard arguments in support of programmed learning instruction have been presented, the fact remains that *learning to read* from a written program requires the *ability to read*.[17] Programmed learning instruction in reading appears to be a future, rather than a present, accomplishment.

Increased use of the paperback as a method of providing for individual needs in reading appears to be a widely accepted trend in the

[16] Robert Karlin, "Machines and Reading: A Review of Research," *Clearing House* (February 1958) : 32:349–352, p. 352.
[17] Jane Levine, "Let's Debate Programmed Reading Instruction," *Reading Teacher* (March 1963) : 16:337–341, p. 337.

field of reading. With the increased use of paperbacks in the classroom, a move has developed to increase the circulation of library books by using paperbacks. The difficulty of cataloguing and the necessity for display are factors reported as reasons for the resistance of many librarians to purchase paperbacks. Convincing arguments are advanced by Vincent Richards, Assistant Director, Fraser Valley Regional Library, Abbotsford, British Columbia, Canada, in support of library circulation of paperbacks. His article in *Revolution in Teaching* relates an experiment involving the purchase and circulation of 15,300 books (900 titles). The cost of these books was $5,000 or an average of 32.7 cents each. Because the books were not catalogued, the cost of making them ready for circulation was only an additional 7.3 cents each. He compares this total of forty cents per book to the average cost of adding one hardbound book of $3.60. The depreciation rate for paperbacks averaged four cents per issue with an average of ten issues before discarding. The hardbound book is expected to average thirty issues or twelve cents per issue. Circulation of the 15,300 books was 68,393 in six months. Six hundred and eleven were discarded; 2,000 useable books were donated. During the six months after paperbacks were purchased, adult circulation of all books was up 15 percent. Although paperbacks accounted for only 15 percent of the total bookstock, they accounted for 30 percent of the circulation.[18]

This experiment in paperbacks for libraries might well be used in middle school libraries. Individual differences can be accommodated at the same time reading interest is stimulated. An increased rate of recreational reading may well increase the overall reading skill of the students.

The presence of an adequate library and a skilled librarian are essential to a developmental reading program for the middle school. NEA and U. S. Office of Education surveys report particularly the absence of qualified librarians in today's schools. Increased emphasis on the library as a resource center is evident currently, but tremendous advances are necessary to effectively fill the needs of the developmental reading programs of middle schools.

Some work has been done to integrate the fields of linguistics and reading, but no concrete programs or evidence of exciting new trends was found in current periodical literature.

Project English is providing research into many phases of the task of teaching English; however, only three out of forty research project titles listed by Mensand[19] indicate a direct relationship to reading. The

[18] Vincent Richards, "The Cheap Paperback Is No Country Cousin," *Revolution in Teaching*, edited by Alfred deGrazia, and David A. Sohn (New York: Bantam Books, 1964), p. 150.

[19] Joseph Mensand, "The Secondary School Principal, The English Program, and Project English," *National Association of Secondary School Principals Bulletin* (February 1964) : 48:53–61.

University of Oregon Project English has the following stated purpose: "Improvement of the curriculum in language, literature (including reading), and written and oral composition in grades seven to twelve.[20] However, emphasis does not appear to be directed to teaching developmental reading in Project English.

One indication of emphasis put on a subject is found in state school and certification laws. Pennsylvania passed a law requiring all students to take a developmental or remedial course in reading during the seventh or eighth grade.[21] Professional preparation for the Basic Norm for junior high school teachers in Oregon includes at least one course in the teaching of reading. School District No. 4, Eugene, Oregon, directed that its junior high schools shall provide one-half hour per day of reading instruction for grades seven and eight.

"Surveys of the status of reading instruction in junior and senior high schools . . . are in general agreement that although new reading programs of some type are increasing, only a limited beginning has been made. Many such programs are remedial rather than developmental or both."[22] This quotation seems to sum up the state of innovations in the teaching of reading. The challenge which confronts teachers of reading is how to put to use in the classroom the knowledge gained from experimentation.

The increased demand for educational specialization seems to offer the possibility of increased difficulty in establishing "every teacher a teacher of reading" as a reality. Demands for inclusion of additional mathematics and science decreases the amount of time available for reading instruction. The school time devoted to foreign languages in the elementary and middle schools must come from somewhere. Even in the field of English, reading appears to be fighting a losing battle against composition, literature interpretation, transformational grammar, and other specific skills in the language arts. Some reintegration of the language arts program must be attempted. In addition, a realistic appraisal of the values attached to different subjects should be attempted. Is learning French or Spanish so important to a child who cannot read English?

Literature

In reading and in literature the trend is away from the deadening exposure to selections such as "Jump, Spot, jump," or our cheerful

[20] *Ibid.*, p. 55.

[21] Ruth Strand, and David M. Lindquist, "Progress in the Teaching of Reading in High School and College," *Reading Teacher* (December 1962): 16:170–177, p. 171.

[22] J. T. Hunt, "The Refinement of High School Reading Skills," *High School Journal* (April 1966): 49:307–313, p. 311.

friends, the postman and fireman. In this changed curriculum, information important to the comprehension of literature is gradually introduced within the elementary grades. Attention is paid to those qualities which give a selection literary value, such as imagery, allegory, and theme. In the effort to develop perception and critical thinking, it is important to go beyond asking questions which deal only with what a character does or what he was wearing.

This approach to literature, based upon the spiral curriculum proposed by Jerome Bruner, begins with the hypothesis that any subject can be taught effectively in some intellectually honest form to any child at any stage of development. In short, to learn the structure of a subject is to understand it in a way that permits meaningful relation to the subject of many other things. Terminology useful in discussing literature, background such as mythology and Biblical stories, and carefully chosen items from the vast field of literature are introduced to children at an early age. As the students grow older, they are given material which requires more from them.

The wise teacher realizes that the same piece of literature does not affect all students the same way. If we give any weight to teaching for individual differences and developing student ability to make wise choices, there must be pupil involvement in the selection of a part of the literature read. If a piece of literature is disliked by the students, it may be well to leave it for something else.

Students of this age frequently acquire an interest in a specific kind of writing. Often it is science fiction, adventure, stories of the out-of-doors, automobiles, or tales with teenage characters and problems. Teacher demands that such a concentration of interest be ended may lead to the student's refusal to read anything. It is better to bring in related stories or stories of a different nature by the same authors. In broadening student reading interests it is desirable to develop reading lists by teacher-pupil recommendation, planning, and selection.

In analyzing the literature taught it is worthwhile to ask why the selections have been made. Frequently something is taught because, "it is good for the students," or, "This is what we were taught," or, "I have always liked this." What we teach can find justification in reasons; one frequently stated is to transmit the cultural heritage. But who is to determine which literary selections best serve this function? Should all Americans be familiar with *Evangeline, Silas Marner,* or *Life on the Mississippi?* Lacking a national curriculum, teacher choices differ with the result that there is little conformity. Too, there is the possibility that literature will become a study of literary history involving intensive analysis of relatively few classics.

Students read also for knowledge. The information is more than that afforded by reference books; it relates to how other people have felt, how they reacted, and their human strengths and weaknesses. It is Macbeth's deterioration of character that is important and the fact that "Brutus is an honorable man."

In reading for pleasure a whole new world opens to the students; there are many worlds. The fantasy of Jules Verne and H. G. Wells, the adventure of Stevenson and Masefield, and the enjoyment found in the poetry of Frost and Poe take us places and open doors which might otherwise not have been found.

The insights and understandings afforded by a well-planned program in literature begin their development in the early elementary school, continuing and expanding throughout one's life.

In view of this it may be seen why increasing stress is being placed upon the need for an individualized literature program which will encourage the development of the reading habit, improve the reading taste of each student, and attempt to meet individual needs, abilities, and interests. At the same time, the students should read some literature as a class, for example, to introduce a unit, to acquaint the class with a type of literature, or to have the whole group enjoy a reading selection together.

Such an approach, which permits all students to acquire the same broad fundamental knowledge plus specifics in terms of ability and interest, should reduce or eliminate the situation in which the teacher of English finds that he can never assume that a student knows any one particular story or literary selection.

In the past, instruction in literature has concentrated upon analysis and literary history. Considerable emphasis has been placed upon a coldly surgical dissection of each literary selection over which a class has agonized. Compounding the difficulty has been the lack of general instruction in fundamentals coupled with the wide variety of selections chosen by different teachers with differing preferences. This is not to say that the students do not know anything—just that they do not know what they know, and what they do know varies widely.

In planning the literature for a course or period of time there are several possible arrangements or combinations of arrangements that may be used, each having its advantages and disadvantages.

Literature may be arranged chronologically, which permits an orderly development but often tends to present the least interesting (to the students) literature first. This arrangement may also become a course in literary history and as such may tend to slight modern literature or literary styles.

Literature may be arranged by types, a method which permits easy combination with other plans but tends to restrict continuity and limit understanding of the development of literature.

The thematic approach, in which literature is arranged by units and themes frequently around student experiences, has been found most satisfactory for the early teens, particularly for grades seven, eight, nine, and ten. This permits broad selection and coverage in accord with student interests but it requires unusually able teachers to direct the study, maintain student interest, and prevent the tendency toward student laziness which independent work may allow. Ideally, the thematic approach stimulates a perceptive analysis of the theme as it relates to the literature or of the literature in its relation to the theme.

In developing, for example, the theme of "Courage," it is possible to use a wide range of material from *Kon-Tiki* to *The Red Badge of Courage*. Students may come to realize that there are many kinds of courage and these may be exemplified by both real or imaginary events which deal with man's feelings, thoughts, and experiences. In this approach, selection of literary pieces is made on the basis of those that have something to say and say it clearly. There is room for writers both old and new, including current writing not of a classic nature.

Whether taught in English language arts classes, Social Studies classes, or a block-time class, some attention needs to be given to the mass media. Time should be allowed for examination of the use of newspapers, periodicals, radio, television, and moving pictures. Indeed, with proper planning and timing, the teacher can take advantage of and make successful use of current mass media in the daily work. Since these materials are with us always and increasing rapidly in quantity and technology, it becomes more important that students are trained in selection, interpretation, and appreciation of such forms of literary expression.

Of increasing importance in the teaching of literature is the extensive availability of inexpensive paperback books in virtually every community in the country. Many, it is true, are unadulterated trash. Yet there are 300 to 400 million paperbacks produced and sold annually in North America, including more than 30,000 titles, a distinct percentage of which are excellent literary selections, both classic and modern. Colorful covers, ease of carrying, comparatively low cost, and the lack of a "textbook look," are all factors tending to lend desirability to consideration of expanded use of paperbacks. A paperback will usually cost less than one-fifth of what the same book will cost in a hard cover and, in library issue, will last at least one-third as long. The advantages to a school English language arts program are obvious. With the same amount of money available, the range, number, and variety of selections is vastly multiplied.

Changes are currently taking place in the approach to teaching literature. Terminology useful in discussing literature is being introduced in the early grades along with carefully chosen selections in a planned sequence. This curriculum spirals upward and outward, providing an ever increasing range of material at an ever increasing level of maturity. Selections chosen because "they are good for you," or because of past use and tradition are required to prove their value. Literary works, both old and new, are included.

In the individualized program considerable emphasis is placed upon the participation of the student in the selection process and upon the efforts to correlate with student interests, background, and experiences. Selections are aimed at developing thought, reflection, and analysis.

Composition

When we teach literature we are exposing students to experiences, thoughts, feelings, and arguments. Proficiency in writing requires more than freedom from errors; it requires thinking, organization, and composing. It is necessary to emphasize content, to have something to say.

Students of the middle grades are much inclined to write about the imaginary and romantic, feeling that their own experiences, thoughts, and feelings are not worth putting on paper. If a class should be writing a description of a house, the early teenager will, on the first try, more often than not devote much time and little imagination to a description of a haunted house (something it is doubtful that any of them have ever seen) rather than his own house.

As the child's interests change so should those things about which he writes. Too often writing is bogged down by a standard assignment in which the student outlines his composition, selects his topic sentences, develops the paragraphs, and hands in his effort. When it is returned with numerous "red gashes" and "wounds," he takes one corrective mechanical step after another, "polishing up" his effort.

Organization is important—more than that—essential to good writing. Of equal importance is perception and critical thinking. There is a distinct loss of student interest and original thinking when the larger part of student effort is devoted to mechanical production, revision, and resubmission, often three or four times, of the same piece of writing.

One study at a major university established a faculty committee representing several departments to examine the prevalence of substandard writing among undergraduates. This committee studied the term papers and examinations of fifteen hundred undergraduates. The most conclusive finding was that good writers tend to be those concerned with organization and with the problems involved in forming relationships. The poor writers are those concerned primarily with mechanics.

This leads one to wonder whether those teachers who have placed heavy reliance upon work with spelling, punctuation, and vocabulary in short, emphasized writing rather than composition—have aggravated this situation.

Arguing for expository rather than creative writing is pointless. Assignments in composition should include creative writing, exposition, description, narration, and argumentation. Whatever is assigned should fall within the planned sequence and should not be a hurried, last minute topic thrown at the class just before the end of the period.

A good assignment is one which provokes thought and elicits a response that is based upon discovery. It begins with some information or a proposition that is supplied. It requires reflection. One might present two conflicting statements such as, "He who hesitates is lost," and "Fools step in where angels fear to tread," and let the students interpret, oppose the statements, or defend one or the other. An assignment such as "My Most Embarrassing Moment," or "What I Did Last Summer," provides little, if any, mental exercise and increases the number of students who dislike writing.

Good assignments are varied. Some topics will fall in a planned sequence, others will be added as daily work permits random choice. Provision should be made for interspersing expository with creative writing, and argumentation and description with these. An assignment which compares two makes of automobiles, two candidates for office, or opposing views on any civic issue presents opportunities for analysis of the effect of emotional arguments as opposed to factual. It is easy to point out the importance of organization and the need for precision and clarity of presentation in this kind of writing.

The closer the subject to the student, the better the results will be. Children usually find it difficult to believe that anyone will be interested in what they have to say about themselves. Asked to describe a room, they frequently let their imaginations run wild with the result that their compositions are nonsense. One way around this is to require that they write a description of the way their kitchen (or living room) makes them feel. Strive for comparisons which are different. Avoid "Our kitchen is about eight feet by ten feet." Help students to find words which really say what they want to say. In an effort to improve their writing by the use of modifiers, students will say that, "It was an impressive sight." Why? What does "impressive" mean? If the child can explain how and why this is impressive, what makes it impressive, he probably will not even use the word impressive. In the same context, children feel safer with phrases such as, "A beautiful view," or "A lovely place." What makes this view "beautiful"? Why is this "a lovely place"? Meaning, understanding, and communication are enhanced by the proper use and selection of words.

Humpty Dumpty, you will recall, remarked that when he used a word, it meant just what he chose it to mean, neither more nor less. He went on to say that it was only a question of who was to be the master. Children can enjoy learning to master words, to make words say what the writer wants to say.

A thorough approach to composition requires work in organizing and developing paragraphs. Proper paragraph construction involves instruction in sentence structure, usage, and logical thinking. A good composition, and this is what a properly written paragraph is, displays unity, coherence, and emphasis. With the growth in ability to write paragraphs, the student learns to put paragraphs together and produces longer compositions, themes.

In organizing the theme, some form of outline can be valuable. The danger in using outlines is that of permitting the outline to become the important result of composition instead of an aid to the completed writing. A short theme of only a few paragraphs may easily require no outline or a short informal outline. Longer compositions will be more easily written and better organized if the plan for the theme, the outline, is carefully written.

The discovery approach, the inductive method, is being used more and more in English composition. More stress has been placed upon the need for students to write well. Sometimes this recognition of the importance of student writing skill has led to the production of quantity instead of quality themes.

Certain other trends are becoming apparent:

1. Increased emphasis on organized sequential instruction concerning specific processes and principles of composition as contrasted with unsequential programs which merely require much writing. The writing begins at the primary level, continues in the upper grades and later.

2. Greater interest in the teaching of composition in the upper elementary grades, rather than exclusive emphasis on writing experiences alone.

3. Greater emphasis on expository writing in the upper secondary grades.

4. More frequent, brief writing assignments of paragraph length or so.

5. Recognition that the traditional book report violates every principle of sound composition taught elsewhere in the program, that it forces students to string together a series of virtually unrelated paragraphs (on setting, on plot, on most interesting incident, etc.), and thus seriously undercuts the composition program being developed elsewhere. In its place, more and more teachers are substituting something which might be called a book review, where students, like professional reviewers, are asked to develop a single idea expressed in each book and to organize their comments around this theme.

If composition is properly taught, the students will be able to express themselves with a reasonable degree of clarity, communication skills will have been developed, and thinking power will have been increased. Writing need not be the fearsome thing that so many students consider it to be.

Grammar

To begin with, the term grammar, as such, has at least two quite different meanings. In one definition, it refers to a series of recommendations prescribing a body of specific usages; in the other definition, it is an attempt to describe the structure of language by means of terminology and a series of concepts which have come down to us from the Greeks and Romans. In the past there has been a heavy concentration on grammar in the study of language, chiefly because of the attention devoted to the classical languages rather than the language popularly used. Interest in the classical languages declined, but the grammar remained, applied now to teaching students how to speak and write in English. The rules derived largely from languages of a static nature have been adopted as the prescription for an ever-changing, dynamic language.

In its prescriptive aspect, classroom instruction and usage employed a form of the language which became a prestige dialect used in the presence of the English teacher and chiefly remembered by its students for the linguistic prejudices it created. With prescriptive grammar goes the concept of prescriptive correctness, distinctions which are clear and readily identified between right and wrong in English usage. Unfortunately, these rules have never presented a true picture of usage, even by the best writers.

Following rules of grammatical analysis, students are taught to recognize and use a terminology of instruction which begins in the elementary grades and is repeated at intervals throughout their schooling. Grammar and language are thus equated—an artificial situation. Compounding the confusion is the fact that experts in English recognize at least four major varieties of English grammar.

That which is usually called *traditional* grammar uses terminology based upon Latin and treats English as if it were Latin. References are frequently made to methods of achieving purity in English, rules are established for all users of the language, and all is evaluated as correct or incorrect. Traditional grammar spends a gread deal of time on sentence analysis, drill on word forms, memorization of terminology, and day after day of exercises designed to demonstrate what is "correct," and, therefore, "right." As a part of this, although vaguely differentiated, is added the study of punctuation, spelling, and capitalization.

Historical grammar is chiefly concerned with the history of English and its relationship to other languages. Historical grammar has had little effect upon classroom instruction except as it has contributed somewhat to the history of the language.

Structural linguistics operates from three main assumptions:
1. Since written language is based upon spoken language, study of the spoken form is especially important.
2. It is important in describing language that form and meaning be separated.

3. In this form of grammar the chief function is the description of language, not an evaluation of what is right or wrong.

In *transformational* grammar the emphasis is placed upon the ways in which new sentences are generated. Exact rules and formulas resembling those used in mathematics are applied to sentence construction in an effort to explain the transformation of the active voice into the passive.

Probably the best grammar is an eclectic approach which uses contributions made by each kind of grammar, choosing from each what is most useful in making clear a point, and teaching what students need most. This requires a minimum of taking apart the sentences in the exercise books and increased efforts to encourage thought and arrive at conclusions inductively.

Too many teachers have felt that they could teach language arts from the security of a direct and objective approach as may be used with history or mathematics. Memorization and drill in rules and definitions conceives of grammar as a static thing. The teacher has the child for only a part of each day and attempts to convince the student that much of the way he speaks and writes is wrong and bad. The child knows that what he hears, learns, and uses at home, on the playground, on television, and in his daily life is real. People understand him and he can communicate with them even though his communication is flavored by the usage with which he has become familiar.

Wherever possible, instruction should be individualized. Since the purpose of all instruction in grammar is to improve the student's communication skills, ideally the program is keyed to the needs of each student. This is generally difficult to achieve in these days of burgeoning enrollments and increased emphasis upon written work with the attendant increase in the number of papers to be corrected.

It is sometimes surprising when we find how many children cannot put together a noun and a verb to form a simple sentence. An easy way to begin instruction in sentence structure is to start with a thing or a name, as, "the dog," or "Mary," and ask the class to tell, in one word, several things which the dog or Mary did. Explain that the class is constructing simple sentences, "The dog barks," and "Mary laughs," and that all sentences must have a subject and a verb. Develop this method and substitute pronouns for subjects. Soon the class will be using direct objects, indirect objects, compound subjects, and compound verbs.

Avoid over emphasis upon diagramming. This can be very wasteful if it is used only to identify the components of sentences made up by others although it may have some value in helping students to construct sentences of their own. Diagramming does impart an ephemeral sense of security to many teachers of English, but it frequently becomes a pointless debate concerning which line goes where, and at what angle.

Whenever possible assignments should be of paragraph length or longer. However, there will be occasions when it will be desirable to use shorter assignments for the purpose of making and illustrating a point or to reinforce and practice what has been discussed in class. Such an assignment should be specific and require student thought. For example, a list of five to ten colorful verbs may be presented which are to be used as a part of an exciting story. Logically, picturesque and vivid modifiers should be brought in as a part of this writing. The entire effort should require planning and organization by the students. These exercises should be directed toward helping children to construct sentences rather than dissect and analyze sentences created by others.

A survey of current thinking about the teaching of grammar includes the following:

1. Grammar is not a set of rules but a description of usage.
2. Grammar for American schools should be based upon American English usage. There are different levels of usage and some are more appropriate in some situations than others. It follows that students should become aware of polite usages.
3. It is not necessary to study grammar to learn any language. Small children learn to communicate without formal grammar instruction. Memorization of grammatical rules is of little value.
4. In providing a terminology grammar may have some use for describing and teaching.
5. Grammar should be taught functionally. Inducing the rules from what one knows and discovers of usage is more valuable than trying to learn proper usage from a set of rules.

Perhaps the most difficult part to treat of the language arts curriculum is the study of grammar. The great majority of teachers were themselves taught a system of prescribed rules and definitions which had historical approval and little else to recommend it. Changes in the study of teaching of grammar are taking place although structural linguistics and transformational grammar are, as yet, not widely accepted nor taught in the public schools.

Children should learn the grammatical terminology in activities that have meaning to them rather than in isolated drill work, and the application of grammatical knowledge should be continual instead of the intensive but sporadic drills and reviews which seem to be so common.

Project English

Project English, begun in 1961 by the U. S. Office of Education, involves a coordinated attempt to improve instruction in English on all levels. It began with the belief that the English curriculum requires a concept, a basic program in English that is sequential and cumulative from kindergarten to and including college. English is regarded as a discipline in its own right, not a catch-all for whatever is rejected by other disciplines nor for content matter given to the teacher of English because it conceivably touches remotely upon some aspect of language arts.

In consultation with organizations and groups such as the Modern Language Association, the College English Association, the National Council of Teachers of English, organizations of principals, administrators, supervisors, and librarians, the U. S. Office of Education made long-range plans to develop a cumulative, sequential language arts curriculum. A prominent aspect of this curriculum is the stress placed upon the interrelationship of literature, language, and composition.

One feature of Project English is the funds available for research studies. Through colleges, universities, or state educational agencies, individuals or groups may present proposals for research that indicate possibilities of contributing to the instruction in English at any level. These studies have examined teachers, textbook materials, teacher training, and pupil learning.

Project English is also concerned with conferences and seminars dealing with needed research in teaching English, such as studies in reading and summaries of research in reading and studies of curricular offerings in English in public schools, colleges, and universities.

Several curriculum study centers have been established across the nation to develop sound patterns for sequential teaching of skills and content in reading, in language, in composition, and in worthwhile materials. The curriculum sequence is based upon both subject matter and what is known of child growth and development. The centers test promising materials and practices, make recommendations concerning curriculum, and develop materials for systematic instruction.

The Oregon Curricular Study Center developed a curriculum in language, literature, composition, and speech for grades seven through twelve. Seven school systems cooperated in this project, opening their classrooms to the testing of new text materials and sending their teachers to training workshops. They assumed that there are two aims of the English curriculum: to improve student control of the basic skills of communication, and to give students command of a body of subject matter—language and literature. It was further assumed that the skills and the subject matter are mutually complementary, and instruction in both is closely coordinated.

The six-year language curriculum consists of the study of transformational grammar, social variations in language, the history of writing systems, the history of the English language itself, and the nature of language.

The literature curriculum focuses on three concepts considered to be basic: the subject, that is, any work of literature must be about something; the form, the author must adopt a particular style; and the point of view the author indicates. One advantage of this plan is that it provides the basis for a really sequential curriculum in literature. These three principles may be examined in very simple selections as well as those which are complex. Another advantage is that the attention of both teacher and student is continually attracted to the literary work itself as a work of art.

Florida State University had as its project the development and testing of three sequential English curricula for grades seven, eight, and nine. A fundamental assumption at Florida State was that there is a new English which is new in concept content, scope, and the learning process. Content of the new English was held to include literature, English linguistics, and rhetoric. English language was studied as content in itself and all versions of grammar, traditional, transformational, and structural are included as well as other aspects of English linguistics such as phonology, usage, semantics, dialects, and varieties of English.

Attention was paid to the development of thematic units which represent concern with four basic human relationships: man and deity; man and other men; man and nature; man and himself. Six thematic categories were established: Man in Action; The Unknown; Decisions; Teamwork; Frontiers and Horizons; and Human Relations. Literature was central to this curriculum but language study was also involved.

At the Curriculum Study Center at Northwestern University, emphasis was placed upon investigation of the study of teaching of composition from grade seven to the college sophomore level. The program in composition was related to reading and language study in accord with the belief that the approach to English language arts is a study of literature, composition, and communication skills.

These changes in the teaching and content of English language and arts are having an impact upon instruction in the public schools. This impact will become more noticeable as teachers trained in these new curricula become more numerous.

What is happening in the English curriculum may not be a breakthrough but it is certainly a step in the evolution of instruction in English language arts. Behind all teaching and learning of English should be the importance of a fundamental approach and understanding as to what is literature, language, and communication—both written and oral. In the attempts to reach the reality of the concept, the new approaches in English seem to revolve around three ideas: the inductive teaching and learning of English, the attempt to establish cumulative steps in the English curriculum, and the importance of literature, language, and communication as basic and interrelated parts of one discipline.

Chapter 7 Bibliography

Bamman, Henry A., Hogan, Ursula, and Greene, Charles F. *Reading Instruction in the Secondary School.* New York: Longmans, Greene, and Co., Inc., 1961.

Betts, Emmett Albert. "Structure in the Reading Program," *Elementary English* (March 1965): 42:238–242.

Broenig, Angela M. "Development of Taste in Literature in the Senior High School," *The English Journal* (April 1963): 52:273–287.

Cawley, John F., Chaffin, Jerry, and Brunning, Herbert. "An Evaluation of a Junior High School Reading Improvement Program," *Journal of Reading* (October 1965): 9:26–29.

College Entrance Examination Board's Commission on English, *Freedom and Discipline in English.* New York: College Entrance Examination Board, 1965.

Commission on the English Curriculum of the National Council of Teachers of English, *The English Language Arts in the Secondary School.* New York: Appleton-Century-Crofts, Inc., 1956.

DeGrazia, Alfred, and Sohn, David A. *Revolution in Teaching.* New York: Bantam Books, 1964.

Fries, Charles C. "Linguistics and the Teaching of Reading," *Reading Teacher* (May 1964): 17:594–598.

Gaver, Mary Virginia. "What Research Says About the Teaching of Reading and the Library," *Reading Teacher* (December 1963): 17:184.

"Growing Pains in Grammar," *The English Journal* (April 1958): 47: entire issue.

Hall, Robert A., Jr. *Linguistics and Your Language.* Garden City, N. Y.: Doubleday and Co., Inc., 1960.

Heath, Robert, ed. *New Curricula.* New York: Harper and Row, Publishers, 1964.

Hook, J. N. *The Teaching of High School English,* 3rd ed. New York: Ronald Press Co., 1965.

Lefevre, Carl A. "A Comprehensive Linguistic Approach to Reading," *Elementary English* (October 1965): 42:651–659.

Mensand, Joseph. "The Secondary School Principal, The English Program, and Project English," *National Association of Secondary School Principals Bulletin* (February 1964): 48:53–61.

Squire, James R., and Hogan, Robert F. "A Five-Point Program for Improving the Continuing Education of Teachers of English," *National Association of Secondary School Principals Bulletin* (February 1964): 48:1–17.

Chapter 8

Social Studies

The disciplines usually included in the social studies in the secondary schools are history, geography, political science, economics, sociology, anthropology, civics, problems of democracy, psychology, and philosophy. Social studies is a descriptive term for these subjects whose content is concerned with human relationships and which include man's relation to his environment, its effect upon him, and what he has done to influence and change such effects and environment.

In a general way it may be said that the purpose of the curriculum in social studies is to develop good citizens and to ensure the preservation of American democracy and our way of life. Frequently, other statements are listed as purposes of the social studies curriculum, including such varied contributions as:

1. To impart a body of factual knowledge.
2. To develop critical thinking.
3. To train our children to make wise decisions.
4. To learn and use a methodology of inquiry.
5. To transmit the cultural heritage.
6. To become aware of the range of human values.
7. To further the growth of attitudes and understandings needed for good citizenship in today's world.
8. To achieve maximum growth and development of the individual.

Recent interest in revision of the social studies curriculum has pointed up the confusion which exists regarding instruction in these areas. Not only is the emphasis different from one school to another, but different teachers cover different topics, subjects, and areas in "social studies," the method of teaching varies widely, and even the school organization may, by prescribing core, or block, or departmentalization, compound the confusion.

The Changing Social Studies Curriculum

Essentially the present social studies curriculum is obsolete; it has remained basically unchanged since the early 1900s. Up to the end of the nineteenth century, the components of social studies were taught as separate, though narrow, disciplines, usually history and geography. Thus, the present social studies curriculum, both in terms of content and organization patterns, is a product of the past and an outgrowth of numerous influences. Among these influences are our philosophies of education, the needs of our communities, social and political forces, the desires and goals of pupils and parents, and the work of various national committees of education. The work and reports of these national committees of education have been vital in shaping our present day social studies curriculum.

The first of these reports was that of the Committee of Ten of the National Education Association which was published in 1893. This committee was formed for the purpose of organizing conferences on various subjects or groups of subjects within the secondary curriculum. The Committee of Ten decided to streamline the curriculum by reducing the number of subjects. For example, physical geography was grouped with natural history, out of which grew general science, while political geography was merged with history. Those who decry the lack of geography in the schools today can likely blame the Committee of Ten for its rather arbitrary decision. In any case, geography all but disappeared from the high school curriculum. It should be noted that the Committee of Ten included bits and pieces of economics, civics, and geography in the history courses; in this fusion lies the probable beginning of the social studies. The Committee of Ten specifically recognized the terminal role of the high school, but in spite of this, recommended that all students should study college preparatory subjects. The humanistic and mental disciplinary ideals and the college preparatory concept function as reflected by the philosophies of the committee members, dominated the program which was recommended by the Committee of Ten.

A series of conferences was organized by the committee, one of which was devoted to history, civil government, and political economy.

Meanwhile, the American Historical Association formed a Committee of Seven to study the history curriculum in American schools. The committee's report of 1899 apparently influenced high school history teaching for many years. The report advocated ancient history, modern European history, English history, and United States history. A later committee recommended separate history courses in the elementary schools that would teach respect for life and property, health, and government. Again, there was emphasis on a broad curriculum. The work of this committee proved to be much more influential than that of the Committee of Ten and presented a series of statements concerning the value of historical study. The need for adequately trained teachers, college entrance requirements, sources, and the use of textbooks were also mentioned in the recommendations of this committee.[1]

The emphasis and demand was on the practical in the early part of the twentieth century. High school enrollment doubled each decade. The inadequacy of the high school curriculum to cope with the expanding number of students resulted in the establishment of the Commission on the Reorganization of Secondary Education Committee on Social Studies by the National Education Association in 1916. This committee submitted a report recommending (1) the one-year course in European or world history on the tenth grade level, (2) problems of democracy—social, economic, and political, and (3) a one-year course in American history. The existence of the junior high school was recognized by the report which recommended a course sequence for the junior high school that included geography, United States history, and civics. These subjects were to be correlated, integrated, or fused. It should be remembered that at this time a junior high education was terminal for a large proportion of American youth.[2]

This National Education Committee went on to attack the recommendations of the Committee of Seven as being based on the naive assumption that all students finished high school and, therefore, completed the full series of courses recommended by the Committee of Seven. Such assumptions, said the NEA, were fallacious; a great many students did not complete high school, and there should, for this reason, be two cycles in the social studies: in grades seven, eight, and nine there should be geography, civics, European history, and American history;[3] a new course, "Problems in Democracy," was to be presented to grades ten, eleven, and twelve. This new problems course, in drawing materials from the spectrum of the social sciences, particularly economics, government, and sociology,

[1] Committee of Seven, *The Study of History in the Schools: Report to the American Historical Association* (New York: 1899).

[2] Dorothy M. Fraser, and Edith West, *Social Studies in Secondary Schools: Curriculum and Methods* (New York: Ronald Press, 1961), pp. 374-375.

[3] National Education Association, *The Social Studies in Secondary Education* (Washington: 1916).

. . . marked the movement into 'social studies' as a unified (if confused) subject and began the drift away from the disciplines.[4]

In 1918, this commission attempted to redefine the role of the secdary school and a new concept of secondary education, as expressed in the report of the Seven Cardinal Principles of Education, provided a much broader view of the role of the secondary school than the narrow program of college preparatory studies advocated by the Committee of Ten in 1893. Thus, in theory, the secondary school was committed to providing a broad education to a relatively large segment of the population in America. The report of the Commission on the Reorganization of Secondary School Education, 1918, has been widely accepted as a statement of general aims for junior and senior high schools. It held that education in this country should be guided by a clear and distinct conception of the meaning of democracy. Each individual within our society should be given the opportunity to develop his knowledge, interests, ideals, habits, and powers to the greatest degree possible. The seven cardinal principles or objectives of the commission attempted to draw up a blueprint which purported to accomplish these ends.

There has been no comprehensive revision of the social studies curriculum since that following the report of the Commission of Secondary School Education in 1918. Since the report of the seven cardinal principles the many reports by the national committees down through the years have been mainly a restatement of these educational goals. There has been a continuing interest in the social studies, however, and a great deal of experimentation in the social studies programs on the individual and state levels. The societal stresses resulting from rapid social and economic changes in the twenties and thirties had an inevitable impact on the social studies program in the secondary schools, now clearly institutions for mass education.

Largely because of the recommendations of the Commission on the Reorganization of the High School, the social studies curriculum still follows the cyclic pattern in most American school districts. The assumption is that an introduction to the different social studies is given to children in elementary school, and that the understandings and concepts are then strengthened and extended by a second presentation of the subjects, in deeper and more difficult levels, in junior and senior high schools.

A common sequence in the cycles places geography in grade four, American history in grade five, and aspects of European history in grade six. Similarly, the courses most frequently offered in grade seven are world geography, American history-geography, and Amer-

[4] Robert W. Heath, *The New Curricula* (New York: Harper and Row, Publishers, 1964), p. 198.

ican history; in grade eight are American history, American history-state history, and American history-civics; and in grade nine, civics, world geography, world history, and state history-civics.[5]

Since the commission recommendations of 1916, 1917, and 1918, there has been little new of value added and little of the old dropped. The American Historical Association and its Commission on the Social Studies published a series of seventeen volumes between 1932 and 1942 in which the Commission designated as major goals for social studies, the creation of socially sound personalities in children, and the achievement of a model society. Nothing in the way of practical suggestions or materials ensued.

There have been changes in society and knowledge, in attitudes and in social responsibility without any corresponding changes in the social studies curriculum in the American schools. Most schools disregard or treat lightly the non-western world. Topics and areas that are difficult and controversial are usually avoided. There is but small attention given to Economics and Sociology and even less to Anthropology and Psychology.

The subject matter that comprises today's social studies is presented in highly sanitized textbooks intended to offend no conceivable interest group; chiefly in a read-recite quiz manner calculated to reinforce both its inanity and its short term retention. . . . Students characteristically regard social studies as a crashing bore.[6]

After a decade of concentration in the physical sciences, however, American scientific achievements made it possible to expand the narrow focus of concern and to evaluate the reshaping enterprise from a less emotional perspective. What has emerged is a realization that we are, as individuals and as a nation, confronted with intensely significant new needs, needs largely insoluable in the scientific laboratory. Harris Dante describes the challenge in this way:

Today we are faced with problems of a nuclear age, with new responsibilities of world leadership . . . ; as well as with great national issues related to education; to the working of our economic system and to the despoiling of the environment. There is also the need to catch up after one hundred years of neglect of the Negro and other minority groups . . . the social studies are destined to play an important part in overcoming these and other problems.[7]

[5] Willis D. Moreland, "Curriculum Trends in the Social Studies," *Social Education* (February 1962) : 26:74–75.

[6] Franklin Patterson, "Social Science and the New Curriculum," in Alfred DeGrazia, and David Sohn, *Revolution in Teaching* (New York: Bantam Books, 1964), p. 289.

[7] Harris L. Dante, "The Social Studies Face the Future," *High School Journal* (October 1965) : 49, 1:30–37. By permission of the publisher, University of North Carolina Press, Chapel Hill, N. C.

In 1962, the U. S. Office of Education gave formal recognition to the increasing agitation for a systematic evaluation and reworking of the social studies by initiating the Social Science Program. This federal support stimulated widespread involvement in curriculum development. Not only have the traditional centers of curricular concern become involved in explorative and developmental efforts, but scholars from the social sciences, universities, foundations, researchers in the behavioral sciences, and many special interest groups have actively sought a part in the change process.

Out of the work of these groups has come a consensus that change, approximating that experienced by the science curricula, is imperative; that much of the antique content and methodology of the social studies is inadequate for meeting the needs of today's youth. James Becker, representing a common viewpoint, argues for change by pointing to two significant phenomena: First, there has been a vast expansion of important content, a result largely of changes taking place in the social science disciplines—history, economics, sociology, anthropology, political science, and psychology. Second, arising in part from the first, there is a recognized inadequacy in instructional methodology.[8]

One of the first serious attempts to bring about a program for evaluating and redefining the social studies was made by Howard E. Wilson. In his address to the annual meeting of the National Council for the Social Studies in 1958, he supported his thesis for a national curriculum by describing what he saw as the typical nature of curriculum-making:

> The history of curriculum-making in the social studies has been characterized by unilateral effort—first the historians, then the educators, and in more recent years state or local committees of teachers. In each case the responsible group saw clearly a part but not all of the job to be done. Historians, for example, could not know the contributions of other social sciences as well as their own. Educators could see clearly the broad goals to be achieved by the schools, but underestimated the contributions which the various disciplines could make to education. Teachers knew much about children's interests and how they learn, but could not possibly be experts in all fields of social studies, including behavioral studies, psychology, and measurement.[9]

Wilson's comment was a preface to more vigorous demands for a substantially more appropriate approach to curriculum development. Goodlad summarizes the current thinking by pointing to several specific needs, among them the creation of a strategy of change based on a

[8] James M. Becker, "Prospect for Change in the Social Studies," *Social Education* (January 1956) : 39, 1:20-22.

[9] Howard E. Wilson, as cited by Donald W. Robinson, "Chaos in the Social Studies," *High School Journal* (October 1965) : 49.

systematic approach, a reordering of priorities, and a careful integration of the efforts of those who can contribute positively to the improvement of social studies offerings.[10]

Although relatively little attention was given to Wilson's recommendations at the time, largely because of the "science myopia," the changes he sought are today being realized within the framework of the current social studies projects.[11] John Michaelis summarizes the character of the work which has taken place since 1962:

> Intensive efforts have been put forth to improve the quality of education and to provide programs of instruction that will contribute to the attainment of more clearly defined purposes. Content has been selected more critically from basic disciplines in the natural sciences, social sciences and humanities. The development of the thinking process has been stressed as a central purpose of education. Attempts have been made to devise better materials of instruction, more effective instructional procedures, and more adequate techniques of evaluation. New patterns of curriculum organization and new designs for units of instruction have been developed with greater attention to fundamental concepts and generalizations. Renewed interest has been shown in the improvement of the curriculum.[12]

Kariel suggests that the social studies changes which will have the greatest long-range impact are those which contribute to an emphasis on analyzing and explaining phenomena rather than the collection and classification of data—a shift from "finding out what social phenomena are in the world to discovering they are there."[13] Such an emphasis agrees closely with the 1961 position statement of the Educational Policies Commission, entitled the *Central Purpose of American Education*. This document, representing the general focus of American education, stresses the importance of developing cognitive processes. Furthermore, the Commission gives an important place in the formation of cognitive abilities to the social studies.

> The social sciences . . . provide an excellent opportunity to acquire knowledge which is of considerable importance in daily living and simultaneously to improve the ability to analyze, compare, generalize, and evaluate information. Individual and social interests alike require that the citizen understand the nature and traditions of the

[10] John I. Goodlad, *The Changing School Curriculum* (New York: The Fund for the Advancement of Education, 1966), pp. 91–102.

[11] Donald W. Robinson, *op. cit.*, p. 3. By permission of the publisher, University of North Carolina Press, Chapel Hill, N. C.

[12] John U. Michaelis, *Social Studies for Children in a Democracy* (Englewood Cliffs, N.J.: Prentice Hall, Inc., 1963), pp. 3–4.

[13] Herbert Kariel, "Updating Instruction in the Social Studies," *California Teacher's Association Journal* (January 1967): 63: 1:29, 33–34.

free society and that he have skill and insight in studying the issues which his society faces. This requires the tools of the historian, economist, political scientist, sociologist, geographer, and anthropologist. The pupil who learns to use these tools and to integrate the insights to which they lead will improve his ability to think wisely about social problems and to acquire information of significance to himself and his society. He will also develop a sense of the complexity of society and the difficulties which lie in the path of those who.would understand it and meet its problems.[14]

In their investigation of the theoretical basis for the current projects, Metcalf and Massailas found the methodology and structure to be drawn chiefly from the work of John Dewey, Griffin, Henderson, Hullfish and Smith, Earl Johnson, Jerome Bruner, and Jean Piaget.[15] Most evident in the new curricula, however, is the influence of the psychological tenets of Piaget and the developmental or "spiral" pattern described by Bruner. In his *Process of Education,* Bruner offers an example of the "discovery" strategy apparent in most of the social studies projects:

A sixth grade class, having been through a conventional unit on the social and economic geography of the Southwestern states, was introduced to the North Central region by being asked to locate the major cities of the area on a map containing physical features and natural resources, but no place names. The resulting class discussion very rapidly produced a variety of plausible theories concerning the requirements of a city—a water transportation theory that placed Chicago at the junction of three lakes, a mineral resources theory that placed it near the Mesabi Range, a food supply theory that put a great city on the rich soil of Iowa, etc. The level of interest as well as the conceptual sophistication was far above that of the control class. Most striking was the attitude of children to whom, for the first time, the location of a city appeared as a problem, and one to which an answer could be discovered by taking thought.[16]

This "discovery" method of instruction has been systematically scrutinized by several researchers. Robert M. Frogge compared the achievement of the two student groups, one taught by an authoritarian method and the other in a reflective situation emphasizing the rational examination of issues. Frogge found little difference in the attainment

[14] National Education Association, American Association of School Administrators, Educational Policies Commission, *The Central Purpose of American Education* (Washington, D. C.: The Commission, 1961), p. 19.

[15] Lawrence E. Metcalf, "The Reflective Teacher," *Phi Delta Kappan* (October 1962): 44:17–21.

[16] Jerome Bruner, *The Process of Education* (Cambridge: Harvard Press, 1960), p. 33.

of factual content, but a far more positive attitude among those students in the reflective environment.[17] Coleman and Kluethe found that simulated socioeconomic games, which employed a "discovery" strategy, "held considerable motivational and instructional potential."[18] A study conducted by Massialas and Zevin tested the effect of the "discovery" approach in a controlled experiment using history students. The results indicated that students were "able to participate in the process of discovery and inquiry"; that they were able to identify and define problems, derive alternatives for solutions, develop working hypotheses from data and previous experiences, test hypotheses by drawing logical inferences, and create plausible generalizations or theories by drawing together all data and supporting hypotheses.[19] In another study, one which has a direct bearing upon the concepts of self-motivation in the learning process, Marks attempted to test the recommendations of J. Lloyd Trump for their instructional value.[20] He found that students who had previously failed under conventional classroom conditions exhibited a measurable degree of growth when exposed to team teaching, small group instruction, independent study, and the liberal use of audio and visual aid to instruction.[21] Evidence of this kind points to the opportunities that may exist for improving educational experiences through the careful use of new techniques of instruction and organization.

In the light of the acknowledged need for content and methodological revision in the social studies, and the increasing availability of resources, it is to be expected that widespread changes should be occurring in the public school programs. Such, however, is apparently not yet the case. Masia, in investigating the structure of the social studies curriculum, found that the typical pattern still reflected the recommendations made by the 1916 Committee on the Social Studies.[22] In a similar study Snyder found, in analyzing his regional profile of the social studies curriculum, that not only were Masia's findings valid, but that the behavioral sciences have been given relatively little attention

[17] Robert M. Frogge, "The Relative Effect of Two Methods of Instruction on Achievement of Certain Modern Objectives," *Dissertation Abstracts* (June 1964) : 24: 5240.

[18] Coleman and Kluethe, "Research Programs in the Effects of Games With Simulated Environments in Secondary Education," U. S. Office of Education, Report #2, 1964.

[19] Byron G. Massialas, and Jack Zevin, "Teaching Social Studies Through Discovery," *Social Education* (November 1964) : 28:384–387.

[20] J. Lloyd Trump, *Focus on Change* (Chicago: Rand, McNally and Company, 1961).

[21] Merle B. Marks, "Trump in Transition," *Social Education* (March 1964) : 28:149–151, 154.

[22] Bertram A. Masia, "Profile of the Current Secondary Social Studies Curriculum in North Central Association Schools: Foreign Relations Project," *Social Education* (January 1956) : 39:1:20–22.

in the existing social studies offerings.[23] These findings are given added credence by the studies conducted by Prpich,[24] Joyce and Weinburg,[25] and Wilkinson.[26]

What is the cause of the apparent resistance to change? The answer to this question has considerable significance with regard to the degree of influence exerted by current projects. First, the gap between curriculum development and curriculum implementation should not be interpreted to mean that the social studies projects have produced no tangible results. Rather, the retarded acceptance and implementation may well be the result of two factors: One, the present lack of a clear pattern for the schools to follow;[27] two, the built-in diffusion and decentralization characteristic of our pluralistic society. "Because the society is diffuse so too are the schools."[28] Change agents, therefore, operate against the force of tradition and the existence of organizations. In effect, a check exists in opposition to radical innovation. On the basis of current trends, however, several distinct changes can be anticipated to appear in the future public school social studies curricula:

1. Greater emphasis on the development of concepts, principles, and methods of the social science disciplines.
2. Stress on the inductive methods of teaching and learning.
3. Integration of previously neglected social science disciplines into the curriculum.
4. Application of the contributions of the behavioral sciences.
5. Intensive investigation of nonauthoritarian teaching strategies.
6. Reduction of the "parochial" western viewpoint.
7. Emergence of new information and retrieval systems.
8. Development of more appropriate evaluation instruments.
9. Wider participation and cooperation in the process of curriculum-making.

If, however, the public schools are to make the needed alterations and benefit from the effort being made, effective communication lines

23 Eldon E. Snyder, "The Social Studies Curriculum in Kansas Secondary Schools," *Social Education* (March 1964) : 28:152–154.
24 Mike Prpich, "An Analysis of Teaching of Current Events in the Social Studies Curriculum in the High Schools of Salt Lake City, Utah," *Dissertation Abstracts* (October 1964) : 25:2323.
25 Bruce Joyce, and Carl Weinburg, "Using the Strategies of Sociology in Social Education," *Elementary School Journal* (February 1964) : 64:265–272.
26 Rachel D. Wilkinson, "Social Studies in the Elementary School," *Social Education* (January 1964) : 84:280–285.
27 George W. Bailey, "Problems and Trends in Junior High School Social Studies," *Dissertation Abstracts* (July 1964) : 25:177.
28 James B. Conant, *The Education of American Teachers* (New York: McGraw-Hill Book Company, 1963), p. 34.

must be established between the projects and the schools, and between the separate projects themselves. The lack of such communications must be considered a major contributor to the "utilization gap" which has occurred between the innovation and application of methods and materials. At least two direct consequences of the absence of effective communications links are identifiable: The multiplying difficulty of selecting appropriate materials, or knowing of their existence, and the disagreement over proper objectives and approaches to change. The professional literature reveals a clear picture of the disagreements arising among the commentators of the contemporary movement. For example, Gall sees history as "all-inclusive" and as the appropriate "bridge between the humanities and the social sciences."[29] Shinn, on the contrary, sees history and geography as the integrator in the elementary grades, and history as the focus for the secondary social science curriculum.[30] Still another point of view is expressed by Lowe, who contends that history should not be taught as a separate subject below the college level.[31] Others argue that students should master structure and that this can only occur within a framework of separate disciplines. Still others are equally insistent that knowledge in the social sciences is by nature integrated and cannot, therefore, be taught separately without losing meaning—that to teach them separately would only produce "little historians, little geographers, and little economists," rather than thinking citizens. Ultimately, it is possible to find advocated any position which can be defined. Arguments such as these, however, will probably have little long-range effect on the social studies curriculum. They will, however, serve to further retard the changes needed in the present social studies curriculum.

Perhaps the greatest potential danger arising from the lack of effective communication systems lies in the possibility that educators at the public school level will interpret the "national" curriculum projects as a panacea for their individual needs and as a replacement for local curriculum-making. Richard E. Gross, a critic of the present emphasis on "national" curriculum work, warns that the revolution in the social studies threatens, "by its apparent lack of cohesion and direction," to be more of a burden than an aid to the public schools. As an alternative, he suggests the creation of regional and national coordination centers, like those established under Project English; these centers would function to prevent unnecessary overlapping and wasting of effort. Such a plan seems to have considerable merit, especially if, as part of

[29] Morris Gall, "The Future of History," *Social Education* (May 1965): 29:269–271.

[30] Ridgeway F. Shinn, Jr., "Geography and History as Integrating Disciplines," *Social Education* (November 1964): 28:395–400.

[31] William T. Lowe, "Where Should History Be Taught?" *The Clearing House* (December 1964): 39:210–213.

their responsibilities, the coordination centers were to collect, organize and make available to schools and school districts, the best material available. The National Science Foundation in 1969 implemented a variation of this plan when it set up six regional training and dissemination centers for Man: A Course of Study. Even under such a hypothetical system, however, it could not be expected that curriculum efforts at the "national" level would solve the special needs of individual schools. As Richard Brown points out:

> Between the lines of all projects is the idea that learning begins with the individual student. Carried to its logical conclusion this means that curriculum must be planned in each individual classroom, ideally for each student. It cannot be planned in Pittsburgh or in Cambridge or in Minneapolis or in Amherst (and be expected to fit the needs of Eugene, Oregon).[32]

With this point-of-view in mind it appears essential that school districts and individual schools continue independent innovative efforts in curriculum-making. Subject matter and cross-discipline teams of teachers, working on the curriculum with the aid of resource specialists, should be an integral part of each school enterprise. To search for a total solution in the newly generated curriculum is to ignore the fact that few communities have problems of the same nature. The point is well made by Leonard Kenworthy:

> Some (schools) need to be shaken loose from excessively slavish teaching of facts. Some need to inject more rigorous attention to fact. Some need to be made alive to crucial issues of our time. Some need to learn to treat their students with the dignity appropriate to a thinking individual. Some need to become aware of modern contributions to social science knowledge and process.[33]

The impact of such a statement should be especially meaningful to our teacher training institutions and the curriculum-makers in the public schools. Whether or not the new materials and methods being created at the "national" level are utilized to produce a better local curriculum depends largely upon the kind and the quality of education pre-service and in-service teachers receive. Subsequent generations of teachers must be given an entirely different kind of educational experience. Likewise, in-service programs in the schools must be designated to provide the new tools to practicing teachers. To do less is to fail in an important way to serve the best interests of our children.

[32] Richard H. Brown, "History and the New Social Studies," *Saturday Review* (October 15, 1966), pp. 80–81, 92.
[33] Leonard S. Kenworthy, "Ferment in the Social Studies," *Phi Delta Kappan* (October 1962) : 49:12–16.

Considerations of Change

While there can be little doubt that the social studies curriculum stands in need of change, there is considerable question as to what kind of change and how it may best be effected. One of the biggest problems is that of effecting peace or compromise between those who advocate separate disciplines in the social studies and those who believe that the best approach is that of a social studies which is a single, integrated discipline. As a part of this difficulty is the divisiveness between the scholar and the public school teacher. The university scholars question the policy of fusing the diverse materials and areas of the social studies and become sharply critical of the common program wherein the child learns first about his family, then his neighborhood, then his community, and eventually, his country and the world. A frequent criticism, and one which contains validity, is that the social science concepts are expected to be fitted into an existing course instead of developing a course to fit the concepts. The past few years have, fortunately, seen a real improvement in the relations of public school personnel and the university scholars and an obvious interest in and effort by the academicians to improve the social studies curriculum.

What shall the social studies teach and how shall it be taught? The problems of content and lag between the usual social studies curriculum and the state of knowledge in the parent disciplines is underlined by recent advances in organization and teaching in other disciplines, notably science, mathematics, and English. Partially, this lag occurs because the social sciences themselves are new and relative newcomers to the academic field. Too, their growth is increasing at a continually accelerating rate. Rapid growth and added knowledge in a number of disciplines cause the social sciences to appear most complex, sprawling, only vaguely related at times, and extremely diverse. The major role given history in the school's social studies program literally makes this discipline the heart and the focus, and all other disciplines often appear to be interlopers. The widening scope of the social studies in turn aggravates another problem, that of securing teachers who are competent in the newer fields—most teachers do not have nor take the time to read, study, and bring themselves up to date in these areas. This leads to an ever increasing reliance upon the safely sterilized textbook—with exercises—which does but little to develop the intellectual processes and critical thinking which we say is so important.

Another factor which adds to the quantity of the material is the change in attitude and scope of social scientists caused by changes in the world situation. Modern technologies have united the globe; current problems have accentuated the need for a worldwide view. Then, too, the particulars of the past that interest man in one age are not necessarily those that interest him in another. This means that the social studies which often fills our courses and our textbooks is very often irrelevant to our society and its problems. Frequently, we find that we devote major emphasis in our grade eight social studies to constitutional problems, to the struggle for responsible government, and to the events leading to independence from, say, British control. This material was of importance and, therefore, of interest to people a generation ago, but is far less so today.

Work to change and improve the social studies curriculum frequently wastes time and effort on such nonessentials as the relative merits of titles. For example, are we teachers of geography, economics, and history, or are we teachers of social studies, unified studies, or core? The pressure and arguments of special interest groups adds sauce to this confusion. Further, how much importance do we need to attach to the Carnegie unit? Specifically, how often and for how long does an individual class meet or need to meet? Still another factor which must be considered relates to the use, effect, and anticipated expansion of such innovations as educational television, programmed instruction, and other developments and techniques.

A survey of the major social studies curriculum projects now underway does not give hope of "salvation." Meno Lovenstein of the Ohio State University Project is exploring economics; the Amherst College Project staff is exploring history. Neither has indicated how other social sciences fit into the scheme of the social studies program. The Greater Cleveland Project, the Education Development Center Project, and the Northwestern University Project indicate concern for the first of the many social sciences but the perspective of each varies from the others. If the differences in these few projects are indicative of the biases of the more than forty major projects now underway, local curriculum builders will receive little guidance in the selection of the discipline(s), for heterogeneity of interests and direction is characteristic of these projects. Yet, two trends may provide guidance to some extent. First, the majority are engaged in a fruitful exercise of identifying the structure which reveals the fundamental concepts and principles of the discipline. Second, almost all of them are devising ways and means of promoting the development of the students' cognitive processes by identifying the mode of inquiry unique to the discipline examined. At this juncture, then, there appears to be no consensus as to what should constitute the social studies program. Nevertheless, this much is clear: the traditional, thematic approach to programming social studies content in an attempt to integrate subject areas are definitely not characteristic of the trend. The present state of knowledge in the social sciences prevent synthesis into a single overarching single discipline.

If, as it has been argued that the development of the modes of inquiry in the disciplines of history and the social sciences is the central concern of social studies education, to whom should this program be beamed? Bruner, whose proposition that "any subject can be taught effectively in some intellectually honest form to any child at any state of development,"[34] implies that the study of the disciplines can be fruitfully conducted at any level by both the mature and the immature alike, by both the "advanced" and the "slow" alike. Piaget, on the other hand, posits a developmental concept relating levels of cognition with an individual's conceptual system which unfolds with maturation. Recent studies based on Piaget's theory seem to indicate that conceptualization takes place in different forms and much earlier than heretofore believed. Further research should clarify the nature of the cognitive unfolding. Bold curriculum experiments are bringing forth increased light.

The apparent success of Senesh of Purdue University who launched a sequence of courses in economics at the primary level supports Bruner's hypothesis. Based on her study of elementary children, Taba hypothesized:

It is possible that the key to individual differences in learning may be found partly in the difference in the amount of concrete thinking an individual needs before formal thought can emerge. . . . It is not beyond possibility that many slow learners can achieve a high level of abstract thought, provided he has the opportunity to examine a greater number of concrete instances than the teaching process now allows.[35]

Bruner, Senesh and Taba feel strongly of the possibility of the so-called "slow learners" to profit from a program of this kind. Downey takes a step further:

If, as is claimed, the process of discovery builds intrinsic motivation, strengthens the memory, and makes learning one's own, the method may very well be more appropriate and more necessary in activating learning in the inept and unaroused student than it is in the case of the naturally motivated and able. . . .[36]

These propositions, if confirmed, will compel us not only to alter our common sense notions of slow learners, but also to reexamine the nature of the social studies curriculum designed for different streams and tracks, and perhaps, even alter the concept of streams and tracks. The argument that the study of social disciplines be limited to the college bound and that the noncollege bound be restricted to courses of practical living, such as family living or consumer education, is being seriously challenged. Disciplined study appears to be for all students.

[34] Jerome S. Bruner, op. cit., p. 33.

[35] Hilda Taba, et al., Thinking in Elementary School Children (Washington: U. S. Department of Health, Education and Welfare, Office of Education, Cooperative Research Project No. 1574) ; (San Francisco: San Francisco State College, 1964), p. 49.

[36] L. W. Downey, The Secondary Phase of Education (Waltham, Mass.: Blaisdell Publishing Company, 1965), p. 114.

The assumption that inquiry is the central task of general education has led us so far to the following propositions:

1. Purpose: The development of disciplined inquiry in history and/ or the social sciences is the central task of social studies instruction.
2. Program: History and/or the social sciences ordered in some form constitute the basis for the social studies program.
3. Client: All students in the junior high school should be disciplined in the social domain of knowledge.

Trends

In examining the activities in the social studies curricular efforts, it is possible to draw some generalizations: more attention is being paid to the history and the culture of the non-western world; better communication is being established among classroom teachers, social science educators, and scholars in the social science disciplines; the repetitious cyclical offerings in social studies will be revamped and, in some cases, abandoned; more recognition will be given to the K-12 sequence and articulation; there is more effort made to draw more heavily upon the contents and concepts of the different social studies disciplines; more emphasis is being given to world geography, world ideologies, and controversial issues; there is a distinct tendency toward "postholing"— that is moving through a social study area in a general way and occasionally stopping to explore in depth; an obvious effort is being made to develop and use the discovery technique, the inductive method.

Summary

Today many educators agree that certain basic concepts, generalizations, attitudes and skills should be emphasized in the social studies program. The pendulum in the past half-century has swung from a substantially departmentalized program toward a diversified and differentiated content. Uneven growth, which affects the social and emotional maturation of the adolescent, especially during the junior high school years, is recognized and supported by the latest modern educational research. The differing patterns of growth and maturation provide the chief basis for providing for individual differences within the junior high school.

The changed nature of modern society caused by the technological, scientific, and population explosion is changing educational goals rapidly and causing some wholly new emphasis in teaching. There is much more attention given to planning, both immediate and long range, for the sequential development of skills, generalizations, and establishing conceptual frameworks. More stress is being placed upon international learnings, the overall world view, as opposed to the largely western cultures previously studied. It has been recognized that there are many unsolved problems in society and that they need serious study and consideration. Materials and content from other social sciences are replacing the traditional dominance of history and geography, and such courses are intended to be more intensive and careful than the cyclical, and often superficial, broad surveys. There is much interest in and increased use of innovations such as programmed learning, team teaching, flexible and block scheduling, use of audiovisuals, and individual programs of study.

In examining sample programs certain generalizations may be made concerning the content of the curriculum: World history has changed materially; no more is it divided into ancient, medieval, and modern European history. American and state history have become almost uniform offerings in the schools; it is apparent that more needs to be done with other social studies disciplines, and educators are attempting to bring in more economics, sociology, anthropology, and political science. Teaching of civics and social responsibility has moved from emphasis upon the student and his community to that of increased knowledge of world affairs and world understandings.

The review of several current large scale projects fails to reveal many distinctively flavored for the early adolescent. Discussion of the "new" social studies for grades six to nine is framed quite often either within the rubric of secondary education or within the total K-12 span.

The reason for this appears to be imbedded in the fact that current curricular conception rests on a theoretical construct not directly related to physical and psychological development while advocates of the middle school subscribe to a conceptual framework whose central axis is founded on the unique personal and social needs of adolescents. The bulk of the innovators in the social studies envision the new programs frame perspective which makes unnecessary the traditional phases of education. Time and experience must weigh the advantages and disadvantages of this trend.

The recent interest and efforts of the U. S. Office of Education and groups such as the American Historical Society indicate that an organized approach to revising and developing the social studies curriculum may finally eliminate the patchwork appearance it has so long endured.

Chapter 8 Bibliography

Committee of Seven. *The Study of History in the Schools: Report to the American Historical Association.* New York, 1899.

DeGrazia, Alfred, and Sohn, David A. *Revolution in Teaching.* New York: Bantam Books, 1964.

Faunce, Roland C., and Bossing, Nelson S. *Developing the Core Curriculum.* Englewood Cliffs, N. J.: Prentice-Hall, Inc., 1958.

Fenton, Edwin, and Good, John M. "Project Social Studies: A Progress Report," *Social Education* (April 1965) : 29:206–208.

Fraser, Dorothy M. "Status and Expectations of Current Research and Development," *Social Education* (November 1965) : 29:421–425.

Heath, Robert W., ed. *New Curricula*. New York: Harper and Row, Publishers, 1964.

Howard, Alvin W. *The Middle School in Oregon and Washington 1965–1966*. Unpublished doctoral dissertation, University of Oregon, 1966.

Keller, Charles R. "Needed: Revolution in the Social Studies," *Saturday Review* (September 1961) : 44:60–62.

Leonard, J. Paul. *Developing the Secondary School Curriculum*, rev. ed. New York: Rinehart and Co., Inc., 1959.

Lurry, Lucile L., and Alberty, Elsie J. *Developing a High School Core Program*, New York: The Macmillan Company, 1957.

Massialas, Byron G., and Zevin, Jack. "Teaching Social Studies Through Discovery," *Social Education* (November 1964) : 28:384–387.

Moreland, Willis D. "Curriculum Trends in the Social Studies," *Social Education* (February 1962) : 26:72–76, 102.

National Council for Social Studies. *A Guide to Contents in the Social Studies*. Washington, D. C.: The Council, 1958.

National Association of Secondary School Principals, Ad Hoc Committee. "Social Studies in the Comprehensive School," *National Association of Secondary School Principals Bulletin* (September 1961) : 45:6–7.

National Education Association. *The Social Studies in Secondary Education*. (Washington, D. C.: 1916).

Robinson, R. W. "Ferment in the Social Studies," *Social Education* (November 1963) : 27:360–364.

Chapter 9

Mathematics

Arithmetic is the foundation of all mathematics,
pure or applied. It is the most useful of all
sciences, and there is, probably, no other branch
of human knowledge which is more widely
spread among the masses.
Tobias Dantzig

A Point of View

If children in the elementary school have been taught to *enjoy* and *use* arithmetic, the job of the mathematics teacher at the junior high school level is much easier.

How many times have you heard some adult say, "I always hated arithmetic," or "I never did get arithmetic when I was in school and I still don't get it."

Many factors may account for the expressed hatred of the various branches of the highly organized system of deductive logic which we call mathematics. Perhaps the knuckles of the intended learner were rapped to indicate failure to give the correct answers. Perhaps the learner did not get a good foundation of understanding in the beginning. Perhaps the learner was conditioned to hate arithmetic because of certain deprivations which were made when learning did not take place.

Just as "life can be beautiful," so can "mathematics be made meaningful." Authors of texts have long attempted to make the subject meaningful by a variety of story problems of real life experiences. One trouble has been, however, that the experiences have had too little real meaning for a host of learners. It is difficult to motivate teenage youngsters with problems about acres of land, bushels of farm produce, or tons of coal when they have had no direct experience in these matters. In the interest of learning fractions, pupils are asked to calculate such problems as the cost of 13 7/8 potatoes at 5 3/7 cents each.

For years we have had junior high school students figuring the cost of buying homes, calculating taxes, tax rates, and insurance costs, and the amount of interest a homeowner pays on a loan, compounded semi-annually. We have done all this in the interest of having children learn mathematics. We have implied that by so doing we were making the subject meaningful! In the junior high school grades most youngsters are several years from marriage and probably even further than that from buying a home. Are we *really* teaching realistically, or are we teaching meaningless subject matter?

It is possible, of course, for us to bring mathematics much closer to the needs of adolescents. They have many interests and needs which, with a little imagination on the part of the teacher, can be capitalized upon to serve as motivation. Many of them have allowances, they want new clothing, they may be supporting a car of some description within three or four years, they have expenses for movies, phonograph records, buying treats for their friends, and so on. Newspapers and magazines abound with possibilities in advertisements, reports of research and invention, building and construction. There is a world of mathematics just outside the classroom door.[1]

It is the contention of the authors that manipulation of objects, which is so prevalent in the teaching of arithmetic concepts in the elementary school, could profitably be carried over to the junior high school. Measurement is taught with rulers, yardsticks, milk cartons of varying sizes, egg cartons, and scales. Fractional parts are taught with a flannel board and fractional cutouts made of felt, cut up aluminum pie pans, and by one inch cubes used as counting blocks.

If mathematics can be made *truly* meaningful for the adolescent, and for the elementary school child before him, there will be no need for them to hate the subject forever.

---

[1] Lee Emerson Boyer, *An Introduction to Mathematics for Teachers* (New York: Holt, Rinehart and Winston, Inc., 1945), p. 3.

An Historical Perspective

Historically, the mathematics curriculum has developed according to the needs of society. During the nineteenth century, with the beginning of the public schools, some uniform and concerted effort was put forth to develop curriculum that might fulfill needs of individuals to assume citizenship obligations as well as prepare people for the professions.

In 1890, the Committee of Ten on Secondary School Subjects recommended changes in the teaching of mathematics. They recommended that geometry be introduced in grammar school, systematic algebra at the age of fourteen, demonstrative geometry follow algebra and be taught two years with algebra. For those not college bound, the Committee suggested bookkeeping and technical arithmetic after Algebra I. During this era, it was assumed that the major value of studying mathematics was one of developing discipline. The Committee did not feel obligated to analyze the content of the course to see if it helped people to solve problems, but dealt with traditional placement in preparation for college or life in the business and industrial world of that time.

The Progressive Education Commission of 1932 began to expand its area of examination by investigating the role of the teacher and how to teach mathematics in order to achieve the aims of general education. This group discussed broad concepts and related abilities used in problem solving. This covered formulation and solution, data, approximation, function, operation, proof, and symbolism. This Committee also gave some consideration to the evaluation of learning.

The Commission on Post War Education was established in 1944 with the idea of providing more adequate training for *all* students according to their needs. The two main points of emphasis seemed to be that a broader and better program should be offered to all learners including slow learners. There was more emphasis placed on functional competence in various areas. A criterion was set up to cover grades one to six, seven to eight, nine, ten to twelve, junior college, teacher education, and multisensory aids for instruction. The more narrow concept of math as a mental discipline was discarded in favor of emphasis on mathematics as a content subject with both mathematical and social aims. Guidance was another major problem considered and a simple framework of nine categories was set up to assist students to select courses according to the vocational goals they planned to follow. The postwar era already offered an expanded vocational opportunity that demanded a greater variety of skills.

The Commission for Mathematics of 1955 was established to review the secondary program to provide more adequate preparation for college entrance. With the rapid development of the space program, the new program was geared toward the superior student going to college. It was recommended that certain broad basic topics include such topics as algebra, geometry, and trigonometry but with emphasis on the modern view of basic concepts, skills, and principles of deductive reasoning. The emphasis was shifted to understanding and applying concepts rather than acquiring new concepts. The trend seemed to be away from specialization but toward emphasizing a well-integrated experience which would enable the student to deal with many problems. The rapid advance of science during this time has created many new occupational areas which also demanded more utilization of new mathematical concepts. Considerable attention was given to improving teacher training and better instructional aids.

Today's Math: The "New" Mathematics

There seems to be little doubt that the new mathematics was swept into the public mind shortly after the successful launching of Sputnik I. In one day, Sputnik I made the competitive position of America clear, forced the country to reexamine its scientific resources, and focused attention on the shortage of personnel, particularly in mathematics, the discipline on which so many other sciences depend. One writer has expressed the view that Sputnik I has done more for the cause of mathematics and mathematicians in this country than they have been able to do for themselves in the past two hundred years.[2] Contrary to the popular belief, the new math programs did not start after Sputnik's success. Rather, the Russian success in their space program gave the drive for a revision of the mathematics curriculum greater impetus. In December, 1951, at the University of Illinois, for example, the deans of the Schools of Education and Engineering in cooperation with the head of the mathematics department appointed a committee to revise the mathematics curriculum in the junior high school. The work of this committee became known as the University of Illinois' Committee on School Mathematics (UICSM) Program.

Change in the mathematics curriculum had to come. The question was, in what direction should research and development take place? Attempts to answer this question resulted in development in many different directions at the same time. The appropriate mathematics for each level has become a stimulating controversy which may not be resolved for some time. Strehler has commented:

> What final form the new mathematics takes—and it is bound to take a more stable form since the whole evolution is inevitable—is only a matter for time to decide. . . . At the moment, the new mathematics is essentially a renewed mathematics—renewed in the attention it has attracted from many interested participants and

[2] Allen F. Strehler, "What's New About the New Math?" *Saturday Review* (March 1964), pp. 84–86.

observers; in the searching reexamination that has been forced upon its pedagogical intricacies; and in its increased importance in an age and society deeply involved in technology.[3]

In addition to the rapid advance of knowledge in mathematics and the increasingly greater demands that it has made on an enlightened citizenry, other reasons for change include: (1) the need for more effective articulation from one grade to the next and from elementary to secondary school; (2) the need for better understanding of the structure of mathematics as essential to a satisfactory and permanent grasp of the subject matter; and (3) the need for improved mathematics programs for children of different ability levels. In referring to the revolutionary nature of the new mathematics, Price has stated:

> The changes in mathematics in progress at the present time are so extensive, so far-reaching in their implications, and so profound that they can be described only as a revolution.[4]

Price would add automation in general and the development of the automatic digital computer in particular to the causes of change in mathematics. He expressed the view that the technological revolution now in progress requires that new mathematics be taught in our schools, that the emphasis be shifted in the teaching of many subjects already included in our mathematics, and that we increase the number of mathematicians and mathematics teachers.

Although most mathematics people agree that there is great need for the new mathematics to solve certain kinds of new problems, some do not approve of the use of the word, "new." Professor W. W. Sawyer, a noted mathematics scholar and author, has denounced the word in connection with mathematics. He noted that most of the mathematics now being introduced into school curricula was known by the nineteenth century at the latest. He went on to say, "We do not serve the cause of education, of mathematics, or of honesty by calling old things new, by making simple ideas appear imposing."[5] What appears to be new is the emphasis being given to topics that were not previously treated at certain grade levels.

A few words of caution have been thrown in the path of the modern mathematics steamroller. Mannheimer has stated:

> The theories of sets, groups and other mathematical structures are the very apotheosis of abstraction. They are the view from the mountain tops, reached after centuries of struggle. Can we seriously

---

[3] *Ibid.*, p. 84.

[4] G. Bailey Price, *The Revolution in Mathematics*, A Report of Regional Conferences in Mathematics (Washington: National Council of Teachers of Mathematics, 1961), p. 1.

[5] Strehler, *op. cit.*, p. 86.

expect our youngsters who are still grappling in the underbrush, to get any of the richness and depth of these concepts?[6]

Mannheimer inferred that mathematical education was too important to leave to the mathematicians alone. They need the help of philosophers, psychologists, and teachers in bringing about desired changes and formulating objectives.

Another note of caution has been sounded to those who would carry revision in mathematics too far. Hannen has expressed the view that we should not abandon what has been taught traditionally in favor of new ideas. New ideas for presenting traditional material should follow a process of evolution rather than revolution. Reconstruction of the curriculum should be largely in the form of deletion of undesirable materials, extension of the present curriculum to challenge superior students.[7]

The mathematics curriculum is currently in ferment. Conflicting claims are made for traditional and new mathematics at all levels. Decisions must be made about the topics included, the sequence of the topics, and the immediate and remote goals of mathematics instruction. Decisions must also be made about teacher preparation to teach the new mathematics. If there are to be wise decisions, they must be based on experimentation and research.

A number of authoritative statements have been added to the literature in recent years concerning the more specific needs of students of mathematics in the middle schools. A. M. Hach,[8] writing in the National Education Association Journal in 1957, stressed several methods of adding interest to junior high school mathematics programs. He prefaced his remarks by expressing the view that since the senior high school can influence only those students who choose to take mathematics in high school some of the emphasis or pressure on the senior high school to train more students in mathematics should be shifted to the junior high schools. Each stressed the importance of fostering interest in mathematics below the secondary level. Of importance is the way in which students are led away from elementary mathematics and into junior high mathematics. One almost gets the impression that Hach considers elementary mathematics and junior high school mathematics as two separate bodies of knowledge with few connecting rods between. Perhaps the interests of the students would not have to be "led away" from one and into the other. Hach went on to infer that the great chal-

---

[6] Wallace Mannheimer, "Some Heretical Thoughts from an Orthodox Teacher," *Arithmetic Teacher* (January 1960) : 53:22–25, p. 23.

[7] Herbert Hannen, "A Look at Content and Its Placement in Elementary Mathematics," *School Science and Mathematics* (November 1959) : 59:614–623, p. 614.

[8] A. M. Hach, "Add Interest to Junior High School Mathematics," *National Education Association Journal* (October 1957) : 46:433–434, p. 433.

lenge was to teach skills in an interesting manner at this level so that boredom would not set in. If students can be taught to seek help when they need it, to take initiative, and to evaluate their own work, they can measure their own progress and enjoy the rewards that go along with such progress. Hach suggested that well organized field work would go far in making mathematics interesting. Devices for measurement and the use of newspaper advertisements for concocting problems can make the subject matter very lively. Hach concluded his message on interest in mathematics with the following statement:

> Children get a thorough understanding of their mathematics when they are challenged to search for the why of a process and when they develop devices and find ways to show the why.[9]

The National Association of Secondary School Principals in cooperation with several state principals associations agreed on some general statements in regard to modern junior high school mathematics at their regional meeting in Atlantic City, New Jersey, in September of 1961. Among the conclusions arrived at were the following: (1) there is a definite need to change junior high school mathematics to include modern mathematics programs; (2) teachers must be trained adequately; (3) all classes except the very low are capable of absorbing "new math"; (4) a good public relations program is necessary to get parents to accept new ideas; and (5) careful articulation is needed between elementary and senior high schools.

One major area of disagreement appeared. Should one well-developed program be totally adopted by a school system or should elements of the newer mathematics be woven into the fabric of the present mathematics curriculum? Dr. Max Sobel maintained that revision of the mathematics curriculum is definitely necessary because: (1) the old program is repetitious and dull, and (2) better preparation is required for the advanced conceptual work in grades ten through twelve.[10] Questions and discussion during the conference brought out the following points of view: (1) A major purpose of the new mathematics is to give algebra and arithmetic a structure based on logical development from postulates such as is done in geometry. (2) Programs set up only for bright students have pitfalls. These students do well at almost all tasks so only a weak evaluation is achieved. Furthermore, average students who show rapid development will still be at a serious disadvantage for moving into faster groups. (3) The Yale SMSG Program is specifically geared for the top one-third of American pupils. New materials are being prepared for average classes. (4) Dr. Morris

[9] *Ibid.*, p. 434.
[10] "National Association of Secondary School Principals' Curriculum Discussion Groups: Mathematics," *National Association of Secondary School Principals Bulletin* (October 1964): 45:44–45, p. 45.

Nadler pointed out that the new program will not eliminate failures in mathematics. Students who lack aptitude and industry will fail as badly as they did with the old. (5) Students find it easier to adjust to the new approach than do teachers.

The controversy between the old and the new probably will continue for some time. That there has been and will continue to be change in the mathematics programs for the middle schools is not in question. What is in question is, "How much change should take place and in what direction should it occur?"

The curriculum challenge at present is undoubtedly the development of new mathematical material. The problems of bridging the gap between traditional content and methodology to the new and challenging modern mathematics approach will probably test the ingenuity of all concerned for some years to come. Some of the questions that must be answered are: (1) What values of the traditional approach should be retained? (2) What criteria shall be used to select newer mathematical experiences? (3) How can some of the new content be integrated into the existing curriculum? (4) How can teachers best become familiar with the new mathematics? These are a few among many questions that must be answered in order to develop a mathematics curriculum that will meet the needs of the students. The latter task of developing a satisfactory curriculum is not an easy matter during a period of rapid change when terminology is being revised, teaching techniques are changing, and books and texts are being revised and rewritten.

Mathematics for Slow Learners

In expressing some ideas on teaching mathematics to disadvantaged groups, Fremont[11] suggested that lack of motivation is one of the sturdy building blocks of the wall of indifference. Students who are beset with many past failures often express little desire to get high grades. Fremont suggests further that these students have been brainwashed with the ideas that they cannot be taught and will not learn; that teachers have worked hard to impress them with this fact. One wonders why Mr. Fremont did not document with reliable evidence such a harsh indictment of mathematics teachers. If they are the conscienceless, unfeeling, indifferent creatures they are made out to be, then a drastic revision of school district recruiting and screening policies and perhaps even of the whole teacher education program in mathematics is in order.

The teacher is the key to nearly any move that is made in destroying the wall of indifference. Particularly, he must know mathematics beyond the level on which he is teaching. He must in addition understand chil-

[11] Herbert Fremont, "Some Thoughts on Teaching Mathematics to Disadvantaged Groups," *Arithmetic Teacher* (May 1964): 11:319–322.

dren and how they behave and learn. He must present lessons effectively and be actively interested in children. In short, a teacher must make a child feel that he is important and that the teacher cares about him. It is Fremont's contention that teacher-training programs have been ineffective in developing these kinds of attitudes. The psychological distance between student and teacher must be reduced if effective teaching is to be accomplished. This is particularly true in the case of slow or disadvantaged students. Mathematical abstractions must be presented as clearly and concretely as possible using many different types of learning materials, e. g. personal folders, workbooks, guest speakers. Fremont suggests that teachers should be imbued with certain ideas and assumptions in regard to the development of their teaching philosophy, such as: (1) all children deserve a chance to achieve to the highest potential of which they are capable; (2) all children want to learn when they come to school; (3) teachers should seek a better understanding of themselves through acceptance of others as they are; (4) teachers should have a strong respect for their students, not just tolerances; and (5) a purpose for learning mathematics must be established for students of all levels of ability, and especially for the slow and disadvantaged.

The authors would agree that most of Fremont's ideas with respect to the development of a teaching philosophy are desirable objectives. On the other hand, it is unrealistic to assume that all children want to learn when they come to school. Many disadvantaged children do not possess a desire to learn when they begin their education. There is little in their background experience that would lead to the formation of such an attitude. Although it is true that many are reached through proper counseling and guidance techniques, some do not respond to efforts to remove the mental barriers to learning.

Shortness of memory and attention span is another problem area of the slow learner. A recently conducted experiment on slow learners in the eighth grade attempted to evaluate the effectiveness of current textbooks in reteaching multiplication of whole numbers. Eight review lessons were used as an instrument of evaluation. Eleven days, eight for instruction and three for testing, were used in the experiment. A pretest was given on the first day followed by eight days of instructional lessons. On the tenth day an immediate recall test was given. Four weeks later a delayed recall test was given. Conclusions of the experimenters were: (1) carefully constructed material can aid in the retention of the slow learner; (2) materials and methods must be such that they help the slow learner to succeed and, at the same time, want to learn the operations of mathematics; (3) if learning materials are not available, the teacher must provide his own; (4) if methods in the textbooks are not appropriate, the teacher must devise his own; and (5) the entire process of learning with the slow learner is a matter of the proper combination of methods and materials.

The study of motivation in the middle schools is difficult for many reasons, one of which is that teacher influence cannot be equated or parceled out so that groups would be comparable with respect to this variable. Boyd Holtan conducted an experiment in which he investigated the relative effectiveness of four types of instructional motivational vehicles on general mathematics students in a unit of mathematics. Programmed materials were used because they randomized teacher influence as well as other factors. Four motivational devices were compared—automobile, farming, social utility, and intellectual curiosity. Fourteen classes of ninth grade general mathematics students were used. The conclusions of the experiment after statistical treatment of data were: (1) the four treatment programs were equally effective in regard to knowledge of mathematics inequalities retained; (2) the high interest related to the treatment vehicle program was more effective in achievement of knowledge of mathematics inequalities than interest not closely related to the vehicle treatment program; (3) the high interest related to the treatment program was more effective in the amount of knowledge of mathematics inequalities retained than interest not closely related to the treatment program; and (4) no achievement or retention advantage of any one treatment vehicle program for a particular interest level was apparent. In regard to the educational implications of the study, Holtan stated, "Any vehicles could be chosen for motivational use providing that they are appropriate in terms of student interest.[12]

In regard to the content of mathematics programs for slow learners at the junior high level, Greenholz suggests that these pupils usually do better at computing than problem solving. They should be exposed to the structure of mathematics, i. e., properties of number systems, nondecimal number systems, etc. They should learn the operations with whole numbers including percent. They should be taught to keep accurate records and to write checks. Teachers should help to develop in the slow learner attitudes of industry, courtesy, self-discipline, and respect for other people. The teachers who are best suited to accomplish this purpose are those who are secure in themselves and have respect for human dignity and individuality. Greenholz prefers a departmentalized program in mathematics for the slow learner in the middle school rather than a core. She took to task the critics of the public schools who suggest that our energies should not be directed toward educating these boys and girls:

> In a few years these young people will pay taxes, vote, serve in the military forces, operate autumibiles, buy and sell, marry, and have more children than an average cross section of our population. We will be supporting them because they cannot find employment. How

[12] Boyd Holtan, "Motivation and General Mathematics Students," *Mathematics Teacher* (January 1964) : 57:20–25, p. 24.

can we, a nation, afford not to educate every child to be the best citizen his talent and ability permits?[13]

Teaching Mathematics to Superior Students

Recent trends in the teaching of mathematics have included programs for gifted and superior students as well as for the slow learner.

In 1957, M. S. Norton wrote:

The use of special enrichment units in mathematics and arithemetic for the capable pupil appears to be gaining wide acceptance by schools throughout the nation. Such units are designed for developing greater insight, interest, and motivation in mathematical pursuits.[14]

Norton goes on to express the view that teachers who have used such units have emphasized their value and are especially enthusiastic about the new interest and motivations which seem to come about through the use of this challenging material in mathematics.

Lawrence Hyman experimented with accelerated programs in grades seven and eight in 1962. The study was carried on in Cleveland, Ohio, and involved the participation of academically talented students in an accelerated program in which both seventh and eighth grade mathematics were taught in grade seven and completed during that year. The program involved a rearrangement of subject matter. One teacher coordinated the entire program working with the principal and other teachers, organizing workshops, and serving as chairman of a steering committee. The Stanford Advanced Arithmetic Test and the Iowa Algebra Aptitude Test were used to evaluate progress. He concluded that: (1) The experimental group of talented seventh graders achieved a median grade equivalent of 11.5 while regular classes scored a grade equivalent of ten; (2) the Iowa Algebra Aptitude Test given to the same group indicated that two-thirds of the experimental group had superior aptitude for algebra whereas slightly more than one-fourth of the regular eighth grade pupils were in this category; and (3) the experimental group was stimulated to do better work in all classes.

Russell R. Baker investigated accelerated mathematics programs for eighth graders in 1964. His purposes were to identify the schools in which accelerated programs were receiving attention to determine principals', teachers', and students' perceptions of the effectiveness of a program in which selected eighth graders were being accelerated into

[13] Sarah Greenholz, "What's New in Teaching Slow Learners in the Junior High School," *Mathematics Teacher* (December 1964): 42: 522–528, p. 527.

[14] M. S. Norton, "Enrichment Units in the Junior High School Grades," *Arithmetic Teacher* (December 1957): 4:260–261, p. 260.

algebra, and to determine the achievement level attained by standard achievement tests. Baker's conclusions were: (1) there is great interest on the part of principals in developing mathematics programs for superior students; (2) there are more programs at the eighth grade level than at the seventh; (3) much conscientious effort is expended in planning programs as well as in subsequent evaluation; (4) there is considerable diversity at the seventh grade level of enriched, accelerated, and combination programs in mathematics; and (5) at the eighth grade level 73 percent of the junior high schools offered accelerated programs in mathematics instruction. Baker's conclusion was that the "success of students, as measured by standardized achievement tests, indicated that the superior eighth graders in this study could successfully take algebra in the eighth grade."[15]

Another method of instruction which is receiving attention in junior high school mathematics is that of programmed learning. Many claims have been made by proponents of the method relative to its superiority in certain respects to other methods. Paul H. Randolph's experiment in programmed instruction with seventh graders in Lafayette, Indiana, showed that students using programmed materials showed amazing gain in achievement over those using traditional materials.[16] The gain was thought to be due to two things—programmed learning procedure and the relatively modern material used. Randolph also concluded that, although students find programmed learning fun at first, they soon tire of it.

The foregoing studies with regard to slow and fast learners have brought out the following points:

1. Lack of motivation appears to be a significant factor in the development of attitudes of indifference toward learning.
2. Teacher training programs probably could be more effective in helping teachers to develop attitudes that would reduce the psychological distance between themselves and the pupils.
3. Slow learners can be helped in the learning process through: (a) developing carefully constructed materials; (b) using methods that will facilitate success in mathematical operations; (c) being placed in the proper ability group.
4. Vehicles for motivating pupils should be appropriate in terms of student interest.
5. The nation cannot afford not to educate every child to be the best citizen his talent and ability will permit.

[15] Russell R. Baker, "Program Provisions in Michigan Junior High Schools for Superior Students in Mathematics," *Mathematics Teacher* (November 1962) : 40:556–559, p. 559.

[16] Paul H. Randolph, "An Experiment in Programmed Instruction in Junior High School," *Mathematics Teacher* (March 1964) : 47:160–162, pp. 160–161.

6. Subject matter for talented pupils could be introduced much earlier than usual, including algebra which could successfully be handled by superior eighth graders.
7. Programmed materials in mathematics may be useful in drill and review areas, but its application to all areas of mathematics instruction is predicated upon further development.

Two Mathematics Projects Used in Middle Schools

University of Maryland Mathematics Project (UMMaP)[17]

The University of Maryland Mathematics Project was undertaken in 1957 as a cooperative enterprise of the departments of mathematics, education, psychology, and engineering at the University of Maryland and four major public school systems in the area. The project was financed by a grant from the Carnegie Corporation. The School Mathematics Study Group assisted with the evaluation of teaching experiences. A number of outstanding junior high school teachers were chosen to participate in lectures on modern mathematics and psychology. Experimental units were then prepared for grade seven.

One problem in traditional mathematics has been that of language. Every effort was made in UMMaP to streamline and improve vocabulary and usage. Efforts have been directed toward distinguishing between mathematical symbols and the ideas or objects they represent, number and numerals, for example. Number may have many different names or symbols as studies in number systems other than base ten show. The important notion is that mathematics is a language within which are sentences represented by symbols.

UMMaP is not completely new. There is still much that is traditional in the project for the middle school. The Maryland system had, at its core, the concept of a mathematical system because the numbers used are structured like any mathematics system regardless of the nature of its elements. For example, the first four units were entitled: (1) properties of natural numbers; (2) mathematical systems; (3) number systems or ordinary arithmetic; and (4) the system of integers under addition.

The three parts of a structure were: (1) definition of the elements of the set used; (2) definition of the operations used with respect to those elements; and (3) proof that the elements and the operations have certain properties associated with them.

It was reported by those who worked with the project that children readily adjusted to the spirit and flavor of UMMaP. Generally, high

[17] H. M. Garstens, "University of Maryland Mathematics Project," *Arithmetic Teacher* (February 1960): 7:61–65.

interest and motivation have resulted from its application. Certain suggestions are offered by the UMMaP people to educators interested in undertaking mathematics revision in their school or district: (1) the team approach should be used, i. e., mathematicians, mathematics educators, supervisors of mathematics teachers, and children should be involved; (2) the team should be structured so that instruction, free exchange, evaluation, planning, and demonstration classes go hand in hand. If educators are to be teachers of children, they must also be students of children.

The primary goal of UMMaP, according to M. L. Keedy, associate director of the project, was to "prepare course materials for a teaching sequence in grades seven and eight that is mathematically and psychologically sound, and appropriate to modern-day needs."[18] Stated somewhat more specifically, "At what maturity levels and with what materials can certain mathematical concepts be taught?"

Four basic principles underlie the UMMaP program: (1) there should be no separation of algebra and arithmetic as it is artificial and detrimental to learning; (2) unifying concepts such as "mathematical system" are used to reduce the total number of basic ideas; (3) emphasis is placed on precision of language to express mathematical ideas; and (4) students should understand mathematics rather than simply learn by rote a variety of manipulative skills. Motivation and retention should be greater when students can be led to make discoveries themselves.

No reliable reports can be made in the absence of statistical compilations in regard to the success of the project. However, some observations indicative of progress can be made. Middle school students are far more capable than has been supposed traditionally. Seventh graders of all ability ranges consistently grasp sophisticated mathematical ideas easily and with less difficulty than their own teachers. Teachers, along with authorities in disciplines, have shown an increasing interest in the work outside education. The importance of the joint effort of experts in different fields in building new mathematics programs would be difficult to exaggerate. The interest in cooperative experimental projects across the country has been great.

The implications of research in the project to date would be difficult to assess completely, but again, some observations can be made:

1. Large-scale curriculum revision should not be undertaken by single schools or even school systems using present procedures.
2. Research teams consisting of subject specialists from all pertinent areas should be used in the process. The cooperation that has been gained between subject matter specialists and education people should not be lost.

[18] M. L. Keedy, "Mathematics in the Junior High School," *Educational Leadership* (December 1959) : 17:157–161, p. 157.

3. No one specific curriculum in mathematics is best for all purposes.
4. One universal result of research is the bringing into focus of shortcomings and showing the need for further work.
5. The realization has developed that the junior high school program is vast, and the UMMaP Program represents only a beginning.
6. Research has caused rapid changes in mathematics programs, largely as a result of financial support of several foundations. It is the job of the universities to accept the responsibility of continuing this work.

School Mathematics Study Group (SMSG)

Between 1923 and 1957 little attention was paid to the seventh grade mathematics curriculum; no unified effort was made in terms of study and revision. In 1958 the National Science Foundation made available a grant of $1,200,000 to the School Mathematics Study Group to prepare and test sample textbooks at the junior and senior high school levels and to study other aspects of the secondary mathematics program.

E. G. Begle, coordinator of SMSG, suggested that the usual curriculum of grades seven and eight was boring to good students and frustrating to weak ones. Definite goals needing identification included the improvement of teaching, the persuasion of more students to study more mathematics, and the insurance that mathematics is appropriately oriented toward the world today.[19] The SMSG material was developed in a manner similar to that of the University of Maryland material. It was recognized that one of the most difficult problems was the blending of the best of the old with new ideas. The goal of both programs was to prepare materials and test them in classroom situations. Another goal was to determine whether the materials contributed effectively to the goals of general education. In the actual preparation of SMSG materials, first consideration was given to mathematical properties. They were written by teams of mathematicians, educators, and grade level teachers. The result was a revolutionary program in mathematics which proponents believed was mathematically sound, psychologically presented, and necessary for intelligent citizenship.

The School Mathematics Study Group has developed a complete sequence from grade seven to twelve:

Grade 7: Numeration; number system; plane geometry (intuitive); and applications of these

Grade 8: Graphs; plane, solid, and nonmetric geometry (intuitive); probability; additional work with number systems; and applications

[19] E. G. Begle, as reported in M. F. Willerding, "A Critical Look at the Mathematics for Seventh Grade," *School Science and Mathematics* (March 1962): 62:215–220, p. 217.

Grade 9:   Elementary algebra
Grade 10:   Euclidean plane and solid geometry
Grade 11:   Algebra and trigonometry
Grade 12:   Elementary functions and matrix algebra[20]

It included the kind of mathematics that SMSG deemed appropriate for today's college-capable student. In addition, SMSG has developed an elementary curriculum which seeks to exploit childrens' intuition. For example, the concept of commutativity is developed early. There are too many cases in evidence today where a child, when asked for the sum of two and seven will reply "nine," but when asked for the sum of seven and two will reply, "We haven't studied the seven's yet!" The SMSG series, like many other projects, is difficult. It unrelentingly asks its reader to think and rarely permits him to "rest in rote."

M. F. Willerding, in evaluating the SMSG Program in 1962, agreed that both the content and organization are in keeping with sound learning principles. The reports of teachers were almost unanimous that the interest of students was improved. The weaknesses according to Willerding[21] are: (1) the material could be more readable in regard to certain printing techniques—type, color, spacing, etc.; (2) many concepts need to be supplemented with additional examples; (3) the practice material is inadequate for reinforcement of arithmetic skills; (4) a unit is needed on how to solve word problems and much help and guidance is needed in this area; and (5) the examples used to illustrate properties of numbers are limited and are aimed at high-ability students.

In general, Willerding was impressed with the SMSG seventh grade material. She suggested that the enthusiasm generated and the achievement level attained by the students using this material leaves no doubt that the new programs will produce more good thinkers and fewer arithmetic haters.

In regard to the duties of the teacher in teaching the SMSG material, Martin commented that the "teaching of SMSG is like charting an unknown course."[22] This does not imply that the material is disorganized or that the teacher's manual is deficient. However, learning a new mathematical language, developing a new point of view, digesting a new philosophy, and clarifying recurrent themes are all challenges to a teacher. Martin expressed the view that most, if not all, subject matter of traditional mathematics is contained in the new, and that the program is enriched by the new.

SMSG is aimed toward discovering new ideas through exercises that depend on intuition. Martin feels that students have a better over-

[20] William Wooten, "The History and Status of the School Mathematics Study Group," *New Curricula* (New York: Harper and Row, Publishers, 1964), p. 42.

[21] Willerding, *op. cit.*, p. 220.

[22] Lillian Martin, "SMSG—One Point of View," *Mathematics Teacher* (October 1962): 55:476–478, p. 476.

view, are aware that mathematics has a structure wherein all elements are related and patterns can be discovered. "Mathematics," says Martin, "can be exciting and thinking can be fun."[23]

The UMMaP and SMSG are only two of the many mathematics programs in existence at this time. The new ideas with respect to content, psychology, teaching, and research represent the state of flux in which the science of mathematics finds itself at the present time. Although some basic patterns are beginning to emerge (mathematical structures, for example), it may take some years before the pendulum comes to rest in a position of stability, if indeed it ever does again. This is the age of research, an age whose technological advances require that mathematics keep pace with them. The changes which are being brought about should be the result of the efforts of teams of interested persons: psychologists, grade-level teachers, mathematicians, supervisors of mathematics, and other professionally competent persons interested in the development of good mathematics programs. Such changes should be based on sound, continuing research programs whose implications for instruction have been clearly spelled out and whose objectives have been appropriately defined in terms of pupil and societal needs. Above all, instructional practices which have stood the test of time should not be abandoned in favor of new and untried practices. Let the new be blended with the old in a synthesis that will meet the needs of youth in a modern, changing world.

Recommendations

Mathematics should be a required part of the instructional program during each of the years of the middle school. It must serve the role of transporting the students from an elementary background with the rudiments of number concepts and geometric ideas, and challenge them to explore the entire breath of mathematics. This exploration, interdependent as it is or development of fundamental skills, can best be implemented in carefully grouped classes.

The regular mathematics program should conclude in grade nine with an understanding of mathematical concepts traditionally associated with Algebra I. However, classes in arithmetic for those limited in mathematical achievement must be available as well as classes in geometry for the mathematically talented. In this way, the schools can provide mathematics education for the talented student as well as introducing mathematics specialization to others.

---

[23] *Ibid.*, p. 478.

Chapter 9 Bibliography

Baker, Russell R. "Program Provisions in Michigan Junior High Schools for Superior Students in Mathematics," *Mathematics Teacher* (November 1962) : 40:556–559.

Dickie, Paul. "A Supplementary Program in Junior High School," *Mathematics Teacher* (January 1962) : 55:55–60.

Fremont, Herbert. "Some Thoughts on Teaching Mathematics to Disadvantaged Groups," *Arithmetic Teacher* (May 1964) : 11:319–322.

Garstens, H. M., et al. "University of Maryland Mathematics Project," *Arithmetic Teacher* (February 1960) : 7:61–65.

Greenholz, Sarah. "What's New in Teaching Slow Learners in the Junior High School," *Mathematics Teacher* (December 1964) : 42:522–528.

Holtan, Boyd. "Motivation and General Mathematics Students," *Mathematics Teacher* (January 1964) : 57:20–25.

Keedy, M. L. "Mathematics in the Junior High School," *Educational Leadership* (December 1959) : 17:157–161.

Mannheimer, Wallace. "Some Heretical Thoughts From An Orthodox Teacher," *Arithmetic Teacher* (January 1960) : 53:22–25.

Martin, Lillian. "SMSG—One Point of View," *Mathematics Teacher* (October 1962) : 55:476–478.

Mayor, John R., and Brown, John A. "New Math in the Junior High School," *Educational Leadership* (December 1960) : 18:165–167.

Price, G. Bailey. "The Revolution in Mathematics," *A Report of the Regional Orientation Conferences in Mathematics*. Washington: National Council of Mathematics, 1961.

Randolph, Paul H. "An Experiment in Programmed Instruction in Junior High School," *Mathematics Teacher* (March 1964) : 57:160–162.

Strehler, Allen F. "What's New About the New Math?" *Saturday Review* (March 1964).

Willerding, M. F. "A Critical Look at the New Mathematics for Seventh Grade," *School Science and Mathematics* (March 1962) : 62:215–220.

Wilson, F. T. Learning of Bright and Dull Children, *Teacher's College Contributions to Education*, No. 292, 1928.

Wooten, William. "The History and Status of the School Mathematics Study Group," *New Curricula*. New York: Harper and Row, Publishers, 1964.

Chapter 10
Science

*Science is universal and constant in the life of
our citizens, and hence to be useful to all pupils,
general science must accept the science of common
things as its legitimate field. The science of
common use and that of the classrooms should be
the same. General science should use any phase
of any special science which is pertinent in
the citizen's interpretation of a worthwhile
problem.*
Reorganization of Science in Secondary Schools,
National Educational Association Report, 1920

A Point of View
Never before, in the history of mankind, has science played a more
important part in the everyday life of each of us. So much of our physical life today is a direct or indirect result of the continuing march of
science. The ever present conflict between advocates of the natural

versus the supernatural continues. There are those who hold, perhaps justifiably, that unless the moral and spiritual win out, the physical and impersonal scientific will eliminate man from the earth.

The primary function of the high school science program is *not* to train students to begin work in scientific jobs the day they graduate. The schools must give pupils instruction in the sciences necessary to serve as a basis for college or university training, vocational training, and environmental competence. The potential of the middle school science program can be similarly described, however, under more specific responsibilities. "The present vogue is to develop a continuous curriculum in science from the elementary school through the secondary school."[1] This speaks of articulation and implies conceptual development.

Similar statements are easy to make, but the maximum value of a science program in the middle school is not easily stated or implemented. The abundance of science programs would surely indicate a trend. The central theme is that education is "to be from within, not from without, and the child, not the subject matter, should be the center of the educational system."[2] This is truly a modern approach to education; it is an unfortunate commentary on education that the quotation is a description of standards used by Pestalozzi for his elementary schools. The history of the middle school has not always remembered this philosophy in teaching or in its curriculum.

The middle school sequence of science courses traditionally is somewhat as follows: grade six, physical science; grade seven, physiology or nature study; grade eight, physiology, if not taught in the seventh grade; and grade nine, physical geography or biology. The physiology courses usually included hygiene. The physical geography courses usually consisted principally of elementary geology, meteorology, and astronomy. This is not meant to imply experience in physics or chemistry.

General Science courses were introduced into junior high schools about 1915, gradually supplanting physical geography in the ninth grade. The broad content of the general science programs probably hastened the change, for it included training in such areas as physics, chemistry, and biology. Perhaps it was fortunate that higher education impeded this trend. Even though many of the ninth grade general science courses persist, an upgrading of high school science has occurred. In 1920, general science in the seventh and eighth grades was given encouragement by the recommendation of the Commission on the Reorganization of Secondary Education. It recommended that it should be

[1] L. H. Clark, R. L. Klein, and J. B. Burks, *The American Secondary School Curriculum* (New York: The Macmillan Company, 1965), p. 242.

[2] Luella Cole, *A History of Education* (New York: Holt, Rinehart and Winston, Inc., 1960), p. 477.

taught five periods a week in either grade, or three times a week in both grades. The feeling was that biological science should be established in the ninth grade.[3] Thus by 1920, seventh grade science covered nature study, eighth graders studied physiology, and ninth grade science was taught as general science. Colleges and universities would not accept ninth grade general science as an entrance requirement. As a result, general science began to move down into the lower grades. By 1930, the pattern of general science in seventh and eighth grades was firmly established. If offered in the ninth grade, it tended to be "more of the same," but not acceptable for college entrance. By 1934, 40 percent of the pupils in seventh and eighth grades throughout the country were enrolled in general science or junior high school science.

Forty years of experience in curriculum planning has failed to stabilize the situation. The only thing that seems to be "in" is the title "General Science." When and what it covers is still variable. The unrest is still present, the main reason being, as Morris Shamos would put it, most people are still ignorant of science.[4] Or, "Either science is basically unteachable (in the usual sense) or we have simply not yet discovered how to do it."[5] His point is well taken. In answer to the need, emphasis in the teaching of science is returning to some of the principles used by Pestalozzi and others years ago. The child is being emphasized. It is safe to say a definite trend exists toward more doing of science by students and less reading and talking about it. The trend started in the elementary schools, then moved to the high schools, and is now being, at least verbally, accepted in the middle school. Experimentation by individuals and in groups is on the increase in regular classes as well as in the form of supplemental projects and activities. More scientists are visiting the classrooms and more students visit laboratories outside the school.

The past ten years have seen the amount of time and number of classes per week increased in general science, especially in seventh and eighth grades.

Some districts now require two years of laboratory sciences for the college-preparatory curriculum and do not recognize general science as one of the sciences meeting college admission requirements. For these and other reasons, in some schools ninth grade general science is being replaced by ninth grade courses in biology or earth science.[6]

[3] W. T. Gruhn, and H. R. Douglass, *The Modern Junior High School* (New York: The Ronald Press Co., 1956), p. 114.

[4] Morris H. Shamos, "The Role of Major Conceptual Schemes in Science Education," *The Science Teacher* (January 1966): 33:27–30, p. 27.

[5] James B. Conant, *A Memorandum to School Boards: Recommendations For Education in the Junior High School* (Princeton, N. J.: Education Testing Service, 1960), p. 30.

[6] Clark, *op. cit.*, p. 247.

General science itself has moved out of the core program organization. In doing this, it is becoming more laboratory oriented for the purposes of more pupil involvement and better articulation with courses to come. This gives rise to two current innovations—the first being a repetition of history where one or more senior high sciences is moved downward, while the second counteracts college pressures with a systematic six-year general science program. In recalling junior high school history, the latter would be the only true innovation.

The latter innovation has one very strong advantage, i.e., a postponing rather than a possible omission of any one concept requiring greater maturity. As an example, the power concept in general science seemingly cannot be grasped by the average pupil until his mental age is higher than 160 months.

Under the category of teaching methods and materials, the middle school years are considered to be unique. Early adolescents are representing a period of profound transition in physical and mental development. This means a practical program of traditional or innovational origin must bear a strong relationship to the elementary school science program and the more disciplined high school courses which follow.

The traditional program of instruction has had the major shortcoming of concerning itself with trivia, or has been organized in such a way that whatever substantive ideas were contained in it are submerged in the morass of detail. "The essence of science lies not so much in seeking out the detailed workings of nature as in trying to understand it."[7] This greater emphasis on application and processes, in laboratory situations, over the development of new processes, is new to the junior high years.[8] New in action but not new in concept, the "experience curriculum" was being voiced for the junior high back in 1946.[9]

This experience or inquiry approach is usually defined as the act of creating individual knowledge by gathering and processing information. The teaching approach is to present a problem episode, and then allow the students to try to construct explanatory models or theories of causation. It has at least eight values which cannot be obtained through the traditional approach.

1. It clarifies the nature of knowledge.
2. Activities shift from storage to processing.
3. Self-esteem is heightened.
4. Students acquire meanings through their own operations.
5. Students become less dependent and more autonomous.
6. Inquiry individualizes conceptual growth.

[7] Shamos, *op. cit.*, p. 29.
[8] J. Stanley Marshall, "Junior High School Science," *Science Education News* (December 1964) : 12:64.
[9] Gruhn, *op. cit.*, p. 99.

7. The learners program their own learning.
8. Unknowns are approached in a manner compatible with cognitive needs.[10]

Scientific investigation is problem solving. A student must solve problems to know what science is. However, he must know *about* science in the sense that it has particular contributions to our culture; it has limitations; it can be approached as a pure subject, a modus operandi for life, or an application to a particular task; it produces knowledge; it produces solutions; it produces problems; and, like everything else, it is what the participants make it—nothing more and nothing less.

One of the most effective ways of mechanically motivating a person is to involve him in an activity in which he is directly affected by the outcome of his participation. In this way, the laboratory or experimental activity can be helpful in motivation. However, the desired learning is accomplished by the student's relating what was done, what was observed, and what it was all about in relation to his experience. This depth of involvement requires more definitive planning by the teacher for producing preliminary and follow-up discussions of the exercise.

Investigation is more important than comprehensiveness in middle school science. This view is outlined by Harold R. Hungerford[11] in a straightforward manner stressing specific skills as being the essence of scientific investigation, i. e., the skills of observation, discrimination between pertinent and irrelevant data, intelligent comparison, ability to hypothesize, experimentation and finding and using information. Such investigatory skills are not developed in the high speed, comprehensive, survey courses that science has typically exemplified in the past. Rather, these skills may be developed through student and teacher inquiry into problems of any of numerous selected topics using real materials which permit study in depth (postholing). Only through such investigation can students be brought to a stage of scientific training and stature which will enable them to gain optimum benefit from the new high school science curricula (e. g., PSSC, CHEM study, and BSCS course materials).

The term "discovery" will be used as follows: (a) A laboratory or experimental exercise utilizes "discovery" when it seeks to derive an answer to a question from the apparatus, organism, situation, or experimental design to which it is directed. The "answers" to the posed questions are not valued as being right or wrong but are interpreted only in reference to the data gathered as it compares to the question

[10] J. Richard Suchman, "Illinois Studies in Inquiry Training," *Science Education News* (April 1963) : 63:4.

[11] H. R. Hungerford, "Investigations in Science," *Illinois Education* (March 1965) : 53:300–301, p. 300.

that was asked. (b) Verbal interaction is denoted as "discovery" when it forces the students to make decisions from data, reading, experience, logic, or creative thoughts that come forth during the discussion. Decision making then requires the group, no matter how large or small, to arrive at some point of agreement from which it can depart. Decision making also requires that the teacher *not* be the authority, but that he be a special form of colleague.[12] The prime value of "discovery" as a technique is that it permits student involvement at many levels, depending upon the capacity of the teacher to allow and encourage such involvement.[13]

The observation skills which are so essential to "discovery" approaches in the sciences need development in both contrived and natural environments. The concepts and observation techniques necessary to both earth and life sciences may be more effectively learned in an outdoor laboratory as suggested by Helen Swonger[14] than just by conventional laboratory means. A plot of land purchased by the county or school district can provide the space, flora, fauna, and land forms with which to plan, construct or re-plan and reconstruct a nature trail offering real phenomena for the scrutiny and analysis by students. Considering available arable land and water resources along with population increases, conservation principles as they may be learned in a real laboratory are going to become acutely important. Exploratory learning experiences under these conditions may enable those who take high school biology later on to profit from the outdoor natural history museums which are becoming more prevalent in senior high schools.

Revision in Science

The typical experience of the junior high student has been to hear a little about science and quite a lot about scientific accomplishments (applied technologies). A true scientific experience we now belatedly realize must include not only "talking" science but also "doing" science. Lecture-demonstration has been thoroughly exploited for its efficiency in dispensing factual content but overlooks the definition of science as experience. The product of science has received ample attention but the process has been largely ignored. A practical reason for this has been economics. We need not belabor the point that many science programs are under-financed.

[12] William Van Til, Gordon Vars, and John Lounsbury, *Modern Education for the Junior High School Years* (New York: Bobbs-Merrill Company, Inc., 1961), pp. 258–270.

[13] Charles B. Wellington, and J. Wellington, *Teaching for Critical Thinking* (New York: McGraw-Hill Book Company, Inc., 1960), chapter 2.

[14] H. Swonger, "Building a Nature Trail to Teach Junior High School Science," *School Science and Mathematics* (April 1965): 65:296–8, p. 297.

Expecting twelve-to-fourteen year old students to sit and read or hear about scientific facts and concepts day after day is both physically and emotionally unreasonable. The case for laboratory learning experiences is strengthened by students themselves who exclaim, "If I find it out myself I remember something ten times better than I can when someone drills me." Elaborate individual laboratory stations replete with sinks, gas, electric and water outlets are not necessary for the laboratory approach in middle schools. It is the spirit of investigation of the teacher and students combined with some equipment and various odds and ends that are essential. Both fast and slow students can wrap themselves around problems they have identified. A single text is inadequate for this kind of learning.

Although textbooks are assuming less importance as singular authorities in secondary science classes, they are undergoing changes in format and content which may render them more effective than ever before. Such a text by Marean and Ledbetter[15] has been designed for ninth grade science entitled *Matter and Energy: The Fabric of The Universe*. The book is short and not heavily laden with facts. It is rather a guide to discovery leading students into opportunities to learn science by doing science. In guiding students toward investigation, their own record books become important documents as records of activities, observations, conclusions and consequent extensions of the hypotheses which initiated the investigation. A pattern some other text writers are following is the inclusion of films, film loops, slides or overhead transparencies which pose leading questions preparatory to direct investigation.

Although there has been considerable emphasis on curriculum revision for senior high schools, some programs include the ninth grade with the sixth, seventh, and eighth grades left virtually untouched. Robert Yager has indicated that science curriculum is like a two-fat-tailed monster with no body, the elementary and senior high school curricula representing the tails and the middle school representing the body. At least in Iowa, some attempt was made to try to adapt a program along the interest lines of the students. However, as most of the other programs seem to indicate, the concern is that of accelerating the students. The apparent success of this particular pilot study is to be questioned because of the nature of students typically enrolled in university laboratory schools.[16]

Although the national programs are the most organized in curriclum development and produce the most spectacular results, they are limited in scope and do not necessarily fit into a school district's K-12

---

[15] J. Marean, and E. Ledbetter, "New Approach to Ninth Grade Science," *The Science Teacher* (April 1966) : 33:18–20, p. 19.

[16] R. E. Yager, "A Junior High School Sequence in Science," *School Science and Mathematics* (December 1963) : 63:719, p. 719.

sequence with meaning. Most of them appear to be unconcerned about the poorly motivated or slow students. On the other end of the scale, few of the programs have provided the operational flexibility to really challenge the abler student.[17]

Several sources recommend the personal involvement of students with equipment as being important, especially for the potential dropout. However, in Ohio considerable success was obtained with techniques based primarily on vividly illustrated materials having several reading levels and appropriately interesting subjects. The spread of reading range was from fourth to tenth grades, although the students were aged sixteen to twenty-one. The strong feature of the program may have been the individuality of the approach, in which each student read what he wanted to, when he wanted to, and requested tests when he felt he was ready.

The teachers' manuals reviewed raise some doubt about the inter-teacher reliability of definitions for inquiry, discovery, inductive thinking, critical thinking, and exploration. If teachers could forget the subject matter long enough to consider the point of view of personal involvement expressed by the Wellingtons,[18] methods of this sort of presentation might fall into a more consistent pattern. Although the Wellingtons disagree with Broudy concerning the student maturity at which certain aspects of critical thinking can reasonably be understood, the pursuance of this sort of thinking will necessitate the teacher's concern for the interests of the individual student in order to get him involved in the "anxiety" of the subject matter.

Thus the exploratory program has merit, especially if it involves the laboratory experience: it is easier for the teacher to contact each student, get some sort of feedback about his interests and degree of involvement in the exercise, and provide direction in terms the individual is more likely to comprehend meaningfully. David Pierson gives some support to this method for learning skills and applying principles to problems in that his study shows principle application to be easier than principle identification.[19] The question may not be one of which approach to use but that of which sequence of approaches, as suggested by Grote. This study showed that students had better learning and retention after a six-week series of exercises in which they used the laboratory approach followed by a teacher-directed approach, as opposed to the reverse sequence. The whole realm of "best approach" is still in ferment, as Hurd indicates in his review of the research.[20]

[17] Lloyd Bennett, "The Present Plight of Junior High School Science," *Science Education* (December 1965) : 44:473, p. 473.

[18] Wellington, *op. cit.*, p. 35.

[19] P. S. Hurd, "Science in the Secondary School," *Review of Educational Research* (June 1964) : 286–297, p. 289.

[20] *Ibid.*, pp. 286–297.

Calandra proposes that the district should not get caught up in the rush and ballyhoo but should evaluate each offering in the light of given criteria. He also encourages interdistrict cooperation.[21] While Hurd suggests that districts need to use more long-range evaluations of the effects of curriculum change upon the students, he further recommends that more research be conducted on the clinical aspects of group dynamics and on the *results* of teaching practices, and less on cataloguing programs.[22] Mayor projects that a district may need to provide two middle school science tracks: one is interdisciplinary at each grade level, and one retains the courses as separate science disciplines at each grade level.[23]

Emphasis on teacher effectiveness is made by Mallinson in describing his finding that some poor teachers caused negative changes in student achievement after a year of teaching. He added fuel to his thesis by citing that students in the ninth grade were less interested although they still asked the same questions relating to science, after three years of science instruction.[24]

Seemingly, all of the new programs attempt to upgrade the level of knowledge and skills, inferring that a considerable portion of the responsibility will fall on the student outside of class. Modular scheduling may again be a help but "required homework" should be done in school without the student option of taking it home. This would improve the student's efficient use of time, improve his work habits and attitudes generally, and would provide the teacher with more accurate feedback concerning the practicality and value of the assignments made. On the other hand, students should be encouraged to do non-graded enrichment work after school. The extent to which a student becomes involved in enrichment work would be an index of his degree of interest, for he would be competing with all other after-school activities on a "no-credit" basis.

"New" Programs

It would seem prudent at this time to include a cursory examination of several programs which represent this "new" curriculum in science. It is not the intent of the authors to provide a thorough analysis of the programs. Therefore, readers are encouraged to investigate the project

[21] A. Calandra, and E. G. Colby, "The New Science Curriculums," *School Management* (November 1964) : 8:75–83, p. 77.

[22] Hurd, *op. cit.*, p. 296–297.

[23] J. L. Mayor, "The Critical Role of Junior High School Sciences," *Journal of Secondary Education* (May 1964), pp. 201, 204.

[24] G. G. Mallinson, "Junior High School Science and the Implication of Science Motivation Projects," *School Science and Mathematics* (October 1964) : 64: 613–624, p. 616.

materials directly. Also, the programs discussed in no way encompass the broad range of innovative projects currently under consideration.

The Florida State Curriculum Study emphasizes several disciplines (math, science, and education) and bases its rationale for the program on the following: (1) The middle school science courses should serve a general educational function. (2) It is proper to ignore the limitations of time, facilities, space, and equipment, assuming that these limitations can be changed by the taxpayers and administrators. (3) The curriculum program of the project begins at kindergarten and proceeds through grade nine, therefore, providing a means of articulation between the elementary and middle school curriculum.[25] Since the junior high school represents a transitional period in mental and physical growth of the student, it seems important that the junior high school science curriculum provide some form of articulation with the elementary school.

The curriculum structure of the Florida University Project begins in the seventh grade with an extension of the fundamental skills developed in the K-6 program. Even though there is a continuing emphasis on processes, there is also an increased emphasis on the accumulation of scientific knowledge and information. The emphasis on the processes carried out in the laboratory situation increases in the seventh and eighth grades.

Throughout all grades the accumulation of knowledge becomes progressively greater. The seventh and eighth grade curriculum attempts to develop a better understanding of the principles of physical science beginning with the properties of matter. The physical science curriculum is divided into two parts: the first deals with the problems of "locating objects in space" (e. g. location changes of objects in terms of forces, velocity, and acceleration); the second deals with the three states of matter and the changes that take place in matter (e. g. chemical changes and chemical bonds). The ninth grade curriculum is concerned with problems requiring organization of scientific processes and knowledge. The curriculum consists of blocks or investigations of three to six weeks' duration. The investigations are discovery-centered, requiring laboratory equipment. The curriculum consists of topics in biology and earth science.

The Secondary School Science Project on *Time, Space, and Matter: Investigating the Physical World*, was a curriculum study sponsored by the Princeton University Department of Geology and supported by the National Science Foundation.[26] The project was piloted by schools in

[25] J. Stanley Marshall, "Junior High School Science," *Science Education News* (December 1964) : 64:12, p. 12.

[26] Frederick L. Ferris, "Secondary School Science," *Science Education News* (December 1964) : 64:3.

eight regional centers. The curriculum was divided into three series of investigations, each being logically dependent upon the preceding series, but building to a climax at the end of each series so that it could be terminal. One, two, or all three series may be completed in a year, depending upon available classroom time and the ability level of the students. The first series centered on "The Nature of Things" involving physical science and mathematics, using instrumentation, measurement, approximation, precision, extrapolation, and interpolation of data. The second series centered upon activities involving "The Regularity in Matter." This series emphasized the behavior and occurrence of matter. Activities which were used in developing concepts and investigations account for the structure of matter. The third series, "Interpreting a World of Change," dealt with the constituents of the earth and how they were formed. This curriculum study provided auxiliary materials which might assist the student in answering questions that arose from his investigation. One form of the supplementary materials is the Science Reading Series, a number of paperback books including special adaptations of work done in science (e. g., adaptations of the work of Galileo). Record books are provided so that the student can record his observations and interpretations. Also, instructional materials were provided for the teacher, as: instructional folios that accompany the investigations, 33⅓ rpm recordings of background information and lectures, sets of quizzes and examinations, and laboratory equipment. This program was designed to help the student understand the nature of the physical world through investigations in science involving observations and inferences.

The School Science Curriculum Project began in 1963 under the direction of Gilbert Finlay and was supported by the National Science Foundation.[27] The committee of the project based its rationale on the following: (1) The child learns best when he is involved, and (2) the teacher must be well informed and capable of implementing the philosophy of a new curriculum approach. Project materials were developed through consultation with research scientists, educators, and teachers. The curriculum approach emphasized inquiry, quantification of data as a tool of investigation, and application of concepts. The study developed eighteen or more units consisting of anthropology, physical science, biological science, and earth science for seventh, eighth, and ninth grades. A teacher would select and teach three topics a year. The topic sequences were concerned with ecology, taxonomy, geology, genetics, and social and cultural development in animals.

The *Introductory Physical Science Project* (IPSP) began in 1963 at the Educational Science Corporation and was supported under the National Science Foundation. The purpose of the IPSP was to replace gen-

[27] Rupert Evans, "School Science Curriculum," *Science Education News* (December 1964) : 64:33.

eral science and to equip students with basic skills and understandings of scientific methods which might help them when they encounter the new science curricula of the high school. The IPSP course introduced the study of matter and progressed to the atomic model. Experiments were written into the text, and laboratory equipment was designed so that it could be set up at the students' desks.[28]

The Earth Science Curriculum Project (ESCP) course was unique when compared with previous teaching methods. Where other courses stressed a comprehensive collection of facts the ESCP stressed that science is "a science of inquiry." The program hoped to challenge the students to explore and discover the answers for themselves.[29] Shea in the same report of the development of the ESCP stated five ways in which the planned program differed from previous tests and methods of science teaching:

1. Fact is carefully kept separate from theory, and both are clearly labeled for what they are. There are many places where the book says: "some scientists think . . ." or "one theory is that. . . ."

2. A separate section of each chapter is devoted to unsolved problems illustrating the fact, to paraphrase Newton, that we are merely standing on the shore playing with pebbles while the whole ocean of truth lies undiscovered before us.

3. No attempt is made for comprehensive coverage of the many disciplines included, nor are the lines separating them emphasized. Instead, each is treated as part of the entire body of earth science.

4. For the first time in any secondary school text on earth science, the interface concept is introduced and developed.

5. The theme of cyclical phenomena is used as a unifying concept and explored at some length. Examples are the rock cycle, sunspot cycle, and climatic cycles of various types.

Most of the innovations in the science curriculum of the middle school have just been produced commercially. From the projects that are still in the experimental stages, insight might be gained through the result of pilot programs, and revisions might be made according to the total development of the child. The advantages and disadvantages of the new curriculum projects in relation to the total development of the child cannot be measured until the results and revisions of the projects have been evaluated. Some of the advantages of the curriculum might be that it helps the adolescent in developing self-direction, respon-

[28] Uri Haber-Schaim, "Introductory Physical Science," *Science Education News* (December 1964) : 64:4.

[29] James H. Shea, "Earth Science Curriculum Project—A Progress Report," *Journal of the National Science Teachers Association* (February 1965) : 32:43.

sibility, independence, self-realization, and cooperation. The curriculum approach involving inquiry, discovery, investigations and observations may help the student approach and solve problems later on in life. Many of the curriculum projects provide only one text. Several texts at different reading levels would probably be more beneficial in meeting the needs of the students. Some of the curriculum projects provide a variety of materials. The flexibility and diversity of these materials are matters that still need to be investigated. Another problem may arise from the lack of teacher training which would limit the use of curriculum materials.

The junior high science projects cited all represent a break with what has been typical of the past but there is no single "best" project for all middle school science programs. Perhaps the best programs are those which will arise locally out of group efforts of dynamic teachers and curriculum workers within a single school district.

Generally, trends of the future for science in the middle school might include:

1. Increase in the variety of science textbooks available for the courses.
2. Less use of a single textbook; greater use of several texts and supplementary material.
3. Fewer larger units each semester: three or four rather than eight or ten.
4. Change from much subject matter to relatively little subject matter.
5. Change from teaching one problem solving method to teaching many relatively unstructured methods.
6. Movement away from the accumulation of facts to understanding concepts and to the development of inquiry skills.
7. Greater stress on quantitative observation.
8. Less emphasis on technology and more on science.[30]

Criteria for Evaluating "New" Programs

The following criteria have been constructed to evaluate the materials being developed for middle school science programs:

1. The approach should be that of "discovery" as defined.
2. The materials should provide a teacher's guide in which it designates for each unit and/or exercise:
   a. The optimal scheduling of the exercise with the reading assignment.
   b. The expected range of student behavior and growth.

[30] C. H. Heimler, "General Science in a State of Flux," *School Science and Mathematics* (December 1964) : 64:755–764, 1964, p. 760.

    c. The function of the exercise in terms of student behavior change.

    d. The relative importance of repeating the exercise for accuracy or proficiency, as compared with the value of moving into the next subject concept or experience.

    e. Lists of materials, supply sources, audiovisual suggestions, and instructions for making equipment, reagents, and media needed for each exercise.

The following is an example of the sort of direction a teacher needs: when students are instructed to measure a line, is it more important for them to get the right answer, discover that measurement is not exact, determine that they need more precision than a plastic ruler can provide, or create measuring devices such as graph paper grid lines (or pencil length, triangulation methods, or notebook paper hole diameters)?

3. The program should be sequential.

4. The program's sequence should be based on developmental and maturational capabilities of the students.

5. The program should be organized toward teaching the major concepts on the basis of increasing complexity.

6. The program's schedule of learning should allow adequate time for discussing and relating the information contacted through inquiry, inference, and discovery.

7. The program must budget time for encouragement of student idea reflection, collateral reading, independently designed creative pursuits, applicative appreciation activities, and intrinsic value appreciation pursuits.

8. The program should be oriented to laboratory learning; the demonstration technique should be limited to those necessary conceptual situations that are too difficult or dangerous for student manipulation, or to those experiences of *primary* importance for which there is insufficient material.

9. The program should allow for flexibility in using programmed techniques, nonreading type instructional techniques, and independent study approaches.

10. The program should include depth study of some topic.

11. The program should relate science to life; it should liberate curiosity at all levels. Considerations such as those discussed in the dialogues written by Robert MacIver should be built into the curriculum.

12. The program should include a teacher training specification that includes in its course of study the content required in the program, the methodology required, and an experience in using the "colleague" approach. This approach should train the teacher to behave in a manner alluded to in the introduction.

13. The program should provide that each of the following types of experiences should occur at least once during each course.
   a. The student is provided a critique on his technique, procedure implementation, results, and interpretation, all of which were accomplished by himself without student assistance.
   b. The student must repeat a procedure until he develops confidence, accuracy, and efficiency.
   c. The student must work cooperatively with a partner to produce an acceptable accomplishment.
   d. The student must function in a large group in several capacities.

Summary

Science is here to stay! The general populace is coming to accept this fact more and more. They realize that much of our national stature in the world is accountable to the fact that we are rich in scientific know-how. The nation is also coming to realize that we do not have a monopoly in the area of scientific development. Although it is recognized that the "survival of the fittest" may well become the "survival of the greater scientific advancement and more deadly weapons," it is reverently hoped that we do not discourage even one budding scientist in the middle school. Scientific advancement can, and must be controlled by equal sociological and moral progress by all of mankind. Just as fire or water can be destructive when out of control, so can the giant which we call science. Science is a universal language. It has given us many luxuries and conveniences, yet it is still in its infancy in terms of potential. We, as educators, have our work in front of us relative to future scientists. What they do with their potential and resultant knowledge is largely up to us as their teachers.

Authorities are in agreement that science should be required in the middle school. Agreement would not however be found to any great extent on how much should be required, or in what form, for that matter. In the business of curriculum development and requirements for graduation, one comes upon many vested interests. The mere weight of self-perpetuation obviates eliminating a course in a given subject area from the curriculum. This is not to say that the authors recommend the exclusion of any of the popularly offered subjects from the middle school curriculum. It is not the existence of a course or a particular title that is important—it is, rather, the method and content involved and the nature of its continued scrutiny and reevaluation.

It is lamentable that the curricular organization of most middle schools does not leave much room for more science offerings. If emphasis is put upon the crafts and industrial art classes, little room is left for science. If music and art are requirements, little room is left for science to expand. If English, social studies, mathematics, and physical education are required at each grade level in the middle school, there is not much latitude for science.

It is the firm conviction of the authors that science should be a requirement in the middle school curriculum. Which "science?" in what order? and for how long? must be a local decision made on the basis of staff training, local interests, facilities available, and financial resources.

Chapter 10 Bibliography

Bennett, Lloyd M. "The Present Plight of Junior High School Science," *Science Education* (December 1965) : 49:468–476.

Calandra, A., and Colby, E. G. "The New Science Curriculums," *School Management* (November 1964) : 8:15–83.

Evans, Robert N. "School Science Curriculum," *Science Education News* (December 1964).

Ferris, Frederick L. "Secondary School Science," *Science Education News* (December 1964).

Francis, G. M., and Hill, C. W. "A Unified Program In Science for Grades Nine Through Twelve," *The Science Teacher* (January 1966) : 33:31–32.

Haber-Schaim, Uri. "Introductory Physical Science," *Science Education News* (December 1964).

Heimler, C. H. "General Science in a State of Flux," *School Science and Mathematics* (December 1964) : 64:755–769.

Hungerford, H. R. "Investigation in Science," *Illinois Education* (March 1965) : 53:300–301.

Mallinson, G. G. "Junior High School Science and the Implication of Science Motivation Project," *School Science and Mathematics* (October 1964) : 64:613–624.

Marean, J. and Ledbetter, E. "New Approach to Ninth Grade Science," *The Science Teacher* (April 1966) : 33:18–20.

Marshall, J. Stanley. "Junior High School Science," *Science Education News* (December 1964).

Shamos, Morris H. "The Role of Major Conceptual Schemes in Science Education," *The Science Teacher* (January 1966) : 33:27–30.

Shea, James H. "Earth Science Curriculum Project—A Progress Report," *Journal of the National Science Teachers Association* (February 1965) : 32:43.

Souers, Charles V. "An Integrated Math-Science Activity for Process Teaching at the Junior High School Level," *School Science and Mathematics* (January 1966) : 66:3–5.

Suchman, J. Richard. "Illinois Studies in Inquiry Training," *Science Education News* (April 1963) : 63–64.

Swonger, H. "Building A Nature Trail to Teach Junior High School Science," *School Science and Mathematics* (April 1965) : 65:296–298.

Section Four

The Instructional
Program, Part II

Overview

This section is written from the same rationale described in the overview of the previous section. It is separated because somehow there is a difference between the content areas included in the two parts. The first has been described inadequately and, to a large extent, inaccurately as "academic," "college prep," "hard subjects," "required," "the core of the curriculum," and "classical subjects." In contrast, those included in this section are referred to, often with derision, as "elective," "superfluous," "activity," "non-academic," or "exploratory." This is unfortunate. It is too bad that humans have no other way to communicate labels except through words which are, all too often, static, classificatory, and limiting. Few would deny that *all subjects* must prepare a person with some end in mind, be it academic, be it active as opposed to passive, be it taken because a student wants to learn, be it challenging, or be it for exploration of self, others, and the environment. Yet, in the attitudes of parents, teachers, and students there is something different about the areas which are included in this section.

Some would call this section the "Unified Arts," others the "Unified Studies," while still others would call it the "Arts Program." Whatever it is called (the authors refuse to add yet another name to the lexicon of middle school educators), it is that part of the instructional program that provides for creative, often non-language expression by the early adolescent. In many districts, the middle school student, for the first time, is involved in classes conducted by specialists in their field.

Chapter 11

Exploration Courses

Throughout the literature appertaining to middle schools considerable attention has been given to the function of exploration as one of the primary roles of the institution. Gruhn and Douglass in the revision of their landmark work on the junior high school defined exploration, in part, to be the obligation of the school to:

1. Lead pupils to discover and explore their specialized interests, aptitudes, and abilities as a basis for decisions regarding educational opportunities.
2. Stimulate pupils and provide opportunities for them to develop a continually widening range of cultural, social, civic, vocational, and recreational interests.[1]

Within most instructional programs, the courses dealing with art, music, home economics, industrial arts, crafts, business education, and foreign language are generally referred to as the exploratory program. This collection of course offerings certainly does have considerable potential for broadening and deepening the creative activities and individual expression contained within each student. But, if exploration

---

[1] W. T. Gruhn, and Harl Douglass, *The Modern Junior High School* (New York: Ronald Press Company, 1956), p. 59.

were to stop here, the middle schools would not be coming near to maximizing their potential for exploration. The early adolescent, losing his dependence and searching for independence and a life the way he sees it, must be permitted to understand (explore) himself, his world, and his relationships with people around him and in school. Thus, the biggest danger in writing a chapter entitled, "Exploratory Courses" is that teachers in the fields not included in the exploratory program will see their task as one not demanding exploration. In the opinion of the authors, every course lends itself toward exploration.

Included in this chapter are short discussions of current concerns in some of the fields usually classed as exploratory courses in the middle school. Each section was written as a separate unit since most schools offer the courses in that way. The "Arts Program" idea, described below, serves as a good framework for efficiently exposing a large school population to the rudiments of several fields; but it is no substitute for a well articulated specialized study of any of these fields. Variable, modular, and flexible scheduling certainly offer a worthwhile alternative to the Arts Program's objective of expanding the exploratory possibilities of the middle school schedule.

Regardless of the perspective a viewer uses, the instructional program is crowded. As the "knowledge explosion" continues at a more rapid pace each year the demands upon the schools will certainly intensify. One solution, suggested by many, is to reduce the number of required subjects and surplant them with a potpourri of elective choices. In grade six or seven, unfortunately, many students are not prepared or able to make realistic choices. Such students often take music because their parents want them to, art because their friends are doing it, foreign language because it is "the thing to do," or home economics because of the popularity of the teacher. Few students actually have a depth of experience which would enhance intelligent choices.

An Arts Program

Why not structure a course in the first year of the middle school which would provide contact with several elective areas so that in succeeding years the students can make intelligent choices? Such a course could, conceivably, offer nine weeks each of music, foreign language, art, and home economics. Other schools, for local reasons, might substitute typing, industrial arts, or crafts, for one of the four listed. The idea behind such an organization would be twofold. It would

1. give each department an opportunity to "sell" itself and its "product" in a concentrated dose designed to interest and stimulate the student into further study in the area.
2. provide a ready-made opportunity for integration of the subject matter of several areas *where such integration* deepens and strengthens a student's understanding of the aesthetic world.

Briefly, the program would be a unification of the arts such as is suggested below.

Dividing the Group for the Year
  Semester Plan
    First half
      Introduction week for all
      Break into four areas:
        Art
        Music
        Industrial arts
        Home Economics
      Evaluation week for all
    Second half
      General group meeting
      Break into four areas:
        Students who were in the art area move to music; music to industrial arts, etc.
      Evaluation week for all
      Display of some work
  Second Semester
    First half
      General group meeting
      Rotate to new area
      Evaluation week
    Second half
      Complete cycle
      Last week for evaluation and display of year's work

Many schools today have closed door policies. This means that the industrial arts, the art, the music, and the home economics areas are separate, and yet in many cases these programs overlap in the teaching process. For instance, the student cannot avoid coming in contact with color and design. He may hear not only extremely narrow and prejudiced points of view, but he has to sit and hear them again many times for a second or third time.

Art in the Middle Schools

Art is everywhere, and to define art is answered best perhaps by saying, "What isn't Art?" Art is not found in a vacuum; it is part of a rich, everyday living. It is the creative and aesthetic illustration and reproduction of experiences in various media, in general; and to the art teacher, those expressions included in the definitions above take visual form.

Art, in the narrow sense, includes not only sketching, painting, and sculpting but also, to some degree, printing, constructing, designing, weaving, and fashion work. In its broadest sense, fine art includes work that is primarily written as literature, primarily aural (music), primarily visual (art), or a combination of all of these, as well as drama and dance.

The Adolescent Artist

In the middle school there exists a special creature who, from the art teacher's point of view, is "new born." The early adolescent, regardless of his experience in art, is suddenly endowed with the ability to "see" the world around him from an entirely new point of view. He may be without skill, generally awkward and poorly coordinated, but he can be extremely emotional, serious, and conscientious. He may have the physical body and desires of an adult, yet at the same time still be a child. In art classes, the teacher often finds the incongruence between the mature appearance of the student and his extreme, immature artistic expressions. To reject the contribution of this student who is trying to express his personality would hamper or destroy further artistic development. Of course, it is not unusual for art teachers to find just the reverse of the above situation—a student with mature critical abilities and perspective but physically unable to reproduce his insights and appreciation.

Adolescence is a period of simultaneous mimicry, of rebellion against adult conventions. In art, adolescents portray this phenomenon by attempts either to create realistic visual effects or to achieve mature abstract or stylistic aims. It is easy for adolescent artists to become discouraged when successful art forms of previous years are no longer possible. Here, the art teacher needs to recall for the students the difference between the non-analytic, uninhibited nature of children's art and the complex, sophisticated attributes of adult art. The middle school artist can be a very interested and willing student so long as his needs are met and successes, regardless of how minor they may be, are provided. His questions need answering—questions about all the things that have been around him for his twelve years which suddenly take on new meaning and relationships. He sees and responds, sometimes for the first time, to designs, to color, to form, etc. The art teacher, an expert in personality expression, needs to understand his student fully as much, and sometimes more, than do the academic instructors.

It must be remembered, however, that the adolescent tends to lose confidence in his own creative ability and expresses himself less and less in a visual manner because of the tendency of teachers to be critical of his activity—especially his imaginative behavior. He often reacts to his own work negatively since he suddenly feels it might be childish when evaluated in terms of his newfound, but not fully understood, system of values. The final product of his efforts becomes very important to him. At that point, art ceases and craft begins.

A major part the teacher plays at this time is to make the adolescent aware of his creative abilities, sensitivities, and skills as shown in his work. If the individual is made knowledgeable concerning his accomplishments in all probability he will feel confident with his work.

The trend today toward individual instruction and the concern on the part of the teacher for the overall development of the adolescent may also be seen in an experimental junior high school. Teachers at Clara Bryant Junior High School conceived a plan for unifying industrial arts, homemaking, and art to the degree that each individual could readily use the three departments as needed.[2] The emphasis in the plan was on each student going his own way with his project. In the course of the program, it was seen that the idea of integration of the program on the physical level—actual freedom of students to move about among departments—was not workable. However, the need was still recognized for the conveyance of information and skills across department lines.

Art's Last Chance

The Minnesota Department of Art Education in 1963 carried out a study to ascertain the effects, influences, and modifications of art education practices and programs since 1957.[3] The nationwide sampling of schools indicated that, between 1957 and 1962, there was an increase in the percentage of time allotted to art programs in the elementary and middle schools. The increase in the percentage of time was negligible in comparison to the increases in time allotments for subjects such as social studies and English. The study also indicated that there was a noticeable drop in the percentage of time allotted to art in the high school. This drop in high school was attributed to the fact that colleges were requiring more work in "solids" such as mathematics, science, and foreign languages. Consequently, many young people today have their last real experience with art in their junior high school years. By this fact, the responsibility placed on middle school art to accomplish its goals in an extremely short period of time and to do so in such a way as to imprint its very nature in thoughts and actions of students cannot be minimized.

Many teachers in the field of art education today are calling for change. Art educators must take some type of strong stand in order to survive in the educational system of the future.

Historical Considerations

Art educators also say that there must be a revival of the interest in creative art that infused the progressive movement in American education during the 1930s.[4]

[2] James LeWis, and Hershel K. Bennett, "A Unified Arts Program for Junior High Schools," *Art Education*, XI, April, 1958.

[3] Reid Hastie, and David Templeton, *Art Education in the Secondary Schools* (Minneapolis, Minn.: University of Minneapolis, 1963).

[4] Robert H. Beck, "The Social Background of Art Education," *Art Education*, National Society for the Study of Education, Sixty-fourth Yearbook (Chicago: University of Chicago Press, 1947).

The 1930s saw perhaps the greatest interest in art in the whole history of education. In essence, this period was marked with a concern for education as a whole and a desire to meet the needs of the individual in his day-to-day living. The Owatonna Minnesota Art Education Project was an effort which actually tried to infuse the idea of "art as a way of life" into a typical American community.[5]

Much research has been done on the history of art education and much effort has been made to identify movements in the field as to the place of art in public schools. Francis Belshe, in a doctoral dissertation at Yale University, has identified briefly several major movements.[6] In chronological order they are:

1. Before 1870, art instruction was considered an educational extravagance, a subject usually found in isolated situations, taught by a volunteer teacher according to his, or her, own method.

2. During the fifteen years following 1870, some form of drawing instruction became part of the public school curriculum in a number of large cities.

3. Walter Smith's work in Massachusetts was influential in promoting "industrial drawing" consisting largely of copybook exercises. Smith's ideas dominated from 1880 until 1900, but were modified by the findings of the Herbartian movement which was concerned with cultural and aesthetic appreciations by the increased availability of inexpensive art materials, by the forming of professional organizations, and by the manual-arts movement.

4. By 1900 came a trend toward the conception of art as central to general education. Such theorists as Dow, Dewey, Bonser, Cizak, and Clark attempted to correlate art with such subjects as history and geography.

Dewey himself influenced the thinking of educators with his book, *Art as Experience*,[7] which gave focus and flavor to the period following its publication. One of the first statements relating to the task of art in education was contained in the book and, in brief, stated that art has the task of restoring the continuity of everyday events, doings, and sufferings that are universally recognized to constitute experience.

A whole generation of theorists followed Dewey and found many meanings and implications in his work. Winslow advocated an integrated school arts program, the correlation of art with other subjects,

[5] For further information about this project, see, *Art in American Life*, The Fortieth Yearbook of the National Society for the Study of Education (Chicago: University of Chicago Press, 1941).

[6] Francis B. Belshe, "A History of Art Education in the Public Schools of the United States." Unpublished doctoral dissertation, Yale University, 1946.

[7] John Dewey, *Art As Experience* (New York: Minton, Balch, and Co., 1934), p. 3.

and the explicit integration of art learnings toward the accomplishment of the general objectives of education.

Read argued, in his book, that art (as he defined it, "creative aesthetic expression") must become the *basis* of education. He believed that art should not be viewed only as an instrument of education. He believed, instead, that the most fundamental aspect of human development existed in "information getting" processes utilized in art.[8]

Both Read and Lowenfeld believed that art should be perceived as growing out of the expressive tendencies of the play of children. These tendencies, however, must be oriented toward spontaneous, yet disciplined ways of working toward maintaining and developing "sensibility" and "imagination." Contemporary art theory tends to reinforce Read's ideas. Langer, in particular, in her philosophy, considers art as a form of symbolization for expressing certain aspects of human experience which have no other medium of expression.[9]

On the whole, most of the research done up until this time to substantiate new methods and movements in the field of art education has been done by psychologists, educational researchers, philosophers, sociologists, and art historians rather than art educators. While this indicates that there was a recognized necessity for progress in art education and that many other fields of learning related, in interest, to art, it also indicates that there was lack of interest on the part of art educators in improving art in education.

This state of affairs soon began to change and is still changing today. Since World War II, significant graduate study has been carried on at such universities as Columbia, Minnesota, Ohio State, Stanford, Wisconsin, and New York. Pennsylvania State University became, under the leadership of Lowenfeld and Beittel, a center for art educators' research.

The trend in research efforts today seems to lean toward the interdisciplinary study of new concepts and new theory in close harmony with related work being done in psychology and education, i. e., creativity, perception, personality development, and curriculum.[10] Previous research seemed to be directed toward providing supporting data for the prevailing doctrines of art teaching.

Content and Method Trends

Particularly in public school art, there seems to have been a gradual shift over the past twenty-five years.

[8] H. E. Read, *Education Through Art* (London: Faber and Faber, Ltd., 1958).

[9] Susanne K. Langer, *Philosophical Sketches* (Baltimore: Johns Hopkins Press, 1962), pp. 92–94.

[10] June McFee, *Preparation for Art* (San Francisco: Wadsworth Publishing Co., Inc., 1961).

1. During the thirties and early forties, emphasis was placed on representational picture-making, commercial art and illustration, craft projects, and the deliberate application of "principles of art and design."
2. Through the influence of Moholy-Nagy's work in Chicago, art instruction, during the late forties and early fifties, centered on a "materials approach."
3. Recent developments in method seem to emphasize the idea of art in "expression" and "visual poetry," and even the traditional crafts are taught in terms of their expressive possibilities. Growing awareness of the actual "psychology of art" has drawn attention to ways of facilitating the creative process and to "self-actualization," and appropriate kinds of creative effort.[11]

Most middle schools have some provision made for art as a part of the general required program. It is usually considered to be an "exploratory" course and is rarely required for more than one year. Since art in the average high school is an elective subject and participated in by relatively few, these courses can be considered terminal for most students.

The *School Arts* magazine, in 1963, conducted a survey of 4,000 of its readers. The majority of readers were involved in art education. In response to a questionnaire, the following facts were deducted:

1. Although some art educators are interested in art education as a product of the mind, many continue to view it as a product of the hand.
2. Many art educators are interested in creativity, perception, and aesthetics.
3. Philosophic and conceptual themes are stimulating to art educators.
4. The art educator-fine arts hostility is fading.
5. Methods, projects, and workshops are still attractive concepts to some art educators.[12]

Ideas, Trends, and Experiments

Widespread acceptance and use of teaching machines in our schools will necessarily involve art teachers in educational issues not initially of their own making.

Innovation and reform are the new watchwords for educators mainly because of the aroused public concern for more "excellence," less "frills," more "standards," and less "life adjustment" in the

[11] J. S. Keel, "Art Education 1940–1960," *Art Education* (Chicago: University of Chicago Press, 1965), p. 46.
[12] Harlan E. Hoffa, "Art as Education," *School Arts* (December 1963), p. 33.

schools. Since art is often thought of as a "frill" and teaching machines are considered by many to be a cure for a great many of education's ills, there will, undoubtedly, be greater emphasis on "basic" learnings, on objective evidence of higher academic achievement. This will tend to draw attention away from subjective activities characteristically found in the art classroom. If non-art activities in the school become more and more committed to the use of programmed instruction, art teachers may be challenged to show cause why art should be in the curriculum at all. The challenge might result in art teachers programming that part of art instruction which requires the learning of factual information.

David Ecker, Associate Professor of Art Education in the School of Art at Ohio State University, has shown particular interest in teaching machines and their possible use in the art education program of schools.[13] He uses teaching machines in the presentation of factual matter related to art and says that a complex machine might present to the student reproductions of artwork in the form of colored slides of film sequences in conjunction with information about the history, style, and methods of production of the works of art. Anything that human instructors can show or say about art, he thinks, can probably be presented on a screen, sound track, or tape. Students could respond to questions with short written answers or small drawings.

This is all very well for factual information, but how are the students provided with activity *in* art—the making of paintings, drawings, sculpture, ceramic objects, and prints? There must be a characteristic behavior in art where it can contribute to the full development of the child, both physically in muscular coordination, and mentally, in providing emotional outlets and creativity. No one can argue that knowledge *about* art interferes with creativity and the growth of the child for which education is concerned, but one can argue that a knowledge of art alone is not enough.

A plan has yet to be formulated which would, through the teaching machines, include all of the many types of behaviors required in art for the student. Creativity may be one trait humans display that machines do not possess.

If this is true, the art teacher may rightly be challenged with the genuine possibilities of programming facts, values, and attitudes concerning art. But he may also view a widespread use of teaching machines in the school as a serious threat to his main objective—the promotion of creative behavior.

Transition

The historical importance and study of art has been both emphasized and ignored during the course of the development of art education. To-

---

[13] David W. Ecker, "Programmed Instruction: Challenge or Threat to Education?" *School Arts* (October, November, December, 1963).

day, we are in a transitional period between the importance placed on the creating of works of art and the study of previous works.

An example of the trend along these lines today lies in the theory of G. Scott Wright, Jr.[14] His approach to the curriculum is based on the fact that man has been creating art for tens of thousands of years. Every society in history has produced its artistic expression. An understanding of man is incomplete without an understanding of his art, and an understanding of his art leads to a deeper understanding of man.

The formal history of art concerned with dates and names has little meaning to the young mind. On the other hand, why man has created art throughout history can be quite fascinating. Each motivation casts a little more light on the nature of man and his universe as he sees it. Although there are various explanations for each work of art, it is possible to make certain generalizations which are valid and illuminating. These generalized "whys" are the content of the curriculum.

The "whys" or general motivations might be: magic, religion, political control, recording of daily events, honoring the great, expression of philosophy, expression of emotion, decoration, and function. In order to present the major motivations in some related way, they can be organized in the traditional chronological sequence of history.

Music

Music, the most abstract of all arts, grows out of a human need to give expression to feelings. From earliest times, it was, and still is, a means of communication between men. It is an emotional outlet which adds meaning to the events of life. The composer, as the writer and painter, speaks through his medium to provide for the layman a better understanding of himself and others—a better appreciation of life.

Appreciation is the principal aim of music education in the middle schools. To increase the capacity for enjoyment and participation, the student must be exposed to idioms, forms, and patterns—the language of music. This appreciation cannot be taught as such; rather, the students must be guided to find the beauty, joy, contemplation, inspiration, or rhythm in available music.

Music education is frequently under attack as an unnecessary extra —a frill in education. Music educators, unfortunately, have frequently attempted to justify the music curriculum with statements such as, "music will improve one's home life," or "music education will improve the health of the students." While such statements may have some truth, their general vagueness and all inclusive scope render the whole music program suspect.

Actually, the music curriculum has some very real values which make it highly desirable to include in the school's course of study:

[14] G. Scott Wright, Jr., "Toward a Curriculum for Understanding—Junior High School," *Art Education* (January 1963), XVI: 1.

music is a part of the culture of many countries; music contributes to one's general joy of living; music is a part of everyone's world; music is a basic and universal mode of communication.

Music can best meet the exploratory functions of the middle schools, as well as its own academic objectives in a dual capacity through general music classes to be required of all pupils in at least some of the grade levels, and through a variety of elective activities designed to meet the needs of those pupils with special interests and abilities.

Probably in no subject field of the public school program is it more important that teachers teach "children" rather than "subjects" than in music. Since music seems to be so much a part of the life of the pupil, the music teacher is in an excellent position to guide him in the establishment of worthwhile attitudes, in the understanding of social responsibilities, and in the need for a sense of unity and cooperation with his fellow students. The teacher must be a student of the early adolescent child and must adapt his teaching procedures accordingly.

The materials and methods of the music teacher cannot be effective unless they are chosen and used with a total picture in mind of the child and his background. The teacher's job today is more important than at any time in the past because of the larger part played by the school in the shaping of each child's character and personality. In effect, the music teacher no longer has the single responsibility of teaching music; he, with his fellow teachers, is responsible to a large extent for what the child becomes as a citizen.[15]

Since the middle school became generally accepted, there has been much controversy concerning the extent to which music should be required of all pupils within the school. If it can be accepted that music is a part of the life of each individual, then there is justification in the thesis that music should be included in the preparation for that life. Probably as a holdover from the traditional music programs of the 6-3-3 or 8-4 plan, it has been the general practice to require music in the first years of the middle school curriculum in the form of a general music class and to offer music in the form of specific electives in the eighth or ninth grades. Since much of the activity of the general music class involves singing, this practice undoubtedly was influenced in part by the "problem" of handling boys' voices during the difficult period of voice change.

A common practice in grades where general music is required is to schedule instrumental groups at the same time as the general music classes. Thus those children who are part of the instrumental program and presumably more knowledgeable musically, pursue their instrumental study without interference with other class work.

[15] F. M. Andrews, and L. A. Leeder, *Guiding Junior High Pupils in Music Experiences* (New York: Prentice-Hall, Inc., 1953), p. 27.

Along with the two years of required music, musical performing groups and activities are usually offered on an elective basis in a heterogeneous manner so that pupils of more than one grade level may meet and participate at the same time in a single activity.

Music education, as is true with many areas of the curriculum, is accepted today without question while for many years its position in the instructional program was highly tentative and controversial at the secondary level.

Music has, on the other hand, been part of elementary curricula since the early eighteenth century. This presence of music in the "common schools" of early America can undoubtedly be connected to the religious orientation of the colonies. Louis Elson, in fact, traces the beginnings of music education in America to efforts to revitalize church singing and the publication of several psalters in the second decade of the eighteenth century.[16]

General Music

The middle school general music class fulfills the general function of continuing the music training begun and developed in the elementary school. General music courses have frequently been condemned or slighted by administrators and disliked by students. When this has been the case the fault could usually be traced to a teacher who was himself disinterested or unenthusiastic about this phase of the music curriculum, or an uncertain, disorganized approach which emphasized nonmusical objectives and involved dreary stress upon musical history or long and painful sessions of listening to records which the teacher liked. There is a place in the junior high school where the exploratory nature may be truly fulfilled in activities which may include listening, singing, playing simple instruments, use of films and filmstrips, reports, and field trips.

The early adolescent has ended a phase of his educational development when he confronts a new school environment, a new type of social and educational organization, and new and different kinds of activities. That he enters into the difficult period of adolescence at the same time does not make this change easier for him at first, although as discussed above, the organization and services unique to the junior high school will undoubtedly compensate for some of the difficulties encountered in his initial adjustment period. He is neither a child nor an adult, and complete understanding on the part of the teacher is necessary to insure desirable relations. Variety of materials and teaching procedures, a key to success in any school, must dictate the music teacher's educational plan if he is to succeed in his job.

16 Louis C. Elson, *The History of American Music* (New York: The Macmillan Company, 1904), p. 9.

The general music class has a legitimate place in the required instructional program of the middle school. Whether it is required each year, only one or two years, as an alternate with another subject, or as a part of some combined course, each school district must decide according to its own objectives and community needs.

It is important to insure continuity and articulation with elementary and high schools; to provide a program that has activity, interest, and meaning, and is not just busy work; and to develop the exploratory aspects of general music as well as attempt to locate latent musical ability and talent.

Several school districts during the last decade have attempted to fuse the general music program with the "core" classes in their schools. Few, if any, such experiments were continued beyond the pilot period. The administrators' inability to find teachers with sufficient content background in English, social studies, music and possibly art was always the primary reason for discontinuance of those "core" programs that were organized with one teacher for each classroom. Fusion of music and social living seems quite unworkable, but there does appear to be ample justification for some correlation under two adequately prepared teachers to give both subjects more meaning.

Possibly the greatest contribution the general music class can make to the curriculum is in the nature of integration of its content with relation to other areas. The organization of units to parallel work in these other areas will require much study and cooperation on the part of all staff members, but it is possible that the rewards in worthy outcomes will more than compensate for the extra planning involved. Music lends itself to practically every classroom situation found in the middle school. For example, the music of every country is correlated with its history and geography. There is a natural connection between both music and literature, and between music and the plastic arts. Music is both an art and a science, and one can hardly imagine presenting a unit in general science on acoustics without involving the study of musical sound. Teachers of physical education have long accepted music as a necessary aid in teaching rhythms.

The school should encourage the correlation of music with other areas and activities. Although some traditional music teachers fear that music will lose its identity through such practice, there are many modern educators who believe that only through such practice can music be justified as a required subject. To quote again from Andrews and Leeder:

> Music, because of its very structure and meaning, is rich material for integration. Since it fosters creative imagination, it may carry a pupil out of himself and identify him with far-off places, great historical events, and generous feelings for all mankind. When music is taught with such a philosophy in mind, it tends to break down the rigid departmental barriers which separate subject matter in the junior high school. If the pupil learns the human meanings of

the folk and art music studied, he sees that music is a picture which reflects the significant thoughts and feelings found in literature, arts, and social studies. Thus music becomes a great integrative force in contrast to the activities phase it occupies in some schools.[17]

As is true in all curricular considerations, music classroom activities, methods, and materials are successful in direct proportion to their ability to reflect students' interests, attitudes, and preferences. This should not be construed to mean that the general music class must be limited to "pop" music, but, rather, that the music teacher should select and present his content—be it classical, theatrical, popular, or whatever—with his listener in mind. The wise teacher works from the immediate pupil musical preferences by easy stages and steps, through popular music to ballads, to semi-classical, to classical material.

The importance of music should be stressed from the standpoint that it plays a part in the lives of all people. As a result, musical performance and participation should be the natural outgrowth of the general music program.

The middle school is in a favored position for music instruction in that its students come from schools and backgrounds which are usually deficient in a musical environment. As a result, the middle school is apt to have desirable special facilities as well as performing groups which appeal to the beginning general music student. Music teachers at these grade levels frequently fail to capitalize on the built-in advantages of finding themselves in a learning situation, characterized by student interest and enthusiasm, which other teachers work hard to create.

Although a certain level of excellence of performance is a prerequisite to a successful music program which stresses excellence for its own sake, it must be emphasized in the middle school that it is more important to promote as widespread participation in and appreciation of music as possible. Along the same lines, a music teacher who presents himself as a teacher who enjoys music will be much more successful with students than one who presents himself as a musician who teaches.

Basically, the general music class is an orientation course in which the pupils are introduced to the history of music literature, to composers, musical forms, instruments, the essence of music theory, and the reading of music. The students, sometimes for the first time, study under teachers who have specialized training in music. The students look ahead with anticipation to choral groups, marching bands, musical performances, and other elective musical activities. The general music class is the place to "sell" music to the inquiring, exploring student; unfortunately, existing programs have not realized the potential.

The general music class may be considered, then, as a culmination of the required music training the child has received in the public schools.

[17] Andrews, and Leeder, *op. cit.*, p. 106.

Its importance lies in the fact that the effectiveness of the teaching of general music will greatly affect the entire music education program in the school system. It may be considered the strategic point in this over-all program, a point at which the most competent teaching is required.

It is generally accepted that the excellence of teaching will depend largely upon the use of an activity approach in presenting the work. Activities that should be considered in every general music class are singing, listening, playing, rhythmic activities, and creative activities. It is obvious that there are many methods of organization in any subject area. A seemingly logical and much used method is that of chronological or historical order. It is doubtful, however, if the historical ranking of units in music has much meaning to the middle school pupil with his sparse knowledge of world history.

Another favorite method is that of ranking according to types of musical activities. As we believe that each of the five types of activities is important in all music teaching in the school, it does not seem wise to separate them in organizing the program. Because the seventh grade course of study in most states deals with the cultures of other countries, a popular plan in developing music units on this grade level is to follow this practice. As the content of the year-long course will remain much the same regardless of organization, it seems wise to follow a plan that will utilize all possible variety of activities in each unit.

The degree to which pupil-planning may be employed will depend upon the experiences and interests of the pupils. Because some units will fit certain activities better than others, it is possible that the same amount of emphasis need not necessarily be given to each activity in all units. In organizing the program into nine units, or approximately one unit per month, it is possible throughout the year to give a balanced emphasis to all the activities over a longer period of time. By the same token, these units are not necessarily equal in the amount of time spent on each, but will vary according to importance, student interest, and time available. Also, as some schools will devote more periods per week to general music than will others, the amount of material to be covered will depend upon each school situation.

All units must be flexible enough to allow deviation from the strict adherence to the unit plans during certain periods of the year when music, especially singing, may be used to special advantage.

Elective Music Activities

Most elective music activities in the middle school curriculum may be divided into two classifications, the vocal and the instrumental. As one of the objectives of music education is to enrich the entire educational program, these music groups may serve the activities program common to all pupils as well as perform a function unique to their own groups. General activities most commonly affected are athletic contests, assemblies, club organizations, special programs and events, and community services. By their very nature, music groups in the elective category are performance oriented, as is much of the music. The prospect of performing before an audience often serves as a powerful motivator and stimulant and many educators believe that participation in performing groups is of great value to the student in conferring a sense of achievement and a feeling of belonging. Although there have been instances of schools offering elective classes in phases of music theory or music history, appreciation, and literature, it is more common to include these studies in the general music program and to consider elective music to be synonymous with performing groups of one kind or another.

In organizing bands, orchestras, and vocal ensembles, there are certain problems which deserve consideration if these groups are to perform their musical functions and also aid in strengthening the overall educational program in the school. Middle school students are extremely curious and any new exploratory courses help to fulfill the functions of the school. These pupils are gregarious by nature with a strong feeling of belonging to groups. They show traits of extreme loyalty and sympathy for others, yet their greatest desire is acceptance among their peers. The rapid rise of interest in musical performing groups in the schools is quite understandable when one considers that the organizations provide natural outlets for these needs which are so prevalent among adolescents.

Although there is much similarity in the general objectives between instrumental and vocal groups, certain factors unique to each are sufficiently different to warrant separate consideration.

Instrumental Music Activities

The instrumental music program is accepted by students with tremendous enthusiasm. The nature of the activity is such that there is little need for motivation in soliciting participation. Ideally, the instrumental program should be offered at a minimum expense to all children. Where this is not possible, the financial resources of the child's family may be an important determining factor in his participation. Many school districts have tried to equalize opportunities by offering school-owned instruments to children of families with limited means but who possess definite ability and interest. Programs based upon the rental of instruments at low cost have also proved successful, and in many schools, parent and community groups have provided much of the band and orchestra equipment. Some schools have developed cooperative arrangements with commercial outlets whereby rental costs may be applied against the purchase price of instruments. It is general practice for school districts to purchase the larger and non-solo instruments necessary to provide balance in the instrumental groups.

The instrumental segment of a music program should endeavor to provide every interested student with an opportunity to explore the possibilities available in instrumental study and, after a decision is made, to encourage further study of an instrument in the hope of gaining a realistic appreciation of music through participation. Some of the same desirable outcomes possible in a good physical education program are found in a good music program, particularly those that deal with teamwork, leisure-time activity, pleasurable and satisfying experiences, and good health habits. Performing good music at a level of excellence commensurate with ability and development of the group should be a means to the above ends, not a desired result itself.

A frequent problem in the middle school instrumental music program is that of scheduling. The fact that the band and orchestra are usually composed of members of each of the grade levels complicates scheduling and may indicate the need for grade level sections during the school day and full band rehearsals held before or after school. Such a compromise would make it difficult to carry out a music program in those communities where a large number of pupils are transported by school buses. Some teachers feel this type of scheduling will tend to downgrade music activities compared to other school classes. As is true of many problems peculiar to the organization of the music program, scheduling difficulties may be best solved through study by and action of all members of the school staff, including administrators and teachers. There is no single "best" way to meet the problem and its solution will depend largely upon local school conditions.

A word of concern may be expressed toward the band or orchestra director who is interested chiefly in developing a balanced instrumental group at the expense of allowing pupils to play instruments of their own choice. This is often true when the middle school is considered merely the recruiting ground for the senior high school groups. Although this objective need not be altogether undesirable, the practice indicates that the music teacher may have forgotten his major purpose —that of meeting the needs of each individual pupil, and he arouses suspicion when his major objective may be that of selfishly developing his own position through the excellence of performance by his groups.

The practice of "weeding out" pupils because of their lack of ability, though interested, is another questionable technique in teaching instrumental groups. Favorable attitudes toward music are basic in selecting and retaining band and orchestra members, and it is often true that pupils who are possessed with a sincere desire to play may ultimately go farther in music than others blessed with greater natural ability. At least their enjoyment will be more sincere, and it is difficult to see any justification in eliminating them merely to raise temporarily the standards of performance. In the modern school, the watchword should be participation rather than performance if instrumental music is to take its place in realizing the general objectives of education.

The kind and number of instrumental groups is often limited only by the interest and enthusiasm of the students and the teacher. In addition to band and orchestra, the groups most commonly found are small performing groups such as a German band, a string ensemble, a string quartet, a pep band, horn ensembles, a swing band, or a pop band, the last two really being variations of the stage band. There has been an increasing interest in stage bands and the number is increasing rapidly. These instrumental groups play music which is chiefly popular and current in nature and appeals to their age group. There is a ready acceptance of their performances at assemblies and related student activities. The justifications for these specialist groups center around the need to create opportunities for maximum student participation, to take advantage of student interest and enthusiasm, and to provide outlets for developing student abilities.

Music educators have indicated a concern over the steady decline in school orchestras. Partially this is because of the flash, noise, and eye appeal of the marching bands. In addition, other factors have also contributed to this attitude: the need for a longer period of time to learn to play stringed instruments which, in turn, implies a strong elementary program; the fact that orchestra music is likely to be less familiar to an audience than choral or band music; the problem that the orchestra does not have as much opportunity to perform; and the absence, in most cases, of a dressy uniform as is found in bands.

Not all bands are marching bands. Many schools encourage the development of the concert band, an instrumental group which plays music chiefly of a non-marching nature. Some of the world's finest bands, such as the United States Marine Band, are of the concert band type. A concert band plays to its audience from a seated position, usually in an auditorium, and since it is not marching, plays more difficult music. The controversy over marching bands is a real and pertinent issue. Discussions as to their value on the college and high school level are nothing compared with the debate of this issue in the middle schools. Some music educators believe that elementary and middle school students should never participate in a marching band. Others feel that these youngsters should march in civic parades only, both for the value of participation and for the public relations benefit and goodwill. At the extreme are those who believe that a band is, per se, a marching band, and the more opportunities there are to march, the better.

The arguments for such bands go something like this: a marching band appeals to all pupils and attracts more students to the music program; properly organized and operated, a marching band is a unit of pride and dignity; it permits individual self-expression and provides a belongingness, esprit de corps, for many who would otherwise never find this gratification; a marching band requires more musicianship and, therefore, discipline and concentration; it develops poise, bodily control, and improved carriage; it provides music for school functions and promotes improved school morale; and it is an excellent public relations instrument.

The disadvantages, faults, and problems of the marching band are claimed to be: a marching band has little to do with philosophic and educational objectives and goals: a marching band is a big part of the entire pageantry in which the young apes the adult; its pageantry snowballs and is likely to include, even in a middle school, drum majors, majorettes, dancerettes, baton twirlers, flag twirlers, flag bearers, and drill team; a marching band often exploits the players and causes serious inroads into class time; a marching band is flashy, misleading as to simplicity, and expensive to outfit; and, finally, a marching band develops bad playing habits, depends largely for its effect upon noise, movement, and entertainment, and, therefore, students could be better taught in another kind of instrumental situation.

It is possible to develop a non-marching band program which will do for the students virtually all that is claimed by the proponents of the marching band at a cost materially less in money, in class interruptions, in undesirable activities and sophistication, and in involvement in related activities. The real question which must be answered of course, is, what music curriculum will provide the best education? What is best for the children?

Vocal Music Activities

The middle school choral program, because of its nature, is not limited in the same respect as is the instrumental program, yet it is confronted with problems of its own. The expense of financing choral music is negligible since song materials will not usually exceed the expense of textbooks found in the average class. Personal cost to pupils is usually slight and in this respect vocal music can reach a much larger number of pupils. Interest in vocal music shown by boys depends largely upon their musical experiences in the earlier grades and in the general music class, their peer group attitudes, the prestige of the singing group, and, most importantly, the satisfaction which they get from it.

The singing groups in middle schools do have a unique problem that has been the concern of music educators for some time. This is the problem of mutation or voice change, most prevalent among boys but present with girls as well in a different way. Some teachers "solve" the problem by eliminating boys completely from the singing program during these problem years. Cooper tried to disprove what he called the "myth" that boys' voices change abruptly and that they should, therefore, be dismissed from singing during the period of mutation. He believed the change is gradual rather than abrupt and the problem lies not so much with the student but with the teacher in failing to meet the problem effectively.[18] Each boy's voice should be carefully classified ac-

[18] Irvin Cooper, "The Junior High School Choral Problem," *Music Educators Journal* (November-December, 1950), pp. 20–21.

cording to range and quality, and music should be selected to fit these ranges. Unison singing, songs in which the boys sing in unison and the girls sing independent parts, part singing using both boys and girls, and all male voice singing with range taken into consideration should make up the nucleus of the program.

Too often, for all practical purposes, the students' singing experiences actually begin in the middle school and, therefore, the music training must assume an elementary level approach. It becomes necessary to develop both the interest and singing ability within the pupils, especially the boys. This can be done in selecting unison songs of great variety and number. Unison singing will develop a certain amount of mastery in control of the voice and the boys will want to begin part singing eventually.

Much of the success in getting boys to like to sing depends upon teacher enthusiasm and the materials selected. Boys like to sing military, western, folk, and popular music. The music teacher who tries to make boys like songs about flowers and raindrops could be asking for trouble. But, by gaining the boys' respect and confidence, it is not too difficult to shift the interest from subject-matter to the music itself so that eventually the boys will want to sing only good music, regardless of the text.

The success of singing among girls has been so obvious that little need be said concerning it. Adolescent girls, as discussed in an earlier chapter, are gregarious, dramatic, romantic, and often so musically inclined, regardless of ability, that "girls only" music activities are quite popular. Girls of this age group do experience a change in voice quality and range, but it is far less than the change associated with boys' voices.

The problem of organization of choral groups revolves mainly around whether or not the boys and girls should be segregated. The solution to this problem will depend upon many factors. There are arguments for both plans and the decision will again depend upon the particular situation in each individual school. The combined chorus is preferred because of its flexibility in the variety of music that may be used; because of the parts, balance, voice range, and tonal qualities; and because it carries out the general philosophy of coeducational, heterogeneous grouping preferred in most American schools. Possibly the inclusion of both plans may be the best solution with both boys and girls organized into glee clubs of their own which meet concurrently during certain periods of the week.

Choirs and glee clubs do an excellent job in serving the functions of the middle school. They may serve both the musically talented youngsters and those who like to sing but are limited in ability. A great variety of music is available which will not only meet the interests of all, but will stand the test of excellent music literature.

Small vocal ensembles, such as boys' glee clubs and barbershop quartets, swing chorus, and girls' glee clubs, are easily organized, but, unfortunately, often exploited. Public performances create motivation, and admission to these small groups becomes a symbol of ability or status. Their small size makes them readily mobile and their large repertoire of novelty numbers, greater than choruses and choirs, makes them highly susceptible to short notice demand and an overload of performances in the community.

Foreign Language

From the beginning of foreign language instruction in American schools the "humanistic" tradition set the pace, i. e., modern foreign languages were taught like Latin and Greek with the emphasis on grammar for grammar's sake and the translation from one language to another. Teachers taught about the language instead of teaching it; they talked about the language instead of talking in it.

According to a survey recently completed by the authors, 10 percent of the student body enrolled in middle schools are experiencing foreign language instruction—one-half in Spanish, one-third in French, and the rest (all less than one percent) divided between Russian, Latin, German, and languages of local interest. This percentage is a composite taken from schools ranging from zero to 100 percent student involvement. As elementary language programs continue to multiply both the nature and the extent of middle school involvement will likewise increase.

Some schools require a foreign language for one year (usually in the seventh or ninth grade); others include instruction as part of the Language Arts-Social Studies program; still others offer it only on an elective basis. No consistent pattern exists as to the means of providing for such instruction. If more states follow the lead of legislation enacted in the California Legislature, foreign languages will be taught one semester each year during the middle school years.

Historical Background

Just what is traditional in language learning? At the close of the nineteenth century in the United States, languages were taught by the grammar translation approach.[19] Methodology was similar to that used in the basic instruction of Latin in the early private colleges. Students were expected to analyze the foreign language; rules of grammar, conjugations of verbs, and long vocabulary lists were memorized. Because

[19] Robert Lado, *Language Teaching: A Scientific Approach* (New York: McGraw-Hill Book Company, Inc., 1964), p. 4.

reading the literature of the target language was often a major goal, students were required to translate, with the help of a bilingual dictionary, the target language into English.[20] There was little, if any, opportunity to hear a native speaker. Nor were students expected to learn how to speak the target language. Teachers, as a rule, were not trained to teach the sound system of the foreign language.

> Those in charge taught about the language instead of teaching the language; they talked about language instead of talking in the language.[21]

Language instruction was limited to the acquisition of three skills—language analysis, reading, and writing.

The offerings in modern language instruction gradually declined until World War II. As the economy-of-time became less important, foreign languages were not generally found in the curriculum below the ninth grade.[22] Particularly during the period of isolationism that followed World War I, Spanish and French classes became increasingly less popular electives.

Entrance of the United States in World War II renewed our involvement in world affairs. Our country lacked men trained in the ability to speak a second language. It was at this time that the foreign language curriculum received much criticism. The United States Army set up a crash program for a very select group of men to train them to speak another language. Native speakers were hired; English was banned from the classroom. Instruction took place daily and lasted from eight to nine hours. The language laboratory, widely acclaimed by many today, first came into use at that time. The program was generally thought to be successful.

From that point on, language learning began to receive attention from many outside the actual field. Descriptive linguistics—the scientific study of language—contributed much to our understanding of the necessary skills involved in language learning. Linguistic field workers in attempting to reduce unwritten languages to paper followed certain procedures. First, they listened to natives to find out what sounds were significant phonemes in order to distinguish meaning. Next, they learned to orally reproduce the sounds so that a phonetic transcription based on the international phonetic alphabet could be derived. After determining the phonology and semantics, they were able to transcribe

---

[20] J. Michael Moore, "Breakthrough in Foreign Languages: The Audio-Lingual Approach," *Journal of Secondary Education* (October 1963): 38:8–12, p. 8.

[21] *Ibid.*

[22] W. Van Til, G. F. Vars, and J. H. Lounsbury, *Modern Education for the Junior High School Years*, 2nd ed. (New York: Bobbs-Merrill Company, Inc., 1967), p. 368.

the syntax. And so it was established that listening and speaking should precede the reading and writing skills.[23]

Psychological theory and educational research also contributed much to the changing emphasis in language instruction. The learning process was discovered to be essentially habit formation. Correct behavior is reinforced by much practice over a long period of time in order to establish the language skills. Acquisition of speaking skills should begin at an early age. Wilder Penfield, of the Montreal Neurological Institute, maintained that the time to begin schooling in foreign languages is between the ages of four and ten.

Children's capacity to imitate is then at a maximum. Their memory is prodigious. Their vocal mechanism is flexible, capable of making a great variety of sounds.[24]

Research also indicated that by the time a child reached the age of nine, his ability to imitate foreign sounds is diminished. He is capable, however, of more and more analysis in language learning.[25] The time had come when foreign language educators had to reexamine former methods and practices in view of the ever increasing scientific research applicable to their field. Thus, the way was paved for the audio-lingual approach.

With the advent of Sputnik the American public was ready to finance quality language education in spite of the fact that the need of thorough language instruction was felt more than ten years earlier. In 1958, the National Defense Education Act passed by Congress legislated foreign languages as defense weapons. Through its various subdivisions (Titles III, IV, VI, VII), millions of dollars were provided for supporting language activities at the elementary, secondary, and college levels. Federal funds were made available on a matching basis to provide new equipment such as tape recorders and language laboratories for the classroom. And on the assumption that better teaching would result in increased interest in foreign languages, the NDEA established the Institute program as a stop-gap measure aimed at teacher education.[26] An institute offered extensive training in the functional skills of listening comprehension, speaking, reading, and writing the foreign language. Applied linguistics, culture and teaching techniques were also included in the program.

In 1959, James B. Conant viewing the curriculum of the high school said that fewer than four consecutive years of the same language was almost a complete waste of time. Throughout the country the movement

[23] Robert Politzer, "The Foreign Language Curriculum and its Shifting Foundations," School and Society (April 17, 1965): 93:250.

[24] Emma Marie Birkmaier, "The Teaching of Foreign Languages," National Education Association Journal (November 1961): 50:16.

[25] Ibid.

[26] James M. Spillane, "Language Institutes Show the Way," National Education Association Journal (May 1964): 53:25.

was to include foreign languages in the seventh and eighth grades. Today, it is not uncommon to find many school districts offering Spanish, French, or German in the fourth, fifth, or sixth grades.

"New" Language Instruction

> If the goal for the learner is a coordinate system (one in which the audio-lingual and the gestural-visual are given primary stress, with the graphic-material coming in later) then a ringing challenge is sounded, a radical transformation called for, a new orientation of procedures demanded, and a thorough house-cleaning of methods, materials, and texts is unavoidable. . . .
>
> The learner plays a dual role, first hearer, then speaker . . . recognition and discrimination are followed by imitation, repetition, and memorization . . . only when he is thoroughly familiar with the sounds, arrangements and forms does he center his attention on enlarging his vocabulary. In learning the control of structure what he may do at first as a matter of conscious choice he will eventually do habitually and unconsciously. Throughout he concentrates upon gaining accuracy before striving for fluency.[27]

These statements by Nelson Brooks have been taken as the basic tenets of an entirely new method of teaching foreign languages. Although there are several new methods in the language field, the Audio-Lingual Method is perhaps the most extreme departure from the traditional grammar-translation method, and also because it is one of the most controversial innovations in any teaching field. The opinions of the authorities are sharply divided and it seems almost impossible to get a calm, moderate reaction to the technique. We often find such vehement contrasts as:

> We now seem to be living in what might be termed the Reign of Terror of the French (and other languages) Revolution. The Audio-Lingual method, whose precise rules are set forth in official pronouncements, reigns supreme. Teachers must swear allegiance to the mechanized, monolithic, pedagogical state or risk being denounced as traditionalists. . . . Such frantic linguistic activity has not been observed since that unfortunate incident at Babel.[28]

> 'La plume de ma tante' is gone with the wind, and good riddance!!
> . . . The old spectator sport has finally become one of the performing arts.[29]

---

[27] Nelson H. Brooks, *Language and Language Learning*, 2nd ed. (New York: Harcourt Brace Jovanovich, Inc., 1964), p. 51.

[28] Rubin Pfieffer, "A Jaundiced Look at the A-LM," *High Points* (October 1964) : 46:22.

[29] Elton Hocking, "Revolution in the Foreign Languages," *National Association of Secondary School Principals Bulletin* (April 1964) : 48:34.

Any new method that inspires such differences of opinion must constitute a rather violent departure from tradition.

But, in foreign language instruction there is no real "traditional" method. Aside from the stressing of grammar rules, translations, and paradigms, the foreign-language teacher has always had considerable freedom in the methods he uses. In fact, Meras wrote: "We should not try to impose one method of study on all students, no matter how successful this pattern might be in special cases."[30] This means that anything which can bring about learning should be used. Another tenet of the traditional method is the de-emphasis of speaking skills in learning the foreign language. "Competence in reading is, as we have said, the single skill that is most likely to be achieved and to be used. While ability to speak a language is a skill which interests students, it will be less used, outside the classroom, than reading."[31] This traditionalist goes on to describe some of the goals for foreign-language learning: the student's increased ability in English, and the development of a feeling for correct speech, for nuances of meaning, and for the etymological relationships of English and foreign words. According to him, the selection of a teaching method depends upon several different things: the type of school and its locality, the student group comprising the class, and most importantly, the skills in which the particular teacher is strongest and feels most confident.

A-LM, on the other hand, can be defined, as:

The audio-lingual approach to the teaching of foreign languages is one in which . . . the student approaches the language, not through a series of rules to be acquired intellectually, but through practice on grammatical patterns which have been prepared according to linguistic principles.[32]

A-LM is based on ideas radically different from the traditional. For one thing, its proponents believe that there is one method that can be effectively used to produce learning in almost all students. They follow certain prescribed procedures and techniques and teach according to specified units and unit segments.

Another difference is the increased emphasis with A-LM on the speaking skills of the foreign language. It favors a definite progressive sequence of the skills of listening, then speaking, then reading, then writing. The audio-lingual skills are thus seen to be not only the basic but the most important skills. The importance of ear-training in developing speaking proficiency is considered especially vital. There are some

[30] B. T. Meras, *A Language Teacher's Guide* (New York: Harper and Brothers, 1954), p. 68.

[31] C. Gullette, and C. Keating, *Teaching a Modern Language* (New York: F. S. Crofts and Co., 1954), pp. 27–30.

[32] Douglas C. Sheppard, "So What is Audio-Lingual?" *Hispania* (May 1961) : 44:292.

strong arguments, both psychological and physiological, for preceding speaking with considerable practice in listening comprehension:

1. Ear-training facilitates speaking. Articulation is dependent upon hearing sounds accurately, discriminating among them, establishing proper auditory sound images, and developing a "feel" for the new language.

2. Concentration on one skill at a time facilitates learning by reducing the load on the student and by permitting the use of materials and techniques geared to the specific objectives and requirements of each skill.

3. When students are required to speak from the outset, the likelihood of errors is increased, apprehensiveness on the part of the students impedes learning, and confidence develops slowly (if at all). When listening comprehension precedes speaking, each student's initial experience includes more correct responses and more frequent positive reinforcement, less apprehension, and more rapid development of confidence.

4. Premature listening to his own unauthentic pronunciations and to that of other students may interfere with the discrimination and retention of correct sound.[33]

These are some of the reasons why in most A-LM classes the students do not even begin speaking until lengthy periods of just listening have been completed. It takes even longer for them to start reading and writing the material. Most classes do not use textbooks until late in the year.

Another difference between traditional and A-LM involves the training of teachers. As mentioned above, one of Gullette's traditional criteria for choosing a method is the teacher's own capability. He is counselled to stay within the areas about which he knows the most. This is a reflection of his own training in the language. His college methods courses have taught him several teaching techniques, but his training usually ends here and in the classroom he is pretty much on his own. On the other hand, with the development of the A-LM program has come the development of the Summer Institute, whereby teachers are specifically trained in A-LM techniques.

A-LM Techniques

Douglas Sheppard has pointed up the philosophy behind one of the basic A-LM techniques:

If language is speech and not writing, it is apparent that phonology

[33] Gerald Newmark, and Edward Diller, "Emphasizing the Audio in the Audio-Lingual Approach," *Modern Language Journal* (January 1964): 48:18. By permission of the authors, Gerald Newmark and Edward Diller, and *The Modern Language Journal*, publisher.

must be taught first, but this gives rise to various problems. If the students work from the written symbol, he will give that symbol the phonological value it has in his native language, and not that of the foreign language. If constant comparisons are drawn between the phonological systems of the two languages, the student will come to look upon the foreign language as little more than a variant of his native tongue. If the teacher arranges phonological drills to include mainly reduced sound segments (syllables and words) the student will be confused by the changing values of the same sound segments in more complex structures. There is also the danger that he will come to feel, albeit subconsciously, that the language is all sound and no meaning.[34]

A-LM's answer to these recognized problems is the dialogue. The teacher presents simple and meaningful utterances between two or more people in a predetermined situation. The students memorize these dialogues, with the help of taped versions in the language laboratory, until they can present them at the normal rate of native speech and with pronunciation and intonation acceptable to a native. The central focus in the dialogue is a real situation which the student can understand. The language is standard, authentic, informal French, as an example. The dialogue is divided into two halves, and, on the tapes, further divided into four quarters. Each quarter must be mastered before going on to the next.

The teacher practices with the tapes until he is certain he pronounces each word correctly, with correct intonation, etc. Before he begins the French he briefly explains what the entire dialogue involves. This is not a word for word translation; he merely wants the students to get a general understanding. Even the rendering into English is a contextual rather than a literal translation, representing the language an average American would use in the situation. One effective way of presenting the dialogue is with stick figures, drawn on the board, for each person. Colored pictures and other props can be used to help illustrate the meaning of specific words. This allows for as much as possible to be given in French, and eliminates such explanations as "disques means records." If the students are ever going to learn to think in French, they must learn to associate French vocabulary words with actual objects, rather than with equivalent English words. The students probably will not see the English version of the translation until quite a bit later. Within the A-LM there exists a further controversy as to whether the students should see the French written and the translation right after they memorized the dialogue, or whether they should achieve a solid pronunciation skill before going on to the written work.

[34] Sheppard, *op. cit.*, p. 293.

Supplement: (Examples)
Quels sont les jours de la semaine?
Les jours de la semaine sont: lundi, mardi, mercredi, jeudi, vendredi, samedi, dimanche.

The supplement presents some useful vocabulary items that may be learned and practiced as part of the daily routine. They are taught by repetition. They add variety to the student's learning experience, and are useful expressions. Authorities agree that A-LM, to be successful, requires many supplements of this sort. The teacher is free to add other materials, the basic criterion being that it does not interfere with the basic learning.

Dialogue Adaptation: (Examples)
Philippe, combien de disques avez-vous? . . . J'ai beaucoup de disques. Paul, combien de disques avez-vous? . . . Je n'ai pas de disques. Aimez-vous jouer aux cartes? . . . Oui, j'aime jouer aux cartes.

The objective of the dialogue adaptation is to relate the dialogue sentences and situations to the personal experience of the students and to aid memorization. These questions and answers may be learned as soon as the corresponding parts of the dialogue have been memorized. It is not the place to introduce new vocabulary or structure; its purpose is to reenter words and patterns in a different context.

Structure Drills: (Examples of each kind)
Repetition Drill
Nous jouons aux cartes . . . (students repeat)
Vous jouez aux cartes . . . (students repeat)
Ils jouent aux cartes. . . .

Person-Number Substitution
(Teacher says) Je . . . (students must finish the phrase, using the structures they learned in the Repetition Drill)
Elle . . . Elle joue aux cartes
Il . . . Il joue aux cartes
Nous . . . Nous jouons aux cartes

Number Substitution
(Teacher gives a phrase using the singular form of the verb, and the students give the same phrase in the plural; or, the teacher gives a plural phrase and the students counter with the singular.)
Je regarde le journal . . . Nous regardons le journal
Nous jouons aux cartes . . . Je joue aux cartes
Il déjeune a midi . . . Ils déjeunent a midi

These are the pattern drills which are used to teach basic grammatical patterns of the language in terms of the language itself. The essence of the work is the presentation of a frame utterance exemplifying a particular point, and the manipulation of this utterance in such a way that the items illustrating the point are varied without changing the essential structure of the sentence. In this way the student's attention is drawn toward the "slot" in which the changes are being made; he learns to properly manipulate the items that can be properly substituted in that slot, and gradually develops an awareness of the pattern he is handling.

However, knowledge of a language can no more be considered the memorization of dialogues than it can be considered the comprehension of traditional paradigms. Thus the students must pass beyond the dialogues; so they are followed by a series of drills and exercises designed to enable them to gain a mastery of structures. The teacher begins to break the dialogue down into structural elements presented in syntactical segments which are normally heard in the language. The students begin to drill on these patterns and, as with the dialogue, they keep at it until they can provide any pattern without hesitation, again with near mastery of pronunciation and intonation. All of this requires perfect pronunciation on the part of the teacher and completely eliminates the old theory that she can base her method on her own capabilities.

According to some authors, the use of the dialogue is consistent with current psychological theory, both Behaviorist and Gestalt. For example, Politzer states:

> The psychology of second-language learning must take into account three important things . . . first . . . the native language interferes with the acquisition of the new one; second, that language is a habit or complex of habits; third, that language is an elaborate system.[35]

Politzer and other A-LM advocates feel that the use of dialogue-centered materials as intended by their authors takes these factors into consideration. Kelley summarizes their psychological application: the use of English during the class is held strictly to a minimum and direct comparison of the mother and the target language is avoided. By thus keeping the target language dominant the phenomenon of interference is reduced. During the learning of the dialogue and the drills which follow, the emphasis is on imitation, repetition memorization. The student is as active as possible. The rewards of a correct response and the correction of an incorrect one are immediate. The student is led to see the patterns of the target language at "morphological and syntactical levels"; i.e., they understand both the structure of the words themselves and the structure and order of words in a sentence. At this point

---

[35] Robert L. Politzer, *Teaching French: An Introduction to Applied Linguistics* (Waltham, Mass.: Blaisdell Publishing Co., 1965), p. 13.

they may begin to make some generalizations for themselves; if not, the teacher may present these generalizations more formally.[36]

One good thing about the use of the dialogue is that it especially seems to please students. It allows them to use the language instead of just talking about it. Another argument in its favor is that it presents speech as far as possible in its natural and normal setting, as it is actually used. But the use of the dialogue has raised considerable controversy. One argument against it concerns the student's ability to express himself in his target language. There is a certain inflexibility in the simple memorization and recall of others' conversations that hinders the development of an ability to create in the language. It is believed by many 'that the overemphasis on methodology limits both teacher and students when a comprehensive picture of the language is the goal.

Another disturbing development, in the opinion of Gifford Orwin, is "the inevitable downgrading of the instructor."[37] When a language course is conceived primarily as an oral one, the teacher's role can often be reduced to that of a parrot. The new mode of teaching seems to lay great emphasis on the "histrionic." In an effort to avoid English, communication is reduced to the most primitive gestures and grunts. This argument is less troubling than those regarding the learning of the language and it would seem to the authors that what Orwin calls "primitive communication" might be effective in teaching the student to produce the language himself, especially with the younger students of the middle school.

These arguments help to point up the many questions that must still be resolved as to the worth of A-LM. As of now, there is little known about its effect on the total development of the child. We can, however, see what areas are most uncertain and which problems most pressing. It must be remembered that the audio-lingual program in general has been accepted without experimental evidence to prove its superiority over traditional methods and, in like manner, the dialogue has been accepted without any evidence to indicate its superiority over other audio-lingual approaches. One point still to be resolved is whether the program takes into consideration the individual student. With a program like this, the teacher must take the whole or leave it; he cannot apply it simply to some of his students. He has to stick closely to the recommended procedures, although he is urged to add supplementary material, such as the learning of songs. This means that he can give less thought to the individual differences among his pupils.

---

[36] See Leo Kelley, "Dialogue Versus Structural Approach," *French Review* (April 1964) : 37:432–439.

[37] Gifford P. Orwin, "Reflections on the Textbook Jungle," *French Review* (April 1964) : 37:557.

We are beginning to get indications that we should give greater attention to such factors as individual differences, attitudinal orientation ability patterns at different ages, and the sequence of training with respect to these abilities.[38]

Can the middle school student do the same work as the senior high student who is taking A-LM at the same level? It may be necessary to revise the program so that all students do not have to move lock-step through weeks of memorization and drilling, all at the same speed.

Another question concerns the learning situation. Does the student learn better in a highly controlled situation, such as the language laboratory, or with more freedom than A-LM provides? Does the method really present speech in its natural setting so that the student learns it much as a child does? Many feel that A-LM is putting natural speech into a completely unnatural and abnormal situation, the classroom, which makes it impossible for the student to learn it by the "natural method."[39]

Is it better accepting the main goal of language learning as the ability to think in the target language or is it better to start from prescribed and artificial sentence patterns or begin with a basic grammar course?

These questions show that there is still a lot of work to be done before A-LM can be accepted as the best method of foreign-language learning. Yet, even its opponents have to admit that it is "sweeping the country," having a great influence on language instruction. Along with other similar methods, all stressing oral work but none as extreme, A-LM has turned emphasis entirely away from the traditional grammar-translation method. Rather than trying to make improvements in the traditional methods, schools which want to improve their foreign-language curriculum are turning to new methods. It may be that A-LM will be as short-lived as it is now important. It can only be hoped that, if such is true, as with many educational trends, it will leave its good qualities behind.

Industrial Arts

The industrial arts program for middle school students has come a long way from the required manual training course for boys which was common fifty years ago. Although it was conceived originally as preparation for a vocation or trade, boys learned to use various tools and machines and worked almost entirely in wood and metal in shop classes. Consider-

[38] Wallace E. Lambert, "Psychological Approaches to the Study of Language," *Modern Language Journal* (March 1963) : 47:116.

[39] Clodius H. Willis, "After You Speak Think," *French Review* (January 1965) : 38:3:398.

able stress was placed upon the value of a good industrial arts program in reducing dropouts.

Changes in society and technology coupled with compulsory attendance laws have drastically altered the role of industrial arts. The program is now considered to be an integral part of general education and, properly taught,

> A good industrial arts program provides a broad interpretation of our whole industrial culture and specifically educates students in the fundamentals of technology.[40]

In its interpreting and relating science, industry, and technology, the industrial arts program fulfills a primary purpose of the middle school, that of exploratory activities. In their efforts to justify the inclusion of industrial arts in the school program, educators have occasionally made some pretty general statements such as, "Industrial Arts promotes good health." Actually, a good industrial arts curriculum has many specific reasons for its inclusion: in addition to the exploratory activities, pupils learn about various industrial occupations and operations; a wide variety of materials and techniques are introduced and used; industrial arts provides activities for the rapidly increasing leisure time available to Americans; opportunities are available in industrial arts for student creativity; students may learn to appreciate good craftsmanship, improving and developing their own work.

Kinds of Shops

When "shop" is mentioned, what usually comes to mind is the stereotyped version of the unit shop common to high schools and junior high schools for so many years. Even today, we hear too often of a middle school wood shop, generally highly productive of bookends and footstools, or the metal shop, which turns out a proliferation of tin can sugar scoops and spindles.

For middle grades the recommended style of shop is the comprehensive general shop. In a well-planned, well-organized, properly supplied and equipped general shop there will be facilities and materials for work in wood, metal, drafting, ceramics, plastics, concrete, leather, textiles, photography, electronics, electricity, radio, welding, forging, lapidary work, graphic arts, and small motor mechanics. All of this and more can be and is being offered in one large general shop in middle schools throughout the country. All activities are not centered around one material, such as wood or metal, but the use of a variety of media in one activity is stressed.

In the problems of organizing and staffing the industrial arts program with general education for all, the most imperative change in

---

[40] K. E. Dawson, "Developments," *National Association of Secondary School Principals Bulletin* (November 1963) : 48:108.

the pattern of curriculum organization is the removal of arbitrary divisions of materials and procedures now in general use in industrial arts.[41]

In providing such a variety of facilities and media the comprehensive general shop best fulfills its exploratory function and can more readily be related to the curricular offerings of the school. In contrast, the limited general shop is restricted in materials and facilities to working with a particular material, such as metal, or a related group, such as electronics and radio. Recommended for high school level students, the general metal shop, for example, involves all kinds of work and activities with metal. The unit shop is usually found in technical schools or the upper level of high school industrial arts work and concentrates upon a specific activity—a welding shop, or steel metal shop in metalwork, for example.

Trends

The theory of the old unit shop has been firmly imbedded in educational and community thinking for many years. Teachers and administrators are beginning to realize the possibilities inherent in the broad general shop. Indeed there is a growing interest in developing a comprehensive shop program on the elementary level and many of the newer elementary schools have included an industrial arts area in their buildings.

The content and method of industrial arts is changing from the severely restricted and compartmented course of study and constructing projects to an understanding of technology, science, and even gadgets of today. The "every boy builds a birdhouse" days are rapidly disappearing in favor of instruction which strives for concept formation and understanding instead of a concentration upon specific skills.

In the attempt to avoid repetition, there is less division into specific areas in elementary and middle school, less coverage of a wider range of materials and facilities, and a delay in specialization or work in depth with one particular material until the upper school levels.

It is not at all uncommon now to find girls in industrial arts classes. These classes may be composed entirely of girls or can be coeducational. In many schools a quarter or semester or even a year may be required of all students, boys and girls. Occasionally, there is a rotation sequence for all students of industrial arts, homemaking, art, and music, such as suggested earlier. A required course of this kind may include basic woodworking, electricity, basic metalwork, crafts, flower and lawn design, working with finishing materials, and small appliance repair.

There is a movement away from large single purpose machines toward the use of smaller, more versatile equipment. In equipping and

[41] Alan R. Seuss, and Daniel L. Householder, "A New Climate for Industrial Arts Education," *The American School Board Journal* (September 1964) : 149:17.

supplying the shop, cost is a definite factor, not only initially for equipment, but for regular supply items. Often a shop fee is charged although it is difficult to justify a fee in a required course in many communities.

Newer teaching methods and techniques are coming into use in the industrial arts areas. Team teaching, programmed instruction, and closed circuit television are making better use of staff competencies, and,

> In lieu of the traditional individual student project, emphasis is placed upon problems which require research, experimentation, product, and process development.[42]

Schools may have, as the enrollment exceeds four to five hundred students, two general shops: a General Shop Heavy, which places emphasis upon electricity, metalwork, forging, welding, concrete work, and small motor mechanics, and a General Shop Light, in which more work is done with small wood projects, crafts, plastics, graphic arts, radio, and lapidary work. Electives in the eighth or ninth grade provide opportunities for specializing in areas such as graphic arts, drafting, wood, plastics, and metal.

Industrial Arts Programs

While course outlines for industrial arts apparently display little variation, in actual practice there is a great deal of difference from district to district and even within districts in what is included in the industrial arts curriculum. The opportunities to work with different materials, tools, and equipment, the degree to which the course is related to other subject areas within the school, the amount of time devoted to the various media and topics, all are limited only by the imagination and creativity of the instructors and the administration, the money available, and the physical facilities at hand.

The Oswego Campus School Industrial Arts Laboratories,[43] grades K-9, provide facilities for woodworking, sheet metalwork, electricity, graphic arts, elementary science, weaving, sewing, and cooking. The laboratory for the upper grades has facilities for drafting and planning, woodworking, metalwork (forging, foundry, welding, sheet metal, and metal turning), electricity, ceramics and pottery, graphic arts (letterpress, bookbinding, block printing, silk screening), small motor mechanics, textiles, and crafts (copper enameling, copper tooling, metal etching, leathercraft, plastics).

---

[42] *Ibid.*, p. 18.

[43] Edward N. Kazarian, "Oswego's New Campus School Industrial Arts Laboratories," *Industrial Arts and Vocational Education* (March 1965): 54:50–52.

The course of study for the sixth and seventh grades includes drafting, woodworking, sheet metal, basic electricity, and crafts. Eighth graders work with ceramics, wood, metal, textiles, electricity, and graphic arts. The ninth grade course of study includes metalwork and power mechanics. Tools and equipment in these Oswego laboratories or general shops include a graphic arts bench, press, loom, potter's wheels, metal bench, ceramics bench, drying cabinet, kiln, scroll saws, woodworking benches, shear and rolling form, metals bench, wood lathes, band saw, jointer, jigsaw, circle saw, metal lathe, grinders, power hack saw, drill press, forge, crucible furnace, welding bench, welding equipment, rock saw, buffers, and table saw.[44]

A northwest Washington middle school, grades six to eight, formerly a junior high with grades seven to nine, includes most of the same facilities and curricula as the Oswego school and, in addition, provides work with radio transmitting and receiving. The school has a transmitter, a federal license and call number, and regularly has a number of students in each grade who have become licensed "ham" operators.

The Bedford, New York, School District built a unified arts area in their middle school.[45] The school enrolls students in the age group of grades six, seven, and eight, and all students, boys and girls, take industrial arts and homemaking.

> Recognizing that the young adolescent finds dignity, intellectual benefit, and psychological values in the often neglected areas of industrial arts, home arts, music, crafts, fine arts, and dramatics, the middle school should provide an appropriate program and housing in a single arts center.[46]

The unified arts area, constructed circularly around the little theater, includes industrial arts space equivalent to two art rooms in close proximity to the art area; a home arts space equivalent to two home arts rooms, so arranged as to encourage a variety of activities for both boys and girls; and an art area and lobby as an exhibit gallery, whose adjacent space is equivalent to two art rooms.

Areas of instruction in this middle school include crafts and metalwork, ceramics, drawing, painting, and three dimensional work,

---

[44] Tools and equipment in these Oswego laboratories or general shops include a graphic arts bench, press, loom, potters wheels, metal bench, ceramics, bench, drying cabinet, kiln, scroll saws, woodworking benches, shear and rolling form, metals bench, wood lathe, grinders, power hacksaw, drill press, forge, crucible furnace, welding bench, welding equipment, rock saw, buffers, and table saw.

[45] Sheldon R. Wiltse, "Developing a Unified Arts Area in an Ungraded Middle School," *Industrial Arts and Vocational Education* (March 1965): 54:45.

[46] *Ibid.*

cooking and laundry, sewing, cutting, and fitting of textiles, wood-working, electricity, and graphic arts.[47]

Los Angeles junior high schools include courses in agriculture, ten weeks required for boys, and elective thereafter for boys and girls.[48] The standard agriculture unit provided for all new junior high schools, and for bringing existing junior high schools up to date, consists of a classroom with a toolroom, storage, lavatory facilities, a lath house, potting room, compost bins, and approximately one acre of adjacent ground. There are texts and a well-defined course of study:[49]

1. Gardening (exploratory) ten weeks: Boys—required instruction in garden tool identification, safety, preparing soil, planting and harvesting a crop, making simple cuttings, and preparation of a notebook.
2. Gardening (elective) twenty weeks. Boys—long term crops of vegetables and flowers, plant identification, advanced plant propagation, simple landscaping, and garden maintenance.
3. Floriculture (elective) twenty weeks: Girls and boys although designed primarily for girls—instruction in the preparation of soil and the planting of flowers, how to cut, preserve, and use flowers in arrangements and corsages, the propagation of plants by seeds and cuttings, plant identification and planting, and maintenance of dish gardens and plantings.

Another district emphasizes a core program centered around the industrial arts area with special stress on auto and electrical appliance repair. Two periods daily are scheduled for one semester with one period available for a related science.

There is considerable variation in the amount of time scheduled for industrial arts by middle schools. Probably the most common arrangement is a block of nine weeks, twelve weeks, or even eighteen weeks required in grade seven for one or two periods daily which rotates with other subjects, usually homemaking and art. Many schools, however, require industrial arts one period daily all year in grade seven and may even require the same amount in grade eight. Other schools have a required program of industrial arts the first year the students enter the school, whether grade six or grade seven, and operate an elective program thereafter.

[47] Areas of instruction in this middle school include crafts and metalwork, ceramics, drawing, painting, and three dimensional work; cooking and laundry, sewing, cutting, and fitting of textiles; woodworking, electricity, and graphic arts.

[48] Lester O. Matthews, "All Students Take Agriculture in Los Angeles," *National Association of Secondary School Principals Bulletin* (February 1962) : 46:78.

[49] *Ibid.*, p. 79.

Summary

The industrial arts program for early adolescents is undergoing considerable change. The old manual training concept is dropped in favor of a general shop program which is a much broader exploratory experience than the traditional rotation of mechanical drawing, wood shop, and metal shop. Courses currently offered in middle schools include a fascinating array of materials and subjects such as landscaping, ceramics, horticulture, small motor operation, electronics, radio transmitting and operating, metalwork, woodworking, and graphic arts. A part of general education, industrial arts should be required to some extent for all students, boys and girls, with additional electives available. The industrial arts classrooms, shops, and laboratories should never be a dumping ground; the courses have much to offer students of all ability levels. A clear relationship is possible, desirable, and necessary with other subject areas in the school, particularly science. There is a real need for thorough understanding of what the industrial arts program can and should be and an equal need for materials, supplies, tools, equipment, and facilities to operate such a program.

Home Economics in the Middle Schools

It is generally agreed that education for home and family living is extremely important for all persons. The stability of the home, the basic unit of our society, is essential to the well-being of a democratic nation. Thus, the preparation of our youth for worthy home membership can well be one of the most valuable functions our schools can perform.

Though this function is a shared responsibility within the total school program, home economics education, in its dealing with all aspects of home and family living, has a special contribution to make. The belief that the home is the most important influence on the individual presents an impressive challenge to home economics education.

Rapid and constant changes in our way of life have been reflected in the shift of emphasis in home economics education. The learning of skills which were at one time necessary for effective homemaking have taken second place in importance to the understanding of human relationships. We work with people rather than tools. No longer is the family an isolated unit, self-sufficient unto itself. We have become a nation of users of someone else's products, instead of producers of our own.

Mechanical devices have taken over much of the physical labor of the homemaker. Present day homemaking calls for a knowledge of problem solving and decision making, of choosing and buying wisely, managing time and energy as well as money, understanding the development of the child, and making the most of home life in the limited hours the family spends together.

The change in the status of women—the impact of her dual role as career woman and homemaker—has affected the role of other individuals within the family. With more family members contributing to the financial support of the home, more members participate in all of the activities of the household so that homemaking becomes a "shared" responsibility. Father helps in the care of the new baby, family council makes cooperative decisions about the purchase of a new car, children assume responsibility for the care of the playroom, and the teenagers work on a family do-it-yourself project. Regardless of whether the scene is a trailer house or a split-level home in the hills, the home has ceased to be labeled "for women only." With this new concept of shared responsibility comes the need for guiding boys as well as girls for satisfying membership in their immediate families, as well as preparation for their own future home.

We can no longer assume that the responsibility for these teachings concerning family life will be accepted exclusively by the home. The very nature of our pattern of living leaves too little opportunity for such learning. Even the traditional teachings of the basic skills are more difficult to administer, and the complexity of this mechanical age, with its atomic ovens, electric blenders, and automatic rotisseries, discourages early experimentation on the part of children. Even childhood imitative play was much simpler in the days when mothers used wooden spoons and brooms. Likewise, problems of management and relationships were less complex. We need to learn how to be effective home-members these days. The school, then, must supplement what the home is able to do.

In view of these characteristics of our home life today, home economics education has had to keep pace with the times. Students must be prepared to be able to use personal and available resources to the fullest potential in order to achieve a satisfying family life. The theme, then, has changed from training efficient housekeepers to developing happy homemakers.

The establishment of the middle school as a unique part of our educational system, designed to meet specific needs of a particular age group, has presented a new challenge. Thus we must have course offerings to help the student in this present stage of development.

The age group which the middle school serves, sometimes referred to as the "tween-age," has its own particular characteristics and needs, developmental tasks if you will—accomplishments which need to be met satisfactorily before an individual can progress to further development. Though no two individuals at any given age are alike, there are basic characteristics which are found to be typical within an age group. It is these characteristics and developmental tasks that are of paramount importance in considering a curriculum which will best serve the age group.

If home economics in the middle school is planned for this particular age group it, too, will have specific characteristics which are in keeping with this philosophy. If the middle school serves a transitional and exploratory function for the pupil, then the home economics program accepts the pupil where he is, fulfills the needs with which he is faced, and establishes a desire for continued growth and development in the field of home and family life. Too often we have failed in these respects. Too often, likewise, a senior high school offering was merely transplanted into a school for early adolescents. The question is not, "Should the student take home economics in the middle school instead of at the senior high level?" but, "How can we offer a program that will stimulate further interest on the part of the student?"

Curriculum

It is difficult to define objectives and curriculum of the middle school program without considering the overall goals of home economics education and considering the program from the vertical standpoint. Home economics education, at whatever level, includes within its scope some work in child care, foods and nutrition, clothing, personal grooming, family relationships, home management, related art, and home furnishings.

At each stage of development the individual is faced with some particular need in each of the areas of home economics. As the individual matures, however, the horizons of interest widen to include a broader conception in each of the phases. The early adolescent, for example, may be interested in knowing how to get along with little children and the responsibilities which a baby-sitter must accept, while the late adolescent will be anxious to understand prenatal care and the development of the infant. During the inner turmoils of puberty the young adolescent is bothered with the problem of making and keeping friends—the middle adolescent with how to act on a date—while the late adolescent is vitally interested in preparation for marriage and family life.

It is important that we build upon experience—that the needs of the age group are taken into consideration. Emphasis is placed on particular phases important to the maturation age of the pupils. No one suggested course could possibly be recommended for home economics education in a middle school. Even if one arrived at a perfect combination within one classroom, schools, communities, and homes differ throughout the nation so that what would fit the needs of students in one locality would not be appropriate for another.

General suggested guides for curriculum planning and course offerings are available in most states. Although originally many programs were planned for the four year senior high school, the trend toward planning for home economics from the elementary years through college is becoming more widespread.

Variation in beliefs and practices regarding the scheduling of home economics in middle schools exists. Some amount, however, is usually required of all girls at some period in the middle school. Sometimes a short unit is required in the sixth, seventh, or eighth grades, with an elective program offered in the eighth or ninth grade. Some educators believe that exploratory experiences should begin at the sixth grade or earlier, while others feel that the eighth grade is the logical place to begin due to learning readiness. Whatever rationale is used, the length of courses at each level vary from nine to twelve weeks to a semester for the lower grades, with thirty-six week courses ordinarily scheduled for the eighth or ninth grade.

With the recent surge of interest in the total school educational program, experimentation and research have taken on new acceleration. For instance, the persistent problem of inability to accomplish some tasks in the fifty minute hour has been largely eliminated through variable, flexible, and modular scheduling techniques. Likewise, the problem of giving the middle school student exploratory experiences in several course offerings each year can be alleviated through similar scheduling techniques or through the "Arts Program" such as described earlier in this chapter.

This "Arts Program" would include a nine week unit of home economics during the sixth grade, for example, during which the students would participate in experiences planned for continuity with as little identification of separate units as possible. Activities might include learning to sew and cook, getting along with others, and social affairs. This type of program has merit when implementing the philosophy that boys as well as girls need preparation in home and family life beyond the highly successful boys' chef clubs in the activity program. It also provides an opportunity for group experiences with members of the opposite sex which has been cited as a need during this growing period. Thus, both boys and girls are learning the importance of sharing home responsibilities, the art of getting along with others, and are gaining an insight into the many facets of home and family life.

The high interest in creating, particularly prevalent in "tween-agers," is met in the opportunities for actual construction and preparation of projects that are challenging enough to provide stimulation, yet not too difficult to prevent achievement or to cause frustrations.

Local Resources for the Program

An awareness of what resources are available for the student to work with in the home setting is necessary to make teaching of home economics meaningful. Many families in poverty areas receiving surplus food are totally unfamiliar with means of preparing these goods in a palatable manner. Girls who have never had a sewing machine in their home and come to school with hems loose, seams open, and clothing torn should be taught how to mend by hand and care for commercially prepared clothing before being taught to sew on a machine. Too often the home economics curriculum dictates that all seventh graders, for instance, must learn to sew an apron. The same principles used to teach how to sew an apron might be put to better use if the girl had some decision making power as to what to make—a shift, a simple A-line skirt, or repairing or remaking already purchased clothing.

The total child's needs must be taken into consideration when planning a meaningful course of study. Social, environmental, psychological, and physical needs of the child should be weighed when deciding what to teach and how. How many homemakers of the future will need to make a white sauce, or bake a cake from "scratch," or make aprons or head scarves? The curriculum should be built upon the needs (present and future) of the students, not the traditional methods that have been handed down over the years.

How, then, should the teacher decide upon the content within the curriculum? Perhaps one might say that, equally important to the characteristics and needs of the students, is the background knowledge of the homes and communities from which these students come. What kind of home life do these students have? Is the population of the community a stable or a mobile one? Do the long hair, changing skirt styles, and oddities in dress of the young generation cause problems with the adults? What socioeconomic implications need to be considered? Do mothers work? Do students assume responsibility for the care of the home? Do students earn spending money, and if so, how do they spend it? Are breakfasts provided in the home and, if so, of what nature are they? How do early adolescents spend their leisure time? These are all the questions which the home economics teachers need to attempt to answer in order to be able to offer a practical and realistic, as well as stimulating, experience in their courses. This information must be gleaned from class discussions, questionnaires, surveys, parent-teacher conferences, orientation meetings, home visits, other teachers, local residents, and cumulative records.

Cooperative planning is vitally important in many directions. The teacher should work hand-in-hand with home economics teachers at the senior high level in defining objectives and goals for the total program. Repetition is good only to the extent that it occurs as a result of careful planning; all too often it just happens to happen. Too many classes, at too many levels, use the same approach to nutrition with the same techniques, the same charts, the same films being used for the same students. With the wealth of possibilities of different approaches, it is important to know the "what" and "how" that others are using.

The content and methodology of home economics is a continual challenge to the teacher in light of the changes in our society. Values concerning premarital sex, drug usage, and the necessity for marriage (love being all that is necessary for a relationship) are constantly being redefined and reappraised by young people. Many times the teacher's values and those of the student are "poles apart." This is not to say that the teacher must change her values to meet those of the student, but, rather, that she must be aware of their feelings and ideas and allow them freedom in the classroom to express and challenge these ideas. Too often a teacher of family relationships, for example, will attempt to impart her values and beliefs to a class. While it is impossible not to let certain biases and feelings come through in teaching human relationships, it is important to keep an open and free atmosphere that will allow students to present their viewpoints also.

How does a teacher of a ninth grade class, for instance, react when a student says, "I plan to go on the pill whenever I find someone I really like, and my mother agrees with this idea." One possibility is to say "that's foolish," or "you know you'd be too young to get the pill." Another is to take this as an opening to discuss what is necessary in a relationship between two people (sex being just one of the ingredients) and ways of dealing with sexual feelings. Labeling the idea as good or bad without exploring where the idea came from, other ways to look at the situation, or hearing other students' viewpoints will never help the student grow or change her beliefs.

Facilities and Equipment

Home economics departments of today are designed to create as real and as homelike a situation as possible within a school room. Facilities for teaching each of the areas need to be provided, with emphasis placed equally upon group and family work, clothing, and food. Gone are the days when each student scientifically experimented with her own individual "pot of porridge," to be tasted, in solitude, at her own individually assigned stool. Emphasis on planning meals for a family, or a group, with the problems of time management involved has afforded opportunities for practical experiences in family life situations. The same belief must be applied to all units, with group work occurring as often as individual work does.

All purpose rooms, or multi-purpose rooms, with areas and equipment provided for all or many of the kinds of activities which constitute modern home economics, have helped to dispel the old cooking and sewing division of the domestic science courses. Even in schools which have planned separate areas for the equipment related to foods and clothing, flexible space and materials are planned so that many phases can be taught within each area.

How these plans are designed will depend upon such factors as the size of school, type of program, location, number of teachers, and anticipated sizes of classes. Some schools with more than one teacher have provided two or more all purpose rooms, so that each teacher has a self-contained room. Some are involving students in related activities so that a variety of centers within the home economics classroom are in use at one time.

It is important that the facilities be attractive and homelike and planned in such a way that students and teachers alike can work individually or in groups with ease. Students will take pride in an attractive home-within-a-school and will help to keep it inviting.

Equipment and supplies should allow for experiences which would be at least as adequate as representative home situations in the locality. With the introduction of school buying plans for major appliances which are available through many companies, the home economics rooms can have a continuous supply of up-to-date equipment at minimal cost.

Chapter 11 Bibliography

Broudy, Harry S. "Educational Theory and the Music Curriculum," *Music Educators Journal* (November-December 1964) : 57:32–36.

D'Andrea, Frank. "A New Basis for Music in the Secondary Schools," *Music Educators Journal* (February-March 1963) : 49:33–36.

Dawson, Kenneth E. "Developments in Practical Arts," *National Association of Secondary School Principals Bulletin* (November 1963) : 47:108–113.

Ecker, David W. "Programmed Instruction: Challenge or Threat to Education?" *School Arts* (October, November, December, 1963).

Gallington, Ralph O. "A Two Shop Limited General Shop Offering," *Industrial Arts and Vocational Education* (March 1964) : 53:30–32.

Gullette, Cameron, Keating, Clark, and Viens, Claude. *Teaching a Modern Language*. New York: F. S. Crofts and Co., 1954.

Hocking, Elton. "Revolution in the Foreign Languages," *National Association of Secondary School Principals Bulletin* (April 1964) : 48:34–36.

Isch, Anthony. "The Benefits of Marching Bands," *Music Educators Journal* (February-March 1965) : 51:97–100.

Kazarian, Edward N. "Oswego's New Campus School Industrial Arts Laboratories," *Industrial Arts and Vocational Education* (March 1965) : 54:50–52.

Kelly, Leo. "Dialogue Versus Structural Approach," *French Review* (February 1964) : 37:432–439.

Lewis, James, and Bennett, Hershel K. "A Unified Arts Program for Junior High Schools," *Art Education*, XI (April 1958).

Maze, Clarence. "Philosophical Basis for Business Education in the Junior High School," *Balance Sheet* (October 1966) : 47:60–62.

Newmark, Gerald, and Diller, Edward. "Emphasizing the Audio in the Audio-Lingual Approach," *Modern Language Journal* (January 1964) : 48:18–22.

Politzer, Robert. *Teaching French: An Introduction to Applied Linguistics*. Waltham, Mass.: Blaisdell Publishing Co., 1965.

Rowe, John L. "How to Meet Changing Needs in Typewriting," *Business Education World* (September 1963) : 44:9–11.

Russon, Allien R., and Wanous, S. J. *Philosophy and Psychology of Teaching Typewriting*. Cincinnati: South-Western Publishing Co., 1960.

Tonne, Herbert A., Popham, Estelle, and Freeman, M. Herbert. *Methods of Teaching Business Subjects*, 3rd ed. New York: McGraw-Hill Book Company, Inc., 1965.

Health and Physical Education

Physical educators have a great as well as a grave responsibility. Educationally speaking, they are in a choice spot, for they have the opportunity to play with children, to observe them at play, and to teach them the enduring lessons of life through an informal play approach. Psychologists tell us that children are their real selves when they play. Educators claim that all people regardless of age learn more, faster, and remember longer when they are doing something they enjoy and when they become absorbed in the adventure of learning.

Children are active creatures and enjoy movement—any kind of movement. They need and seek activity to help in the proper development of bones, muscles, tendons, and ligaments. A child also seeks status through activity. Hear the youngster who says, "Watch me!" or "I can do that." They enjoy testing their strength and skill and experiencing the "feel" of new activities. In fact, we associate activity so much with children that we regard the inactive child as one who is ill.

It is recognized that activity can promote learning. This learning, however, at times may not be desirable, but there is learning. That the child is capable of "doing something" is the basis of learning experience. Physical education seeks to use the basic drive for activity to promote and guide these learning experiences into channels of proper growth and development of the individual.

Physical education gives the teacher an excellent opportunity to observe the child in an active social setting and to become more familiar with the characteristics of the child in light of this experience. Physical education can help children to become more skillful, accept their limitations, and gain status in the eyes of their playmates.

The middle school years are a good time for establishing the ideals of democracy through cooperation, good sportsmanship, good leadership, loyalty, and tolerance in activities of great interest. It is a period when pupils can be motivated easily. Furthermore, since children need much more vigorous physical activity than is provided by twentieth century living, they are entitled to daily teaching-learning situations in which movement of sufficient intensity, duration, and meaning is given the dominant role.

Physical Education

An all-around program in physical education should be offered. The program should include some activities of social value in larger groups and heterosexual relationships. All pupils should be encouraged to become proficient in at least one activity and at least average in several activities.[1] Leadership-followership opportunities should be provided. Whenever possible, pupils should be given responsibilities which may help them to develop qualities desirable in leaders.

Physical education is an integral and indispensable phase of education. It is concerned with the growth, development, and adjustment of youth by means of a systematic program of physical activities and related experiences selected and organized according to social and hygienic standards which contribute to the total fitness, growth, and development of the child primarily through physical activities and directed toward specific outcomes. Physical education is both a means and an end. It is a means in that it provides a medium for optimum growth and development of the child. It is an end in itself because physical fitness and the acquisition of desirable skills are needed for full living.

The values of physical education are valid for education. Other areas cannot make the contributions to the development of the individual that physical education can. Since its values are important and necessary to all students, it is a part of a general education. In the middle school it is the universal practice to require physical education in all grades. Activities are the sole direct means of producing certain desired developments and adjustments of youth. These youths must acquire primary interests and skills in the activities. Associate and concomitant values, such as physical conditions and attitudes, are acquired through participation, under proper conditions, in the activities.

[1] Karl W. Bookwalter, *Physical Education in the Secondary Schools* (Washington, D. C.: The Center for Applied Research in Education, Inc., 1964), p. 42.

Physical education aims at the optimum development of the physically, mentally, and socially integrated and adjusted individual through guided instruction and participation in total-body activities selected according to social and hygienic standards. The aim of physical education is to provide an opportunity for the individual to act in situations that are physically wholesome, mentally stimulating and satisfying, and socially sound.[2]

Physical education refers to the process of education which goes on when you are concerned with activities that develop and maintain the human body. Through a well-directed physical education program, students develop skills for the worthy use of leisure time, engage in activity which is conducive to healthful living, develop socially, and contribute to their physical and mental health.

Physical education requirements are prescribed by state law or regulation, with their implementation the responsibility of the local unit. Cultural and geographical characteristics, as well as the health status of students, will determine, to a large extent, what is included in a local program of physical education. Specific community interests must also play a part. Program emphasis will frequently differ from one locale to another as a result of traditions that have been established and perpetuated.

It is within the province of local authority to offer programs which go beyond established minimum requirements. Properly organized, a well-balanced physical education program provides the development of all aspects of personality, including the mental, physical, emotional, and social. The experiences are arranged to provide for sequence and continuity and, therefore, to contain a place in the program for all students, including the handicapped. Provision is made for coeducational activities and with a flexible program, the interests of all students are met on an efficient and economical basis. The activities should be so varied and the skills required so broad in nature that even the child with the poorest physical ability can find some satisfaction of success in an activity.

Physical education is one of the category of experiences through which the child's needs may be met. An effort should be made to help each student explore himself and develop an adequate self-concept based upon knowledge of his own assets and liabilities.[3] A complete physical education program in the schools includes participation by pupils who cannot fully engage in the program provided for those who are medically capable of engaging in all activity offerings. Every effort should

---

[2] Victor T. Trusler, *Fundamentals of Physical Education* (Minneapolis: Burgess Publishing Co., 1950), p. 29.

[3] Ann E. Jewett, and Clyde Knap, eds. *The Growing Years—Adolescence*, (Washington, D. C.: American Association for Health, Physical Education, and Recreation, 1962), p. 48.

be made to include students in those phases of the regular program which might benefit them. Modifications should be made so that every student, regardless of physical capacity, may engage in some kind of physical education activity. Functional efficiency is highly dependent on energy supplies, on growth and development, and on habits of recreation. Moreover, physical development, sociomotor skills, posture, and group-cooperative experiences contribute to the student's social status. Social status refers to the degree of prestige one attains in the social groups with which one comes in contact. Physical experiences that foster growth, develop skilled movements, increase and redirect energy supplies, furnish opportunities for success in social experiences, and resolve frustrations are examples of physical education.[4]

Physical education, through its emphasis on wholesome activity, group participation, skills for self-expression, proficiency and ease in movement, recreational and social tastes and skills, self-appraisal, and desirable attitudes furnishes an excellent background and a fruitful means for satisfaction of human needs. There is psychic and physical therapy in enjoyable motor activity, and a means of self-expression in sports, in the dance, and in physically active fun. The nature of the program makes an increase in biological fitness concomitant.

The true function of physical education deals with realistic contributions made by these programs to the overall and avowed purposes sought by the school in its total curriculum. The supervised program of physical education also provides the school child with those tools of participation in recreation that enable him to spend his leisure time pleasurably and beneficially in out-of-school days and after-school years. Moreover, the games and sports, the team play, the group enterprises are good bases for incorporating social attitudes and understandings and democratic principles of living.

Physical education is the only area of the school program specifically charged with the responsibility for developing and promoting the physical fitness of pupils. This is one objective that uniquely belongs in this field. Raymond Weiss of New York University asked in "Memorandum," publication of the Oregon State Department of Education, "Should physical fitness be our ultimate goal? It should be a prerequisite. The ultimate goal should be the development of a positive attitude towards physical activity and physical education."[5] Thus, the physical education teacher should assess each student's physical fitness at the beginning of the school year. Those who are physically fit should be taught sports, games, gymnastics, skills and other activities. Those who are not fit should be put in remedial groups until they overcome their deficiencies.

[4] Elwood Davis, and Earl Wallis, *Toward Better Teaching in Physical Education* (Englewood Cliffs, N. J.: Prentice-Hall, Inc., 1961), p. 6.

[5] Ralph J. Dyson, "Memorandum," Oregon State Department of Education, September 21, 1964.

The Physical Education Program

The physical education program should offer opportunities to learn a wide variety of skills. Some students will not have the readiness to learn some skills. Because maturity, structure, and strength are important factors in the success of performing the skills, standards of achievement should be set up on a basis of classification by structure and function.

There should be a daily period of physical education, and at least ten minutes of the physical education period should be devoted to vigorous activity. A wide variety of activities should be provided to aid in all-around development of boys of different growth patterns. Strenuous activities are needed for developing physical fitness, but teachers should be alert to signs of exhaustion or unusual fatigue among the boys. Basic skills for extracurricular activities should be given as well as the skills leading up to the regular class programs. Physical education can challenge students intellectually by including historical information about the various activities offered as well as data concerning terminology, fundamentals, and rules.

To meet the needs and interests of all youth, the program is usually organized as follows: adapted physical education, the intramural sports program, the extramural sports program, and the interscholastic athletic program. Each is essential and no physical education program is complete unless all four are developed. In addition, each aspect is organized in relation to the other components of the program. Finally, all are integrated and coordinated so that teaching and learning are purposeful and effective.

Depending upon the geographical area and the interests of students and teacher, some thirty or more sport activities and various exercises are taught in the basic program. The program includes aquatics, posture work, dual and individual sports, self-testing activities, formal activities, games and relays, sports of higher organization, rhythmics and dancing, contests, apparatus, and tumbling and stunts. The listed activities serve as the medium through which education takes place; thus, physical education uses physical activity for the identical purpose that mathematics, for example, employs numbers, symbols, and formulas.[6]

The activities at this level must be selected with care because of the anatomical and physiological nature of the student. Pupils at this level are susceptible to fatigue, are in a period of rapid growth, and find it difficult to coordinate their actions, which results in awkwardness. The program should become neither a patchwork of games chosen to amuse children nor a series of formalized body-building activities. It should

---

[6] Clifford L. Brownell, "The Role of Health, Physical Education, and Recreation in the Space Age," *National Association of Secondary School Principals Bulletin* (May 1960) : 43:6, p. 6.

seek to educate through the motor experiences, consider games as educative media, and recognize the need in children for developmental activities. The activities should be taught not simply explained. All too frequently, the boys' program consists of softball, basketball, and volleyball. These meager programs are not examples of the application of this criterion, but an abuse of it. On the other hand, a mere smattering of experiences in a multitude of activities can lead to little but distaste and disinterest.

Activities must progress from simple to complex, single to combined, from beginning through intermediate to an advanced level. Rules may be modified to restrict time and space. There should be unity in the nature of the activities which are organized. Conditioning or warm-up exercises should be chosen so as to favorably affect the muscle groups and joints involved in the vigorous or essential activities of the day. For unity and safety, there should be an orderly progression from the less vigorous to the most vigorous and a tapering off by the close of the period. There must be careful supervision by qualified personnel of all physical education activities at this period in order that the student may experience optimum development. The physical education teachers on the middle school level should be specialists.

During each daily lesson, physical capacities need to be stimulated to peak motor performance. Activities must be chosen on the basis of how well they achieve this objective. The entire body must be involved and exercised at a level far exceeding the casual, and yet choices must show cognizance for mind-body unity and accommodate concomitant learnings that serve the total being well. The whole of the lesson, when put together, must both exercise the body and produce valuable learning. Lessons failing to accomplish this merit something less than the label of physical education.

There are a number of basic reasons for requiring suitable wearing apparel for physical education. A primary advantage of some kind of standard uniform is to enable students to perform in the various activities with ease, unhampered by restrictive garments. Also, attractive costumes provide for a general atmosphere of cooperation and pride in appearance. Hygienically, the ease of checking and supervising the cleanliness of uniforms also makes it advisable to use them wherever possible in the physical education program. Exceptions to this requirement are often necessary when neither the school nor the parent can afford the cost.

Physical educators must make certain that approved sanitary practices are observed by students in the program. Hygienic activities should be those which will aid the pupil to maintain personal cleanliness and to improve personal appearance.[7] Showers after activity participa-

---

[7] Karl W. Bookwalter, "What We Know about Fitness," *National Association of Secondary School Principals Bulletin* (March 1956) : 39:43, p. 43.

tion are to be required of all students wherever conditions permit. High standards of sanitation and health practice should be maintained at all times in gymnasiums, locker rooms, shower rooms, lavatories, and swimming pools. The physical education program can serve as an excellent laboratory experience for putting into effect many of the facts and knowledges acquired in health education and safety.

During the sixth and seventh grade, introduction of simple coordination exercises can be made with emphasis on response, rhythm, and balance, with attention given to group games of low organization, relays, and modified team-game skills. Good sportsmanship and desirable personality reactions are urged in all activities.

The program in the eighth grade can include seasonal sports with an opportunity to play the game in learning situations where the emphasis will be on fundamental skills and rules of play.

In the ninth grade, more advanced skills in games and sports can be included and activities made progressively more challenging to the students' ability. Motorability testing and self-testing activities should be given as well as a proportionate increase in the amount of body-building exercises. Progressive upgrading of all activities should be maintained through the ninth grade.

Health Education

The middle school is designed for and owes its existence to its ability to meet the common and individual needs of boys and girls in early adolescence. The recognition of its responsibilities in the area of health education is basic to achieving these fundamental goals. The school has a direct civic obligation to provide an environment (both physical and mental) which is not only conducive to good health and safety but promotes the development of desirable health concepts and practices.

A student's health is determined by many factors, and the responsibility for its maintenance is vested in many public and private agencies and organizations in addition to his family. A well-conceived school health program involves the efforts of the home, the school, and the community, each performing a distinct function, but all interdependent, working cooperatively for a common goal.

School health education is a broad area. It encompasses all phases of school living, from school site to school lunch and from curriculum to administration and custodial services. The following discussion will attempt to focus on that part of the school health program embodied in the instructional program.

That the importance of good health has been recognized by governments internationally, nationally, and locally is apparent by the existence of such agencies and organizations as the World Health Organization at the international level, the Department of Health, Education and Welfare at the national level, and the State Departments of

Health and their subdivisions at the state and local levels. Huge sums of money have been budgeted and innumerable laws and regulations have been established for the development and maintenance of conditions which contribute to the satisfactory health of individual citizens. Health is recognized as being involved in all phases of any action directed toward raising a standard of living and increasing productivity, efficiency and happiness.

Health has always been recognized by educators as a fundamental or basic quality in individual effectiveness. The National Security Council, in a statement relating to responsibilities of schools in health education, indicated that when schools do a good job in health education they lay a foundation for a lifetime of sound health habits which strengthen the whole community and the whole nation. This statement is not idealistic, unrealistic, or theoretical. The principle is sound and can be illustrated by comparing certain aspects of high standards of living—malaria control, venereal disease control, productivity, for instance—with the level of education of the people in a given country.

Education of the individual toward an increasing awareness and acceptance of responsibility to himself and to society is another well-accepted educational aim. Frequently, the implications of this objective of education are not related to or associated with the subject or the area of learning, called health instruction. But, again using an example of progress that has been achieved, it can be seen that the improvements in sanitation, the improvements in diet as evidenced by the steady increase in the physical stature of Americans, the virtual elimination of rickets, and the control of communicable diseases have all resulted from the efforts of public health organizations and a health-educated public. Frequently, it is not recognized that these changes and improvements have been brought about by an increased awareness and acceptance of responsibility by the individual for his own health and for the welfare of others.

The health instruction phase of the school health program carries a large proportion of the responsibility for the development of habits, attitudes, and information which have contributed to the comparatively good quality of health Americans enjoy today. Health instruction in today's schools cuts through the mythical walls which separate the biological and sociological categories of learning, selecting parts from each and reuniting them into a new whole. It capitalizes on the health experiences of students, interprets the mystical, and helps to allay fears and worries through understanding and knowledge. It identifies the needs and interests of students and gathers them together within the curriculum for exploration and investigation. It is more than merely learning what is best for the individual; it is more than just learning the facts. Rather, it is a striving toward the development of attitudes and behavior which are conducive to the promotion and maintenance of health.

The student should grow in his realization of *how* to act in the promotion of health and in knowledge of *why* such behavior is biologically and sociologically sound.

Adults are universally interested in health, as can be observed by the tremendous sale of patent medicines, the huge quantities of advertising about health products and health conditions, and conversations which are frequently marked by discussions of deviations from normal health. In general, these interests are not as strong in young adolescents; however, these students are beginning to develop an intense interest in certain areas of the health instruction program. Adolescents share the adult interest in such things as good figures or physiques, mental ease, and personal attractiveness. Havighurst in his "Developmental Tasks and Education"[8] lists "accepting one's physique and accepting a masculine or feminine role" as a fundamental developmental task of adolescence. He goes on to say, that

> since we teach boys and girls to evaluate themselves so largely on the basis of their physical development, we must expect this to be a source of interest, pride, assurance, doubt, worry, or inferiority feeling depending upon the accident of the individual's particular physique and pattern of growth. Many problems of behavior and low achievement in school can be solved by reassuring boys and girls that they are 'normal' even if their pattern of development is not that of the average person.

The student is arriving at an awareness of himself and a more realistic feeling of his relationship to a group and the group's relationship to him. He is becoming aware of the influence of his family and particularly that of his parents, brothers, and sisters. He is growing toward more and more self-direction and independence and enlarges his social group from family and school to the community. Gaining freedom and independence from parents and other adults is another developmental task of adolescence. As he gains more freedom a new realm of choices opens to him and he needs guidance and knowledge to help him form the attitudes which direct his behavior and which help him to avoid unfortunate choices in his initial stages of economic and emotional independence.

Basic Concepts in Health Education

Repeated emphasis has been given to the necessity of planning the health curriculum around the needs and interests of the student. On the basis of health implications drawn from general needs of early adoles-

[8] Robert J. Havighurst, *Developmental Tasks and Education* (Chicago: The University of Chicago Press, 1948), pp. 30–32.

cents presented above, certain health needs common to sixth, seventh, eighth, and ninth graders can be specified. In turn, these common needs can be used to form the framework of the instructional program in health.

Statements of health needs common to all middle school youth have been made by a number of different authorities. Although the statements vary in their manner of presentation, all of them include areas of health information relating to the structure and function of the human body, personal care, nutrition and food, first aid and safety, disease, public or community health and sanitation, alcohol, narcotics and tobacco, rest, exercise, health fads and fallacies or consumer health, and mental health including emotional adjustments, family life, and sex education.

Various states have attempted to identify the common health needs of youth and have recommended courses of study to meet these needs. For example, North Carolina includes instruction in the following areas:

alcohol education; cancer; cleanliness (personal) and grooming; community health; dental health; developing wholesome life relationships; eyes, ears, nose and throat; first aid; heart and circulation; nutrition education; posture education; rest, work, relaxation and recreation; safety education; and sanitation.

These areas of instruction are repeated in each grade with the emphasis and concepts differing according to the maturity of the student.

Texas recommends that at the eighth or ninth grade level consideration be given to:

the development of increasing responsibility for and desirable attitudes toward personal hygiene such as care of the skin; adequate grooming, sleep and rest, changes associated with puberty; nutritional health; mental and emotional health; the body, its structure and action; standard first aid practices; health fads and fallacies; and common communicable and noncommunicable diseases and their control.

Oregon, following a cyclic plan of instruction, recommends for the middle school these units:

development of the body; personal hygiene (including alcohol, stimulants and narcotics); nutrition and foods—kinds, care, and use; safety and first aid with stress on safety; effects of exercise; safety and first aid with the stress on first aid; community health and sanitation; and mental and emotional health; choice and use of health services and health practices (consumer health); community health and safety including industrial safety, civil defense, driver education and recreational safety; and the control of communicable and noncommunicable diseases.

Any school using the common health needs of youth as a basis for curriculum development should remember that however useful listings may be, it does not obviate the necessity of determining the particular interests and needs of the children in a given community and school. Certain techniques may be used to determine the emphasis to be given within the particular teaching situation. These techniques include a review of the school health records which contain the results of screening tests, teachers' observations, health examinations; sociograms; teacher-nurse conferences; tests of knowledges, attitudes, and habits; student interest surveys; home visits; class discussions; and a study of the health of the community through such sources as the health department and official and voluntary agencies.

The areas of instruction relating to alcohol, drug, and sex education are sometimes greeted with some degree of emotional response on the part of communities, administrators, teachers, and even students. Because of fear of community reaction, administrators sometimes refuse to let such topics be introduced into the curriculum; because of inadequate knowledge and preparation and the resulting feeling of insecurity, teachers may avoid including such topics in classroom discussions. When opportunity for discussion and study of controversial issues is not provided in the classroom, teachers and administrators are failing in their obligation to students. Early adolescence is the age when children are beginning to experiment, when they are beginning to seek adult status, and when they begin to feel most strongly their inadequacies and, as a result, sometimes turn to undesirable behavioral outlets.

Sex education should be included in the health instruction program where it seems most appropriate. This subject matter can be an integral part of the teaching of health, science, social studies and home economics. Classes may be mixed or segregated. It is most desirable to teach social hygiene to boys and girls together. This subject should be approached in a natural, matter-of-fact manner. Teachers should be well informed so that instruction is scientifically and socially sound rather than merely a repetition of the teacher's individual attitudes.

Instruction about the effects of alcohol and drugs on the human body is mandatory in most states but statutory requirements unfortunately have little relationship to the effectiveness of such instruction. Alcohol and drugs, as used today, are creating problems of great magnitude because they are so often disruptive to personal, social, and economic well-being. Continued social pressures exerted by friends and acquaintances, movies, advertisements, and television make it necessary that each community face these problems. The most promising approach seems to be through public education. The aims of instruction about alcohol and drugs are consistent with the aims of general education—that is, the development of a well-adjusted individual—one equipped to make the necessary adjustment in life with a feeling of adequacy and security.

For this reason emphasis at all age levels should be placed upon good mental health. Scientific information in many fields helps pupils develop attitudes and reactions to varying situations and to base their own behavior upon known truths. The student is desperately seeking social acceptance by his peers. He is often faced with the problem of being able to say "no" when his judgment indicates that this is what he ought to do. At the same time he needs to learn acceptable ways of having fun—acceptable to himself, his peers and the adults who are responsible for him. Middle school students can begin to understand some of the social and economic problems related to alcohol and drugs; these might well be taught through units concerned with safety, family living, or health. Here again youth must be helped to differentiate fact from opinion. Misconceptions and misunderstandings concerning these topics should begin to clear up as his knowledge, based on scientific fact, increases. An understanding teacher will encourage individual children to feel free to discuss personal problems privately. Individual problems related to the use of alcohol and drugs by members of their own families may occur occasionally. A teacher who will listen sympathetically and without showing undue emotion can help the youngster acquire security in his relationship with himself.

Interscholastic Athletics in the Junior High School

The question of whether interscholastic athletics should be a part of the educational experience found in middle schools has long been debated. Neither side in the argument has achieved much success in changing the attitudes and opinions of the opposing group. In the beginning of the junior high school movement in the United States many school systems organized their schools on the same pattern as that of the senior high schools within the same system. This tendency was especially notable in their athletic programs. Many schools introduced the accepted athletic activities that had been sponsored for years in high schools and colleges. Football, track and field events, baseball, and basketball all became a part of the interscholastic program. Rules for games were usually modified so they more nearly met the level of ability of the students. In essence, the interscholastic program was simply stepped down from the nine-to-twelve grade level to the seven-to-nine grade level.[9]

Since about 1930, questions have been raised regarding the advisability of considering the junior high school as a young high school as far as its athletic program was concerned. With the expansion of the junior high school concept into that of a middle school, the feeling is more prevalent that the chief athletic interest of the middle school

[9] Charles E. Forsythe, *Administration of High School Athletics* (New York: Prentice-Hall, Inc., 1954), p. 417.

should be largely intramural in nature. This policy is more in keeping with the basic principles of the school. The intramural program enables more students to play more games, to extend and broaden their interests, and to improve their skills. It is usually possible to satisfy the desire of students of this age for competition if the intramural program is handled properly.

However, this trend toward intramural athletics is not universal. A few states, among them Pennsylvania, Indiana, Kansas, and Michigan have definite regulations for athletic competition. Such states have felt it was preferable to set up standards knowing that certain schools would engage in interschool play.

Arguments for Interscholastic Sports

Proponents of this philosophy point out that there is a definite need for an athletic program in the school. Each teenage student possesses an abundance of energy and natural tendencies toward physical activity. What could better satisfy these urges and desires of youth than a well-balanced program of athletics, organized properly and supervised adequately? In addition, it is pointed out that this type of program would afford worthwhile activities for many youths who have too much leisure time. It is obvious that most children have an inherent desire for competition. If the school does not provide an outlet for these desires, the youngsters will seek release in other areas of the community. This is especially true when one watches the growth of such programs as Little Leagues, Kid Football Associations, and similar sports which are community sponsored. Those who favor interscholastic sports for middle school youth claim that since it is impossible to eliminate the natural competitive tendencies in our youth, the school should fulfill this function.

Our society is competitive in nature, not just in athletics alone. By the time a boy is in his early teens, he should be exposed to some of this competition. Not all boys can derive enough competition from intramural sports to satisfy their desires. The place for the skilled boy is in competition against other boys that have the same ability. This is usually the interschool situation.[10]

Usually opponents of interscholastic competition in the middle schools claim that the physical strain involved is too great on a person of this age. Hollis Fait, Director of the Physical Efficiency Laboratory at the University of Connecticut, has this comment on the subject:[11]

[10] Burt Droste, "The Advantages of Interscholastic Sports at the Junior High School Level," *School and Community* (February 1960), p. 17.

[11] Hollis J. Fait, "Should the Junior High School Sponsor Interscholastic Athletic Competition?" *Journal of Health, Physical Education, and Recreation* (February 1961), p. 38.

Summarizing the evidence available of the results of certain physiological studies, it may be said that there is nothing to indicate that
the heart or the kidneys of the normal youngster may be damaged
by the strenuous work required of him in competitive interscholastic play.

However, the research done in this field has been limited and somewhat inconclusive. There is a great deal of conflicting evidence at the
present time. Competitive athletics are a physiological, psychological,
and sociological experience and to be complete research should include
all three areas. Sociological and psychological investigation is generally
regarded as less accurate than direct physiological research. Yet to
approach the study of the effects of athletic competition upon young
children purely on physiological implications would denote a lack of
understanding of the problem. Many of the claimed attributes of an
interschool athletic program are psychological and sociological in nature. Besides the physiological advantages of the development of physical fitness, good health, and mental alertness, such factors as improved
social relationships, ethical conduct, and spiritual growth are personal
values claimed. Research has been conducted which indicates that children who participate in competitive athletics exhibit greater popularity,
social esteem, and personal and social adjustment. However, if personality or character changes occur because of participation in competitive
interscholastic sports at the junior high school level, these are so slight
that they cannot be determined with the psychological instruments now
available.

In 1958, the American Association of Health, Physical Education,
and Recreation, a division of the National Education Association, conducted a survey of 2,329 separately organized middle schools. The results indicated that a little more than 85 percent of the schools had
some program of interscholastic athletics.[12] In a similar survey the
National Parent-Teacher sent questionnaires to a representative group
of school superintendents across the country. They were promised
anonymity and requested to speak their minds. Asked if they agreed
with Dr. James B. Conant that there is an almost vicious overemphasis
on interscholastic athletics, the superintendents said no by a five-to-one
margin.[13]

Although sheer weight of numbers does not make an activity correct, it is easily seen that there is an overwhelming majority of schools
that are conducting interschool athletic programs. In spite of the criti-

---

[12] Creighton J. Hale, "What Research Says about Athletics for Pre-High
School Children," *Journal of Health, Physical Education, and Recreation* (December 1959), p. 20.

[13] Raymond Squires, "Are School Agers Athletics Happy?" *School Activities* (April 1961), p. 229.

cisms of the programs, the students, parents, and a large number of administrators support such a program.

Arguments Against Interschool Athletics

During the past thirty years there has been a great deal of criticism directed toward those schools that are engaging in interschool sports for the early adolescent. Various individuals and groups have come out against this practice.

In 1952, a joint committee of representatives from five organizations—the National Education Association; The National Council of State Consultants in Elementary Education; the Department of Elementary School Principals; the Society of State Directors of Health, Physical Education, and Recreation; the American Association of Health, Physical Education, and Recreation—after three years of study published the following statement concerning interscholastic athletics for children: "Interscholastic competition of a varsity pattern and similarly organized competition under auspices of community agencies are definitely disapproved for children below the ninth grade."[14]

In 1954, after three years of careful investigation, the Education Policies Commission of the National Education Association and the American Association of School Administrators published a report concerning interscholastic athletics in which the following statement appears: "No junior high school should have a school team that competes with school teams of other junior high schools in organized leagues or tournaments. Varsity-type interscholastics for boys and girls should not be permitted."[15]

When James B. Conant made his study of the junior high school one of the areas he was greatly concerned about was the area of extra-curricular activities. Dr. Conant made the following statement: "Interscholastic athletics and marching bands are to be condemned in junior high schools; there is no sound educational reason for them and too often they serve as public entertainment."[16]

Why have so many people frowned on the idea of athletics? Probably the most important argument against competitive athletics for this age group is the physiological aspect. As early as 1938, authors were condemning junior high sports on the basis that the boys and girls of this age are undergoing very rapid physical development and the

[14] American Association of Health, Physical Education, and Recreation, "Desirable Athletic Competition for Children" (Washington: National Education Association, 1952), p. 14.

[15] Educational Policies Commission, "Problems and Policies" (Washington: National Educational Association, 1954), p. 36.

[16] James B. Conant, *Recommendations for Education in the Junior High School Years: A Memorandum to School Boards* (Princeton: Educational Testing Service, 1960), p. 83.

hard training necessary to build strongly competitive teams may easily overtax the body and cause permanent damage.

In 1946, a questionnaire was sent by C. L. Lowman to 900 orthopedists throughout the nation, requesting an opinion on the limitation of competitive sports in these grades. A return of 43 percent was obtained. Sixty-seven percent of the orthopedists felt interscholastic activity below the tenth grade level was unwise.[17]

This action taken by recognized leaders in the field of physical education should bear considerable weight because its chief consideration is the physiological aspect of the problem. It is not an attack against competition but against some of the circumstances under which competition is conducted for children of this age.

Besides physiological reasons, another important negative argument is that the program affords only a few the opportunity for competition. Nearly all students of this age are keenly interested in athletics, but under the conventional system only a very few have an opportunity to compete. The experience of playing athletic games should be a part of the education of all children and the opportunity should be provided for this experience. The students' interest in athletics is sometimes so intense that they are satisfied only when they participate in the program. The concept of interscholastic athletics involving a so-called varsity team representing one middle school, some claim, does not provide a desirable educational program at this level.

Frequently psychologists oppose interscholastic athletics for these youth because they feel that high pressure competition may lead to strong emotional reactions which might have adverse effects upon the individual. Under the conventional form of interscholastic athletics the entire student body becomes so imbued with the idea of "beating" someone else that without safeguards they can become poor losers and poor sportsmen.

Another argument presented against the interscholastic athletic program is that the accident rate is higher for boys participating in athletics than is the rate for non-participants. Proponents of this claim that the additional importance of winning and such factors as the urging of the coach, the presence of rooters, and the interests of the community in the team serve as an emotional stimulus to drive participants to greater exertion than they would be motivated to in a sandlot game, and it is this which brings about the greater number of accidents.

Recommendations and Conclusions

The program of athletics in any school should be tied to the program of education. Thought should be given not to more and enlarged sports programs so much as to that of getting more young people to partici-

[17] C. L. Lowman, "The Vulnerable Age," *Journal of Health, Physical Education, and Recreation* (November 1947), p. 635.

pate. It is agreed that they need emotional and physical outlets and they should be subjected to a wisely directed program of intramural and interscholastic athletics. Even though the authors favor an interscholastic program under restrictions such as are listed below, there is really no need to present the case for interscholastic athletics in the middle school. Even without such educational blessing it is a "going concern." Protesting to no avail are medical men, mental hygienists, psychologists, sociologists, educators, and parents. Not only has the competition been increasing it has been moving downward into the other elementary grades.

Where do educators stand? In 1963, the National Association of Secondary School Principals took the following stand:

We feel that the association cannot take a firm yes or no position on this question. Whether or not a school has an interscholastic athletic program will depend largely upon the tradition of the community and the philosophy of the school district in which it is located.

Emphasis must be on health, safety, sportsmanship, leadership development, fellowship, and the importance of teamwork in success. The program must be child-centered and definitely not high school centered.

The program must be limited. The number and type of sports must be carefully selected. There is much evidence that body-contact sports, such as football, are unsuited for the junior high boy. Most contests, if not all, should be played in the afternoon. The number of schools in the league and traveling distance between them should be kept at a minimum.

Mass attendance, to swell income for the sports program, should be discouraged. Newspaper and television publicity should be kept at a minimum. Administrative control of the program must be maintained diligently by the principal. Every effort to enlarge or glorify the program should be carefully scrutinized and measured against the standard: 'Is this for the welfare of the students participating and morale of the student body?'[18]

In the final analysis the question becomes: "Can the money, time, and energy devoted to an interscholastic program be justified?" The authors suggest that a school administrator could reply affirmatively to this question if the following recommendations of the American Medical Association have been followed:

1. A daily period of physical education for all boys and girls that includes a wide variety of activities and emphasizes careful instruction adapted to individual needs.

[18] James Jordan, "Interscholastic Athletics—Yes or No?" *National Association of Secondary School Principals Bulletin* (October 1963), p. 5–6.

2. Opportunity for all boys and girls to participate in an informal play and intramural program that includes a number of team games as well as appropriate individual and dual sports.
3. Interschool sports *only after* above and if:
   a. A medical examination including a thorough review of health history before and as needed during each session.
   b. Careful matching of players by age, height, weight formula or other equitable basis.
   c. The best obtainable equipment for play, properly fitted to each player and with practical adaptations.
   d. A coach in charge who understands child growth and development, as well as first aid and conditioning, and the sport concerned.
   e. A physician present at all contests and readily available during practice sessions.
   f. When an injury occurs during the course of a contest, the physician in attendance will determine the athlete's ability to continue play.
   g. During practice sessions, in potentially serious injuries, particularly to head, neck, or spine, the injured player will be removed from play, placed at rest, and given the immediate attention of a physician.
   h. Emphasis will be placed on skillful performances, maximum participation, healthful play, and good sportsmanship rather than championship schedules and all-star teams.
   i. On all matters of procedure and practice not covered by these policies, the first consideration will be the health and welfare of players.
   j. No games with schools who do not follow this system.

Chapter 12 Bibliography

American Association for Health, Physical Education, and Recreation. *Fitness for Secondary School Youth.* Washington: National Education Association, 1956.

Bookwalter, Karl W. *Physical Education in the Secondary Schools.* Washington, D. C.: The Center for Applied Research in Education, Inc., 1964.

————. "What We Know About Fitness," *National Association of Secondary School Principals Bulletin* (March 1956): 39:43.

Brownell, Clifford L. "The Role of Health, Physical Education, and Recreation in the Space Age," *National Association of Secondary School Principals Bulletin* (May 1960): 43:6.

Conant, James B. *Recommendations for Education in the Junior High School Years: A Memorandum to School Boards.* Princeton: Educational Testing Service, 1960.

Davis, Elwood, and Wallis, Earl. *Toward Better Teaching in Physical Education.* Englewood Cliffs, N. J.: Prentice-Hall, Inc., 1961.

Droste, Burt. "The Advantages of Interscholastic Sports at the Junior High School Level," *School and Community* (February 1960).

Dyson, Ralph J. "Memorandum," Oregon State Department of Education, September 21, 1964.

Educational Policies Commission, "Problems and Policies." Washington: National Education Association, 1954.

Hale, Creighton J. "What Research Says About Athletics for Pre-High School Children," *Journal of Health, Physical Education, and Recreation* (December 1959).

Jewett, Ann E., and Knap, Clyde, eds. *The Growing Years—Adolescence.* Washington, D. C.: American Association for Health, Physical Education, and Recreation, 1962.

Jordan, James. "Interscholastic Athletics—Yes or No?" *National Association of Secondary School Principals Bulletin* (October 1963).

Lowman, C. L. "The Vulnerable Age," *Journal of Health, Physical Education, and Recreation* (November 1947).

National Committee on School Health Policies, *Suggested School Health Policies.* Washington: National Education Association, 1956.

Squires, Raymond. "Are School Agers Athletics Happy?" *School Activities* (April 1961).

Trusler, Victor T. *Fundamentals of Physical Education.* Minneapolis: Burgess Publishing Co., 1950.

Chapter 13

The Library–An Instructional
Materials Center

Despite the long neglect of the junior high school library, there are
certain encouraging trends and new innovations in the teaching and
learning process which are raising the status and usage of the library
in the middle schools. It has been predicted that by the year 2,000 the
library will replace the classroom as the center of learning.[1] If this prediction is to be fully achieved, then rapid acceleration of the pace of
development is imperative. However, the crucial role of the library in
the education of boys and girls has been recognized by most forward-
looking educators, and a dynamic library program is now considered to
be an essential part of the modern school.

The secondary school library has developed from a prerogative of
the wealthier schools in the more highly developed areas to an all but
universal part of the American secondary school in urban areas.[2]

[1] Louis Shores, "The Medium School," *Phi Delta Kappan* (February 1967):
49:285.

[2] "The Secondary Teacher and Library Services" (Washington: National
Education Association, Research Division, November, 1958).

The major characteristic of recent development is the increasing identification of the library with the school's total educational program. The active school library today is much more accurately described as an instructional materials center, and is frequently so called by educators in order to give emphasis to its important supportive role in the total school program. In this context, the library is ready to serve as a center for films, filmstrips, tapes, records, pictures, maps, and other media quite as readily as with traditional books, periodicals, and pamphlets. There is a full range of materials, equipment, and accompanying services directed by librarians who are competent media specialists knowledgeable about resources in all their various forms. Today's librarian works with the teacher as an educator and a teammate. Greater emphasis is being placed on the need for school librarians to have not only knowledge of modern media programs but also of curriculum trends, instructional methods, the psychology of learning, and the processes of reading, listening, and viewing. The curriculum of today's schools is planned to meet the needs, interests, and abilities of all pupils. This necessitates the creation of the teaching-learning environment which allows for pupil activity broad in scope and utilizing a wide variety of instructional materials. In the light of these requirements, it is logical to expect that the school library becomes the workshop for pupils and teachers alike. The curriculum that values student inquiry, choice-making, core and block-time programs, independent study, and exploration has brought about an increased awareness of the need for a much expanded school library program. It is estimated that in the middle school of the future students will spend from twelve to fifteen hours a week in school doing independent study, including such activities as reading, writing, listening, viewing, and working with programmed instruction and automated devices.

As the school undertook more comprehensively the responsibility for educating "all the children of all the people," the long, dormant potential of the library began to develop into today's instructional materials center. It started by making its way out from under stairs and out of dark and dingy storage rooms which were so often supervised by a teacher whose purpose and qualification was no greater than that of guarding the books from being lost. It has been not more than fifty years since the first full-time librarian was employed in a school. It is understandable that students felt the early day school library was a place to be avoided unless one's presence there was inescapable.

Historical Background

Libraries have a long and distinguished history. Their origin can be traced back to the very beginnings of education. Babylonian youth studied in the libraries of their great temples, and the scholars of Alexandria are said to have walked the colonnades to the great library with their teachers. The school library as we know it today has developed most significantly during the twentieth century. But libraries since their inception have been associated with the schools in some way. In 1835, the United States began to pass laws providing for the organization of school district libraries. As early as 1876, nineteen states had some type of law designed to promote public school libraries.[3] However, the nineteenth century concept of the school library was predominately concerned with the books themselves and not with the services. Early educators did not realize that books alone do not make an adequate or effective library. Many of these early libraries were merely classroom collections, but even after the collections became centralized, they were predominantly book centers and were not coordinated with the curriculum and activities of the schools.

After passing through various periods of development from 1835–1900 the libraries were affected, along with other phases of secondary education, by the signs of dissatisfaction. The interrelationship between libraries and educational trends is apparent in many ways. It is possible that the presence of books and other materials in the schools contributed to the development of newer ideas of education which brought about expanded programs and helped to break away from some of the tradition surrounding the old school. Still, the situation of libraries remained essentially the same for many years.

It is generally conceded that by 1935—due largely to state participation, professional efforts of library and education groups, and the large measure of financial assistance of such foundations as the Carnegie Corporation, Rosenwold Fund, General Education Fund, and the Rockefeller Fund—the library:

> . . . changed from an unwanted outside agency to the center of all school activities. Such school work as project problems and units is built around books, magazines, newspapers, clippings, maps, pictures, slides, and exhibits. All of these are used by the librarian.[4]

The school library was given considerable emphasis in the first *Evaluative Criteria* published in 1940. The section on the school library made an attempt to evaluate both the quality and the quantity of available library service. It dealt with questions concerning minimum budgets, qualifications of librarians, services to teachers and students, and the physical aspects of the library, such as accessibility, adequacy, and attractiveness. The "Statement of Guiding Principles" for the library suggested that the library

> be a center of the educational life of the school, not merely a collection of books. It should provide the reading and reference facilities

---

[3] U. S. Office of Education, *Know Your School Library*, Office of Education Leaflet No. 56, Know Your School Series (Washington: Government Printing Office, 1940), p. 1.

[4] A. J. Middlebrooks, "The School Library 1900–1935," *American School Board Journal* (June 1936) : 92:20–22.

necessary to make the educational program effective. The library should provide pupils with valuable means not only of extending their knowledge and understanding, but also of developing desirable leisure habits.[5]

Such statements reflected the possibility of moving from a "book oriented" to a materials-oriented library. It was not, however, until the 1950 edition that the library was designated as a resource center of instructional materials, and significant recommendations were made as to the necessity of having audiovisual materials, qualified library staff and clerical assistance, and implications were made that the librarians should participate in curriculum development. The "Statement of Guiding Principles" in the *Evaluative Criteria,* 1969 edition, went a step further to outline the specific organization and purpose of the instructional materials center. Its 1969 edition stated:

> In recent years . . . there have been developed many new and wonderful devices which, while they cannot and should not replace books, offer their own unique contribution to the same ends, namely the recording and communication of ideas. Schools have developed an integrated administration unit, generally called the instructional materials center, which furnishes all the services usually associated with the library, and in addition provides the services connected with audiovisual materials, radio, and television.

> . . . The major purpose of the instructional materials center is to serve the established aims of the total educational program by (1) providing a rich variety of materials, including books and other printed materials, recordings, still and motion pictures, filmstrips, and other audiovisual materials and resources for use by teachers and students as individuals and groups; (2) offering leadership in developing techniques for the use of various materials by the teachers and students; (3) making available facilities, services, and equipment necessary for selection, organization and use of instructional materials; and (4) furnishing facilities for and assistance in the production of instructional materials and displays.[6]

No doubt the *Evaluative Criteria,* 1969 edition, shares the credit for new developments in library programs, but it must be recognized that an earlier statement of the American Association of School Libraries in 1956 pointed the way for this development and directly affected the philosophy which was stated four years later in the *Evaluative Criteria* and *Standards for School Library Programs.*

Today's education demands the fusion of all school activities into a complete pattern of learning experiences, wherein the library as an

[5] "Cooperative Study of Secondary School Standards," *Evaluative Criteria* (Washington, D. C.: 1940), p. 51.

[6] *Evaluative Criteria,* 1969 ed. (Washington, D. C.: National Study of Secondary School Evaluation, 1969), p. 257.

integral part of the total school program has an equal share in the responsibility for achieving the educational goals. With increased emphasis in the educational philosophy upon intellectual excellence, individual differences, changes in curriculum and changes in methods of instruction, there is a need for a sizeable increase in the amount and kind of materials for which the library will be responsible. For these reasons the concept of the instructional materials center, where books are just a part of the whole, has evolved.

The Library's Role in Meeting the Needs of Youth

As some of the needs of the early adolescent youth who constitute the population of today's middle school are different from their counterparts in other grades, then also should their library facilities be different. The student population has a broader range of interests than students at any other level. Adolescents are usually eager to explore new areas, but frequently are unable to sustain concentrated attention if there is not an immediate satisfaction gained. The student achieves satisfaction if he is able to locate materials that reinforce his interest. These interests can be fostered by a library with a wide variety of richly stimulating materials covering broad areas and extensive depth.

Often these new interests encompass the world of people. Early adolescent boys and girls are curious about their own age-mates and people all over the world, and their reading habits reflect this interest. Although there is great variation in reading ability among individuals, most studies show that a greater number of books of a recreational nature are read during these years than at any other comparable period. Girls show a strong preference for juvenile fiction about dogs, horses, and other pets. Their preference changes somewhat by grade nine to an interest in mystery, adventure, romance, and books on making things. Boys' early interests involve mischievous pranks, fights, races, sports, and adventure. Mystery, adventure, science, and travel are more representative of boys' reading interests at ninth grade level. Both boys and girls are enthusiastic about magazines and paperbacks. The adolescent seems to have many interests and as a result engages in many activities. Interests are susceptible to change, development, and adult influence, and this variation in interests has important implications for the total library program.[7] In any case, the school library must be ready for continuous adaptation to constantly changing student interests and curricular developments if it is to really fulfill its purpose.

Middle school students are more emotionally receptive to new ideas and experience than at any other time in their lives. There are still

[7] Roland C. Faunce, and Morrel J. Clute, *Teaching and Learning in the Junior High School* (Belmont, Calif.: Wadsworth Publishing Co., 1961), pp. 41–42.

traces of lingering childhood, yet the stirrings of adulthood are apparent. The young adolescent is in a state of transition, and he needs vast resources to help him expand his horizons in this tenuous and vital period of rapid growth and development. He wants to know more about himself and his relationships with other people. All the world fascinates his imagination, and he needs books and materials to stimulate his fancies. Creativity should be demonstrated in the bountiful decoration of the library; there should be art objects, displays, unusual plants, imported artifacts—anything to ply his inquisitiveness. The atmosphere should be lively and exciting, stimulating and challenging.

The student is at an age in his development when he is at a high point of impressionability and responsiveness. This unique stage must be met with appropriate library resources. Transitional printed materials and audiovisual media which are easily accessible to the student must be readily available. There should be a variety of activity programs to involve the students in library experiences. Such a library will help to increase the pupils' understanding of themselves and their world, and will help boys and girls in maturing to young adulthood.

The librarian, without whose training and enthusiasm the library is merely a repository, must have an interest in and knowledge of pupils of this level. He must come to know the boys and girls as individuals, and encourage them vigorously in their present interests while introducing them to unexplored ones. He must have a warm, friendly interest in every student and in every staff member. People should feel welcome in the school library. The good librarian must be able to bridge the gap between materials and the problem at hand. He saves the students and teachers time by focusing relationships within a field for greater clarity. And he helps to individualize learning.

The Librarian's Role
In Providing Services
To Improve the Curriculum

School librarians must first of all be teachers, at least in their working relationship with boys and girls; librarianship is their specialized responsibility. They must be considered an integral part of the teaching staff, intent upon promoting instructional goals. Librarians must know the nature of all areas and departments of the school including the counseling and guidance program. The librarian should expect to spend a considerable amount of time working with individual faculty members in helping them to relate their program of studies to the library services and materials; new teachers may want special help. Another major aspect of such activity is that the librarian will learn from teachers how to make library services most relevant to the curriculum.

The librarian must work with the teacher as a teammate. He provides many good book and non-book materials representing different areas of interest, as well as a variety of reading levels. But there is also a strong service emphasis, and the librarian must work with the teacher to provide these services most effectively. Benjamin Willis said:

> The better the teacher, the greater is the demand made by her on the library and on the services of the librarian. The better the teaching, which leads to and develops from the library, the greater the demand made on it by the students.[8]

Close working relationships between the teacher and the librarian are vitally important to the success of the library program. It is the teacher's responsibility to recommend materials for purchase, inform the librarian of classroom activities, confer with her prior to a new unit, check on the availability of materials, note any demand for similar materials by other classes, and discuss methods of using the materials to greatest advantage.

The librarian in turn must administer a well-organized library. There must be sufficient personnel, including professional librarians, adult aids, and secretaries, to offer the services necessary to an active school program. A competent materials specialist who understands the particular needs of the instructional program enables teachers to teach more capably. Librarians are learning more efficient means of facilitating the educational process. Some of these are as follows:

1. Make readily accessible an unrestricted range of materials which are current, authentic, and pertinent.
2. Make available bibliographic materials in the professional fields of the teachers so they may keep informed of new materials.
3. Work with the teacher in constructing bibliographies related to a unit of study.
4. Assist teachers in selecting materials needed for teaching and plan with them methods for using them.
5. Facilitate the teachers' use of varied techniques by supplying a wealth of enrichment materials.
6. Work with teachers to provide meaningful experiences designed to stimulate students' interest in reading and research.
7. Plan with teachers experiences in library instruction related to units of study.
8. Be alert to providing assistance to teachers in learning effective use of all library resources.
9. Go to classrooms, talk to teachers, and make them aware of materials which may serve their various programs.
10. Watch for and follow changes in subject matter and teaching approaches.

[8] Benjamin C. Willis, "School Librarian: Coordinator," *Better Libraries Make Better Schools*, edited by Charles L. Trinkner (Hamden, Conn.: The Shoe String Press, Inc., 1962), p. 50.

11. Have materials ready for large groups of students as well as individuals.
12. Work with teachers to provide special services such as individual attention to a gifted student, assistance for an eager committee, an exhibit relating to classroom activities, or a visit from a resource person.

The library serves all activities of the school, including those which may be termed extra-class, such as weight watchers clubs, sports clubs, foreign language clubs—anything in which the students may have an active interest. There should be no area in the school program which is not influenced in some way when there is a creative, dynamic librarian and a functional and functioning library.

The concept of the instructional materials center should not be limited to students' use. It can be used to bring forth the constructive use of teachers' talents. Teachers in today's schools will hopefully have more scheduled time for planning. Teachers will have the opportunity to use the instructional materials center more fully; this will inevitably lead to requirements for new and unique physical facilities, materials, and services in the library. Such centers will become the "supermarket of knowledge." As Posner says,

> It (the library) is an idea center and a dynamic aid in promoting the primary objectives of the school district, namely individualized instruction for students and promoting the professional growth and knowledge of teachers.[9]

Working areas, teaching tools and professional resources must be available to staff members as needed. There should be files of bulletin board ideas and materials, community resource files listing knowledgeable people of the community to talk to on a variety of topics, and listing interesting places to visit. There should also be a range of periodicals covering all of the areas of professional concern to the faculty and administration. This requires well-organized and well-staffed learning resource centers serving students and staff alike.

Relationship of the Library to Patterns of Curriculum Organization

The concept of curriculum in education has gradually changed through the years. The curriculum is less often patterned to be a static learning design. It is now emerging as a dynamic working plan which changes as needs of the young adolescent emerge and change. No two individuals are alike; each must grow in his own way. While schools may provide

[9] A. N. Posner, "The Instructional Materials Center as a Means for Constructive Use of Teachers' Talents," *California Journal of Secondary Education* (April 1960) : 35:251.

guidelines directed toward common goals, curriculum experiences must remain unique for every individual learner. Such a program demands a broad range of learning resources consistent with the varying needs, the extensive interests, and the diversified learning levels which characterize every classroom group. John Ratliff maintains that a facilitating environment conducive to healthy growth must be provided for the student to approach his full potential.

> That environment must be rich, extensive, and accessible almost to the point of being in the way . . . It is within the special province of the librarian and library to provide the facilitating environment, but the responsibility is not theirs alone. This is why libraries are changing to learning materials centers and why the concept of a librarian as just a caretaker of books is no longer acceptable. The multiplicity of forces from a diversity of directions is changing the schools and will continue to change them . . . As what is already known about junior high school pupils is incorporated into teaching practice, more books of broader scope and more diversified learning materials will be needed.[10]

The librarian should be actively involved as a resource person in curriculum development. The library collection should be built in terms of the curriculum and should include all types of learning materials. Through working with curriculum committees, the librarian becomes aware of program additions and changes, and is alerted to resulting library needs to support these programs. Then too, teachers and curriculum coordinators may have only limited knowledge of materials that are available, and may draw from the librarian's expertise in this area. School librarians are most effective when they work with teachers through the instructional program and have an active part in planning.

Patterns of curriculum organization are undergoing more rapid change than ever before, and placing greater demands on the library. The kind of curriculum that we are trying to carry on today cannot be successful without adequate learning tools. Cyphert states:

> There is a definite relationship between the curriculum organization of a junior high school and the instructional use which teachers and students make of the library . . . While the core curriculum is benefiting more from classroom library experience now, it also appears to have the most to gain from an increasingly effective approach to making the use of a variety of quality resources an integral part of learning procedures.[11]

[10] John A. Ratliff, "Newer Teaching Methods and the Library Program in the Junior High School," Alice Loher, ed. *The School Library Materials Center: Its Resources and their Utilization* (Champaign, Ill.: The Illinois Union Bookstore, 1964), pp. 82–83.

[11] F. R. Cyphert, "The Core Teacher and the Library," *Education* (November 1962): 83:149. Copyright 1962 by The Bobbs-Merrill Company, Inc., Indianapolis, Ind.

The core or block-time program is one curriculum organization which demands more material than most traditional content organizations. Since problem-solving and investigative skill development are basic in the philosophy of the core curriculum, the library becomes the major resource and service aid to the core teacher. Core demands from librarians more individual and group help than ever before. If core works as planned, many of its major objectives and characteristics are pursued and realized in the library. The library can only meet the needs of the program if it has a vast materials selection, including much of recent publication dates. Since the library is a prime educational agency in core programs, students must be given more rigorous training in the use of instructional media resources. The librarian and the teacher should work together to plan meaningful library activities related to class learning experiences. The librarian must also work with the teacher to guide and encourage students to explore and investigate.

Another pattern of organization which usually results in increased library use is team teaching. Ratliff says,

> If this approach (team teaching) to teaching fulfills its possibilities, the increase in quantity and quality that will be needed has hardly entered our imagination, and it will require an accessibility that will make most libraries out of date. The thoughts of it are staggering.[12]

Team teaching employs such learning techniques as increased use of modern technology, independent study, and problem-centered teaching, all of which require an active, well-equipped instructional media center.

The problem-solving approach to learning found in the core curriculum and team-teaching requires a flexibility which must become a characteristic of the school program, especially in time allocations and staff utilization. The library must also be characterized by flexibility in such matters as student traffic flow and patterns of media use.

The final goal of problem-solving, the development of an original idea by the student, gives special emphasis to a relatively new service of the media program, the production of instructional materials. The student's idea, resulting from his creative inquiry, must be presented in some form to communicate to others and to furnish evidence that the idea has been fully developed. Where the student of the past would have merely written a report, today's young student may wish to make a sound tape, a set of transparencies and photos, or a three-dimensional model. The product may often be created by the student himself rather than by someone else for him. For this reason, the production areas must be available to the student.

The modern library is intended to be heavily used, not just looked at or talked about. Therefore, pre-planned instruction in the effective and efficient use of the library becomes a must. The library's role in

[12] Ratliff, *op. cit.*, p. 81.

library instruction has undergone a radical change in the modern program. Instruction has in the past been regarded as the responsibility either of the librarian or the teacher alone; often it was taught as an isolated experience without reference to pupils' other learning. Sometimes instruction was given in a classroom far removed from the library setting. Such a program was simple to organize and administer, but there is considerable evidence that these formal lessons were quite ineffective. Also, they were so uninteresting that they created in the student an actual dread for the anticipated library visit.

There has been a growing belief among educators that efficient library skills and healthy attitudes toward library use would be more successfully developed if taught in a participative research situation using a problem-solving approach. In such a situation the planning is done by the cooperative unit of classroom teacher, librarian, and the students themselves. The teachers and the librarian should have frequent meetings to coordinate the research activities of their students and to discuss possibilities for viable problems. Relevant tools can be introduced by the librarian and teacher as a team whenever the materials are pertinent to the problem at hand. There should also be a variety of self-instructional devices available for use as the need arises. Such media would include filmstrips, eight millimeter filmloops, diagrams, and brief programmed packages developed by the library for this very purpose. This sort of direction encourages student initiative and independence, and is an asset in the development of an inquiring approach to education.

Developments Leading to Library Innovations

Most of the middle schools, according to recent surveys by the U. S. Department of Health, Education and Welfare and by the American Library Association, seem to have instructional materials centers, but great strides of development must take place if they are to fulfill their potential. At this point in time, their use by students and teachers is more limited than is satisfactory. Contributions have been made by various organizations toward strengthening the role of the library in schools. Some of these will be discussed in the following paragraphs.

The Staff Utilization Commission was established in 1956 to provide for a four year program of experimentation in more than 150 junior and senior high schools. The five salient features of the program were team-teaching, variable schedule, provision for instructional assistants, variable class size, and use of mechanical and electronic aids in teaching. The implementation of the program called for certain definite standards from the library. For example, if a program called for 40 percent of the time to be allotted to independent study, it was expected that there would be provision for instructional materials and space in the library where this time could be effectively utilized. The large group instruction which covers another 40 percent of the time could also be effective only if there is wide use of instructional media.

However, the traditional libraries of the 1950s could not provide services and facilities to meet these specifications. The publication of various pamphlets describing the experimental program stirred up concern among many school librarians and gave the impetus for beginning steps to be taken. Conferences were held by the various state branches of School Library Associations and Associations of Secondary School Administrators. There were a number of articles written in bulletins about the implications of the experimental program for the library, its personnel, materials, and policies. Surveys and research were conducted to determine existing conditions of libraries.

Under the 1965 Education Act school libraries and teachers were given an unprecedented opportunity to develop the creativity and the quality of their offerings to students. Although all titles of the Act may be seen in the light of library services, Title II was directed specifically toward their development. Under this title, federal funds were provided for all types of library resources to be used by teachers and students, such as books, audiovisual equipment, and instructional materials.

The third recent contribution to innovation in library programs is the Knapp School Libraries Project. This endeavor was made possible by a grant of $1,130,000 to the ALA to support a five-year project of the American Association of School Librarians "to demonstrate the educational value of a full program of school library services."

Specifically the grant provides to each of six schools:

1. Purchase of additional library books.
2. Salary of an additional librarian.
3. Purchase of additional audiovisual materials and equipment.
4. Half-time salary and other expenses for half-time field workers who are appointed by a cooperating teacher training institution.

The Knapp project was a further extension of team teaching and was quite complimentary to its use. The program called for a very efficient librarian who could sell ideas to both teachers and students, and train them through in-service and assistance. The Knapp library plan included the rooms for conference and small group discussion which provide a relaxed atmosphere where activity is carried on with its usual noise, and where the stillness of traditional libraries seems to have disappeared. The libraries were kept open late in the evening for teacher, student, and public use. Teachers shared the responsibility of staying in the library for assistance to the students, and thus the supervisory role of study halls were changed to one of service. The plan provided for work space for teachers and students, and for a graphic art center with art technicians who would prepare most of the aids required by teachers.

There seems to be no disagreement that these developments may be called innovations, and that their differences from traditional programs are genuine. These differences are apparent from the tremendous growth and importance of libraries in middle schools, which indicate a complete change from quiet storage of books to the activity of a research center. In fact, it will be difficult to imagine a noisier place (unless it is a gymnasium) because here students are actually working. Students must be given freedom to browse and to go up to talk to each other because activity and research are not possible if the students are jammed into and hushed in their seats. Following reflection and the perception of a new idea, a student often wishes to have it appraised by his peers. The exchange offers a standard by which the student sees and measures his personal growth. The young adolescent is particularly receptive to group participation and the sharing of ideas with his age-mates. The school must provide flexible facilities and scheduling that will allow time, space, and instructional materials for both group work and individual study. There is need for movable adjustable walls to facilitate new ways of organizing learning settings. Such accommodations will create areas for group work and yet provide quiet areas for individual work.

Provisions must be made so the library is available to the staff and students at all times. The scheduled library visit plan is no longer considered efficient in the schools of today. Another obstacle to the full utilization of the library is scheduling of study hall classes in the library facility. This places students in the library whether they need to use it or not, and forces the librarian into a role of supervisor and disciplinarian. This restricts free and independent use of the library's materials and the possibility of conferences with the librarian concerning projects. The use of a library in this manner limits its potentialities and those of its staff. To perform effectively, the library must be free to receive its patrons at any time of day, before school, during, and after. Many schools find it useful to extend library hours to evenings, weekends, and summers so the students, faculty, and often the community can make use of its facilities. Such flexible scheduling arrangements make it possible for individuals and groups of all sizes to use the library on a need basis.

Only if the students feel the library is theirs will they really use it. If there are too many restricting rules, if the atmosphere is stuffy and unpleasant, if the rooms are dull and uninviting in appearance, if the furniture is uncomfortable and rigidly placed, students will reject the library as a formidable place where they will go only if necessary rather than as a focal learning center. The success of the library program depends on many things—personnel, materials, space, facilities, and above all, cooperation, enthusiasm, initiative, and imagination of the library staff and teachers.

The issue which remains to be resolved is to provide full recognition to middle school libraries as an integral part of the school program. More research is desired concerning the relationship between effective library utilization and various teaching methods and techniques. Investigation is required in the provisions colleges and universities as teacher training institutions are making for instructing their graduate students in the development of library skills, and in the use of library materials as aids to teaching in the middle school.[13]

More cooperation and leadership are needed from administrators since much of the leadership for all phases of school programs rests ultimately with the principal. It is he who assumes the responsibility for establishing and expanding its services. He must exhibit the same concern for the library as for the instructional program. Strong communication lines must be open between librarian and principal to establish an innovative, functioning, and realistic library program.

Conclusion

The goals of education cannot be fully achieved without an instructional materials center with a wide variety of challenging resources and the services of an adequate staff and an able imaginative librarian. The evolving middle school library program is so integrated with the instructional program that it is in effect the mainstay of the curriculum. An innovative library program contributes to the total development of the child and reinforces the learning process. Learning affects all around development, and facilitating learning and meeting the needs of the young adolescent are the aims of today's library.

Chapter 13 Bibliography

Cecil, Hener L., and Heaps, W. A. *School Library Service in the United States.* New York: The H. W. Wilson Co., 1940.

Cyphert, F. R. "Junior High School Libraries Develop Investigating Skills," *Clearing House* (October 1958) : 33:137–139.

Fargo, Lucile F. *The Library in the School.* Chicago: American Library Association, 1959.

Gaver, M. U. *Every Child Needs a School Library,* American School Library Association, 1962.

Hartz, F. R., and Samuelson, R. T. "Origin, Development, and Present State of the Secondary School Library as a Material Center," *Peabody Journal of Education* (July 1965).

Posner, A. N. "The Instructional Materials Center as a Means for Constructive Use of Teachers' Talents," *California Journal of Secondary Education* (April 1960) : 35:250–251.

[13] Cyphert, *op. cit.,* p. 182.

Ratliff, J. A. "Junior High School Libraries Must Be Different," *National Association of Secondary School Principals Bulletin* (November 1959): 43:Pt. 3:61–65.

————. "Newer Teaching Methods and the Library Program in the Junior High School," Alice Lohrer, ed. *The School Library Materials Center: Its Resources and Their Utilization.* Champaign, Ill.: The Illinois Union Bookstore, 1964.

Shores, Louis. "The Medium School," *Phi Delta Kappan* (February 1967): 49:285.

Sloan, Thelma. "Working with Teachers—A Cooperative Business," *National Association of Secondary School Principals Bulletin* (November 1959): 43:Pt. 3:153–156.

Witt, Paul. "High School Libraries as Instructional Materials Centers," *National Association of Secondary School Principals Bulletin* (November 1959): 43:Pt. 3:112–118.

Section Five

Institutional Support Programs

Overview

Every agency, institution, or organization cannot be expected to "do its job" without considerable assistance and expertise from administrative and ancillary personnel and related programs. This is especially true in relation to educational institutions in general and the middle school in particular. This section attempts to discuss the roles, responsibilities, problems, and trends revolving around the student activities and guidance program and the administration, organization, and evaluation of the school. The reader will note that this section is student and staff oriented rather than emphasizing building or material in keeping with the rationale of the book first delineated in the preface. Without a doubt, a book could be written and needs to be written about the ideal middle school plant, the administrative activities necessary to "run" a middle school, the rationale, modes, and means of continuous evaluation of a school and school program, the ideal middle school guidance program, and appropriate student activities in the middle school. Such was not done in this section.

Again, this section was written with the intent that the classroom teacher would better understand the programs and personnel working in administrative and support functions designed to enable him to maximize his instructional effort in the classroom. In Chapter 4, it was noted that student activities were an integral part of the instructional program. The chapter on student activities in this section discusses the problems and responsibilities associated with administering a student activities program.

Chapter 14

Student Activities

One of the major differences between the elementary and the secondary school is exemplified in the role played by student activities. In general, the experiences included in this category differ from the more traditional aspects of the curriculum in at least three important respects. They ordinarily meet less often than five times per week; in most cases they do not carry academic credit; and student participation is usually voluntary rather than required.

The major enterprises constituting the activity program include student participation in school government, school assemblies, social activities, school clubs, and athletics. In addition to the above, some schools include journalism, music, speech, and drama in their activity programs; in other schools, however, one or more of these activities are so closely integrated with regular class work that they are really not "extra-class" at all. In fact, a basic principle of a good program of school activities is that it should grow out of the regular class work and remain closely related to it. In good programs, the dividing line is never sharply drawn. The term "curriculum" as commonly used today connotes *all* the experiences in which students engage under the supervision of the school. Thus, the term "extracurricular" is obsolete with reference to school activities; not only are these activities *part* of the curriculum, they are an essential and integral aspect of the modern school program. As such, they require the same thoughtful planning that every other aspect of the total program requires.

General Principles of Student Activities

The most important principle relating to school activities is that they, in common with all other aspects of the curriculum, should be developed and directed in terms of educational objectives. Although many schools have progressed to the point where objectives play an important role in course of study construction and other aspects of curriculum development which relate specifically to classroom work, they have been much slower in adopting the same concept to the non-classroom activities.

Care must be exercised, too, lest the program of school activities cater to a select few members of the student body. The composition of the student body of every school changes considerably, not only from year to year but during the course of any one year. Thus, even if a program of activities meets the needs of a school at a specific time, the assumption cannot be made that the program is, therefore, adequate at another time.

Just as schools provide guidance to students in the choice of courses (and educational guidance becomes especially important during these adolescent years), so should they recognize the importance of guidance in the choice of school activities. Each student's tentative program should be considered as a whole. The establishment of reasonable controls against over-participation will at the same time make available more opportunities for the "under-participant." Thus, the desirable goal of participation for every student will be more nearly realized.

The extent to which the school activity program is successful in achieving its maximum potential will be determined to a large extent by the care with which the sponsor is chosen and the general attitude and policy of the school toward the role of school activities in the total program. Activities will, in general, function best when the sponsor is just as carefully selected as are the teachers of regular classes. Pupil preferences concerning sponsors might well be taken into consideration by the school administration, but serious problems will often develop if the final decision does not rest with the principal of the school. Many of these problems will involve "teacher load."

Schools which recognize activities as an integral part of their total program take this concept into account in assigning responsibilities to individual staff members. The practice, fortunately decreasing, of first making sure that each teacher has a full teaching load and then adding extra-class responsibilities as an appendage—in some cases almost as an afterthought—cannot be defended. The use of a formula (such as that devised by Douglass[1]), can serve a very useful purpose in gaining

[1] Harl R. Douglass, "Teaching Load Crisis in Secondary Schools," California Journal of Secondary Education (May 1957) : 32:295–299.

for student activities their rightful place with reference to the teacher's total load. Criteria applicable to teacher load policy have also been developed by the National Study of Secondary School Evaluation.[2]

Should teachers receive extra pay for activities they perform in addition to their actual classroom assignment? This question has been raised on numerous occasions in recent years. As a result, some school boards have adopted extra pay schedules, supplementing regular teacher salary schedules, which cover the amounts of extra compensation to be paid for each of the various types of so-called extra duties which it is expected teachers will perform. On the other hand, in many school districts these duties, largely extra-class in nature, are looked upon as a part of the teacher's contractual obligations to be performed without extra pay. It would seem that tenable arguments favoring extra pay for extra-class responsibilities would break down if such responsibilities were taken into account when the teacher's total assignment was considered.

Since careful planning is one of the most important characteristics of any successful activity, it is highly desirable to utilize a school activities calendar in considering the scheduling of activities for the school year. The period prior to the close of one school year is not too early to start thinking about plans for the next. Exact dates and events need not be determined at that time; however, an overall tentative program is not only desirable but essential if conflicts and related problems are to be minimized. The intelligent use of the activities calendar holds promise for alleviating many a sponsor's complaint that there just "aren't enough weekends in May!" The nature of some of these activities requires that they be held at or near the close of the school year. However, a reasonable amount of foresight might well provide for the scheduling of more activities than are now scheduled during the fall and winter months.

As noted above, planning is essential for each specific activity as well as for the program as a whole. A useful technique in insuring that this planning will not be overlooked is the practice of requiring that a written authorization be executed for a specific time (e.g., two weeks) prior to each activity. Thus, a class or club desiring to sponsor an event might be expected to list such items as the proposed budget, various committee assignments, anticipated janitorial help needed, and the names of chaperones. Many schools have developed forms such as the one in Table X to implement this planning.[3] It must be remembered that no activities are *inherently* contributors to the attainment of educational objectives; they merely have potential. Unplanned and inade-

[2] National Study of Secondary School Evaluation, *Evaluative Criteria* (Washington, D. C.: American Council on Education, 1969).

[3] *The Student Council Handbook* (Washington, D. C.: National Association of Student Councils, 1967), p. 135.

quately supervised, they may operate in a manner detrimental to the best interests of all concerned. Careful planning is essential if the school program is to capitalize upon its tremendous potentialities.

Table X.   Request for Approval of School Activity

Must be submitted at least two weeks prior to date requested

Name of Activity_____

Sponsoring Organization_____

Date to be Held_____

Place_____

Time_____

Anticipated Expenses and Receipts (itemize):

Names of Chaperones:

_____   _____

_____   _____

_____   _____

Committee Assignments: (refreshments, program, clean up, etc.)

_____   Approved:
President, Sponsoring Organization

_____   _____
Advisor   Principal

_____   _____
Date   Date

There is no more perplexing problem in the area of school activities than the one suggested by the question, "At what time shall they be held?" In the final analysis, each school must answer this question for itself. However, some general comments are in order at this point.

Many schools have adopted the "activity period" as one approach to the problem of time. A carefully planned and administered activity period can prove valuable in providing the necessary time for at least some of the school activities. The mere provision for such a period, however, will guarantee nothing. Poorly administered, it will result in much wasted time on the part of students and faculty alike, disciplinary problems which are detrimental to school morale, and conflicts in group meetings.

Many schools have approached the "time" problem in other ways. Some of these are the following:
1. Utilization of part of the noon period.
2. Utilization of time before and after school. In many cases this requires the adjustment of school bus schedules in some way.
3. Utilization of non-school days and of evenings (evenings prior to school days are avoided in many schools).
4. Scheduling of specific group meetings and activities on school time, as needed. Since a large number of such activities require only a short period of time (one half hour or less), they may be scheduled during the last few minutes of some period during the school day. If these last minutes of academic classes are ordinarily utilized, as they should be in the conventional schedule, for supervised study, the pupils actually are asked to substitute out-of-school time for in-school time for the purpose of study, in return for the privilege of participating in the activity during the regular school day. The practice of regularly excusing one or more pupils from various classes to participate in activities cannot be defended, and the conscientious junior high school faculty will not tolerate it.
5. In the case of activities in which the entire school participates, (e.g., assemblies) both the procedure described above and the shortening of all periods an equal amount, have been found generally more acceptable than eliminating one or more entire periods for such activities.

One of the areas in which much progress needs to be made is that of the recognition of achievement in school activities. Probably the two most universal methods of according recognition are through publicity and through awards. Even a casual examination of school and community newspapers will reveal that in many schools certain activities receive much more space than do others, often out of all proportion to their educational importance. There is much that a school can do to improve this condition. In many schools, too, the awards made to participants in certain activities are more prominent, both in size and accompanying prestige, than those made to participants in other activities. In an effort to equalize such recognition, some schools have developed awards systems which recognize all aspects of activity participation. One method is the establishment of a school citizenship award based upon a point system which specifies, within a range, the recognition to be given for various types of participation in the activity program.

Whatever the method employed, schools are long overdue in modifying the practice of paying lip-service to the desirability of avoiding overemphasis upon certain activities on the one hand and perpetuating conditions which encourage this overemphasis on the other.

Studies have shown that pupil participation in activities is limited by the economic costs involved. Since such items as musical instruments, athletic equipment, school publications, textbooks, and laboratory supplies are necessary in a well-rounded educational program, the use of district funds for their financing is the desirable ideal. In cases in which this ideal is not yet attainable, other means should be taken to avoid the exclusion of pupils because of the "accident of birth." Assistance given to pupils in obtaining work experience to help defray activity costs is one approach to the solution of this problem. Financing, at least in part, from student body funds is another. In recent years, federal programs have done much to assist local districts in financing their educational activities.

In addition to the types of expenses listed above, there are numerous miscellaneous items which are of interest to students but are less closely allied to the school activity program itself. While the school should not attempt to dictate to pupils how their money should be spent, there are ways in which overcharging and needless expense can be avoided. Dealing with salesmen through student-faculty committees and exercising control over the adoption of official emblems, insignia, and clothing are examples of practices common to many schools.

Another problem relates to activity funds. One member of the staff, either the principal or someone appointed by him, should serve as financial adviser to the student body and should be in charge of student body funds. This person should be bonded. Numerous opportunities should be provided for students to gain valuable experience as treasurers of school organizations, and activity advisers should share the responsibility for student body finance; however, it is essential that this be carefully organized under one head. Among his duties are the establishment of a sound bookkeeping system, the development of various business forms (e.g., requisitions, payment orders, and checks), and the establishment of working arrangements with local banks. Although within the student body itself there should be separate accounts for each school activity which handles money, the bank should carry a single student body account. All student body checks should be countersigned by the financial adviser. It is imperative that written requisitions or purchase orders accompany every request for goods and services. Good business procedure requires that periodic (at least annual) audits of student body accounts be made by disinterested parties. Many school districts provide for this at the time of the audit of district accounts.

Student body money-raising policies need to be carefully established. No activity can be justified solely on the basis of financial return. The use, for example, of candy and soft-drink dispensing machines in schools, except in connection with social activities, is difficult to justify, especially when basic health principles are considered. Standard prices for concessions to be sold at school activities should be adopted.

The final general consideration to be dealt with here concerns other educative agencies within the community. Education and schooling are not synonymous terms. The school is the formal agency established for educational purposes. However, a large part of one's education is obtained outside of school. In fact, sociological studies have shown that the family, the peer-group (gang, clique, etc.), commercialized agencies (motion picture, radio and television, press), and organized youth groups (e.g., churches, youth clubs, boy and girl scouts) exert even more of an influence upon education than does the school. This influence is not always positive, but all of these agencies have positive potentialities. It is the responsibility of the school to give guidance in the selection of out-of-school activities and encourage vigorously those activities and agencies which can assist in the attainment of educational objectives.

One valuable service the school can render in this matter is to assist in the development of community leadership in youth-serving agencies. It must be recognized that the youth problem is a community as well as a school problem. In many communities, school personnel, by virtue of their interests, training, and experience, are the ones best qualified for positive leadership in youth groups. However, the automatic assignment of teachers to such positions is not necessarily the best policy. A strong case can be made for the point of view that many teachers assume too many responsibilities in the area of youth leadership—that their out-of-school contacts and energies should involve contacts at the adult level also. In promoting the concept that the welfare of youth should not fall entirely upon the school, the encouragement and preparation of parents and other non-teachers for leadership roles in youth groups might well be the primary concern of school leaders.

The use of bulletin boards and assembly programs to publicize and otherwise encourage the work of non-school educative agencies is another method of attack upon the problem. The use of school facilities by such agencies is still another approach. In many communities the school provides the best, if not the only, facilities for certain non-school activities. Since the problem of when to permit the use of school facilities by non-school groups and when to deny such use is at times a difficult one, it is highly desirable that the governing board of the school district adopt specific policies. These should include requirement of a written application for the use of school facilities by the organization concerned, the setting of fees, and the like. Each application should be considered individually, and no one individual should be charged with the responsibility of making final judgment.

The community calendar, listing approved non-school, as well as school functions, is a useful and valuable clearing-house for dates and a further means of publicizing worthwhile community activities. In many communities such a calendar is administered by the school, in others by the newspaper or some other non-school agency.

Student Participation in School Government

The public school is potentially the most effective laboratory yet devised in which young people may learn and practice the principles of democratic government. Although as recently as thirty years ago the idea of pupils not having a place in the management of the school had to be explained often and defended vigorously, today almost every school (elementary through college) has some form of pupil participation in school administration. The fact that membership in the National Association of Student Councils has increased from 283 to many thousands today is certainly due in part at least to the realization that the student council's contributions to the administration and well-being of the school are so great as to make it an essential part of the educational program.

The basic aims and objectives of student councils as found in an examination of several hundred student council constitutions have been listed by Willard Bear[4] in *The Student Council in the Secondary School*.

To develop good citizenship attitudes and practices, including:
  Understanding how a representative democracy works
  Fostering correct sentiments of law and order
  Teaching respect for constituted authority
  Gaining practice in self-direction
  Training in leadership and fellowship
  Accepting responsibility
To promote good relationships, including:
  Individual and group student relationships
  Student-faculty relationships
  School-community relationships
To develop and maintain good school spirit
To assist in directing and managing student life activities
To provide a forum for student expression and the exchange of student-faculty views
To promote the general welfare of the school
To provide a training ground for developing leadership
To promote scholarship
To help solve problems that arise in the school
To uphold school traditions
To help each student find a place in the school
To develop high ideals of personal conduct

The above list includes only those most commonly mentioned and is by no means complete. Each student council should have its own set of goals and these should be worded to express its particular aspirations.

[4] National Association of Student Councils, *The Student Council in the Secondary School* (Washington, D. C.: National Education Association, 1962).

General objectives represent desirable ends toward which one directs his energies but never reaches in their entirety. Therefore, a student council's general objectives normally will remain fairly constant. Revisions are made only as the attainment of an objective is approached and sights need to be set a little higher or when new purposes emerge.

The effectiveness of student participation in school government is sometimes seriously limited because of inadequate concern for certain important preliminary considerations. The following five points merit the attention of those who would set the stage for sound council operation:

First, there must be a clear understanding, on the part of the student body, of the fact that any and all powers it may possess are powers which are *delegated* to it by the administrative head of the school. Legally, this official is charged with the responsibility for the proper functioning of the school. Thus, a school is *not* a true democracy— rather it is a laboratory in which, under guidance, students may learn and practice the principles of democracy. The wise administrator will delegate powers to the student body to the extent, and only to the extent, that the student body demonstrates its willingness and ability to assume the responsibilities which accompany such powers.

Second, since effective student participation in school government is desirable in a school, and since at best it is difficult to achieve, the selection of the faculty adviser to the student council is a matter of crucial importance and should be made with the utmost care. If the principal himself does not assume this role, he should delegate it to a member of the staff who has a sound knowledge of the administrative relationships involved, who has good rapport with students, and who has an interest in and enthusiasm for the assignment. Many failures in student body operation can be laid directly at the feet of the administrator who acts unwisely in the appointment of the adviser.

Third, students should receive adequate guidance directed toward assisting them in learning to select their most capable fellows as candidates for student body offices. Athletic ability, social competence, and the possession of material goods may or may not accompany leadership potentialities. All too frequently they are the primary criteria upon which student officers are elected. Oftentimes, the effectiveness of the student council's work is hampered considerably by the election to office of those already engaged in a variety of activities. A carefully planned and guided pre-election campaign, possibly culminating in an assembly at which each candidate makes a statement of his platform, may bring little-known talent to the attention of the student voters. Many a school has enjoyed the benefits of outstanding student council operation under leadership uncovered in just this way.

Fourth, student body officers should be installed in a dignified ceremony in which the principal of the school participates. Such an activity provides an excellent opportunity to reinforce the students' and faculty's understanding of the basic principles underlying successful student council operation and, thus, to set the stage for the new set of officers.

Finally, provision should be made for the training of student body officers after they have been elected. A desirable practice is that of assigning a faculty member to train student leaders in the techniques of leadership. This assignment may be assumed by the student council adviser, a speech teacher, or by someone else specifically qualified for the position. The success of any group enterprise is closely related to the ability and skill of the leader. The development of this ability and skill should not be left to chance. In a similar manner, faculty assistance will usually prove valuable in the training of secretaries, treasurers, and other student officers.

The successful student council is an active organization. It is difficult, if not impossible, for a council to occupy a position of any really significant leadership in the school unless it is constantly engaged in promoting worthwhile activities. It is neither necessary nor desirable that the council itself sponsor every project in which the student body is engaged; in many instances it is preferable that it give encouragement and support to other groups.

School Clubs

Probably the spontaneity of student activity at its best is to be found in the well-organized school club which brings together a group who have a common interest. The program of such a group makes possible a wide variety of satisfying experiences and also presents many opportunities for pupil initiative and resourcefulness.

The relatively informal, elective nature of the club program makes it possible to achieve certain basic objectives more easily than is the case in regular classes. And even in those schools which are able to realize these objectives through class work, the club program serves to reinforce and enrich the more formal program.

The student council should assume a leadership role with respect to school clubs. It is desirable for the council to bring together club presidents for several meetings throughout the school year to discuss problems of mutual interest. In matters that affect the entire school, clubs cannot do the job as effectively as the student council where club organization is considered as only a part of the work of the council. Any club member representing specific club interests may appear before any session of the student council and present his problem for consideration. The council, however, has many other duties and responsibilities to the club program, over and above simply hearing club problems as they may be brought to the attention of the council. The council, for example, should help new organizations to get started. The representatives of a group which wishes to organize as a club should appear before the coun-

cil and state all pertinent facts concerning the proposed new organization. They should indicate, for example, why it is being organized, who
may belong, where it will meet, how much it will cost, who will be its
faculty adviser, and many other facts of a similar nature.

The final authority for the control and conduct of the various school
clubs should rest with the student council. This means, of course, that if
the council can grant a charter, it can also withhold a charter if, for
any reason, the council believes that an already existing club serves
adequately the purposes for which the new club is proposed. The council may also withhold a charter if it is not satisfied with the organizational plans as presented. It is understood, too, that the clubs of the
school must give an annual accounting to the student council. At the
end of the year, representatives of the clubs should appear before the
council to describe the year's activities, tell what projects were carried
through to successful completion, and give any facts which would tend
to show that the club has played a vital role in the school activity program. If the council feels that the club has justified its existence, the
charter should be extended for another year; on the other hand, if the
club has done little or nothing, the council may place it on probation for
a specified time or revoke the charter.

It must be borne in mind that not all students are going to be interested in clubs. In order to serve everyone, the council should try in as
many ways as possible to get those activities started which will interest
all students. It should suggest new clubs and new activities and projects
which existing clubs might carry on. It should take the initiative in
starting an organization if the council feels that a particular need or
interest is not now being served.

School Assemblies

In most schools, the assembly is the only activity in which the entire
student body comes together in one group. This fact alone gives it potentialities that are not present in any other aspect of school life. The
assembly presents unique opportunities for the development of school
spirit and school unity. It offers innumerable chances to enrich the rest
of the school program. It is unfortunate, therefore, that pupils and even
faculty members in some schools regard the assembly as a thing apart—
as a welcome interlude offering relief from the usual school routine and
as an opportunity to loiter around or to take a trip downtown. Carefully
planned, executed, and evaluated, the school assembly program can capitalize upon its great potential as a vital, dynamic aspect of the curriculum.

If the school assembly program is to serve the function suggested
above, it must be carefully planned. The practice of the automatic
scheduling of time for assemblies at regular intervals, with a last-

minute rush to improvise each program, does not lead to a valuable kind of educative experience. The planning of school assemblies is a real challenge involving much time, energy, and hard work, and fully justifies and requires carefully thought-out-organization.

It is desirable that there be an assembly planning group, advised by a member of the faculty and including both student and faculty members. In some schools, student council members serve as student members of the assembly committee. However, because of the importance of spreading responsibility among many pupils, and because the well-organized and functioning student council will have many other responsibilities, it is suggested that there be a minimum of overlapping in the membership of the two groups.

Ample opportunities exist in most schools for developing assembly programs which utilize pupil talent. Some schools make no use at all of "outside" programs, and many schools utilize them only occasionally. Certainly the school that relies heavily upon outside performers is not capitalizing upon the rich potentialities that exist within the school itself.

The assembly planning committee should make every effort to include a wide variety of assembly activities. The following are some suggestions of typical programs.

1. *Dramatics.* Early adolescents usually enjoy drama. Skits and one-act plays make excellent assembly programs, and such programs provide a high degree of motivation for the participants. This, of course, is true for all individuals and groups who have the opportunity to perform before an audience.

2. *Music.* Several worthwhile assemblies might come each year from musical groups. In this area as well as in dramatics and others, the adviser has a real opportunity to assist in the aesthetic development of pupils. The potentialities of group singing as a desirable assembly activity should not be overlooked. Under competent leadership almost any group will actively participate and will enjoy the experience. Group singing is helpful in building morale. Many schools include some singing in all assemblies.

3. *Amateur or student talent programs.* This type of program provides opportunities for uncovering hidden talents within the student body. Tryouts sometimes provide enough material for several assemblies. This kind of program is almost always entertaining, and schools generally report a high degree of success with it.

4. *Observance of special days and seasons.* Observances of anniversaries of historical, patriotic, and spiritual significance in the local community or in the state, nation, or the world at large make very appropriate assembly programs. They afford excellent opportunity for correlation with the total curriculum, especially in the field of social studies, language arts, music, drama, and science.

5. *Student body election campaigns and installation of officers.* These have been discussed previously. They are appropriate prior to and following each general student body election. Installation ceremonies might also include officers of groups within the student body.

6. *Award assemblies.* The presentation of awards before the student body provides another worthwhile type of assembly program. It is desirable to schedule such presentations several times during the school year. This policy has the advantages of making it possible for pupils to receive awards shortly after they have been earned, and also avoids the extra-long awards assembly at the close of the year.

7. *Assemblies presented by departments, classes, clubs, and other school groups.* Some of the most worthwhile assembly programs are those presented by departments and classes within the school. These can be very valuable in acquainting pupils with the school offerings and in demonstrating vocational and avocational values of the various offerings. The same can be said of assemblies presented by clubs and other school organizations.

8. *Motion pictures.* Generally speaking, motion pictures are most effective educationally when used with small groups, preferably in connection with a specific topic being studied. Occasionally, however, the general importance of a motion picture justifies its use in an all-school assembly program. Films with unusual historical, literary, civic, patriotic, or dramatic value may be used to advantage as assembly programs. Films, wherever used in the school, are most effective when they can be discussed with pupils both before and after the showing. The educational value of all assemblies will be increased by adherence to the same principle.

9. *Student body meetings.* The student body meetings may be considered as a type of assembly program. Some schools distinguish between the two, while others do not. In schools of the former category, a common policy is that the student body president presides at student body meetings and the principal or another faculty member presides at regular assemblies. Regardless of specific practices, student body meetings are an important type of all-school activity.

This list of nine types of assemblies is far from being all-inclusive— athletics, for example, is an obvious omission. In order to demonstrate the potentialities for a year's program of assemblies built around these areas, the following figures taken from the assembly records of a particular middle school are presented. These should not be considered as recommendations; they merely attempt to point out the vast possibilities available within the school itself: dramatics, four assemblies per year; music, six; student talent, one; observance of special days or seasons, four; student body election campaigns, one; awards, three; presentations by departments, classes, clubs, and other school groups, seven; motion pictures, one; student body meetings, eight; total, thirty-five. This school thus provided a wide variety of programs on the average of about one per week throughout the school year, without drawing upon commercial agencies.

School Parties

Parties and other social activities provide, potentially, an excellent means of developing desirable skills, habits, and attitudes in human relations. They also offer, potentially, excellent recreational outlets. The word "potentially" is used very deliberately, because unless extreme care is exercised in the planning and carrying out of social activities, these activities not only can fail to achieve their objectives but can also contribute heavily to the development of asocial and antisocial behavior patterns.

The effective school social program will not only attempt to supplement, support, and strengthen desirable activities already available within the community, but will do all within its power to assist community groups and organizations to provide additional youth services for which a need exists. Youth clubs, churches, service clubs, boy and girl scouts, and 4-H clubs are just a few of the organizations with which schools should cooperate.

It is desirable that the officers and members of organizations within the student body assume the major responsibility for planning and conducting social affairs. Thus, a variety of committees, possibly utilizing every member of a school group, would provide responsibilities for a large proportion, perhaps all, of the student body members at some time during the school year. One aspect of the evaluation which should be an integral part of every school function would be an appraisal of each pupil's discharge of such responsibilities.

As in all education, the emphasis should be upon pupil learning. The role of the teacher should be that of a guide in facilitating that learning. Progress toward the goal of achieving ability in intelligent self-direction is especially attainable in the school's social program. An adult-dominated social program will fall far short of achieving this objective.

Social events in which the entire student body is eligible to participate provide one important means of widening the students' scope of friends and acquaintances and offer an excellent method of achieving school unity. However, a school which schedules all-school functions to the exclusion of activities for organizations within the school is likely to overlook some important potentialities which the smaller groups may achieve. The modern middle school is a much larger institution than many of its students have ever before attended. Primary group values to which they were accustomed in their earlier school experience are in danger of disappearing entirely unless specific efforts are made to perpetuate them and to increase them. The feeling of "belonging," so essential to healthy personality development, can be fostered to a higher degree, generally, in activities where primary, rather than secondary, group relationships are fostered. Identification with and loyalties to small groups are desirable, just as they are to large ones. This suggests, in even the smaller schools, a balance between all-school activities and activities designed for groups or grades within the school.

There is a tendency in many schools to consider "social activity" as synonymous with "dancing." Dancing is an important type of social activity in most schools but a program limited to dancing is grossly inadequate. The school must recognize that some pupils may not know how to dance, while others, particularly the boys, may not care for that particular activity. Even were such not the case, the social program cannot hope to serve the pupils satisfactorily if it is not characterized by variety.

Individuals and groups within some communities find that their religious and other beliefs conflict with educational philosophy concerning certain aspects of the social program. Such individuals or groups have a right to these beliefs, and the school should be cognizant and considerate of them. Certainly, no pupil should be forced to participate in any activity which conflicts with his religious attitudes or beliefs.

It must be remembered that in addition to providing opportunities for the practicing of desirable attitudes, habits, and skills, the school social program has the responsibility for instruction as well. In many instances, lack of pupil participation in social activities, or the practice of unsocial or asocial behavior, is due to lack of knowledge or skill. In the light of this, many schools provide instruction in social skills as an integral part of the curriculum. In some situations this instruction is provided in the form of a school activity. In others, it is one aspect of the physical education program. The scheduling of boys' and girls' physical education classes at the same time, when feasible, makes possible the scheduling of heterosexual activities of various types during the regular school day. In addition to the social skills themselves, matters of social conduct and mores should be considered an essential phase of the school's responsibility.

Other School Activities

School Publications

School publications, and in particular the school newspaper, provide perhaps the most effective channels of communication among the various individuals and groups who interact with the school. They are invaluable in their potentialities for conveying information, for conferring recognition for work well done, for stimulating effort toward school improvement and for providing a documented history of the institution. Well managed, they can also furnish opportunities for educational growth of pupils in such areas as writing, business management, and intelligent reading habits and attitudes. They are important instruments in the promotion of morale, harmony, and unity within the school community. Particular care must be taken to see that all aspects of school life are fairly represented and treated.

Obviously certain groups are more active and newsworthy than others. The same applies to individuals. But a situation in which items concerning a relatively small number of groups and individuals appear time after time, and in which large segments of the student body are neglected, is not wholesome and should not be tolerated. Even more serious, if not done in a light, anonymous spirit, is the practice of including personal items of a "gossip" nature in the columns of school publications.

Speech and Drama

The primary contribution which every field of learning should make in the middle school is in the area of general education. Thus, instruction and practice in oral communication should be specifically provided as an integral part of every English class. Certainly teachers of English are generally in the best position, by training and because of the fact that they ordinarily are in contact with all students, to assume the major responsibility for speech training. But the task cannot be left to them alone. Diction, mechanics of expression, vocabulary, enunciation, and tone, as well as clarity and discrimination in thought, should be the concern of every teacher in the school to the limit of his ability. The English teacher can make a valuable contribution to the educational program by assisting other staff members in discharging this responsibility.

A school which has provided for speech requirements in general education is often able to enrich its offerings by providing certain elective experiences. These should be designed for those pupils who will most likely profit from them because of special abilities, interests, and needs. Certain vocations (law and teaching, for example) require greater skill in oral expression than do others.

In some middle schools, classes in speech are offered as electives on the regular daily schedule. Other schools provide for specialized speech activities as part of the activity program—often as a club. Such a group can serve any of a wide variety of purposes. It can assist in the training of student body officers and others whose responsibilities require competence in oral expression. It can plan and present programs for the information and entertainment of school and community organizations. It can furnish valuable experiences for individuals desiring to improve their skill in communication. Regardless of the various ways in which schools may attempt to meet the challenge of an adequate speech program, it is imperative that each institution make a wholehearted effort to provide general speech activities for all pupils and specialized activities for some.

Drama has always appealed to people of all ages. This appeal is particularly strong in the case of young people, as indicated in an earlier section. The fact that the medium of drama provides excellent opportunities for rich educational experiences in addition to enjoyment has led school leaders to capitalize upon it in the development of their programs. When the concept of drama is broadened to include role playing, both formal and informal, and when appreciation from the aesthetic standpoint is accepted as an educational objective, as it definitely should be, it follows that drama should receive attention as part of the general education of all pupils. Certainly within the classroom will be found many ways in which drama can play a part. The comparatively new fields of socio-drama and psychodrama can be utilized at this level. The study of dramatic works, in connection with language classes especially, provides a fruitful means of developing appreciations. Even though all students cannot usually participate actively in dramatic productions, intelligent audience participation can be fostered. Although some school drama programs concern themselves almost entirely with the comparatively few who actually take part as members of a play cast, the potentialities for general education should be continually examined and developed.

As in the case of speech, many schools make provisions for the needs of certain individual students in the area of drama over and above the program of general education. In some schools, an elective course in drama is offered. The drama club as a part of the student activity program is also found in middle schools.

As in all other school activities, the speech and drama program should definitely seek and strive for variety. Certainly classical works deserve a place in the dramatic activities, both from the appreciation and production standpoints. But the narrowness of a strictly classical emphasis is to be avoided. The principle of starting where the pupils are and guiding them progressively to appreciation, understanding, and interpretation of various levels of excellence is especially important in this area. Other things being approximately equal, recency and timeliness should be sought rather than discouraged or minimized. Much that is contemporary, much that is "light," is in every way suitable for consideration in the school's program.

Music Activities

As discussed in an earlier chapter, care must be taken lest the sole or primary concern in the music program be for the specialist or the specialized group. Bands, orchestras, and advanced vocal activities are valuable and important additions to a good program of general education, but they are not a substitute for such a program. The development of curricula, whereby, music and other aesthetic fields may become vital in the experience of all pupils is, judging from educational practice, one of our major unsolved school problems.

Attention should be given to understanding and appreciation as well as to performance. Since we generally learn to understand and to appreciate most fully those things which we have actually experienced ourselves, it is highly desirable that all pupils be given opportunities to develop their own aptitudes, abilities, and interests to the maximum. This places a tremendous responsibility upon the school to provide a wide variety of aesthetic experiences within the program of general education, in order that all may benefit from such experiences and also that individuals demonstrating a high degree of special aptitude, ability, and interest may be identified for additional, more specialized work. In middle schools, music supervisors, when available, can render important service in assisting teachers in many areas to correlate music with their particular subject. Nor should the opportunities outside the classroom itself be overlooked. The assembly, for example, is rich in possibilities, as suggested earlier.

First of all, assemblies in which specialized music groups perform can be among the most valuable experiences provided by the school. Thus, during the course of a school year, assemblies might be presented by the school band, by the school orchestra, by smaller instrumental groups and soloists, and by various vocal groups and soloists. Such programs can be made especially worthwhile under the direction of a leader who gives particular attention to the potential values for the audience. Explanations, interpretations, and demonstrations of many varieties of music can be given in order that the assembly be maximally effective and meaningful to participants and audience alike. Many schools plan regularly for several assemblies of the above type during each school year. The use of radio programs, recorded programs, and visiting music groups likewise can be valuable, either as supplements to or in place of school music groups.

A second desirable use of the music assembly, and one which might easily be tied in with the foregoing, involves audience participation in group singing. The value of music in building morale has long been recognized. To this value, when capable leadership is present, can be added that of increasing knowledge, understanding, and appreciation of music. The skilled and capable music director can capitalize greatly upon the opportunities which are present in the school assembly program.

As has been pointed out in previous sections, public schools have responsibilities in the field of special, as well as general, education. In the area of music, this suggests such groups as the chorus, the band, and the orchestra. Like many other activities, music groups first appeared on an "extra-class" basis. Their value once was admitted

302   Institutional Support Programs

begrudgingly, and their "respectability" with reference to more traditional offerings questioned. Although this attitude may still be found to persist in some instances, great gains have been made in the direction of scheduling music classes and groups of various kinds within the regular school program. Pupil enrollment in these groups is usually based upon one or a combination of several factors, including aptitude and ability as indicated by such criteria as special aptitude tests and teacher judgment, expressed interest on the part of pupils, and flexibility of the class schedule. Certainly the inclusion of these specialized music groups within the regular school curriculum is desirable and is possible even in smaller schools, in many of which the employment of a music specialist to serve both elementary and secondary schools facilitates the development of programs which otherwise might not be feasible.

In larger schools, both beginning and advanced groups have been organized, with the instructor's judgment used as the major criterion for scheduling pupils in one or the other group. This type of organization obviously makes possible an enrichment not easily attainable in smaller institutions.

In cases where local considerations make it impossible to provide for music classes and groups within the regular school schedule, such groups can be organized on an extra-class basis. This sometimes makes possible the participation of pupils who for some reason or another are unable to enroll in a regular class. Some schools utilize both plans in combination. Thus, a school band and chorus scheduled as regular classes and an orchestra organized on an extra-class basis makes greater participation attainable on the part of some pupils than would otherwise be possible.

Chapter 14 Bibliography

Armstrong, Robert L. "In Defense of Student Councils," *Clearing House* (April 1965) : 39:481–483.

Bulletin of the National Association of Secondary School Principals (October 1964) : 48:entire issue.

Douglass, Harl R. "Teaching Load Crisis in Secondary Schools," California Journal of Secondary Education (May 1957) : 32:295–299.

Dyer, J. Pope. "Assembly Programs Students Want!" *Clearing House* (October 1963) : 37:113.

Erickson, Ralph. "Growing Up or Growing Older?" *School Activities* (April 1965) : 36:3–10.

Fedder, Ruth. *Guiding Homeroom and Club Activities.* New York: McGraw-Hill Book Company, Inc., 1949.

Frank, Letitia. *The Student Assembly,* Monograph of the National Association of Secondary School Principals. Washington, D. C.: 1965.

Frederick, Robert W. *The Third Curriculum.* New York: Appleton-Century-Crofts, Inc., 1959.

Fretwell, Elbert K. *Extra-Curricular Activities in Secondary Schools.* Boston: Houghton Mifflin Company, 1931.

Gruber, Frederick C., and Beatty, Thomas Bevard. *Secondary School Activities.* New York: McGraw-Hill Book Company, Inc., 1954.

Hearn, Arthur C. *Evaluation of Student Activities,* Monograph of the National Association of Secondary School Principals. Washington, D. C.: 1965.

Hudson, Bruce M. "Leadership Among Ninth Grade Students in The Extra Class Organizations," *National Association of Secondary School Principals Bulletin* (February 1962): 46:254–255.

Johnston, Edgar Grant, and Faunce, Roland C. *Student Activities in Secondary Schools.* New York: Ronald Press Company, 1952.

Kilzer, L. R., Stephenson, H. H., and Nordberg, H. O. *Allied Activities in the Secondary School.* New York: Harper and Brothers, 1956.

McKown, Harry Charles. *Activities in the Elementary School.* New York: McGraw-Hill Book Company, Inc., 1938.

————. *Extra-Curricular Activities,* 3rd ed. New York: The Macmillan Company, 1952.

————. *School Clubs.* New York: The Macmillan Company, 1929.

Miller, Franklin A., Moyer, James H., and Patrick, Robert B. *Planning Student Activities.* Englewood Cliffs, N. J.: Prentice-Hall, Inc., 1956.

National Association of Student Councils. *The Student Council in the Secondary School.* Washington, D. C.: National Education Assn., 1962.

National Study of Secondary School Evaluation. *Evaluative Criteria.* Washington, D. C.: American Council on Education, 1969.

Platzer, Karl H. "Selective Processes in a Junior High School," *National Association of Secondary School Principals Bulletin* (February 1962): 46: 255–256.

Remmers, H. H., ed. *Studies in Extra-Curricular Activities.* Lafayette, Ind.: Purdue University Press, 1950.

Roemer, Joseph. "The Emergence of Extra-Curricular Activities," *School Activities* (March 1965): 36:entire issue.

Sterner, William S. *The Student Council Advisor,* Monograph of the National Association of Secondary School Principals. Washington, D. C.: 1963.

The Student Council Handbook. Washington, D. C.: National Association of Student Councils, 1967.

Wesche, Lilburn E. "The Student Newspaper," *Clearing House* (March 1963): 37:438–439.

Wood, Donald. "Archaic Student Clubs," *Clearing House* (October 1964): 39:91–114.

Chapter 15

Guidance
in the Middle School

Guidance, when defined as a continuing process concerned with determining and providing for the developmental needs of all students,
should be an essential component of the students' educational experience in the middle school. During the period in the student's life when
he is undergoing many changes in relation to his physiological and psychological growth, he needs an educational experience, i.e., the middle
school, which focuses its attention upon the "tween-ager." Knowledge
of the student who is served by the school is essential if he is to have a
unique and individual educational experience. The only way to design
an individual educational program for the student is to learn as much as
possible about him. This requires a concentrated effort of the administration, teachers, counselors, parents and other staff members.

Guidance, when viewed as an integral part of the work of the faculty in the middle school, is the responsibility of every staff member.
Guidance cannot be viewed as a supplementary service provided by
clinical experts but must be viewed and operated in harmony with the
total program. However, it should be realized that some aspects of
guidance must be separated from instruction because teachers are not
specially trained nor do they have the time for these functions.

304

Guidance also can be defined as the provision of services which will assist students to solve their problems—problems which they themselves have identified. A few years ago a well-known psychologist summarized adolescent problems as identified in more than a dozen separate studies. Table XI lists those problems which were mentioned most frequently in these studies.[1] A careful examination of the topics will reveal that they are not those which are ordinarily included in typical courses of study in the middle school. While it is true that some of these topics, particularly those in the school and study area, lend themselves to correlation with course work, it would be unrealistic to assume that they will receive adequate consideration unless the faculty makes a deliberate effort to accord them such attention—this is guidance.

The scope of the guidance program may be described as the material within the basic problem areas confronting students—educational, vocational, personal, and social similar to those used in Table XI. The scope could also be described by function—information-giving, counseling, placement, and follow-up. The authors suggest, however, that the scope of the middle school guidance program has been best delineated by Mauritz Johnson in his text on guidance.[2]

Guidance roles and responsibilities can be classified into four levels —meeting immediate needs, meeting long range needs, providing consultation services, and providing long-term treatment. The first and second levels fall within teacher responsibilities, the second and third levels are in the purview of the school counselor, while the fourth level is reserved for the school psychologist.

The first level—meeting immediate needs—is the responsibility of the entire school staff but particularly that of the teachers as they work with the students in the educational program. The student's needs that can be best served through immediate teacher attention constitute the depth of guidance assistance necessary at the first level. The teachers, through interaction with the students, contribute to the personal and social growth as well as the academic development of the students. It is important that the teacher be aware of the student's needs and desires. Many problems that the student has are compounded or alleviated within the classroom setting depending upon the teacher's ability to establish for the student a feeling of security, to promote positive peer relationships, a feeling of belonging, to provide an understanding of self and to gain competency in subject matter. The first level of guidance service could be called preventative or developmental. All children need this type of developmental guidance and the classroom teacher

[1] From Table 51, from *Psychology of Adolescence*, 5th ed., by Luella Cole. Copyright 1936, 1942, 1948, 1954, © 1959 by Holt, Rinehart and Winston, Inc. Copyright © 1964 by Luella Cole. Reprinted by permission of Holt, Rinehart and Winston, Inc.

[2] Mauritz Johnson, Jr., *Junior High School Guidance* (New York: Harper and Row, Publishers, 1961), pp. 237–238.

Table XI.   Problems of Adolescents

School and Study Problems	Percent of Samples with Problems
Wondering if one has enough ability to do the work	59
Being unable to speak before a group	53
Worrying over examinations	51
Daydreaming while studying	51
Being unable to concentrate	47
Being unable to express oneself in speech or writing	41
Not knowing how well one is doing	40
Being unable to plan time	34
Having too many activities that interfere with study	32
Being unable to take notes	27
Needing help in selecting courses	26
Problems Related to Vocation	
Not knowing what work is suitable for one's abilities	56
Needing experience in different kinds of work	49
Needing help in discovering one's abilities	43
Not knowing where to look for a job	35
Needing to learn how to budget money	28
Needing help in learning about openings in different fields	28
Needing to earn money now	27
Not knowing how to act during an interview	24
Personal–Social Problems	
Wanting to be more popular	54
Fear of making social errors	43
Wanting to make new friends	42
Feeling inferior	41
Wanting to be more attractive	38
Having no one for a chum	38
Feeling unable to converse	35
Worrying over correct manners	34
Being too easily hurt	31
Not knowing what is right or wrong	28
Fear of meeting people	28
Being left out of things	26
Having no one with whom to discuss problems	26

without fanfare or planned activities is best situated, if qualified, to conduct this type of guidance.

The second level of guidance can be characterized by teachers or counselors dealing with individuals who are concerned with a long range personal decision that demands greater depth than that which is involved in the first level. Many students develop a relationship with teachers or counselors and seek advice in areas of course selection, program planning, vocational information, and personal problems. Many schools promote this relationship by providing opportunities for group guidance activities which highlight typical problems in these areas. Some middle schools further promote this service by assigning teachers to be advisors to groups of students whom they teach so that they can perform the function within the normal operation of the school day. This type of individual guidance is usually of short duration and serves to locate students with problems which cannot be alleviated in group or short conferences. These students are referred to a teacher or counselor with time available and such service constitutes the third level of middle school guidance.

The third level of guidance is primarily the responsibility of a trained counselor. The authors firmly believe that this individual must be someone with classroom teaching experience, with considerable time available, and without administrative assignments; but the authors withhold judgment as to whether the counselor should be teaching at the same time that he carries a counseling assignment. The general pattern is that schools employ counselors who devote the entire day to counseling and related activities. The full-time counselor, who is found most often in large schools, may avoid loss of time and effectiveness by refraining from changing his role of counselor to teacher and vice-versa. He is free from the many instructional responsibilities which may hinder his effectiveness as a counselor. He is likely to develop stronger professional ties with the guidance field and to achieve a higher level of technical competence than would be the case if his responsibilities were divided. On the other hand, the full-time counselor lacks the opportunity to observe pupils in the classroom situation, and it is out of these situations that many of the vital counseling problems arise. Thus, the arguments of time and authority-figure image which demand a full-time counselor are diminished to a considerable extent by the valuable insight a teacher-counselor can have concerning a counselee who is also a student in another relationship. However, this argument is resolved at the local level; the authors are assuming in this chapter that sufficient time is provided the counseling function so that there is the equivalent of one full-time counselor for every 250-300 students. This counselor would be working with students who have been referred by faculty members or with students who have come to the counselor themselves. These students have concerns in such depth that the services of a professionally trained counselor are mandatory.

The fourth level of guidance occurs when the student's needs are beyond the training or capabilities of the counselor. The student is then referred to a psychologist or another appropriate professional person. This type of problem usually requires long term treatment and demands the continued involvement of both teacher and counselor so that the work being done can be complemented in the school experience.

Guidance, at any level, is too important to leave to chance. It is not enough that guidance be "everybody's business," although every member of the staff must play a role in an effective guidance program. Nor can the school's guidance function be satisfactorily performed during activity periods, passing in the hall, or in spontaneous "feeling" sessions. What is needed in every middle school is a program which regularly reaches every student, every year he is in school, in both group and individual guidance relationships. While the key to the efficient operation of such a program is the school counselor, the most important member of the guidance function is the classroom teacher.

The School Counselor

The school counselor plays an extremely important consultant role in the operation of a school guidance program. Even though he is an experienced educator with special training in one area, an office in the administrative section of the school, and unassigned time available, it is imperative that he be considered a member of the teaching faculty and not a member of the school administration. Furthermore, the counselor must be a professional person, educationally oriented, highly knowledgeable in the area of child development, with a broadly based multi-disciplinary background in the behavioral sciences and a high degree of competence in human relations. With this background in training and experience, as a member of the teaching faculty he will have responsibilities divided into three areas: consultation, counseling, and coordination.

Probably the most underused and yet potentially the most significant contribution of the school counselor to the middle school is his role as a consultant to administrators, teachers, and curriculum developers in the area of growth and development, human relations, and adolescent problems. In curriculum development, for example, who is better trained to estimate the effect a proposed school program will have upon the physiological, psychological and cultural dynamics currently acting upon the child in the middle school? The curriculum must be appropriate to the student's needs and level of development if classroom teachers are to make maximum use out of group guidance activities. In addition, the counselor is especially qualified to supplement gaps in the training of middle school teachers in (1) school and social pressures that affect the middle school student; (2) awareness, identification, and understanding of the problems of the student; (3) methods of creating a safe learning climate in the classroom; and (4) assessment of the individual learning difficulties and the relation of any diagnosis to instruction. The authors lament the fact that teacher training institutions do not prepare teachers who already have these competencies. Until they do, the counselor can serve a very significant role in this regard.

The obvious role of the school counselor, of course, is the conducting of individual private conferences with students who are in need of such activities. These students may be identified and referred to by other professionals in the school or may be ones who initiate the conferences themselves. The counselor, many times, becomes an intermediary between the student and the problem, even those within the student, and provides an adult listening post for the early adolescent. His status as a member of the teaching faculty enables him in this regard to consult with a colleague, as opposed to a subordinate, about difficulties in the classroom setting which are influencing or being influenced by an individual student's problem.

The third role of the middle school counselor is to perform a coordinating function relative to the total guidance program. He facilitates the movement of students and their records from school to school and from grade level to grade level. He organizes and chairs "staff conferences" which attempt to help students, teachers, parents or the school attack an immediate problem. He provides in-service assistance to teachers relative to their group guidance function. And, he serves as a resource person or an expediter of resources of the school and community for whomever has need of his services.

Thus, although the school counselor is often referred to as the Guidance Director for a school, the authors see his various roles as basically supplemental to the teacher's activities in the guidance program. The conferences he has with students often grow out of classroom activities, group guidance discussions, or teacher student relationships. The consultant services he provides are designed to make the teacher better prepared to assume guidance responsibilities within the classroom setting. The coordination of services and materials similarly is an integral part of his commitment to the teachers as the focal point of the entire guidance program.

The Role of the Counselor in Discipline

The school, of course, is only one of the agencies in society which influence behavior. The family, the peer group, and the so-called mass media (the press, radio, television, and the motion picture) are examples of potent non-school educative forces. In some cases the effect of these forces upon the student complements the work of the school, and in other cases is antagonistic to it. Thus even in the finest schools, constructive, preventive approaches to student problems are not always successful, and corrective measures are called for. This does not mean, however, that guidance should then step out of the picture. To do so would be somewhat analagous to having a physician agree to try to keep a person healthy, but then to refuse to have anything to do with him should he become ill.

It should be thoroughly understood, though, that the responsibility for the maintenance of order, the preservation of safety, and the protection of property rests squarely upon the principal of the school. The principal may delegate some of his authority to carry out this function and he may hold others responsible for various phases of it, but he cannot evade or lessen his own responsibility.

In some schools, authority in disciplinary matters is delegated to a vice-principal or other administrative officer. It is regretable that in other instances, counselors or other guidance functionaries are given this assignment. In such cases these staff members have two separate roles. It is impossible to make the distinction clear to the students concerned.

Professionally, of course, everyone involved with the educational process is interested not only in the establishment of certain conditions but also in facilitating the optimum development of each individual student. For this reason, the guidance viewpoint is essential in the administration of discipline. Johnson and others[3] propose a "discipline ladder" which should be helpful in insuring a consistent and systematic approach to problems which might arise. This outline is suggestive only; each school should develop its own in accord with local conditions. Each step in the ladder assumes that previous action was not sufficiently effective; otherwise, of course, there would be no need for it. The order of steps should not be rigid, some will need to be repeated, and some used longer than others. The important consideration is that each school should have a well-understood, systematic, rational approach to the problems of discipline.

The Teacher's Role in the Guidance Program

Our discussion thus far has focused upon the work of the counselor in guidance. Every effective program, however, involves all members of the staff. The classroom teacher's role, though different from that of others, is the most important. Good teachers on the one hand make it unnecessary for certain problems ever to reach the counselor, and on the other, are able to strengthen and supplement the work of the counselor by stressing applications of general principles to specific situations and subjects. So vital is the teacher's function in the school guidance program that it will comprise the remainder of the chapter.

It will be recalled that in the preceding section, the discussion of various steps in approaching problems of discipline suggested that if

3 *Ibid.*, pp. 131–132.

previous action had been sufficiently effective, subsequent action would be unnecessary. But "previous action," in matters of citizenship and discipline as well as in other situations involving guidance, is usually "classroom teaching." In other words, the most promising and effective way to reduce the number and difficulty of problems requiring involvement of guidance personnel is to bring about a more effective learning climate in the classroom itself. It is for this reason that the classroom teacher is the key figure in the guidance program.

Individualization of Instruction

The teacher's competence in understanding and appreciating the fact of individual uniqueness manifests itself in the classroom in many ways. Data of various kinds concerning each student are at the teacher's fingertips, perhaps assembled in individual folders filed in the classroom. Blanket assignments from class sets of required material are replaced by considerable flexibility worked out on an individual or small group basis. Supervised study within the class period is provided, during which time students receive individual help from the teacher. Objectives are clearly understood, progress toward their attainment is assessed consistently, individually, and frequently, and this progress is recorded in understandable terms. Conscientious efforts are made both to analyze causes of difficulty and to evaluate or remove such causes.

Detecting Problems

Every teacher has the responsibility of identifying some of the factors that may be creating problems not yet recognized by the counselee. Some of the indications of such problems have been well summarized by Erickson:[4]

1. Individuals showing unusual tensions.
2. Individual behavior varying widely from the mores of his group.
3. Individuals continually unable to decide on a course of action, unable to come to decisions.
4. Individuals showing extreme lack of interest or enthusiasm.
5. Individuals continually resorting to attention-getting or overly aggressive behavior.
6. Individuals overcompensating by excess enthusiasms, extreme devotion to typical hobbies or interests.
7. Individuals whose goals and possibilities are not in harmony.
8. Individuals showing lack of faith in self, overdependence on others.

[4] Clifford Erickson, *The Counseling Interview* (New York: Prentice-Hall, Inc., 1950), pp. 30–31.

9. Individuals not making progress commensurate with their aims.
10. Individuals showing sudden and contradictory changes in behavior.
11. Individuals whose abilities and interests are regularly not being utilized.
12. Individuals resorting to antisocial or infantile behavior.
13. Individuals unable to make adequate social adjustments anywhere along the line.
14. Individuals who regularly fail and who seldom have any opportunities for success experiences.
15. Individuals who have acquired handicapping habits or attitudes.
16. Individuals whose basic needs are insufficiently cared for.

Vocational Planning

Even though there is little place in the middle school for vocational *training*, vocational *guidance* is essential. The primary objective of such guidance should be to develop in students career consciousness and occupational awareness in place of a selection of "the" job. In other words, it is not important that students at this level settle upon a definite occupation, but that they *not* settle upon a completely unrealistic one. This involves both realistic self-appraisal and the development of a valid picture of the world of work.

Another contribution which teachers can make to the middle school guidance program is to help students understand the vocational aspects of the subjects they teach. Who, for example, should be better able than the classroom teacher to explain how and why social scientists utilize the field of mathematics in their work? And by the same token the English teacher should be best equipped to show that one's ultimate success in any study or in any vocation is likely to depend very largely upon his competence in the written and spoken language. These examples are perhaps not as obvious as are other vocational values of specific school subjects, but they are of great importance, none the less, in vocational adjustment and success.

Group Guidance

The primary role of the classroom teacher in the middle school guidance program is in relation to group guidance activities, discussions, and seminars.

One group guidance approach, the homeroom, involves most, if not all, of the faculty. In many schools, one or more periods per week are scheduled for group guidance. Time is sometimes provided by scheduling separate periods or modules for guidance purposes; in other instances, one of the regular periods might be lengthened. This approach has the best chance to succeed when two conditions are met: first, that the time is utilized for guidance purposes only, and all of the students assigned to the group are involved; and second, that the faculty members assigned as group leaders have the skills and competencies necessary. These competencies may be thought of as falling into two different but related categories. There are those competencies that are associated with interpersonal relations including a sincere interest in human beings, an ability to establish effective rapport with young people, and the ability to apply what is known about individual differences, motivation, and interests. Secondly, there are specialized competencies in the field of guidance including basic knowledge and skills in interviewing, psychological testing, and the interpretation of data. Thus the "homeroom" approach to group guidance makes exacting demands of a large proportion of the total faculty of the school.

A variant of the above method draws upon the proposals and recommendations of the Commission on the Experimental Study of the Utilization of the Staff in the Secondary School.[5] Many aspects of the school's group guidance program lend themselves very well to large group presentations, with follow-up in small group sessions. It is important to recognize, however, that to Dr. Trump and his colleagues, a small group is made up of fifteen or fewer people in order that the potentialities of group process and interaction might be capitalized upon to a greater extent than is ordinarily possible with a larger number of participants.

A third group guidance approach is based upon correlation with regular classwork. If the group guidance program is to reach all students, it follows that such correlation must take place in a course which enrolls all students. Other considerations being approximately equal, the most logical subject field with which to correlate group guidance is the social studies, since it is ordinarily a part of the required program for all students. The well-prepared social studies teacher of today combines a basic interest in and understanding of the problems of young people with a broad understanding of the contributions which his subject field can make to the solutions of such problems. To such a teacher, a consideration of these problems enhances rather than hinders the social studies program. The school which is interested in correlating group guidance with social studies should have an excellent chance of success in doing so.

A "rule of thumb" proposed by many guidance authorities is that approximately one-fifth of the time ordinarily allocated to a regular subject be devoted to group guidance each year. This is roughly the equivalent of one class period per week. Thus, if group guidance were correlated with social studies, the proposed time allocation would

[5] J. Lloyd Trump, Dorsey Baynham, and Commission on the Experimental Study of the Utilization of the Staff in the Secondary School, *Guide to Better Schools* (Chicago: Rand McNally and Company, 1961).

schedule approximately four-fifths of the year's social studies time to social studies and the remaining time to guidance. In the most effective programs, the two areas would lose their separate identities at many points.

It has been shown in earlier sections that the social studies program often is part of a block of time constituting two or three periods of a seven-period day. When a second subject field is included in this block of time, the subject field ordinarily is language arts. A three-period block including social studies, language arts, and guidance has been found to be feasible in many middle schools. This presumes, of course, that the teachers have competencies in all three of the fields involved. The authors have already pointed out that effective guidance requires special competencies on the part of the faculty members concerned; they feel just as strongly that when two or more traditional subject fields are included in the same time block, the teacher to be maximally effective must have competencies in each of the subject fields.

Let us assume for the moment that a hypothetical school is organized on the basis of a seven-period day, with a three-period block of time provided for social studies, language arts, and group-guidance. Thus there are fifteen periods per week devoted to the three areas. This would make possible, as an illustration, the equivalent of eight periods for language arts, six for social studies, and one for group guidance. This ratio could be varied, within limits, but in any case it would provide for group guidance while at the same time providing more, rather than less, than the traditional five periods per week each for language arts and social studies. This should make it easier to provide, for example, for library usage, supervised study, and other sometimes-neglected learning experiences.

Recent developments within American society have made it increasingly difficult to find teachers with the versatility to handle adequately the three-period block described above. In the first place, the "knowledge explosion" poses a serious problem for the teacher in keeping abreast of developments in one, to say nothing of two, subject fields. It would take a remarkable teacher indeed to meet this challenge. Especially is this so since the trend toward early identification of gifted students, with accompanying curricular modifications, has resulted in learning experiences formerly reserved for the senior high school now being utilized in the middle school.

The foregoing sections have illustrated a variety of ways in which the teacher makes direct contributions into the total guidance program. There is no one or specific way that every teacher should operate but, rather, that each school must ascertain what variety of roles are necessary for its particular situation to the end that, as proposed earlier, the guidance program reaches every student regularly during each year of his school career.

Guidance Materials

Fortunately, many very useful materials are available for implementing the school guidance program. They will be considered here under two headings. First, an organized, comprehensive "total" program followed by brief descriptions of a selected group of miscellaneous materials which through the years have proved to be valuable supplements to the programs in many schools.

Two of the most widely used comprehensive programs of group guidance are those published, respectively, by Science Research Associates[6] and the American Guidance Service.[7] The publications of both of these organizations demonstrate convincingly an awareness of the typical problems of adolescence as discussed at the beginning of this chapter. Both of them present readable, down to earth material dealing with these problems. Both are worthy of careful consideration by every school. The authors have selected the American Guidance Service (AGS) materials for a somewhat detailed description at this point, in order that the reader may be familiar with one way in which a group guidance program might be organized.

The AGS program utilizes three basic themes for use with early adolescents. These are entitled, *"About Growing Up," "Being Teen Agers,"* and *"Our School Life,"* and, although providing for flexibility, are basically intended for use in grades 6-9. For each of the three themes, a student text, a set of classroom charts, and a teacher's guide are provided. The chapter titles from the student texts provide an overall summary of the content. Each text includes thirty-three topics, suggesting the possibility of considering an average of approximately one topic per week throughout the school year.

Other Guidance Materials

Your High School Record—Does It Count? by Robert D. Falk,[8] merits a place in every middle school. It consists of facsimile copies of letters actually addressed to high school principals by colleges and prospective employers seeking information relative to students and former students of the school. Questions relating to specific personality and character traits, on the official stationery of well-known institutions and businesses, do a great deal to strengthen the school's hand in encouraging the development of strong personality and character traits.

Additional guidance tools could be a daily log and diary (Tables XII and XIII) which a student could use to budget his activities at school

[6] Science Research Associates, 259 East Erie Street, Chicago, Ill. 60611.
[7] American Guidance Service, 720 Washington Avenue, S.E., Minneapolis, Minn. 55414.
[8] Robert D. Falk, *Your High School Record—Does It Count?* (Pierre, S. D.: South Dakota Press, 1965).

and home. The relationship of good habits in school to success in later school life is a concern of both counselor and student. These tables could establish a wise use of time and thus help build good study habits, attitudes, and skills.

Inventory of Social Traits

Table XI lists many problems which are classified in the "personal-social" category. The accompanying Inventory of Social Traits (Table XIV) is an example of an instrument which can be used to assist students in assessing themselves in this area. It can also serve a valuable purpose as a basis for solving personal-social problems.

The Inventory consists of a list of "Yes" and "No" questions whose purpose is to ascertain the individual's habitual responses to certain situations. The data from such an instrument, together with related data, facilitate the study of probable cause-effect relationships in specific cases. Frequently the Inventory arouses the interest of the faculty in personnel work, and it invariably creates a high level of interest among students. Students typically desire to know "how they came out," and will ordinarily take the initiative in arranging for interviews to discuss the findings. Thus the vitally important matter of establishing rapport becomes relatively easy as counselor and counselee discuss possible implications in the questionnaire and especially in the counselee's responses to the specific items.

The value of inventories of this type is dependent upon the attitude of the individual responding to it. If he considers it an effort on the part of others to investigate his private life, little if any value is likely to result. On the other hand, its greatest potentialities will be achieved if students think of it as a fairly objective instrument of self-analysis, the results of which may be used to meet some of their most baffling problems more effectively. Because of the need for student cooperation, ample time should be taken to help students understand and appreciate the instrument's potential values.

The Student Handbook

The student handbook is an indispensable document in the effective school, and as such, it provides a ready-made asset to the guidance program. Table XV lists specific topics included in the student handbook of a particular school. These topics are representative of the contents of school handbooks in general. A recommended practice is that of using the handbook in the group guidance program at the beginning of each school year, for as long a period of time as deemed desirable in the individual groups. Undoubtedly, much more time will be required at the lowest grade level. At the upper grade levels, since much of the material will be basically similar to that studied earlier, the time allocations would be adjusted accordingly.

Table XII.   Time Distribution Data Sheet

Directions: On this sheet, record the things which you do and the hours of the day at which they are done. Using Monday as an example, the following entries might be made: Sleep 12–7:10, Dressing 7:10–7:45, Breakfast 7:45–8:15, Walking to school 8:15–8:40, Classes 8:50–12:00, Lunch 12:10–12:45, Leisure 12:45–1:10, and so on for every hour of each day of the week.

Mon.	Hours	Tues.	Hours	Wed.	Hours	Thurs.	Hours	Fri.	Hours	Sat.	Hours	Sun.	Hours

Table XIII.   Time Distribution Sheet

Name_____   Date_____

In the form below summarize the hours spent each day on the items indicated in the left column. When this has been done for each day enter the amount of time spent on each item during the week in the column on the right.

	Mon.	Tues.	Wed.	Thurs.	Fri.	Sat.	Sun.	Total for Week
Classes								
School Activities								
Study and other school work								
Outside work and home duties								
Leisure								
Meals								
Sleep								
Miscellaneous								
Daily totals	24	24	24	24	24	24	24	168

Table XIV. Inventory of Social Traits—Grades 7, 8, and 9

Name_____ Date_____ Grade_____

Directions: The following has been prepared to help you make a self-analysis of your social characteristics. Read each question carefully and answer it sincerely. Do not stop to ponder each answer. Let each answer be the first one that comes to your mind. Indicate your answer to each question by drawing a line under "Yes" or under "No."

You will have as much time as you need, but do not dawdle. As you know, this information is strictly confidential.

Yes No 1. Do you like to go to parties?

Yes No 2. Do you talk much in a group?

Yes No 3. Are you popular with the opposite sex?

Yes No 4. Do you always try to see that newcomers meet the others in your group?

Yes No 5. Have you ever been captain of your team, chairman of a committee, or president of a club?

Yes No 6. Is it hard for you to make friends?

Yes No 7. Do you feel uneasy with a group of new students?

Yes No 8. Do your classmates slight you?

Yes No 9. Do you go off with a few friends at a party or other group gathering?

Yes No 10. Do you think that most of the students are snobs?

Yes No 11. Do you have many friends?

Yes No 12. Do you know many games to play at parties?

Yes No 13. Do you like to make new friends?

Yes No 14. Do other students like to work with you?

Yes No 15. Have you ever been asked to choose sides for a game or contest?

Yes No 16. Do you often think that people are making fun of you?

Yes No 17. Do you think school clubs are a bore?

Yes No 18. Would you rather use your spare time by yourself doing what you please than to be with a group of friends?

Yes No 19. Are other students always teasing you?

Yes No 20. Are parties and dances too stupid to be any fun?

Yes No 21. Do you enjoy being with other students at recess?

Yes No 22. Do you like to share things with others?

Yes No 23. Do you like to work in a group when someone else is the leader?

Yes No 24. Would you like to be a leader?

Yes No 25. Can you lose in a game without being very much upset?

Table XV.   Student Handbook

The following headings have been adopted from the student handbook of an outstanding junior–senior high high school. They are reproduced here in the hope that they might prove helpful to other schools.

Introduction

Philosophy of the school

School creed or citizenship code

Subject offerings

Graduation requirements

Daily schedule

Attendance

Marking system

Guidance program

College entrance requirements

Job placement

Pupil-parent-counselor conferences

The work of the deans

The work of the school psychologist

The work of the assistant principal

The work of the principal

Health services

Other special services

National Honor Society

Assemblies

Other student activities

Elections

Songs and yells

Student conduct

a. halls

b. auditorium

c. vehicles

d. cafeteria

e. fire drills

f. library

Data Concerning Counselees

The effective guidance program utilizes a wide variety of information concerning every student in the school. Included will be material in the following categories:

1. Identifying data and material (e.g. name, address, phone, birth-date, photograph).
2. Scholastic achievement.
3. Information concerning citizenship, personality, and character.
4. Psychological data (e.g. mental ability, achievement, interests).
5. Physical data (health, physical characteristics).
6. Mental health data (e.g. emotional adjustment, conflict symptoms, significant limitations).
7. Data on use of leisure time (e.g. out-of-school activities and achievement, employment, hobbies, chums).

8. Pertinent socio-economic data (e.g. parental background, occupation, and education; home conditions and influence; neighborhood and other environments).
9. Information concerning educational and vocational plans, and reasons for choices.

It is recommended that these and other pertinent materials be assembled in manila folders alphabetically arranged, and that they be the primary responsibility of the counselors. In many school systems, these cumulative folders are instituted at the elementary level, and copies of basic material, and in some cases the entire folders, accompany the student to the middle school. In situations in which such guidance data are not available at the elementary level, it is very important that the school take the initiative in securing certain information concerning its future students at least several months prior to their entrance.

There is no more important single responsibility to be assigned to the lowest grade counselor than that of assisting each prospective student in working out a tentative long-range program of studies. Since this projected program must logically precede the development of the schedule of classes, it should be worked out in the spring of the year.

In most cases, the students for the first time will be faced with the problem of making choices from among several elective offerings. The counselor should assist the student and his parents in understanding the significance of the various kinds of data necessary for informed decisions.

Testing and Guidance

The following seven points concerning the relationship between testing and guidance are important to keep in mind as decisions relative to scheduling junior high school students are considered.[9]

1. Although a large-scale testing program in the junior high school grades can be effectively used in many ways (e.g. diagnosis, placement, evaluation), its major purpose should be guidance.
2. Standardized test scores, properly interpreted, provide data which can aid the pupil in his self-understanding and decision-making.
3. The use of ability and achievement test scores, with proper safeguards, precautions, and qualifications, can be valuable for purposes of prediction.

[9] Adapted from "Resource Materials: Large Scale Programs of Testing for Guidance," Educational Testing Services (Princeton, N. J.: March 1968). Material is abridged. Reprinted with permission.

4. Standardized test scores are by no means the only source for such information, but will be most effective when properly combined with observations and other data.
5. Even when combined with other data, test scores will not tell a pupil beyond all doubt whether he will succeed or fail in his choice.
6. The junior high school represents a timely period in which to administer a program of standardized testing for guidance, since prediction at this level is practical and appropriate in terms of both the psychological development of individuals and the organization of our school systems.
7. Although the junior high school period offers an optimum opportunity for guidance testing, testing should not be restricted to this period. Rather, the entire guidance program should be built upon previous activities and lead into future ones.

The question as to how much information about test results should be revealed to students and their parents is a very important one. Should scores on group tests of mental ability be disclosed? If standardized achievement tests are utilized, should the results be forwarded to parents? How can discrepancies between such scores and report card grades be explained? These are examples of the many questions concerning test results which frequently arise and concerning which the school should establish a clearly defined policy.

The authors suggest that parents have the right to be the recipients, of whatever information the school has about the potential, the achievement, and the difficulties of their children. Furthermore, the school must see that the information is communicated in as understandable and usable a fashion as possible. For example, difficulties arise with Intelligence Quotients (IQ) which are numbers that are often seen as a fixed characteristic of the person tested—as something much more than the mere single test score that it really is. The effect often is that of a final conclusion about the individual rather than that of one item of information useful in further thinking and planning. Few things interfere more effectively with real understanding than indiscriminate reporting of IQ scores to parents, especially so in light of cultural inaccuracies found in the last few years. Also, grade placement scores of various kinds are less likely to cause trouble than IQ scores but, still, they require careful attention.

For example, a seventh grade student with grade placement scores of 11.2 for reading and 8.8 for arithmetic does not necessarily rank higher in reading than in arithmetic when compared to other seventh graders. This is because progress in arithmetic is more dependent than progress in reading on what has been taught, and thus is spread over a narrower range at any one grade. *Percentiles* probably are the most informative numbers to use, provided that it is made clear (1) that they refer to the percentage of individuals whose performance the student has equalled or surpassed, rather than the percentage of items answered satisfactorily, and (2) who, specifically, are the individuals with whom the student is being compared.

The problems posed in the foregoing paragraph have led some schools to the practice of utilizing numerical data only incidentally or not at all. This leads to a brief discussion of verbal techniques utilizing descriptive comments like the following:

"Your scores are similar to those of people who do very well in advanced mathematics."

"People scoring approximately as you do usually become bored with jobs of a routine nature." ·

"Studies have shown that success in that particular college generally requires more success in English than you have had so far."

In short, the school requires basic test data concerning each of its students, and this information should be conveyed to the students and their parents. It should be presented in terms they understand. But, in most cases at least, descriptive terms rather than numbers promise to help achieve the most satisfactory results.

A Reminder

This discussion of the middle school guidance program should suffice to support the authors' contention that not only does the classroom teacher have a place in the total guidance program, but that no program can be maximally effective unless each staff member has a well-defined role within it. These roles should be spelled out in detail at the local level, committed to writing, and reviewed periodically, to the end that each student may continuously receive the assistance he needs in arriving at valid decisions affecting his life.

Chapter 15 Bibliography

American Guidance Service, 720 Washington Avenue, S.E., Minneapolis, Minn. 55414.

Cole, Luella. *Psychology of Adolescence.* New York: Holt, Rinehart and Winston, Inc., 1962, pp. 579–582.

Crow, Lester D., and Crow, Alice. *Readings in Guidance.* New York: David McKay Company, 1962.

Erickson, Clifford E. *The Counseling Interview.* New York: Prentice-Hall Inc., 1950.

Falk, Robert D. *Your High School Record—Does It Count?* Pierre, S. D.: South Dakota Press, 1965.

Johnson, Mauritz, Jr., and others. *Junior High School Guidance.* New York: Harper and Brothers, 1961, pp. 131–132, 237–238.

Science Research Associates, 259 East Erie Street, Chicago, Ill. 60611.

Trump, Lloyd, and Baynham, Dorsey. *Guide to Better Schools.* Chicago: Rand McNally and Company, 1961.

Chapter 16

Organization and Administration
of the Middle School

Administration exists for the purpose of facilitating the operation of the school's total educational program. The key person in any school's success is the principal. This is not to say that the principal is necessarily the most able individual on the staff; it is rather to emphasize the fact that because he is the chief administrative officer, he holds the most crucial leadership role in the school. It is not to be expected—in fact, it is not possible—that he be more competent in the various subject fields than are the teachers of those subjects, nor that he be more able in the area of guidance or student activities, than those having responsibilities for guidance, and activities in his school. The nature of the principal's job is such that to be maximally effective he must be a generalist rather than a specialist. He must have a clear-cut picture of the total field of education, with special emphasis, of course, upon the needs of the particular age range with which his school is concerned. He must understand and help his co-workers to understand the relationship of all of the activities of the school. He must, in collaboration with his co-workers, assist in the planning of educational experiences which will provide for each student the best possible utilization of the available educational resources.

Much has been written and spoken in recent years relative to the "democratic" concept of administration. Democratic administration has been contrasted to authoritarian administration on the one hand, and laissez-faire administration, on the other. There is no real disagreement with the proposal that neither of these two extremes is appropriate to the modern school. But what is democratic administration? Since misunderstandings sometimes exist concerning the meaning of the term, the authors have spelled out below their proposal for a working definition of the concept.

Democratic administration might be defined as administration which provides, for *all* constituents of the school community, the right and the opportunity to share in determining the purposes and policies of the educational enterprise. It seeks to avoid the extreme concentration of power, the unshared responsibility, and the regimentation of authoritarianism on the one hand, and the disorganization and unrestrained freedom of the laissez-faire concept on the other.

The principal who would administer his school democratically must first of all be a philosopher in the broad sense of the term. Since the purpose of education is to transmit, maintain, and improve the culture of which it is an integral part, the educational leader must be a student of the culture, philosophy, and tenets upon which it is based. The key values of American democracy may be summarized briefly as follows:[1]

1. The belief that human life, happiness, and well-being are to be valued above all else.
2. The assertion that, within the limits imposed by nature, man is master of his own destiny; that within these limits man has the right to control his own destiny, in his own interests, and in his own way.
3. The assertion that the people are sovereign and that governments derive their just powers from the consent of the governed; that consent is thus the major social bond; and that human beings are not the mere instruments of the state.
4. The belief that government for the people can be assured only if there is government by the people.
5. Faith in the ability of men to govern themselves wisely; and the belief that the distribution of such ability follows no social or economic lines.
6. Faith in human intelligence, and the belief that by exercising thought man can build a better world; hence, the belief that human happiness and well-being can best be advanced only if there is an unrestricted play of free intelligence upon all problems and difficulties. Hence,

[1] Harold C. Hand, *General Education in the American High School* (New York: Scott, Foresman and Company, 1942), pp. 5–6. Copyright 1942 by Scott, Foresman and Company.

The guarantees given to freedom of thought, belief, speech, assembly, and press—freedoms which are not to be abrogated or curtailed by any majority, these freedoms are in fact placed above the law.

The determination to maintain these freedoms as the necessary condition for creating new minds, and the realization that whoever denies any of these freedoms to that degree stifles intelligence.

The determination that differences shall be resolved and consent engineered only through persuasion based on reason.

The high valuations placed on integrity and fair play and the inclusive tolerance of all creeds and all political faiths.

7. The belief that all human beings are intrinsically of equivalent moral worth; hence, the determination that the dignity and worth of each person shall be respected at all times and under all conditions.

The good life, however conceived, shall be made equally available to all persons without favoritism. Equal justice shall be guaranteed to all persons; equal educational opportunity shall be guaranteed to all; the opportunity to engage in gainful employment, under decent working conditions and at a fair wage, shall be assured to all adults; and undeserved poverty shall be abolished. Tests of the validity of all policies and arrangements shall be made in terms of what each does, or promises to do, for the welfare of human beings; and, furthermore, all such evaluations shall be made in terms of individual well-being.

The happiness and well-being of each person shall count equally in all valuations and in the framing of all social policy.

8. The assertion of the right of individual freedom—the right of persons to resist excessive social pressures; the recognition of the right of each person to think his own thoughts, speak his own mind, and worship in his own way so long as he does not thereby deny the same right to others.

General objectives for American education must be derived from our basic tenets. The widely-known Seven Cardinal Principles of Secondary Education and the Purposes of Education in American Democracy, published by the National Education Association, are examples of objectives which have exerted considerable influence on our school programs. Thoughtful consideration and understanding of the philosophical basis of American democracy and its implications for education must be an integral part of the effective principal's professional equipment.

A second demand which democratic administration makes of the principal is that he be a good organizer. This involves the ability to translate educational objectives into broad categories of "things to be done," to formulate a plan of organization through which they *can* be done, and so to select and assign personnel that they *will* be done as effectively as possible.

Fox and Schwartz have enumerated the overt signs of good organization as follows:[2]

1. Morale is high—instructional and noninstructional staff enjoy working at the school.
2. Personnel know what is happening in the school and throughout the system.
3. Communication flows upward and horizontally as well as downward—the principal also knows what is taking place.

Schools attempting to implement present-day educational objectives must provide for a broad and varied program. This will include curriculum development, guidance and health services, extra-class activities, and much besides. It is the principal's responsibility to see that no student need is overlooked in the total program of the school.

No more challenging problem exists for the principal than that of selecting people for the various roles of responsibility within the organization. A democratic administration requires that the principal make the most effective possible use of personnel. To achieve this he must be familiar with each individual's training and experience background. But this is not enough. What about their interests and aspirations, health and vitality, and ability to function effectively with other people? What shortcomings do the staff as a whole possess, and what gaps remain to be filled as replacements and additions become necessary and justifiable? Many a well-meaning principal has failed in the essential area of organizational ability.

The third major requirement which democratic administration exacts of the principal now comes into focus. He must *exemplify* the democratic concept of leadership. A democratic administration requires that to the best of his ability the principal must liberate and utilize the intelligence of all his partners in the educational enterprise. His responsibility does not end with the appointment of a student council adviser, a custodian, a secretary, or the chairman of a curriculum committee. His function with respect to these individuals and to all others with whom he is associated is unique. He must understand the relationship of the various aspects of the school program to each other and to the program as a whole; and he must assist his colleagues to develop an understanding of these relationships. For example, he would ordinarily lack the competency of his English teachers to develop units of work in composition. However, he should be able to assist these English teachers in understanding general educational objectives and in seeing the

[2] Willard Fox, and Alfred Schwartz, *Managerial Guide for School Principals* (Columbus, Ohio: Charles E. Merrill Books, Inc., 1965).

need for developing courses of study in English which are designed to contribute in the best possible way to the attainment of those objectives. Similarly, he cannot be expected to have acquired the sponsors' specialized knowledge of each of the various student activities. He can and should, however, possess an understanding of certain problems common to many activities (such as finance, eligibility requirements, and meeting time) and be able to guide the staff toward the discovery of satisfactory solutions. He must understand that whereas the citizens of the community lack the experience and training to make technical contributions to the development of the educational program, these citizens do have a role at the policy level which they can and should exercise. He must recognize that within the limits of their experience and maturity, students, too, have a rightful part to play if they are to learn and practice the ways of democracy. In short, the principal has the responsibility of molding individuals and groups into a smoothly working team.

Democratic administration can thus be seen to exact three requirements of the principal. He must be a philosopher, an organizer, and a leader. Only to the extent that he exemplifies all three of these qualities will his school assume its crucial role in the present and future well-being of American democracy.

Now that we have introduced this chapter by dealing with basic philosophical considerations, let us apply them to actual problems of the junior high school. What are some of the most persistent ones? On the basis of their work with several thousands of teachers and administrators over the span of many years, the authors have classified these administrative problems under six headings:

1. *Student citizenship and discipline*
2. *Absence of students from class*
3. *Evaluation of students' work*
4. *Administrative interference with classwork*
5. *Teacher load*
6. *Faculty meetings*

It is very likely that most of the major administrative problems facing any given junior high school appear, directly or indirectly, on the above list. However, no school should ever assume that necessarily to be the case. Fortunately, there are instruments available which make it possible for any school to ascertain beyond any reasonable doubt what its faculty believes to be the major problems of the school at a particular time. Among the most widely used instruments of this kind are those developed by Hand[3] and by Bentley and Rempel.[4]

[3] Harold C. Hand, *What People Think About Their Schools* (New York: Harcourt, Brace & World, Inc., 1948).
[4] R. R. Bentley, and A. M. Rempel, *The Purdue Teacher Opinionaire* (Lafayette, Ind.: Purdue Research Foundation, 1964).

The authors feel very strongly that high staff morale is the most important ingredient in a good school. They likewise believe that there is no sounder approach to the achievement of high morale than that of the entire staff working cooperatively upon basic problems which they themselves have identified. In facilitating this process, it is essential that some systematic means be utilized whereby the feelings of all staff members can be assessed. Because of the valuable help which Hand's instrument has rendered many schools throughout a long period of time, selections from it are given below:

Do differences in discipline among the teachers in your school (some too strict, some not strict enough) keep the pupils from getting as much as they could from their school work? (Check one.)

————1) Yes.

————2) Uncertain.

————3) No.

How would you rate your own morale at the present time? (Check one.)

————1) Very high.

————2) High.

————3) Fair.

————4) Low.

————5) Very low.

How much of your time is spent in "police duties" (hall duty, cafeteria or playground supervision, etc.)? (Check one.)

————1) Far too much.

————2) Too much.

————3) About the right amount.

————4) I have no "police duties."

In your opinion, how does your total work load compare with that of the other teachers in your school? (Check one.)

————1) I think I am carrying the lightest total work load.

————2) I think I am in the bottom ¼ in this regard (¾ do more work than I do).

————3) I think I am in the middle ½ in this regard.

————4) I think I am in the top ¼ in this regard (¾ do less work than I do).

————5) I think I am carrying the heaviest total work load in our school.

On the basis of the careful appraisal of staff morale which an instrument such as the one discussed above facilitates, there will be little doubt in the mind of the analytical administrator as to what constitute, in the judgment of his staff, the school's major problems. The principal's primary administrative function now becomes that of providing the leadership whereby the staff, supplemented from time to time by various other individuals and groups, can attack these problems and help develop tentative solutions.

There is no more effective avenue for the study of school problems than the faculty meeting. The successful solution of any school problem involves the process of bringing all pertinent educational theory and related knowledge to bear upon a specific situation. Thus the faculty meeting is potentially a valuable means of in-service training and professional growth available to the school staff. The extent to which this great potential is achieved depends far more upon the leadership exerted by the principal than upon any other factor. Certain characteristics must be present if faculty meetings are to become truly effective professional experiences for the entire staff of the school. These characteristics are discussed here under four separate but interrelated headings.

1. *Faculty meetings should concern themselves with real problems of the school as identified by the staff.* One of the major causes of teacher dissatisfaction with faculty meetings is the amount of time devoted to matters which should be handled elsewhere. If an affirmative answer can be given to the question, "Can this particular matter be dealt with satisfactorily in some other way?" the subject in question has no legitimate place on the agenda of a faculty meeting. Most routine announcements are in this category. Many reports likewise might best be put into writing, duplicated, and placed in teachers' mailboxes. There will be too little faculty time available for matters which require the consideration of the entire group if care is not taken to eliminate the nonessentials.

An excellent first step in the development of effective faculty meetings, as suggested above, is that of providing a means whereby each staff member may propose a list of school problems which he deems important. These individual proposals might then be classified and tallied, and an order of priority established on the basis of frequency of mention or some other criterion. There is, as has been pointed out, no basic list of problems common to all schools. However, there are certain categories of problems that are persistent in schools generally today. Any of these, or any others with which a particular staff might indicate concern, would provide an excellent faculty meeting theme.

2. *Faculty meetings should be characterized by a cooperative approach to the solution of the problems selected for consideration.* The effective principal will exercise his leadership in such a way that each member of the group has the opportunity, and will be encouraged, to make his contribution to the business at hand. The principal will recognize three points in this connection: (1) that one of the essentials in the rational solution of specific problems is a reference to basic policy; (2) that the most effective way to insure that basic policy will be carried out is to involve in the process of policy formulation those who will

be concerned with its execution; and (3) the members of a faculty, because of the intelligence, training, experience, and interest which they bring to the problem of policy formulation, can be relied upon under wise leadership to do a better job than any individual or small group could possibly do alone. Non-faculty groups, such as custodians, office workers, student leaders, and interested parents have frequently rendered valuable service in helping to solve school problems. A problem considered as "ours" is more likely to be solved satisfactorily than is a problem regarded as "his" or "theirs."

3. *If faculty meetings are to achieve their maximum effectiveness, the policy that "every member participates" is necessary.* One of the major stumbling blocks limiting the effectiveness of the faculty meeting in many schools grows out of the fact that all staff members do not take part regularly. If the potentialities suggested above are to be realized, the time for meetings must be set so that *all* members of the faculty are free to participate. Since the principal's time schedule is likely to be more flexible than that of members of the teaching staff, the selection of the time for meetings might well be delegated to the faculty. Again, faculty members with relatively light responsibilities in student activities might be guided by the suggestions of those whose extra-class assignments are heavy. The time at which the faculty meets is comparatively unimportant; the active participation of every staff member is essential.

4. *If faculty meetings are to achieve their maximum effectiveness, those responsible for their planning must keep constantly in mind the fact that such meetings ordinarily represent, for each participant, just one of many worthwhile and necessary activities in an already busy day.* In many institutions, the period following the close of school on a specific day of the week is selected as the regular time for faculty meetings. It should be borne in mind that a brief period of relaxation is especially beneficial to those who have just completed a full and sometimes hectic day in the classroom. A fifteen or twenty minute "breather" between the close of school and the start of the meeting might well be provided as a socializing and refreshment period. Attention should be given to the comfort of the group and to the attractiveness of the meeting place. Meetings should start promptly and end not later than a previously established time for closing. Thus if the last period in a particular school program ends at 3:30 p.m., the starting and closing times for faculty meetings might be established as 3:50 and 5:00, respectively. Faculty members are certainly due this much consideration, and the favorable reaction thereto is bound to be reflected in their work.

The above represents a brief review of some of the ways in which faculty meetings can become effective professional experiences. Under the direction of an understanding and competent principal, the faculty meeting will occupy a crucially important role in the improvement of the total school program. The following sections deal, in some detail, with persistent administrative problems of the junior high school.

Flexible Scheduling

During the past decade, secondary schools have shown a great deal of interest in modifying the conventional class schedule, in which classes usually meet five days per week for periods ranging from forty to sixty minutes each in length. Trump and Baynham[5] summarize what they call "the school of the future" in part as follows:

The organization of instruction provides classes with fifteen or fewer students especially for small-group discussion.

The organization of instruction provides many more opportunities for individual students' independent study, inside school as well as outside, both during and after school hours.

These schools assemble large classes of from 100 to 150 students, or even more, whenever the educational purpose calls for it.

"The school of the future" recognizes the relationships among various aspects of learning: what happens to students when they take part in small classes for purposes of discussion; when they work in a relatively independent manner in laboratories, libraries, and cubicles; or when they listen to or view a demonstration or explanation in the setting of large group instruction.

Through the use of teacher assistants and team teaching, these schools make possible the full professionalization of teaching. Staff specialists, community consultants, general aides, clerks, and instructional assistants, along with professional teachers, work together. In relation to the total number of students, the school employs more adults, but fewer adults need to be professional teachers.

Such educational facilities are characterized by a flexibility that allows change, as future needs and events dictate. These school programs use government buildings, stores, cultural centers, offices, and industrial establishments for independent study, and persons from these institutions come to the school in the role of consultants to help teach the students. School facilities provide for use of television, radio, disc recordings, video and audio tape recordings, films and slides, mockups, models, museum materials, and many kinds of printed materials such as books, pamphlets, and periodicals. Automated and other programmed instruction devices are used in laboratories and independent study areas.

As each individual school devotes itself to developing the best possible educational program for its particular students, it will of neces-

[5] J. Lloyd Trump, and Dorsey Baynham, *Guide to Better Schools* (Chicago: Rand McNally Company, 1961), pp. 24–38.

sity consider ways whereby the flexibility of its schedule might be increased. What is important is not the adoption of a better schedule in the same manner that we adopt "better mousetraps," but, rather, the adoption of time allotments to meet the needs of the instructional program.

Valley Junior High School Case Study[6]

Since their inception, the middle schools have been "half way houses" in American education and it was no different in Carlsbad, California, than anywhere else when the district governing board called upon the school administration to take a long, hard look at the program while planning a new school. The dissatisfaction was rooted in a general feeling shared by many teachers and parents that junior high school education had over the years taken on the image of an impersonalized, mini-high school: a kind of institutionalized "Skinner box" with children marking time while being properly prepared for high school. There was an uncomfortable lingering concern that somewhere between elementary and high school the early adolescent became turned off about learning, disillusioned with school, suspicious of adults, and apprehensive about his ability to measure up to what people expected of him.

However fair or unfair the charge might have been, the question raised was worth examining: "Is there a better way of organizing the learning experiences of twelve and thirteen year old students?" Was the only alternative to a subject-centered, departmentalized, rigidly scheduled program (even under the name of "Flexible Scheduling") that of an elementary self-contained classroom? If so, could one teacher be expected to know enough about all subjects to provide suitable lessons for thirty individual youngsters who were at a high point in their receptivity for learning? Was there a way of teaching early adolescents drawn from the best elements of both the secondary and the elementary schools?

It was with these thoughts in mind that the superintendent appointed a committee to sit down with an architect, study the matter, and translate educational concepts into school design. The principal was appointed to be chairman of the committee and to work with teacher groups as they gathered information and submitted proposals.

The first question that the committee focused upon was one which dealt with the educational needs of the early adolescent. There was complete agreement in the necessity of considering this question in order to know what the school should be designed to accomplish.

[6] Case study printed with the permission of the author, William E. Moore, University of Oregon, past principal of Valley Junior High School, Carlsbad, California, 1966–1969.

The end result of many lively discussions was a belief in the desirability of developing a school program which had two prominent characteristics: (1) The school was to have a strong guidance orientation which provided the child with the direction and security to make the transition from childhood into adolescence with the least amount of turbulence and disruption. The early adolescent, it was believed, needed instruction from teachers who knew him well, not only in terms of his abilities and achievement levels but also as to his learning styles, interests, experiences, health, and self-perception. (2) The school was to provide the child with an instructional program taught by teachers who were well grounded in content fields. The early adolescent, it was thought, was ready for learning in depth and would respond well to teachers who have such specialized preparation and can communicate the interest and excitement of their chosen fields.

In effect, what was wanted was the best of an elementary program with its strong orientation toward guidance and individual developments and the high school program with its pattern of specialization and subject matter emphasis. It seemed to the committee that junior high programs across the country were suffering from an improper balance of these two components, but the question was how to make it operational.

As the meetings progressed, an organizational scheme for instruction began to emerge which seemed to accommodate the goals. A program was envisioned, built around teaching teams of six or seven teachers. Each teacher on a team would have specialized training in one or two subject matter areas with some additional skills or interest in such fields as testing, audiovisual, counseling, etc. By careful selection of team members as to their subject preparation and special skills, the team could teach the entire range of the curriculum.

The team would meet together regularly and plan lessons which made the greatest provision for the individual strengths and needs of the children. They would have complete control over the scheduling of time, student grouping, equipment, and facilities so that the instructional plan would not be dictated to by a fixed schedule. This team of teachers would, it was believed, learn to share each other's understanding about the individual children as well as methods of teaching more effectively.

Each team would have approximately two hundred students. These boys and girls would work under the team's direction for the two years of junior high without interruption.

The students were to be assigned to homeroom classes on a heterogeneous basis. A balance in abilities, achievements, numbers, sizes, and ethnic background would be sought in the initial programming and as new students entered they would be placed in classes where the balance would be maintained. The homeroom class would become an identity for scheduling purposes, thus allowing the team of teachers a convenient means of communicating with each other about each group. As the team program developed, regrouping would be done by combining segments of one class with another.

The Valley Junior High School has been in operation since 1966 with an enrollment of approximately 800 seventh and eighth grade students. They are divided into four groups of 200 with each group housed in a classroom building known as a "pod."

Within the pod, there are six classrooms centered around a large multi-use room. Four of the classrooms have folding partitions which make it possible for teachers to arrange groups of students in varying sizes. These rooms are carpeted to provide the acoustical properties necessary for large group instruction. The other two classrooms in each pod are especially designed for science and art activities. The pod also includes a small satellite reference library, a seminar room, a teachers' office area, and a teachers' aide work area.

The small reference library within each pod houses a permanent collection of books as well as books and other materials requested from the main library for specific units of study. With this arrangement the materials are within fifty feet of any classroom and accessible at all times. Each pod library is capable of handling approximately a thousand books.

Under the leadership of one team member who serves as the team leader, the six teachers plan programs for the 200 students. They determine how long a particular lesson is to last, how many students will be in a group, and which classes the groups will be drawn from. The time factor which they must work within is 240 instructional minutes per day but guidelines are given in terms of minutes per week to provide a maximum of flexibility. During the remaining time each day, the students are outside the pod receiving instruction from other teachers in physical education, applied arts, and Spanish while the team of teachers meets to plan, coordinate, and evaluate their program. Thus, the team operation permits the members to make any changes they desire without complications. Once the team agrees on what it wishes to do, it is only a matter of blocking in the time available for the six teachers and the six classes. With such control over the schedule and the time to plan free of classroom responsibilities, teachers are able to continuously examine the effectiveness of their teaching and look for ways by which new ideas can be introduced.

This plan made it unnecessary for the district to purchase, lease, or share in the expense of a computer to help in placing students and teachers into classes and time periods of their choice and need. It also enabled the district to avoid the biggest disadvantage of the computer assisted scheduling procedure, i.e. that a computerized schedule becomes as rigid and as inflexible as the schedule it replaces. With the computer, hours of juggling schedules by hand or key-sort is done in a relatively short time; but once the schedule is set, changing it becomes a problem unless the computer is readily available and all the information has been collected and prepared for processing. Minor or short term changes are generally so impractical that desires of individual teachers or teams to modify their schedule to facilitate some other use of time, student groupings, etc., are usually beyond their control or privilege.

The guidelines provided for the leaders in planning the instructional program are:

1. Each child is to receive per week a minimum of:
    400 minutes—Language Arts and Reading
    200 minutes—Social Studies
    200 minutes—Mathematics
    160 minutes—Science
    120 minutes—Fine Arts
2. Lessons which can be as effectively presented to 100 students as thirty are to be planned for the larger group.
3. Lessons to be planned should permit each student to work at an appropriate level and to progress at his own speed.
4. Regrouping of students should be based upon specific terminal objectives.
5. Language development and study skills are the concern of each teacher and should be taught in all classes.
6. Each child is to experience success.

The time requirement in Spanish, physical education, and applied arts is also set up on a basis of minutes per week. Spanish is studied both years for twelve weeks, 200 minutes each week; physical education is also studied for 200 minutes a week; applied arts is taken for twenty-four weeks each year and is divided into three areas of home economics, industrial arts, and arts and crafts. These teachers work together in much the same manner as the pod team teachers. The class time, student groupings, coordination of program, etc., are arranged through frequent meetings.

The students remain in their pod with the same teachers for both the seventh and eighth grade years. This provides a greater opportunity for the teachers to maintain continuity because they know the students and have had control for two years. Students who are together as a group become comfortable with one another and are emotionally prepared to learn without the intervening factor of a constantly changing classroom climate compounded by needs to establish new relationships every time the bell rings. It also contributes to the desired guidance relationship between the teachers and the students which is essential to meaningful planning.

Careful team planning is critical to the success of the program. It spells the difference between the departmentalized operation with its emphasis upon the group, and the smooth use of time, numbers, and space for meeting individual needs as theorized in team teaching. To facilitate such planning, the teams have a daily period of time free of students for all members to sit down together and discuss the complex factors inherent in deciding what should be taught, to whom, in what groups, for how long, and in what ways. The process of making such determinations requires that each teacher bring to the meeting his thoughts and needs as they pertain to the development of the particular phase of the curriculum to which he is assigned. He must be able to say, "Next week, I'd like to do these things . . ." As each teacher unfolds his ideas, the team's secretary records them and makes them available to the team at its next meeting.

At this meeting the discussion focuses on how the choices of each member might be accommodated. This entails the drafting of a schedule which identifies large and small group activities for each day, if desired, and provides sufficient time in all subject areas for each group. Consideration is given to plans for those students who have special needs. The team arranges their program through regrouping, scheduling more time for independent study, or providing tutoring sessions.

One team at the school was able to carry out a program which has taken this process one step further. They discussed, at length, ways by which the students could assume more control over their own learning. There was, in the teachers' judgment, flexibility for them, but not for the students, to make choices. The team believed there were some days when the classes scheduled were not needed by all students and the students would profit more by engaging in independent study. The team decided that, given the responsibility, students would learn to use time wisely and improve their rates of learning. Based on this concept, the team worked out a procedure which involved the following:

1. On Wednesday and Thursday each teacher submits a "work request" for the coming week. It shows what group the teacher wishes to see, for what purpose, and for what period of time. It does not show the day or the sequence. The team leader takes these and puts them together to eliminate any possible conflicts. The schedule is duplicated and distributed to all students. It indicates what days classes will meet, the time, class size limit, and whether the class is required of all students.

2. The following Monday, all classes meet on a rotating basis with each teacher. The teacher uses the day to set goals for the week, to arouse interest, and to explain the schedule for the next three days.

3. Each student plans his own schedule for Tuesday, Wednesday, and Thursday. He must attend certain classes, but can choose from the others, based on the purpose of the class and his own perception of his needs. When he is not in class, he is in independent study with access to the library and certain other materials and equipment. One or two teachers always supervise the

study and provide assistance as needed. Attendance in classes is recorded by the teachers on a master class list. This controls the size of the class and provides an accounting process for record keeping.

4. On Friday, the same schedule as Monday is followed with each teacher evaluating the progress made toward the goals.

The teachers are enthusiastic about the program, expressing the belief that they are able to use time more effectively, provide more individual attention, and do a better job of planning for their classes. They feel the students are also becoming more responsible for their own learning and more secure in their abilities to achieve success. At the same time, the teachers are far from being satisfied that the optimum potential has been reached. They are working on the further development of a "performance curriculum" which provides for continuous progress and terminal goals. They are searching for more effective ways of keeping track of student progress and ways of communicating with parents. They are certain the independent study time is more productive for some than for others and that young adolescents, being as they are, have need of structure which can only come about through careful planning in team meetings.

From an administrative standpoint the Valley program has distinct advantages. The more significant ones are:

1. Instructional leadership is built into the team organization. The team leader carries responsibilities for planning and implementing programs which make good utilization of personnel, equipment, time, facilities, and materials. He becomes a more skillful teacher personally through this process and is in a position to raise questions with other team members which can be discussed in team meetings and contribute to deeper understandings.

2. New teachers are provided more support and help. They work closely with experienced teachers and learn how to teach in a variety of ways.

3. Programming and scheduling is reduced to a minimum. Once the student is placed in a homeroom class, the decisions are made by the team.

4. Discipline, guidance, and counseling are integral parts of the team operation with all members contributing their understanding to the problems that arise. The principal sits with the team in conferences which may include a student and/or his parents. They call upon the district staff from pupil personnel services for testing and consultation as the need arises, but the primary line of service comes from the team.

The school principal in this program must be extremely sensitive to the subtleties of team relationships and operation. He must respect the position of the team leader in regard to the leadership process and not undermine his role by unconsciously taking leadership away in team meetings. At the same time, he must be in close touch with each team's program and offer advice or guidelines for consideration which are consistent with the direction of the total school district. The principal is responsible for the decisions which they make and he must weigh carefully the consequences of their choices. Plans which are poorly conceived can result in frustration and embarrassment for the team members and produce a tendency to retreat to safer grounds. On the other hand, the principal must encourage experimentation and provide the psychological support to ease whatever concerns the team members may feel about the experiment failing. It is only through his support and encouragement that the program will move. It is only through a break with past patterns of teaching operations that the junior high will ever become sufficiently flexible to serve the needs of young adolescents.

Opening and Closing the School Year

The success of any school year depends to a considerable extent upon a carefully planned opening and an equally well-planned closing. A successful school opening requires a great amount of study and organization during the preceding winter and spring months. Much of the requisite study will be based upon data concerning the prospective student body, especially the incoming class. Information relative to academic and nonacademic abilities, interests, and achievement represent the absolute minimum upon which the school program of the early adolescent should be based. It is highly desirable that such information be supplemented by additional guidance data, as suggested in the chapter devoted to that topic. Personnel data as a necessary basis for scheduling students has become even more important with the increased attention which individual needs are now receiving. For example, there is at the present time much more instruction than heretofore in algebra at the seventh and eighth grade levels. Likewise, instruction in foreign language is being instituted at earlier grade levels than was the practice even in the recent past. Curricula in other fields are being revised, too. The implications for school administration are tremendous. Much of the counseling and guidance in preparation for elective subject formerly provided to eighth graders must now be made available at the sixth grade level. The "block" method of scheduling, in which groups of students are scheduled together throughout the day, must be replaced at least in part as legitimate attention is given to individual needs.

It thus becomes a major responsibility of the school to provide the guidance required to enable each student, with the assistance and approval of his parents, to work out a tentative program. Ideally, this should be an integral part of a more comprehensive program—one that projects itself over the entire period of secondary school attendance. So individualized should this projected tentative program be that it should be a matter of sheer coincidence that the programs of any two students be alike. This is an especially valid point of view when it is recognized that an important function of the middle school is that of broadening one's interests and activities and expanding one's personal contacts, not restricting them or confining them to a narrow range.

The development of the tentative program should include provision for alternate or elective choices. This will enable scheduling to proceed uninterrupted in those inevitable cases in which conflicts show up in the master schedule of classes. Since much of the work on the master schedule might well be done during the summer months, it is especially desirable that students' alternate choices in the event of conflict be a matter of written record prior to the closing of school for summer vacation. In this way it should be unnecessary, except in very rare cases, to contact students during that period.

It is also desirable to include extra-class activities in addition to regular classwork in the student's tentative program. This is certainly in accord with the philosophy that the student's program must be considered as a whole rather than in part. School activities become especially important at the secondary level and are an integral part of the modern middle school. It is desirable that all students participate in extra-class activities. However, it is of paramount importance that such participation not be at the expense of any other aspect of the student's work. Therefore, it is essential that the counselor be aware of the fact that a given student plans to participate in the drama club, the production of the school newspaper, or one of the music groups. Such interest and participation bear an essential relationship to the particular pattern of subjects for which the student should enroll.

It is important that the first day of school be as normal a day as possible, in every way. Good administration requires that maximum utilization be derived from the relatively short time that students attend school. The contention that several days are required to get things under way at the beginning of the school year has been demonstrated to be false by many well organized schools which open and close at the regular time, whose cafeteria and buses operate on their regular schedules, and all of whose classes meet on the first day of school.

It is true, of course, that during the summer months, new families will have moved into the school community. This need not affect a smooth school opening to any marked degree. In the first place, new youngsters of school age, and their parents, should be urged through several media to complete registration prior to the opening of school. It is customary for schools to be open for this purpose for a short period prior to the first day. Although it is still conceivable that there will perhaps remain some who may not have been reached in this way, their number should not be large. Special provision for registering them on the first day should be made in such a way that the operation of that day's program will not be adversely affected.

The mechanics of the first day vary from school to school. One highly satisfactory procedure will be outlined in detail here. Such a procedure starts with an all-school assembly presided over by the principal. This assembly should be carefully planned, brief, and designed to "set the stage" for the year which lies ahead. The principal is the appropriate individual to set this stage. One third to one half of the students, in addition to many of the faculty, may be new to the school. Here is their first opportunity to see the school "in action." Attitudes and habits established at the outset are likely to persist for some time to come. Therefore, every effort should be made to insure the establishment of a positive, desirable climate from the outset.

Following such introductory remarks as the principal may see fit to make, the procedures and schedule for the first day should be carefully explained and the importance of following them meticulously should be pointed out. Copies of the daily class schedule for each student, determined on the basis of spring registration in most cases, should be in the students' possession. It is recommended that these be followed without change the first day. If they have been made out with the care suggested above, requests for changes of program will be few indeed. All requests should be in writing on an appropriate form, and should include the reason for the proposed change. The mere fact that such procedures have been set up will tend to reduce requests based upon superficial or otherwise questionable reasons. Whatever small number of requests that the school sees fit to grant can be acted upon following the close of school the first day, with the change taking place the following morning.

It is important that all classes meet the first day for approximately an equal amount of time. The schedule card should be presented by each student to each of his teachers to be endorsed as evidence of official registration in the class. Many schools prefer to have the completed card countersigned by the parent or guardian before being filed in the office as the official program for the year.

Careful attention to the details of closing the school year is equally as important as the provision for a smooth opening. Certainly there will be various activities, many of which culminate major projects of the school year, which must be scheduled during the closing school days. In a faculty meeting several weeks prior to the close of school, these activities should be discussed and a schedule for them made out. It has been demonstrated many times by time-conscious principals that no class needs to be interfered with more than twice, at the most, for any purpose whatever, during the final two or three weeks of school. After the various closing activities have been listed and scheduled, the day-by-day program for the closing weeks should be duplicated and publicized with every variation from the regular schedule noted and lists of affected students appended.

It is highly desirable for each student to "check out" of each class and activity during the final days of the school year. A simple form will suffice for this. It should provide space for each teacher with supervisory responsibility for the student to indicate by signature that the student is "in the clear." This means that all school property has been either returned in satisfactory condition or suitable compensation made, and that the student's record is complete in every way. On the basis of such a "clearance slip" properly executed and filed, the student is granted final credit for the school year.

Issuing or mailing of report cards after school has been closed rather than just prior to closing will help to eliminate the confusion which otherwise might characterize the final days of the school year. Many teachers prefer to administer examinations and other culminating activities as near to the end of the year as possible, and this is difficult to do if grades must be determined and recorded prior to the close of school. An extra day or a weekend in which to attend to these clerical details will be appreciated by staff members generally and will benefit the school program as well.

Evaluating Progress of Students

Some of the most serious and challenging administrative problems in the middle school are related to the problem of evaluation of students' work. These problems are likely to be especially acute if evaluation policies differ considerably, as they frequently do, from policies to which students and parents have become accustomed in the elementary school. Whether or not such differences exist, a sound program of evaluation requires that certain basic considerations be taken into account.

1. The objectives of each learning experience, in order to operate effectively, must be understood by, and accepted by all of the parties concerned—and especially by the students.

2. Evaluation of students' work should be in terms of their progress toward the attainment of these objectives.

3. Since specific objectives will differ from class to class, the desirability of correspondingly different bases for evaluation from class to class should be considered. In some schools this has resulted in the development of different report cards for different subjects.

4. Students should at any time be able to ascertain the status of their progress in any class. Students should be encouraged to evaluate themselves on the basis of course or unit objectives. Teachers should compare these evaluations with theirs, study critically any major discrepancies, and attempt to account for them with a view toward their elimination or reduction.

5. "Progress reports" should be used by the teacher between regular marking periods to communicate with the home. This will ordinarily improve the chances of interested parents to assist in formulating solutions "before it is too late," as well as to commend praiseworthy work on the part of students, especially in cases in which marked improvement has been noted.

6. In order to reduce confusion in the interpretation of evaluative symbols, the desirability of separate evaluations in achievement and in citizenship should be considered.

7. Since evaluative symbols are likely to be misunderstood, unless carefully defined by the users, the school should develop definitions for each symbol if they find symbols necessary, and should include these definitions on every report card or other instrument on which such symbols are employed.

Dr. William M. Griffin of Boston College developed a plan for measuring the quality of independent study. Griffin, as quoted in *Secondary School Curriculum Improvement*, proposed the following definitions, which should be of interest and possible use to those seeking to evaluate behavioral characteristics of students, either in independent study or in other learning activities.[7]

A student performing effectively in independent study is one who:

1. Perceives things to do. For example: pursues instructional leads for further study . . . compares various sources of information . . . asks relationship-type questions . . . integrates information from different subject-matter fields . . . summarizes findings and places them in correct frame of reference.

2. Personalizes learning. For example: casts about for a project of real interest and value . . . gives own unique reasons for doing what is done . . . prepares a plan to structure the study . . . distributes work schedule to allow for other commitments . . . expresses satisfaction in a task of own selection and implementation.

3. Exercises self-discipline. For example: accepts limits of the school without denying self . . . displays sustained and conscientious industry . . . seeks procedural authority for own point of view and actions . . . works in harmony with others in groups of two or three . . . cooperates in maintaining climate for individual work.

4. Makes use of human resources. For example: initiates contacts with appropriate teachers and other persons . . . shares interpretations, interests and ideas in good exchange . . . comes prepared for conference discussions . . . uses contacts to clarify thinking with pertinent and relevant questioning . . . investigates suggestions which are offered.

5. Makes use of material resources. For example: broadens own knowledge through related readings . . . makes use of tapes, records,

[7] J. Lloyd Trump, and Delmas F. Miller, *Secondary School Curriculum Improvement* (Boston: Allyn and Bacon, Inc., 1968), pp. 358–359.

and illustrative material to expand knowledge . . . displays deftness in locating library material . . . recognizes and uses the tools of the study area . . . constructs special materials and devices for use in the work.

6. Produces results. For example: works at appropriate pace and follows through to completion . . . plans projects which are subject to accomplishment . . . states clear objectives . . . displays habit of getting down to work . . . finds applications for a creative idea.

7. Strives for improvement. For example: seeks advice from competent people . . . corrects errors on one's own . . . studies authoritative sources for best practices . . . uses group sessions to test out ideas and clarify issues . . . evaluates material in the light of personal experiences and firsthand knowledge.

Attendance Problems

In secondary schools generally, problems involving student attendance are among the most challenging and persistent of all. Carefully and thoughtfully evolved policies governing attendance are essential in every middle school, at which level irregular attendance is frequently the first overt indication of incipient trouble which if allowed to pass unheeded may lead to serious consequences.

There is no doubt that the best approach to good attendance is good teaching. Teachers who give more than lip service to the ideal of instruction which takes into account the wide variety of abilities, interests, and needs typical of every group of students provide the school's best deterrent to irregular attendance. Every school should do its utmost to improve attendance through improved instruction.

Unfortunately, however, the positive approach suggested above will not in every case prove effective. Nor should the school be unduly discouraged if it is not 100 percent successful in all of its efforts and undertakings. It is unrealistic to attempt to administer any secondary school on the assumption that rules with "teeth" in them can be dispensed with in dealing with the few (and in good schools they *will* be few in number) who are not reached by positive means. It is likewise unrealistic and unfair, in the light of the effect of non-school agencies, to hold teachers entirely responsible for the fact that positive approaches are not always successful. The following illustrate important characteristics of schools which have been relatively successful in solving attendance problems:

1. A program emphasizing analysis of individual students and the development of activities suited to their needs.

2. The conviction on the part of the faculty that there is no adequate substitute for school attendance—that absence can never be fully compensated for—and the ability to convince students and parents of the validity of this point.

3. Strict accounting procedures which will identify absentees accurately and promptly.

4. Carefully formulated and thoroughly understood policies governing absence, tardiness, and makeup work, and their relationship to student achievement.

Problems Involving Student Conduct, Discipline, and Self-Direction

Closely related to the kinds of problems discussed above are those having to do with citizenship generally, and conduct specifically. In many ways, the early adolescent presents a greater challenge to the teacher's motivational ability than does the child in the elementary school or even the older adolescent and the young adult in senior high school and college. Since no amount of subject matter mastery on the teacher's part can be of much avail in a chaotic setting, the successful teacher's equipment must include personality and character traits, understandings, and techniques which are conducive to the establishment of a healthy learning situation. Ideally, as in the case of attendance problems, good citizenship in the classroom results from good teaching. But good teaching is not always enough. Not in every case will even the truly outstanding teacher motivate every student toward constructive activity. In good schools the number of such instances will be few—but in these schools, too, the administrative means for handling them will have been worked out very carefully and utilized when necessary. A few important considerations follow.

It is essential that there be some basic questions raised and policies developed by the faculty as a whole. What, in general, is meant by "good discipline?" What are the respective roles of administration, faculty, and students in promoting it? To what extent should the teacher attempt to handle his own disciplinary problems? At what stage, and under what conditions, should the teacher seek administrative assistance? What should be the relationship between citizenship and academic marks? These are some of the key questions which must be raised and answered.

Fortunately, teachers have powerful allies in disciplinary problems —the students themselves. Studies have shown that an overwhelming majority of adolescents want to learn—and that they admire most teachers who are able to provide a setting conducive to learning. In many schools, students have helped considerably in establishing such a setting by proposing guidelines for their own conduct. Oftentimes students have shown themselves to be more exacting than their elders in regard to citizenship codes.

It is important that insofar as possible each problem arising in a classroom must be solved at the classroom level. This is true for two reasons. First of all, no administrative or other school officer can possibly assume the major responsibility for any single unit within the school; this responsibility must always rest with the teacher. Secondly, the effectiveness of teachers in disciplinary matters is likely to be substantially reduced if they continually seek assistance from outside the classroom.

Teachers should be helped to understand that disciplinary problems usually do not arise all of a sudden; they ordinarily cast their shadows before them. An observant teacher will be on the lookout for symptoms. Oftentimes, a word in private, a moved seat, or a little special attention during supervised study will eliminate an impending problem. Checking cumulative records and conferring with guidance and administrative personnel often proves helpful. The imaginative, creative teacher ordinarily is successful in all but a very few matters involving student conduct and citizenship. In those few exceptions, strong administrative policy is essential. No student, parent, or taxpayer should be allowed to confuse democracy with license!

If administrators are to be in a position to render effective assistance in the solution of disciplinary matters, they must have adequate knowledge of the situation. It is the expectancy in many good schools that teachers submit to the office in writing, usually on a specially devised form, information relative to cases in which there is a likelihood of their needing assistance at some later time. Such a procedure affords a dean, counselor, or administrator the opportunity to do some preliminary work on the case, and in a manner that need not involve the teacher to the extent that his rapport with the student might be adversely affected. Furthermore, if and when, after exhausting his own resources the teacher finds it necessary to call for assistance from others, the aid rendered is likely to be much more effective because of the prior knowledge.

The kinds of administrative policies discussed in the preceding sections provide the important foundations for a good school. Once formulated, their understanding on the part of those who are most concerned cannot be left to chance. Parents must be informed through bulletin, letter, newspaper, and any other media the particular school might select. In certain cases it is desirable to secure the signatures of parents and guardians as evidence that the policies have been read, and, it is hoped, understood and approved. It is recommended that these policies, in addition, be made a part of the student handbook and that specific provision be made in a required class (other things being equal, social studies is the most logical place) for the thorough discussion of these policies. In some of the most effective schools known to the authors, the student handbook becomes the subject matter for the first unit in each social studies class at each grade level every year.

Selection and Professional Development of the Staff

The kind of educational program described in the foregoing pages will call forth administrative leadership of the highest order. This leadership will be evidenced in no more important way than in the selection and improvement of staff members. For no matter how up-to-date and adequate the school plant, regardless of the number and excellence of instructional aids, and irrespective of the cooperation of parents and other groups, it is primarily and fundamentally the faculty who determine the quality of the school. Good schools ordinarily give careful attention to policies like the following in the selection of staff members:

1. Vacancies are anticipated early enough in advance so that the best available candidates can be considered.
2. Qualifications desired in candidates are carefully thought out and listed in writing.
3. Staff needs, described in detail, are listed with major placement agencies both within and outside of the state.
4. Personnel data on candidates from various agencies are examined meticulously, and candidates for each vacancy are ranked tentatively in order of preference.
5. Further study is made of the top candidates. This might include visitation "on the job," personal contacts with present and former employers and others who know the candidates well, and personal interview. Top candidates are reranked if necessary.
6. The vacancies are filled on the basis of the principal's recommendation to the superintendent, who in turn recommends employment to the board.

Of equal importance to care in the selection of the professional staff is the necessity for providing for orientation to and growth on the job. An increasing number of schools are assisting new teachers in solving problems of housing and in other ways becoming members of the community in which they will teach. In working out the new teacher's assignment, the effective principal pays careful attention to areas of preparation and to nonacademic and extra-class interests as well. The tendency to load new teachers heavily is avoided. Rather, an effort is made to give the teacher the benefit of a moderate load during the year or two that adjustment to a new job—and sometimes to teaching itself —is being made. The successful principal is especially conscientious in providing the new teacher with supervisory assistance, particularly in the first days and weeks of the school year. In teaching, probably to a greater extent than in most undertakings, a great deal depends upon a good start.

The principal should assume the leadership in providing the setting within which each faculty member may grow to the utmost of his ability. Through staff organization each teacher should be enabled to contribute maximally to curriculum development. Professional library materials should be accessible to assist staff members with this important work. There is a growing tendency for school districts to help teachers to relate their graduate study to their work on the job. Some districts subsidize, partially at least, summer school and extension work on the part of faculty members. This is especially defensible and desirable when the professional study program is determined in the light of the particular school problems under consideration.

It should be the business of the principal to understand the professional goals and aspirations of each staff member and to help them evaluate and enhance their progress toward those goals. An important trend is in the direction of comparing each staff member's self-evaluation with his evaluation by the principal of the school. This is often done in an annual teacher-principal conference.

There will ordinarily be many opportunities within the school for providing tryout experiences for teachers, who, for example, aspire to administrative positions. Since the qualities required by the successful administrator differ considerably from those required by the successful teacher, it is a great advantage for the prospective administrator to "get his feet wet" under the direction of a wise leader. The careful delegation of responsibility in such areas as discipline, attendance, supervision of buildings and grounds, and direction of social events will serve a dual purpose. It will strengthen the services of the school in these areas, and in addition afford valuable on-the-job training to the prospective administrator.

The Principal's Leadership Role Illustrated

The foregoing sections have considered various aspects of junior high organization and administration. The material which follows describes a hypothetical situation based upon practices found in many schools which are attempting to implement the ideas expressed earlier.[8] This description is, of course, presented for purposes of illustration only. It is not expected that any school would follow precisely the practices found in our mythical Tucker Middle School.

Two years ago one of the opinion polls mentioned in this chapter was administered to the Tucker faculty. This instrument served a most useful purpose in helping the staff to identify what seemed to them to be the school's major problems. The problems themselves were not unusual ones for a middle school—in fact they were quite typical—and all were related, directly or indirectly, to the instructional program. There was, for example, some concern about discipline. The need for more specific policies relative to report cards, marking, and other aspects of pupil evaluation was evidenced. Interference with class work was considered excessive by several. "Must extra-class activities be scheduled at the expense of other phases of the program?" asked some. Others would cheerfully eliminate the public address system.

These matters were important, first of all, because they represented the major problems in Tucker Middle School as viewed by the faculty at a specific time. As such they provided the best possible take-off

[8] Adapted from Arthur C. Hearn, "Columbus High School Organizes for Curriculum Development," *Bulletin of the National Association of Secondary School Principals* (February 1959): 214:67–72.

point for a program of school self-improvement. Secondly, Principal Marvin Lee and the faculty had agreed that these problems would serve as the basis for a series of faculty meetings during the current school year. Each problem was to be discussed thoroughly by the entire staff, with basic policy to be determined as the outcome of careful deliberation.

In the first meeting of the series, the matter of discipline was considered. (It was noted that several items in the teacher opinion inventory related to discipline—and not without good reason.) A single meeting did not provide sufficient time for this particular problem at Tucker. Nor was the staff able to reach satisfactory conclusions on some of its other problems in that short a time. In each case, however, agreements were eventually reached and guiding principles established.

Relatively early in the series of meetings, the staff came to an elementary but basic and fundamental realization. It was the recognition of the fact that appropriate and defensible solutions to specific problems must emerge from philosophical considerations. Stated in a different way, every school needs to come to grips with the problem of education objectives. It needs to agree upon a statement of purposes which is understood by and acceptable to all of the "publics" involved. Of these publics, the staff is an important one—but it is only one.

So while continuing its work on the problems of immediate concern and importance, the staff undertook to develop in its own mind a proposal for a set of guiding educational principles. Recognizing that several excellent statements of educational objectives were available, the faculty reviewed the major pronouncements; they eventually selected the statement of the Educational Policies Commission, outlined in the publication *The Purposes of Education in American Democracy*,[9] as providing the best starting point in its particular situation. Although the staff, for its own purposes, accepted the Commission's wording with few revisions, it was convinced that, to be truly effective, such a statement must involve other groups—especially the parents and the students.

A considerable amount of rephrasing was deemed necessary in order that the objectives might be usable with these and other "publics." In the course of this work, the staff was agreeably surprised to discover that these groups evidenced much more interest than had been anticipated in educational objectives and the ways in which schools were endeavoring to attain them. The Tucker faculty had been led to believe, because of the efforts of a relatively small, but vociferous minority, that certain extra-class activities comprised the primary, if not the sole interest of the community as a whole, insofar as its secondary schools were concerned. Tucker was not the first school to assume, erroneously, that a particular minority represented the sentiments of an entire com-

[9] Educational Policies Commission, *The Purposes of Education in American Democracy* (Washington, D. C.: The Commission, 1938), p. 154.

munity; neither was it the first to discover, gratefully, that a community is likely to demonstrate more interest in objectives, curriculum, and guidance than in any other aspects of the school program—when steps are taken to insure an adequate sampling of public opinion.

The implementation of the objectives next engaged the staff's attention. This led first to a thoughtful examination of the school's course offerings. After informal consultation and discussion with other teachers in his teaching field, each member of the staff developed a series of brief, written statements in which he described each of the courses included in his teaching assignment. These statements contained course objectives, an outline of general course content, teaching methods employed, basic and supplementary instructional materials, and proposals for the evaluation of students' work. The entire set of statements thus represented, at least in outline form, the school's course of study as viewed at that particular time by individual staff members. As such, it comprised a significant document, regardless of the shortcomings inherent in any "first attempt." It represented a starting point from which further development could, and eventually did, take place.

With these thoughts foremost in mind, Principal Lee arranged to have the individual statements assembled and mimeographed so that each member of the faculty could have a copy of the complete document. This not only gave each teacher an opportunity to view each departmental offering as a whole, but also provided an overview of the program of the entire school. There were many almost instantaneous reactions—nearly all positive and constructive—when the document first appeared. Overlappings as well as omissions in the school's offerings were noted. Many staff members suggested that they could do much to rectify these and other shortcomings; a few wanted an immediate administrative "green light" to prove it. Principal Lee was justifiably delighted with the progress attained in approximately one year of faculty concentration on the instructional program.

At the beginning of the ensuing school year, significant further steps were taken. In order that staff collaboration on a more organized basis be facilitated, curriculum committees representing each of the major areas of instruction were established. In addition to the more traditional committees (e.g., social studies, industrial arts, mathematics), three others were instituted. One of these was in the area of health. It included representatives from the fields of social studies, physical education, science, and homemaking. Tucker Middle School was seeking to free itself from the idea that health instruction should automatically be assigned to physical education.

Another committee was established in the field of guidance. This group, too, cut across traditional subject matter lines. It included representatives from English, social studies, and counseling. Its major function was to come to an agreement concerning the topics in the field of guidance with which the school should concern itself, and then to make proposals relative to the ways in which the school should implement this responsibility. Thus the allocation of specific guidance topics as units within various required courses was recommended. Materials published by American Guidance Service[10] and Science Research Associates[11] were found to be most helpful in developing the group guidance program.

The third additional committee represented the field of extra-class activities. Tucker Middle School had long given lip service to the concept that these important aspects of the school program were a vital part of the total curriculum. Unfortunately, however, this philosophy had not been translated very effectively into practice. Here was an opportunity, in developing the administrative organization for curriculum development, to move another big step forward in solving one of the secondary school's most perplexing problems.

Each of Tucker curriculum committees operated under the direction of a teacher-chairman. Principal Lee and Vice Principal James Turner served as *ex-officio* members of each committee. Time did not, of course, permit their attendance at all of the meetings of every committee; however, their availability on call to act in a consultant capacity and to provide encouragement constituted a very important ingredient of the total program.

Each committee assumed the responsibility for developing the appropriate departmental (and in some cases interdepartmental) courses of study for the school. Committees varied in the number of meetings held during the year as well as in their methods of operation. This inevitably followed from the atmosphere of freedom within which the various groups worked and from the differences characteristic of the people involved. The general attitude of the faculty was one of enthusiasm and of conviction that a necessary and important piece of work was being done. Every member of the staff thus had the opportunity to make his unique contribution to the success of the entire school.

So comprehensive was the work of some committees that these group meetings, to a large extent, substituted for general faculty meetings during the course of the year. Principal Lee wisely took into consideration the total demands made upon the time and energy of the staff, and reassessed, with the help of his colleagues, the entire pattern of the school's faculty meetings. As a result, the time devoted to curriculum development was provided largely through reorganization of the time already devoted to meetings of the professional staff, rather than by adding activities to those already in existence. The positive effect of such a policy upon morale and upon the school program as a whole was readily discernible.

Of especial significance as an outcome of the faculty's deliberations was the development, by several curriculum committees, of depart-

[10] American Guidance Service, 720 Washington Avenue South East, Minneapolis, Minn., 55414.
[11] Science Research Associates, Inc., 259 East Erie Street, Chicago, Illinois, 60611.

mental objectives which were specifically related to the general educational objectives already agreed upon by the staff as a whole. The several curriculum committees had studied a large number of subject area courses of study and other curriculum documents developed by the various school systems. Materials of this nature are available by the thousands. But an examination of the documents revealed a startling situation. In all but a small minority of cases, there was no clear evidence of any recognized relationship between the subject areas with which they were concerned and the total educational program of the school. The Tucker faculty recognized this condition as one which helped to justify the criticism that secondary school teachers are all too often competent in their own fields but unconcerned with the program as a whole. The staff sought means of correcting what to them was a serious shortcoming. The mathematics committee, for example, developed the following statement as the first of four objectives in that subject field:

To contribute in all ways possible to the attainment of the objectives of education, and *in particular* to those relating to the following:

speech	personal economics
reading	consumer education
writing (including	critical judgment
spelling)	(including systematic
numbering	thinking and reasoning)
listening and observing	

The above statement (along with similar ones developed by committees in other subject fields) is very significant to the Tucker faculty. It suggests, first of all, a cognizance of general educational objectives and a recognition of the fact that the first responsibility of mathematics, as of any other field, is to contribute to the attainment of these general objectives. Second, the statement implies recognition of the fact that mathematics (again, as well as other fields) has a *particular* responsibility to emphasize certain objectives not especially identified with or limited to any one subject field (e.g., speech, reading, listening). Finally, there is recognition of the fact that the field of mathematics because of the nature of its content is an especially advantageous position to emphasize certain other general objectives of education (e.g., number, personal economics, logical reasoning).

Obviously, the mere fact that a group of teachers in a school has viewed departmental objectives in the light that Tucker mathematics teachers have does not guarantee that those teachers and their teaching are necessarily better because of it. However, there is a decided likelihood that such would be the case. And certainly the *absence* of departmental and course objectives stated in terms of the general objectives of education leaves a faculty "wide open" to many fair and basic questions which any thoughtful observer might raise.

The several committee chairmen form the school's general curriculum committee. This committee's function is to coordinate the work of the separate groups. University and State Department of Education leaders serve as curriculum consultants and are most helpful in assisting with the overall planning. Several committee chairmen have already reported on their progress at general faculty meetings. There is general agreement that the work being done constitutes a most valuable and effective program of in-service education.

The Tucker faculty recognized that this brief account of their efforts to date represents only a partial progress report of a dynamic, continuous process which is never finished. Undoubtedly, a similar account written at some later date will indicate further progress in curriculum development; it assuredly will reveal some differences in approach, in content, and in method.

The work of Tucker Middle School will perhaps offer some suggestions to other schools as they study their own instructional problems. However, the very nature of the curriculum dictates that every successful program must be in many respects unique. To attempt to do just as someone else has done constitutes one of the most serious possible mistakes in a curriculum development program. The most tragic situation of all, however, exists when there is no specific provision for an all-school approach to the improvement of the school's curricular offerings.

The Need for Committing Policies to Writing

This chapter has dealt with matters which may, and often do, "make" or "break" the school. They are matters with which most, if not all, teachers are vitally concerned. It is important that misunderstandings concerning these matters be reduced to a minimum. This suggests the necessity of putting all basic policies into writing and publishing them in a faculty handbook. Such a document might well be of a loose-leaf type, so that new or revised material can be duplicated and inserted in the appropriate place. Such a handbook should become the manual of school operation. It has become in many schools the basis for discussion and study on the part of the entire staff prior to the opening of each school year, and as often as necessary at additional times. The commitment of basic policy to writing gives staff members a feeling of security in knowing definitely the school's present position on important matters. This feeling of security is a major factor in staff morale, and is, therefore, closely related to the success of the school program as a whole.

Chapter 16 Bibliography

Alexander, William M. "The Junior High School: A Changing View," *National Association of Secondary School Principals Bulletin* (March 1964): 48:15–24.

Bentley, R. R., and Kempel, A. M. *The Purdue Teacher Questionnaire.* Lafayette, Ind.: Purdue Research Foundation, 1964.

Bossing, Nelson, and Cramer, Roscoe. *The Junior High School.* Boston: Houghton Mifflin Company, 1965.

Bulletin of the National Association of Secondary School Principals (May 1951): 13–24.

Conant, James B. *Recommendations for Education in the Junior High School Years.* Princeton, N. J.: Educational Testing Service, 1960.

Council on Junior High School Administration. "Ten Tenets of Junior High School Administration," *The Clearing House* (February 1964): 38:329–332.

Douglass, Harl. "1950 Revision of the Douglas High School Teaching Load Formula," *The Bulletin of the National Association of Secondary School Principals* (May 1951): 35:13–24.

Educational Policies Commission. *The Purposes of Education in American Democracy.* Washington, D. C.: The Commission, 1938.

Fox, Willard, and Schwartz, Alfred. *Managerial Guide for School Principals.* Columbus, Ohio: Charles E. Merrill Books, Inc., 1965.

Frey, Sherman. "Articulation Between the Junior and Senior High School," *The Bulletin of the National Association of Secondary School Principals* (October 1963): 47:35–43.

Grambs, Jean, and others. *The Junior High School We Need.* Washington, D. C.: Association for Supervision and Curriculum Development, 1961.

Hand, Harold C. *General Education in the American High School.* New York: Scott, Foresman and Company, 1942.

_____. *What People Think About Their Schools.* New York: World Book Company, 1948.

Hearn, Arthur C. "Columbus High School Organizes for Curriculum Development," *The Bulletin of the National Association of Secondary School Principals* (February 1959): 214:67–72.

Lien, Ronald. "Democratic Administrative Behavior," *The Bulletin of the National Association of Secondary School Principals* (March 1964): 48:31–38.

Lowe, Alton. "Three Schools Within a School," *The Bulletin of the National Association of Secondary School Principals* (February 1962): 46:47–51.

McCleary, Lloyd, and Henchley, Stephen. *Secondary School Administration.* New York: Dodd, Mead and Company, 1965.

National Study of Secondary School Evaluation. *Evaluative Criteria for Junior High School.* Washington D. C.: National Study of Secondary School Evaluation, 1963.

Stone, William J. "Communities of Learning in a Large Junior High School," *The Bulletin of the National Association of Secondary School Principals* (February 1962): 46:52–58.

Trump, J. Lloyd, and Baynham, Dorsey. *Guide to Better Schools.* Chicago: Rand McNally Company, 1961.

_____, and Miller, Delmas F. *Secondary School Curriculum Improvement.* Boston: Allyn and Bacon, Inc., 1968.

Van Til, William, Vars, Gordon, and Lounsbury, John. *Modern Education for the Junior High School Years.* Indianapolis: The Bobbs-Merrill Company, Inc., 1961.

Chapter 17

Evaluation
of the Middle School

It is highly important that every school continuously be concerned with the question, "How satisfactory a job are we doing?" Provision for evaluation of all aspects of the school's program thus becomes a major responsibility of the junior high school administration and staff. This concept has been true in theory, of course, since the beginnings of schools. However, it is only in recent years that the evaluation of schools as an integral part of the total educational program has won widespread acceptance in practice.

During the 1920s the testing movement came into its own and since that time has made great progress. The number and kinds of instruments have increased tremendously. There has been an accompanying qualitative growth. Without question, the availability of standardized measuring devices has had much to do with the increased attention which educational evaluation has received. A major part of this chapter will be devoted to a discussion of some of these instruments. First, however, the possibilities of evaluation solely through the use of local data and personnel will be briefly reviewed. Just as intelligent attention to standardized instruments, including a careful study of both their possibilities and their shortcomings, has proved so valuable in many schools and school systems, so has misunderstanding and partial understanding brought about serious problems. The glamor of the printed word has led many individuals and groups into dangerous pitfalls. Rarely, if ever, for example, will a standardized instrument apply without reservation or interpretation to a local situation. In no case can the human factors be eliminated nor can any program of evaluation be defended without a carefully planned follow-up of the results.

Principles and Procedures of Evaluation

The foregoing statements suggest the desirability of stating briefly at this point some principles which are basic to any sound program of evaluation. These include the following:

1. *Evaluation should be based upon stated objectives.*
2. *Evaluation should involve all who are concerned with the program being evaluated.*
3. *Self-evaluation should be supplemented by evaluation which utilizes outside assistance.*
4. *Evaluation should be comprehensive; it should concern itself with all aspects of a given program.*
5. *Evaluation should be continuous.*
6. *Evaluation should utilize a variety of instruments, techniques, and data.*
7. *Evaluation should identify both immediate and long-range goals.*
8. *Evaluation should be constructive.*

The Check List

Three of the best-known evaluative instruments, discussed in the following section, utilize the check list procedure. In general, these instruments emphasize self-appraisal on the part of the local staff, followed by visitation by a committee of educators from outside the local community. This committee's function is to study the school's self-evaluation and to revise it on the basis of its own observations and deliberations. The visiting committee's written report ordinarily includes commendations relative to those characteristics of the school deemed worthy of particular recognition, and recommendations concerning conditions or practices which the local staff is asked to study with a view toward possible change or revision. These instruments typically involve the use of basic data concerning students and community, and a carefully-formulated statement of educational philosophy developed by the local staff. This philosophy then becomes the basis upon which each aspect of the school's program is evaluated.

The Opinion Poll

A second approach to appraisal is through the opinion poll. The use of this technique is based upon two premises: first, that the effectiveness of any program is conditioned by the attitudes of all persons who are concerned and, second, that some systematic effort to appraise these attitudes is necessary if conclusions are to be reliable and valid.

Techniques and materials designed to obviate guesswork in this type of evaluation have been developed and applied successfully in public school situations. Some of the most useful are described by Hand.[1] In pointing out the necessity of this kind of approach, Hand states: "Principally, there are three very serious limitations inherent in personal observations or other unsystematic methods of appraisal. These are (1) the influence of unrepresentative observations, (2) the reluctance of people to be frankly critical, and (3) the influence of the observer's opinions and interests."[2]

Questionnaires for use in opinion polls can be developed by any school faculty. Questions concerning attitudes toward the school program might well be based upon criteria such as those which constitute the concluding section.

Behavioral Changes of Pupils

Education, after all, is primarily concerned with behavior. A check list might attest to the fact that certain provisions and facilities exist in a school, at least on paper; an opinion poll might indicate that certain individuals and groups hold certain beliefs concerning the school program. Data gained through the use of these techniques are extremely useful, and when such data are positive and favorable, there is, of course, more likelihood of the school's having a sound program of activities than when the data are negative and unfavorable. However, it must be borne in mind that evidence based on these two criteria is not a guarantee that the school program is or is not educationally effective. This suggests that an attempt be made to appraise pupil behavior patterns in relation to expected patterns.

The effective school will recognize and capitalize upon the fact that readily available local resources and data provide an excellent basis for self-appraisal. Some of these are discussed briefly in the following paragraphs.

Attendance

Records of pupil attendance are required by law in all states. Every teacher and administrator has an important responsibility in the compilation of such records. But how often are these data recognized and utilized for their potential in evaluating the school program? One such use, for example, is that of comparing total school attendance to total school enrollment. Thus, if attendance is much below 95 percent of

---

[1] H. C. Hand, *What People Think About Their Schools* (New York: World Book Company, 1948).
[2] *Ibid.*, p. 26.

enrollment, the effectiveness of the school program might well be questioned. An unfavorable ratio suggests to a professionally minded staff the possibility of the school's doing a less than adequate job of meeting the needs of its particular student body. Further investigation and study might confirm this possibility; in most cases it definitely will. On the other hand, some other cause or causes might be identified. In any case, the process will involve evaluation.

Scholarship

A second kind of easily accessible data is that which concerns the pupils' academic records. Studies based on this material are likewise extremely valuable in appraising the work which the school is doing. For example, a school must take cognizance of the situation relative to the number and percentage of students making unsatisfactory records in their classes. In the best schools, each individual instance of a student achieving less success than his abilities promise is accepted as a challenge to the faculty, and specific and intensive efforts are made to correct the situation. Certainly, an unsatisfactory academic record is indicative of a problem worthy of professional attention, and the existence of very many such records suggests serious shortcomings in the educational program itself. The staff's analysis of the situation and the steps taken to correct it constitute a vital and important means of evaluation. If, for example, it is found that a large proportion of failures occur in algebra, some specific questions immediately suggest themselves. Probably the basic one is this: "Upon what criteria is enrollment in algebra determined?" or, perhaps even better, "What kinds of assistance does this school provide in order that each student may make an intelligent decision as to whether or not he should enroll in algebra?" The effective junior high school finds it possible to sharply reduce instances of unsatisfactory work in algebra by providing guidance based upon several criteria. Some of the most widely used include teacher judgment, previous academic record in mathematics (arithmetic), scholastic ability, and competence in arithmetical computation and comprehension.

Citizenship

A third type of information to which the staff of any middle school ordinarily has ready access is that which relates to citizenship. Forward-looking schools recognize that the accumulation of basic data relative to students' progress toward the attainment of civic goals are fully as important as information concerning academic progress. An instrument designed to assist a school in appraising citizenship and character traits (Table XVI) published by the Oregon Association of Secondary School Principals, is reproduced in these pages. Even if such

Table XVI. Inventory of Character and Personality Traits

To the evaluator:

The importance of character and personality in effective living is well recognized. Your thoughtful consideration of the following people will serve at least two purposes. It will assist the school in making valid appraisals in answer to inquiries from colleges, governmental agencies, and prospective employers, and even more important, it will furnish data for individual counseling and guidance.

1. Outstanding   2. Very Good   3. Fair   4. Poor   5. Very Poor

Name	Energy, Drive	Industry	Enthusiasm	Judgment	Personal Appearance, Neatness, Carriage	Leadership	Social and Civic Responsibility, Service and Cooperation	Courtesy, Manners	Dignity, Poise, Self-Control	Regular Attendance, Promptness	Study Habits	Comments

data are not available in such organized form, most schools' records will contain information relative to the citizenship of students. A study of such data constitutes an excellent approach to the problem of school evaluation.

Criteria for Evaluation

The preceding sections have attempted to show that every school has at its fingertips a large amount of data which are invaluable in appraising the effectiveness of its program. Every program of school evaluation must take cognizance of such information and utilize it in seeking to improve the quality of services rendered. The program of evaluation might well use this information as the basis upon which it is built, without reference to published evaluative instruments. Many schools have operated in just this way. An increasing number of schools, however, have supplemented such a program by using one or more of the several excellent published materials which are now available. Three of these will be discussed at this point.

Texas Criteria

A detailed set of criteria was developed through the collaboration of several professional groups in Texas.[3] This instrument, as do the others included here, emphasizes the self-appraisal and improvement aspects of evaluation. Guiding principles in developing the criteria were taken from the Charter for Junior High Schools in Texas[4] and include the following:

1. The junior high school is a program of education, not merely a building, nor a collection of grades, nor a school unit with a principal in charge.
2. The junior high school is a program of education that should be derived from the nature and needs of the persons it serves.
   The nature and needs of the twelve- to fifteen-year-old youngsters are such that a uniquely different educational program is indicated.
3. The outstanding characteristics of pupils between twelve and fifteen are (1) their manifold and wide variations one from another and (2) their common concern with passing from one style of life orientation to another.
4. The program of the junior high school is unique enough to demand different personality traits and special preparation for teachers who work in the school.

[3] *Criteria for Evaluating Junior High Schools* (Austin: The Texas Study of Secondary Education, 1954), p. iii.
[4] *Ibid.*, p. iii.

5. Many of the time-honored features of present junior high school programs need to be thoroughly reexamined in terms of changed demands and changed life patterns for modern youth.

Utah Criteria

In 1960, the Utah State Department of Public Instruction published the most comprehensive junior high school evaluative instrument to appear up to that time.[5] This document was the result of nearly six years of collaborative effort on the part of the Department of Public Instruction and the Secondary School Principals Association in Utah. It devoted itself to three primary purposes: to define the characteristics of a good junior high school; to establish effective ways and means of evaluating junior high schools; and to provide a means by which responsible agencies can stimulate and assist junior high schools to continuous growth.[6] The principles upon which the instrument is based[7] assume that the criteria should:

1. Include for evaluation those elements of an educational program that will meet the needs of junior high school youth and will serve the basic functions of a junior high school such as integration, exploration, differentiation, guidance, socialization, and articulation.
2. Be valid in that they measure that which they purport to measure.
3. Be reliable in that there will be a rather high degree of consistency in the results obtained when they are applied to a wide variety of schools by many different individuals.
4. Call for data which will reveal the philosophy of education to which the school subscribes, the characteristics of the students of the school, and the characteristics and needs of the community which the school serves.
6. Evaluate the activities carried on by the staff rather than evaluate the performance of individuals who make up the staff.
7. Evaluate behavioral outcomes and provide suggestions as to how and where such outcomes may be observed.
8. Define terms where needed.
9. Call for recommendations from both the school and the Visiting Committee regarding plans of action to follow-up the evaluation.
10. Call for data upon which to base in-service training programs.
11. Encourage frequent reevaluation.
12. Stimulate individual teachers and faculties to improve their effectiveness.

[5] *Junior High School Evaluative Criteria* (Salt Lake City, Utah: State Department of Public Instruction, 1960).
[6, 7] *Ibid.*, pp. xi, xii.

The Utah criteria provide for both a self-evaluation by the school itself and appraisal by a visiting committee. Each of these groups is guided in its work by four sections which are concerned respectively with characteristics of junior high school students, needs of junior high school youth, functions of the junior high school, and data pertaining to the particular student population and school-community. Of particular interest, in the first of these sections, is the enumeration of characteristics of students, accompanied in each case with implications for the junior high school curriculum.

National Study of Secondary School Evaluation

In 1963, the National Study of Secondary School Evaluation (NSSSE) drew upon a quarter century's experience with secondary school appraisal by publishing an instrument designed specifically for the junior high school. The original material was extensively revised in 1970. This material seems destined to enjoy widespread acceptance and use, and so is described in some detail at this point.

The steps involved in developing the NSSSE criteria included: observing the work of the Junior High School Committee at an annual meeting of the National Association of Secondary School Principals; securing opinions from leaders in junior high school education and state supervisors of secondary education relative to the need for evaluation materials for junior high schools; enlisting the aid of faculties of junior high schools in securing suggestions for changes in the 1960 edition of the *Evaluative Criteria* (designed for secondary schools generally) to serve junior high schools better; securing leaders in junior high school education to help with the development of the criteria; developing the materials for junior high school evaluation at a workshop held in St. Davids, Pennsylvania, in the summer of 1962.[8]

The materials stress the fundamental importance of developing statements of philosophy, objectives, and functions for each junior high school. As stated in the Guiding Principles,[9]

1. The junior high school is unique owing to the age and nature of the students enrolled. Every school needs a carefully formulated, comprehensive philosophy of education. A school without philosophy and objectives would be as aimless as a society without constitution and bylaws. The philosophy and objectives of the school and the characteristics and needs of its students together determine the nature of its program. The philosophy is a framework of basic principles of education which expresses the staff's convictions on such essential points as the scope of the school's responsibility for the education of youth, the nature of the edu-

[8] *Evaluative Criteria for Junior High Schools* (Washington, D. C.: National Study of Secondary School Evaluation, 1963).
[9] *Ibid.*, p. 7.

cative process, the content and methods of instruction, desirable types of student activities, and the outcomes to be attained. This philosophy gives direction to the objectives and affects every policy and every activity of the school. The objectives of the school are the philosophical principles reduced to specific aims. The school's philosophy is also closely related to the characteristics and needs of the young adolescents whom it seeks to serve.

2. Each school should be free to determine and develop its own educational philosophy, so long as this is consistent with the principles of American democracy, consistent within itself, and consistent with the needs of early adolescent boys and girls.

3. In a school evaluation, the philosophy and objectives of the school bear the same relation to the evaluative procedures as they do to the operation of the school. The entire evaluation is a kind of ratio of accomplishment, a judgment upon the extent to which the school is actually accomplishing what it is properly trying to accomplish. During the self-evaluation the staff studies every policy, every program, every attitude and procedure, measuring them against the formed philosophy and objectives and against the nature and needs of the students.

4. The philosophy of a junior high school should therefore be based on:
   a. An understanding of the characteristics of early adolescent boys and girls.
   b. The responsibility of the school for the maintenance of the fundamental concepts of American democracy.
   c. The responsibility of the school to help the student plan for, and meet, his present and future needs.
   d. An understanding related to the present knowledge of the nature of learning.
   e. The responsibility of the school to assist the student in practicing democratic processes.
   f. An understanding of the relationship of the school to other institutions and agencies in education.
   g. The unique position of the junior high school in the educational program of the school district.

5. In preparing a statement of objectives, the staff, perhaps with the cooperation of students and parents, should set forth in specific terms what it is trying to do to meet the needs and interests of early adolescents in accordance with its statement of philosophy. The statement of objectives should be related to such items as:
   a. The general objectives of the district.
   b. The characteristics of the community and the student population.
   c. Other educational agencies that might affect the school.
   d. The obligation to prepare the youth for the duties of adult citizenship in a free American society.

    e. The rapid physical, mental, social, and emotional changes of students.

    f. The need to continue the development of skills and the increase of knowledge.

    g. The provisions for a wide range of experiences and activities for all students.

    h. The needs of students for preparation for further education.

    i. Evidence from follow-up studies of former students.

6. The statement of functions of the junior high school should be based on the abilities, unique needs, concerns, and problems of all early adolescents. It indicates the direction to be followed by a professional staff in planning a program of studies. There is a direct relationship between the quality of the total educational program and the degree to which teachers and administrators implement the stated functions in the program of the school. Thus, the statement of functions provides criteria for evaluating and improving the school.

The school staff must, initially, define the philosophy, objectives, and functions of its school. Evaluation of the program, both by the local staff and by the visiting committee which is strongly recommended, should basically be in terms of the extent to which the program implements the philosophy, objectives, and functions as accepted by the particular school in question.

In addition to the statements referred to in the foregoing paragraphs, data which describe the local school and community are essential. As stated in the Guiding Principles,[10]

1. The junior high school exists primarily for the benefit of young adolescents of the community or the group which it serves. The types of people, their vocations and interests, their religious beliefs, their tendencies and prejudices, their abilities, their racial characteristics, their hopes and prospects regarding the future, their customs and habits, the similarities and differences of groups within the community are different from those of other communities. The distinctive characteristics and needs of the people and groups of people of the school community, particularly those of the youth, should be known. But every school community inevitably is interrelated with other communities and is a part of larger communities, particularly the state and the nation. The school should, therefore, adapt its general philosophy, specific purposes, and its educational program to its own community and to the larger communities of which it is a part.

2. Basic data concerning students should include at least enrollment by grades, age-grade distribution, academic and other aptitudes and interests, stability, withdrawals, educational intentions, and

10 *Ibid.*, p. 11.

vocational intentions. Data concerning the community should include: population statistics and related data, occupational status of adults, educational status of adults, financial resources, composition of the community, and community agencies affecting education (educational, recreational, civic).

The importance of the foregoing statements and data cannot be overemphasized. Only after meticulous and painstaking attention to this basic material can the most effective appraisal of an educational program take place.

For convenience, the educational program may be thought of as including the program of studies, student activities, and guidance services. In turn, the program of studies includes the various subject fields, usually twelve in number at the junior high school level.[11]

In the sections which follow, a set of criteria for the evaluation of the middle school program is proposed. These criteria are based upon three kinds of written sources:[12] basic documents concerned with tenets of American democracy, purposes of education, and needs of youth; textbooks, pamphlets, and periodical literature dealing with the school; and evaluative instruments and other professional materials devoted to the problem of appraising educational programs.

An attempt has been made to propose here an evaluative instrument which is easy to administer, which identifies major criteria in each area of the school's educational program, and that is specific rather than general in its emphasis. Twenty-two criteria have been identified and classified into the three categories enumerated above. In each case, a basic criterion is stated. Following each such statement, a few specific questions relating to it are raised. The purpose of these questions is to suggest the kinds of evidence that should be sought in ascertaining the degree to which the school's program is actually in accord with the criterion.

The importance of this last point cannot be overemphasized. It is of crucial significance if the school is really serious in its desire to improve itself. Many examples exist of schools in which well-formulated statements of principles or objectives have been developed and published. However, the achievement of this step, essential though it is, is not enough. Objectives are theoretical guides to action. They must be translated; the general must lead to the specific; actual practice must be appraised in terms of the stated objectives. The basic purpose of the following instrument is to assist schools in doing this.

A variety of ways in which the criteria might be used will be apparent. The following procedure is proposed.

---

11 Art (including crafts), business education, English, foreign languages, health education, homemaking, industrial arts, mathematics, music, physical education, science, and social studies.

12 See bibliography at the end of this chapter for further information on these sources.

1. The principal designates a student-faculty committee on evaluation. The makeup of this committee will, of course, vary with the individual school. It should, however, be representative of both the staff and the student body.

2. The committee studies the criteria carefully and decides what revision, if any, might be desirable to improve its use in that particular school. The committee might wish, for example, to add other specific questions to the illustrations given under the various program.

3. The committee formulates plans for involving the faculty, student body, and others in the evaluation program.

4. Data and other evidence called for in the questions are gathered for ready reference, together with any other material which might prove useful in the evaluation.

5. A rating scale is developed for use in evaluating the program on each of the thirty-two basic principles. A five-point scale (outstanding, very good, fair, poor, very poor) should prove adequate for this purpose in most cases.

6. The committee agrees upon a tentative rating for each of the thirty-two criteria, and supports each evaluation with a brief written statement.

7. These evaluations are made available to the faculty for consideration and study.

8. The tentative evaluation becomes the subject for consideration at a faculty meeting or faculty meetings, in which the tentative ratings may be revised prior to acceptance by the faculty.

9. Consultant service is engaged. There is nothing to preclude the earlier use of consultants and schools are encouraged to use them at any stage deemed desirable. Our delay in mentioning them earlier grows out of the conviction that directed self-appraisal constitutes the most effective kind of evaluation.

The number of consultants is a matter for local decision. However, one to three would seem to be quite satisfactory in most instances. The consultant or consultants should have adequate opportunity to study the results of the school's self-evaluation, to visit the school in action, to confer with appropriate personnel, and to propose revisions in the self-evaluation, including the proposed plan of action.

10. The evaluation as revised is accepted by the school board and serves as a constant reference as the school continues to engage in its program of self-improvement.

Program of Studies

1. *The program of studies is based upon the philosophy, objectives, and functions of the middle school.*

    a. Has the school developed clearly formulated written statements of philosophy, objectives, and functions?

b. Is there clear-cut evidence that these statements provide the basis for the development of the school's instructional program?

2. *The program of studies is based upon needs of young adolescents.*

   a. Is the school continuously guided, in its development of its courses of study, by a written statement of the needs of young adolescents which the staff understands and accepts?

   b. Is there clear-cut evidence that the program of studies differentiates between the common and the individual needs of all the students in the school?

3. *The staff is so organized that each member has the opportunity to contribute maximally to the improvement of the instructional program.*

   a. Have functioning faculty committees been established for each of the subject areas included in the program of studies?

   b. Are these committees charged with the major responsibility for developing courses of study or study guides for each of the offerings which comprise the program of studies?

   c. Are specific provisions made whereby the work of the committees is coordinated with the school's total program (including extraclass activities) and with both the program of the elementary school, on the one hand, and the senior high school, on the other?

4. *There is clear-cut evidence of administrative leadership which provides the kinds of services conducive to the development of an effective instructional program.*

   a. Are provisions made for the services of consultants to teachers and others engaged in curriculum development?

   b. Is the school library and instructional materials center an integral part of the school's instructional program?

   c. Has a functional professional library been established?

   d. Have the possibilities of flexible scheduling, team teaching, large and small group instruction, and independent study been explored thoroughly?

5. *All courses within the program of studies are concerned with and capitalize upon their opportunities to emphasize the following:*

   a. development of citizenship traits

   b. development of study skills

   c. favorable attitudes toward physical and mental health practices

   d. development of skills in reading, writing, speaking, and listening

   e. correct usage of grammar, spelling, handwriting, and vocabulary

   f. use of number concepts

   g. development of leisure time skills

   h. development of awareness for aesthetic values

6. *Provision is made for periodic and continuous appraisal of the school's instructional program.*

   a. Which of the following procedures are used in appraising the school's program, and in what specific ways:

follow-up of former students and graduates; interviews with parents and students staff discussions; analysis of school records; utilization of outside consultants.

b. In what specific ways are the findings and results of evaluative procedures implemented?

Student Activities

1. *Student activities are considered as an integral part of the curriculum of the school.*
   a. Is a committee on student activities included among the school's curriculum committees?
   b. Are student activities represented in the committee responsible for the overall direction of the school's instructional program?
2. *The objectives of student activities grow out of the objectives of education.*
   a. Do student activities have clearly formulated written objectives?
   b. What specific evidence is there of the relationship between the objectives of activities and objectives of education as a whole?
3. *The activity program is designed to meet the needs, interests, and abilities of all students.*
   a. Has a survey of student interests been made during the current school year?
   b. What percentage of the present student body has at least one specific assignment, in an activity, for which the students have a clearly defined responsibility and are held strictly accountable?
   c. What percentage of the present student body is actively participating in the activity program?
4. *The school provides guidance to the student in the choice of activities.*
   a. Is proposed activity participation included along with proposed class enrollment in individual students' program planning?
   b. What other specific evidence is there that activity participation is considered in relationship to each student's total school program?
5. *All regularly enrolled students are eligible to participate in student activities.*
   a. Is the research evidence concerning the effect of activity participation upon scholarship clearly understood by the staff?
   b. Are eligibility requirements for participation in school activities consistent with such evidence?
6. *Each activity is sponsored by a qualified staff member appointed by the principal.*
   a. Is activity sponsorship considered in relationship to the sponsor's specific competencies, experience, and interests?
   b. Is activity sponsorship considered as an integral part of the sponsor's total assignment?

7. *Time schedules are arranged in such a way that interference between activities and classes is reduced to an absolute minimum if not entirely eliminated.*
   a. As a general policy, does the *classroom teacher* have the final say concerning exceptions to the above principle?
   b. Do activity periods or similar administrative arrangements make it possible for some activities to utilize "school time" without affecting "class time"?
8. *Recognition accorded to each activity bears a reasonable relationship to that activity's place in the total educational program.*
   a. Does the proportion of newspaper space accorded to any activity suggest an exaggerated importance of that activity in the total program?
   b. Does the size and prominence of certain activity awards suggest a similarly exaggerated importance?
   c. Are any worthy activities slighted in terms of publicity and awards?
9. *Participation of students in activities is not limited by economic circumstance.*
   a. Have sound policies of financing student activities been developed and implemented?
   b. Is every student eligible to participate in any activity regardless of whether he can pay for it?
10. *The school activity program is carefully and methodically coordinated with other educative agencies within the community.*
    a. Have data been gathered concerning the community's non-school educative agencies, such as youth membership groups, recreational organizations, and service clubs?
    b. What specific examples reflect the coordination of school and community activities?

Guidance

1. *Guidance services are an integral part of the school's total educational program.*
   a. What specific evidence is there to indicate a close relationship between the guidance program and the needs of young adolescents?
   b. In what specific ways are the school's guidance services coordinated with the program of studies and the student activity program?
   c. In what specific ways does the guidance program utilize the services of community agencies?
2. *Administrative, guidance, and instructional staff members have clearly defined responsibilities in the guidance program.*

a. Are responsibilities carefully delineated in the school's student and faculty handbooks?

b. Is there specific evidence that both students and faculty members understand clearly these responsibilities?

3. *The guidance program is designed to serve all students, both individually and in groups, throughout each of the middle school years.*

a. How, specifically, does the school provide group guidance for all students each year?

b. How, specifically, does the school provide individual counseling for all students each year?

4. *The guidance program is concerned with problems not ordinarily identified with the typical middle school subject fields but which are far too important to leave to chance.*

a. How, specifically, does the school assist students with such problems as the following:

projecting a long-range program of studies

selecting student activities

planning a realistic time schedule

understanding his academic strengths and weaknesses

developing desirable study habits

b. How, specifically, does the school assist students with such problems as the following in the area of *vocational* guidance:

understanding the relationship between job success, citizenship, and character traits

understanding, in general, the kinds of activities that comprise the world of work

c. How, specifically, does the school assist students with such problems as the following in the area of *personal* guidance:

moral and spiritual values

social etiquette

friendships

grooming

health habits

5. *The guidance program has available and utilizes several kinds of information concerning each student.*

a. How, specifically, is personal and family information used in the guidance program?

b. What use is made of psychological data concerning academic aptitude, achievement, and interests?

c. What additional kinds of information are utilized, and in what specific ways?

6. *The guidance program is concerned with behavioral outcomes.*

a. What evidence exists that students are becoming increasingly self-directive?

b. In what specific ways is the guidance program related to problems involving student scholarship? student citizenship?

Chapter 17 Bibliography

Criteria for Evaluating Junior High Schools. Austin: The Texas Study of Secondary Education, 1964.

Douglass, Harl, and Gumaer, Harry. "Junior High Accreditation," *National Education Association Journal* (October 1965).

Douglass, Harl. "Junior Highs Evaluated and Accredited," *National Association of Secondary School Principals Bulletin* (February 1963).

Evaluative Criteria. Washington: National Study of Secondary School Evaluation, 1969.

Evaluative Criteria for Junior High Schools. Washington: National Study of Secondary School Evaluation, 1963.

Garbarini, Mark. "Expedited Evaluation," *Michigan Education Journal* (May 1964).

Gillespie, R. L. "Evaluation: A New Approach," *National Association of Secondary School Principals Bulletin* (October 1965).

Howell, C. E. "Measuring Rod for Junior High Schools," *Clearing House* (March 1948).

Johnson, Mauritz, Jr. "Three Things to Look For in Evaluating a Junior High School," *School Review* (March 1956).

Junior High School Evaluative Criteria. Salt Lake City, Utah: State Department of Public Instruction, 1960.

McGlasson, Maurice. "Let's Think Through Proposals for Junior High Accreditation," *National Association of Secondary School Principals Bulletin* (April 1964).

Manlove, Donald C., and McGlasson, Maurice A. "Principals and Standards for Junior High School Education," *Bulletin of the School of Education,* Indiana University (July 1965).

Nickerson, Neal C., and Gruber, Arnold. "Evaluating the Junior High School," *National Association of Secondary School Principals Bulletin* (September 1961).

Sparks, Paul, and Baughman, Dale M. "Improving the Quality of Junior High Schools: A Statewide Plan," *National Association of Secondary School Principals Bulletin* (October 1965).

Trump, J. L. "The Dynamic Junior High School Program," *National Association of Secondary School Principals Bulletin* (March 1964).

Wyatt, Sidney L. "Utah Develops Junior High Criteria Partially as An Aid in Improving Staff Utilization," *National Association of Secondary School Principals Bulletin* (January 1959).

Index

National Study of Secondary
   School Evaluation, 286, 362
New language instruction, 227–234
New math, 169–173
Noar, Gertrude, 39
Norton, M. S., 176

Olson, Carl, Jr., 99
Open pod facility, 104
Opinion poll, 356
Organization, 117–118
   See also Administration
Organizational plan, 3
   closing school, 341–342; of Mid-
   dle School, 324–353; opening
   school, 339–341
Orwin, Gifford P., 233
Ossification, 33
Oswego Campus School Industrial
   Arts Laboratory, 237–238
Our School Life, 315
Owatonna Minnesota Art Educa-
   tional Project, 209

Peer acceptance, 322–323
Percentiles, 322–323
Performance curriculum, 338
Physical education, 247–253
   definition, 247; program, 251–
   253
Physical endurance, 34
Piaget, Jean, 87, 155, 162
Pierson, David, 191
Pod (classroom arrangement), 335
Politzer, Robert L., 232
Posner, A. N., 273
Price, G. Bailey, 170
Principal, 325, 347–353
Pringle, G. O., 14
Programmed learning, 177
Progressive Education Commis-
   sion (1932), 168
Project English, 135, 144–146
Public relations, 55

Pupil behavior patterns, 357–360
   attendance, 357–360; citizenship, 358–360; scholarship, 358
Purposes of education in American
   democracy, 349

Randolph, Paul H., 177
Reading, 127–135
   ability, 36; corrective, 130; developmental, 130, 131, 132, 135;
   organization, 130; remedial, 128,
   130, 135; research and experimental programs, 128–130;
   trends in teaching, 133, 135
Realschule, 6
Rempel, A. M., 328
Richards, Vincent, 134

Sawyer, W. W., 170
School arts survey, 211
School assemblies, 294–297
School government, 291–293
School Library Association, 277
School Mathematics Study Group,
   172, 180–182
School parties, 297–298
School publication, 298–299
Science, 184–199
   curriculum project, 194; gen-
   eral, 185–187; motivation in,
   188; new programs, 192–198;
   value of, 187–188
Science Research Associates, 315
Self-contained organization, 95
Sesamoid bone, 33
Seven cardinal principles of educa-
   tion, 151
Shallock, Del, 50
Shamos, Morris H., 186
Sheppard, Douglas, 229–230
Shinn, Ridgeway F., Jr., 158
Shop, 235–236
   See also Industrial Arts
Single-discipline team, 104
Smith, Walter, 209

PRINTED IN U. S. A.